Hip Hop's Inheritance

Hip Hop's Inheritance

From the Harlem Renaissance to the Hip Hop Feminist Movement

Reiland Rabaka

LEXINGTON BOOKS
A division of
ROWMAN & LITTLEFIELD PUBLISHERS, INC.
Lanham • Boulder • New York • Toronto • Plymouth, UK

Published by Lexington Books
A division of Rowman & Littlefield Publishers, Inc.
A wholly owned subsidiary of The Rowman & Littlefield Publishing Group, Inc.
4501 Forbes Boulevard, Suite 200, Lanham, Maryland 20706
http://www.lexingtonbooks.com

Estover Road, Plymouth PL6 7PY, United Kingdom

British Library Cataloguing in Publication Information Available

Library of Congress Cataloging-in-Publication Data
Rabaka, Reiland, 1972–
 Hip hop's inheritance : from the Harlem renaissance to the hip hop feminist
movement / Reiland Rabaka.
  p. cm.
 Includes bibliographical references and index.
 ISBN 978-0-7391-6480-8 (cloth : alk. paper) — ISBN 978-0-7391-6481-5 (pbk. :
alk. paper) — ISBN 978-0-7391-6482-2 (electronic)
 1. Rap (Music)—United States—History and criticism. 2. Hip-hop—United
States. I. Title.
 ML3531.R23 2011
 782.4216490973—dc22   2010052497

Printed in the United States of America

For the artists, activists, and insurgent intelligentsia of the Harlem Renaissance, Black Arts movement, *and* Feminist Art movement

For the faculty, staff, and students of Booker T. Washington High School for the Performing and Visual Arts (i.e., "Arts Magnet") *and the* University of the Arts

And, as with all of my work, for my mother, grandmothers, and great aunt

Marilyn Jean Giles
Lizzie Mae Davis
Elva Rita Warren
Arcressia Charlene Connor

Nkosi Sikelel' iAfrika . . .

Contents

Preface and Acknowledgments: Of the Black Souls Who Sang Neo-Sorrow Songs at the Dawn of the Twenty-First Century

And so by fateful chance the Negro folk-song—the rhythmic cry of the slave—stands to-day not simply as the sole American music, but as the most beautiful expression of human experience born this side the seas. It has been neglected, it has been, and is, half despised, and above all it has been persistently mistaken and misunderstood; but notwithstanding, it still remains as the singular spiritual heritage of the nation and the greatest gift of the Negro people. —W. E. B. Du Bois, *The Souls of Black Folk*, p. 251

OF THE NEO-SORROW SONGS AND THE NEW BLACK POPULAR CULTURE: RAP MUSIC AND HIP HOP CULTURE

Readers familiar with my previous work may wonder why a scholar with expertise in interdisciplinary and intersectional critical social theory would write a book aimed at contributing an intellectual history and critical theory of hip hop culture. The answer to this very valid line of questioning lies, in part, in the lifework and legacy of W. E. B. Du Bois, who has been a major preoccupation of mine, literally, all of my intellectual and political life. To this day, I can vividly recall the first time I read or, rather, tenaciously tried to read *The Souls of Black Folk*. I will never forget the exhilarating feeling I had when I first flipped through the book's tattered pages in my junior high school's library. I almost immediately noticed that each of the book's four-teen chapters opened with poetry and an African American spiritual. I stopped, then and there, in the middle of the aisle, stock-still, in unmitigated awe. I clumsily placed my backpack on the floor and sat on top of it, intensely enthralled and eager to read whatever words and wisdom followed such beautiful poetry and melody. As I started to read *The Souls of Black Folk* I began to think that Du Bois, or so it seemed to me even at this young age, ironically was able to eloquently express something—as the French might say, *je ne sais quoi*—with the written word that most of the folk in the various communities that I was reared and raised in both delicately and decidedly danced around.

Opening *The Souls of Black Folk* with the classic query "How does it feel to be a problem?," I felt that Du Bois (1903) had reached across nearly a century to speak to me, inspire me, and gently guide me along life's journey (pp. 1–2). Reading, and then regularly re-reading *The Souls of Black Folk* throughout my adolescence, I became convinced that Du Bois had also grappled with and earnestly attempted to grasp "the strange meaning of being black,"to use his famous phrase (p. vii). Truth be told, as I look back on them now, his words were simultaneously inspiring and deeply depressing. It was as though reading his weighted words had somehow transported me back to those long hot summer evenings in the Caribbean and Texas where I sat with my grandparents on the porch listening to music that was filled with both celebration and sorrow as the sun set on the horizon. What was it about the African diasporan experience, especially the African American experience, I wondered, that caused generation after jockeying generation of musicians to keep coming back to the beautifulness and ugliness of black life-worlds and black life-struggles?

I knew from first-hand experience that it was not simply black secular music that accented the joys and blues or, rather, "the strange meaning of being black" in America. Because I played drums in a Baptist church band between the ages of five and eighteen, I was well aware of the fact that black sacred music also expressed the agonies and ecstasies of African American life and culture. However, for what seemed to be a very long time, my mind raced and rumbled as I desperately attempted to reconcile the duality and polyvocality of African American music and popular culture.

It was the last chapter of *The Souls of Black Folk*, "The Sorrow Songs," that provided initial answers to my questions concerning the range and reach of black music. After all of the lyrical historical studies, sophisticated social commentary, and pioneering political analysis in *The Souls of Black Folk*, even as an adolescent I noticed that Du Bois concluded the book with an eye-opening discussion of the profundity of the music of black folk. Why would Du Bois, undoubtedly one of the greatest minds black America (nay, America) has produced, give black music such pride of place, going so far as to include it in a volume on the most pressing social and political problems confronting African Americans at the dawn of the twentieth century? Not one prone to mealy-minded meandering, with characteristic calm and clarity Du Bois answered this question when he sternly stated in "The Sorrow Songs":

> Little of beauty has America given the world save the rude grandeur God himself stamped on her bosom; the human spirit in this new world has expressed itself in vigor and ingenuity rather than in beauty. And so by fateful chance the Negro folksong—the rhythmic cry of the slave—stands to-day not simply as the sole American music, but as the most beautiful expression of human experience born this side the seas. It has been neglected, it has been, and is, half despised, and above all it has been persistently mistaken and misunderstood; but notwithstanding, it still remains as the singular spiritual heritage of the nation and the greatest gift of the Negro people. (p. 251)

As I transitioned from adolescence to adulthood, from church drummer to jazz drummer, and from apolitical integrationist to critical social theorist and radical political activist, my relationship with African American music, and black popular culture more generally, drastically changed. Having attended Booker T. Washington High School for the Performing and Visual Arts (i.e., "Arts Magnet") in Dallas, Texas, and then the University of the Arts in Philadelphia, Pennsylvania, my young adult years were spent immersed in African American aesthetic history, culture, and theory. I came to see that the black music and black popular culture of my epoch was being—as Du Bois said so long ago—"neglected," "half despised, and above all . . . persistently mistaken and misunderstood." However, even as an undergraduate student, I had reservations and critically questioned whether hip hop culture, with its seemingly unrepentant embrace of bourgeois materialism, sexism, and heterosexism, was a part of the august tradition of African American music that Du Bois declared to be "the singular spiritual heritage of the nation and the greatest gift of the Negro people." I thought to myself back then: How could my generation's contribution to "the singular spiritual heritage of the nation and the greatest gift of the Negro people" regularly celebrate carpetbagger capitalism and seek to dominate and discriminate against women and homosexuals? What was it about my generation and our music and popular culture that made it seem to me and so many others to be radically at odds with the best of the black aesthetic and the African American musical tradition?

In high school I had been exposed to the artist-activists of the Harlem Renaissance and the Black Arts movement, but it was not until I studied with the controversial feminist cultural critic Camille Paglia at the University of the Arts that I was provided with the aesthetic history and theory needed to critically engage, not simply the past, but also the present. Furthermore, Paglia's critical cultural feminism also had a profound impact on me, as her brand of feminism seemed to be as critical of "high culture" as it was of "low culture," as critical of conservatism as it was of liberalism. Nothing was off-limits or out of bounds for Paglia, and her free-wheeling critiques of everything from religion and education to art and athletics radically altered my relationship with rap music and hip hop culture.

Graduate work in African American studies and women's studies at Temple University further impacted my relationship with and interpretation of rap music and hip hop culture. In graduate school Molefi Asante, Kariamu Welsh, Maulana Karenga, Lucius Outlaw, Lewis Gordon, Sonia Sanchez and Amiri Baraka, among others, taught me that it was not enough to simply appreciate the history of African American aesthetic culture but, even more, that I must be willing and able to bring interdisciplinary and intersectional critique to bear. Obviously many aspects of the intellectual history and critical theory of hip hop culture I advance in the following pages is decidedly at odds with several of my mentors and intellectual elders' conceptions of rap music and hip hop culture. However, for me what is most important throughout this book is to place hip hop culture within the wider stream of historic African American cultural aesthetic traditions and sociopolitical movements. When this happens—which is to say, when hip hop culture is connected to, and compared and contrasted with previous African American cultural aesthetic and sociopolitical traditions and movements—rap music and hip hop culture are radically redefined and, in some senses, re-historicized and re-politicized, and finally seen for what they really are: nothing more than the ongoing evolution of black music and black popular culture.

In short, as will be repeatedly echoed throughout the chapters to follow, black popular culture has always been and remains more than merely "popular culture" in some neutral or free-floating "postmodern" sense. This, of course, is on account of African Americans' particular and peculiar historical relationship with European (as well as other non-European) American cultures, social conventions, and political institutions. In other words, black popular culture in many instances is inextricable from black political culture, because only the most "white folk-friendly" African American politicians and social leaders are halfway given a hearing in "mainstream" America. As a matter of fact, for several centuries black popular culture has provided one of the only avenues available for African Americans to raise their concerns and express their issues both *intra-communally* and *extra-communally* (i.e., both *inside* and *outside* of the black community). This means, then, that there is much to be learned from critically studying the origins and evolution of black music and black popular culture and their relationship with and long-buried bequests to rap music and hip hop culture.

Hip Hop's Inheritance is predicated on the premise that hip hop culture simultaneously converges with, and diverges from, previous African American cultural aesthetic traditions and movements. In other words, it argues that hip hop culture can be situated both *within* and *without* the African American cultural aesthetic tradition because, whether conscious of it or not, hip hop culture has inherited a great deal from, not only previous African American cultural aesthetic traditions and movements, but also antecedent African American sociopolitical traditions and movements. To put it as plainly as possible, hip hop culture can be said to be squarely situated *within* the stream of historic African American cultural aesthetic traditions and movements when and where its schizophrenic embrace and rejection of both black and white conservatism, liberalism, radicalism, and revolutionism is taken into consideration.

Unlike previous works in Hip Hop studies, *Hip Hop's Inheritance* arguably offers the first book-length treatment of what hip hop culture has, literally, "inherited" from the Harlem Renaissance and the Black Arts movement. By comparing and contrasting the major motifs of the Harlem Renaissance and the Black Arts movement with those of hip hop culture, all the while critically exploring the origins and evolution of black popular culture from antebellum America through to "Obama's America," *Hip Hop's Inheritance* demonstrates that the hip hop generation is not the first generation of young black folk preoccupied with spirituality and sexuality, race and religion, entertainment and athletics, or ghetto culture and bourgeois culture. This means, then, truth be told, instead of representing a completely new black youth culture, in many ways rap music and hip hop culture have, however unwittingly, recycled several racial, sexual, and cultural myths and motifs bequeathed by antecedent African American youth-inspired cultural aesthetic traditions and sociopolitical movements—perhaps, none more than the Harlem Renaissance, the Civil Rights movement, the Black Power movement, and the Black Arts movement.

However, no matter how much hip hop culture may seem to fit nicely and neatly *within* the stream of historic African American cultural aesthetic traditions and movements, there are several ways in which it can be said to staunchly stand *without* or, rather, outside of the African American cultural aesthetic orbit. Consider, for example, the enormous influence that several non-African American (or, rather, not exclusively African American) cultural aesthetic traditions and sociopolitical movements have had on the origins and evolution of hip hop culture—perhaps, none more than the Women's Liberation movement, the Homophile movement, and postmodernism. In short, *Hip Hop's Inheritance*, taking interdisciplinarity and intersectionality seriously, employs the epistemologies and methodologies from a wide range of academic and organic intellectual/activist communities in its efforts to advance an intellectual history and critical theory of hip hop culture. Drawing from academic and organic intellectual/activist communities as diverse as African American studies and Lesbian, Gay, Bisexual, and Transgender (LGBT) studies, women's studies and postcolonial studies, history and philosophy, politics and economics, sociology and ethnomusicology, *Hip Hop's Inheritance* calls into question one-dimensional and monodisciplinary interpretations or, rather, misinterpretations of a multidimensional and multivalent form of popular culture that has increasingly come to include cultural criticism, social commentary, and political analysis that not only challenges previously held conceptions of U.S. popular culture, but also longstanding and lethargic perceptions of African American culture, especially African American underclass and working-poor youth culture, African American women's culture, and African American homosexual culture.

OF GIVING THANKS AND PRAISE: SAYING *ASANTE SANA* TO MY FAMILY AND FRIENDS, TO MY COLLEAGUES AND COMRADES

Hip Hop's Inheritance is not simply an intellectual exercise concerned with contributing an intellectual history and critical theory of hip hop culture. Much more, it also stands as a testament to what the many people who have contributed to my personal, professional, and radical political development have taught me. Each chapter of this book bears the imprint of the diverse— although often disconnected—intellectual and political arenas and agendas I draw from and endeavor to establish critical dialogue with. As a consequence, the list of academics, organic intellectuals, activists, archivists, institutions, and organizations to which I am indebted is, indeed, enormous. Such being the case, I hope I may be forgiven for deciding that the most appropriate way in which to acknowledge my sincere appreciation is simply to list individuals below without the protracted praise each has so solemnly earned. My deepest gratitude and most heartfelt *asante sana* (a thousand thanks) is offered, first and foremost, to my family: my mother, Marilyn Giles; my grandmothers, Lizzie Mae Davis (deceased) and Elva Rita Warren; my great aunt, Arcressia Charlene Connor; my older brother and his wife, Robert Smith II and Karen Smith; my younger brother, Dwight Clewis; my nieces and nephews, Journée Clewis, Dominique Clewis, Kalyn Smith, Robert Smith III, Ryan Smith, and Remington Smith; my father, Robert Smith I; my grandfathers, Joseph Warren (deceased) and Jafari Jakuta Rabaka (deceased); and, my innumerable aunts, uncles, and cousins throughout the Americas, the Caribbean, and Africa.

　　An undertaking as ambitious as *Hip Hop's Inheritance* would have been impossible without the assistance of colleagues and comrades, both far and wide. I express my earnest appreciation to the following fine folk, who each in their own special way contributed to the composition and completion of this book: Sonia Sanchez; Amiri Baraka; Camille Paglia; Walter Dallas; Kariamu Welsh; Lucius Outlaw; Lewis Gordon; Eduardo Bonilla-Silva; Rhonda Tankerson; Nedra James; Lamya Al-Kharusi; Denise Lovett; Adam

Clark; Elzie Billops; Sigmund Washington; Patrick DeWalt; Awon Atuire; Stacey Smith; Toroitich Chereno; De Reef Jamison; Anthony Lemelle; Troy Barnes; Zachary Epps; Ursula Lindqvist; Tiya Trent; Stephanie Sparling; La'Neice Littleton; Tim Allen; Howard Wallen; Janette Klingner; Vincent Harding; Marvin Lynn; David Stovall; Gloria Ladson-Billings; Daniel Solórzano; George Junne; Subini Annamma; Darrell Jackson; Deborah Morrison; Radia Amari; Stephanie Krusemark; Eva Torres Henry; Stephany Hope Wilson; Mpozi Tolbert (deceased); the National Association for Ethnic Studies (NAES); and the Association for the Study of African American Life and History (ASALH).

I cannot adequately convey the depth of my gratitude to the National Council for Black Studies (NCBS) for providing me with the critical feedback and fora to deepen and develop my relationship with the wider world of American studies, critical race studies, cultural studies, women's studies, sexuality studies, postcolonial studies, black radical politics, and critical social theory. I have been presenting my research on Africana critical theory at NCBS's annual conferences for more than a decade. Along with saying *nashukuru sana* (very special thanks) to NCBS in general, I would be remiss not to single out several members whose key contributions and intellectual encouragement have made the present volume possible. I, therefore, express my earnest appreciation to the following NCBS colleagues and comrades: Molefi Asante; Maulana Karenga; James Turner; Delores Aldridge; James Stewart; Martell Teasley; Mark Christian; Ronald Stephens; James Conyers; Charles Jones; Sundiata Cha-Jua; Perry Hall; Shirley Weber; Barbara Wheeler; Alfred Young; Bill Little (deceased); Munasha Furusa; Akinyele Umoja; Fred Hord; Terry Kershaw; Jeffrey Ogbar; Scot Brown; Alan Colon; Abdul Nanji; Christel Temple; Patricia Reid-Merritt; Kevin Cokley; Salim Faraji; Cecil Gray; and Ricky Jones.

The faculty, staff, and students in the Department of Ethnic Studies and the Center for Studies of Ethnicity and Race in America (CSERA) at the University of Colorado at Boulder deserve special thanks for their patience and critical support. *Nashukuru sana* to our steadfast staff, especially Sandra Lane and Tiya Trent, for always being there and lending a struggling brother a helping hand. I am also deeply indebted to my colleagues and comrades who selflessly serve on the faculty in the Department of Ethnic Studies, each of whom have patiently listened to me rant and rave about the "hyper-corporate colonization of hip hop culture" over the last couple of years. I say *nashukuru sana*, especially, to professors William King, Deward Walker, Daryl Maeda, and Seema Sohi, who have consistently supported both my teaching and research endeavors over the years.

Several libraries, research centers, special collections, and archives hosted and helped me transform this book from an inchoate idea into its fully realized form. I am indelibly indebted to the directors, research fellows, and staffs of: the Hip Hop Archive and the W. E. B. Du Bois Institute for African and African American Research, Harvard University; Arthur A. Houghton, Jr., Library, Harvard University; Schomburg Center for Research in Black Culture, New York Public Library; Nicholas Murray Butler Library, Columbia University; Institute for African American Affairs, New York University; Elmer Holmes Bobst Library, New York University; John Henrik Clarke Africana Library, Africana Studies and Research Center, Cornell University; Charles L. Blockson African American Collection, Temple University; Center for African American History and Culture, Temple University; Center for Africana Studies, University of Pennsylvania; August Wilson Center for African American Culture, Pittsburgh, Pennsylvania; Center for American Music, University of Pittsburgh; Center for Popular Culture Studies, Bowling Green State University; Center for Black Music Research, Columbia College Chicago; Karla Scherer Center for the Study of American Culture, University of Chicago; Center for Popular Music, Middle Tennessee State University; Center for the History of Music Theory and Literature, Jacobs School of Music, Indiana University; African American Cultural Center, University of Illinois at Chicago; Bruce Nesbitt African American Cultural Center, University of Illinois at Urbana-Champaign; African American Cultural Center, North Carolina State University; H. Fred Simons African American Cultural Center, University of Connecticut at Storrs; Moorland-Spingarn Research Center, Howard University; John Hope Franklin Collection for African and African American Documentation, Rare Book, Manuscript, and Special Collections Library, Duke University; Carter G. Woodson Center for African American and African Studies, University of Virginia; Robert W. Woodruff Library, Atlanta University Center Archives; Manuscript Sources for African American History, Special Collections, Emory University; John L. Warfield Center for African and African American Studies, University of Texas at Austin; Center for African American Studies, University of Houston; African and African American Collection, University Library, University of California, Berkeley; Institute for Advanced Feminist Research, University of California, Santa Cruz; Ralph J. Bunche Center for African American Studies, University of California, Los Angeles; Blair-Caldwell African American Research Library, Denver Public Library; Center for Media, Arts, and Performance, Alliance for Technology, Learning, and Society (ATLAS) Institute, University of Colorado at Boulder; American Music Research Center, College of Music, University of Colorado at Boulder; Howard B. Waltz Music Library, College of Music, University of Colorado at Boulder; Department of Musicology, College of Music, University of Colorado at Boulder; African American Materials, Special Collections, Norlin Library, University of Colorado at Boulder.

My publisher and I would like to thank and openly acknowledge Stephanie Sparling, who graciously granted permission to use her triptych for the book cover. Majoring in both art and Africana studies at the University of Colorado at Boulder, I have been able to witness Stephanie's extraordinary growth and development over the years. In my mind, her cultural aesthetic, artistry, and activism are the epitome of the best of what hip hop culture has to offer, not simply the present, but the future. In short, she is one of those rare and remarkable human beings who is—as is so often said of Romare Bearden, Duke Ellington, and Audre Lorde—"beyond category."

My editor, Michael Sisskin, and the Lexington Books editorial board deserve very special thanks (*nashukuru sana*) for seeing the potential in this book project and gently prodding me along during the many months it took me to revise the manuscript and prepare it for production. Michael's keen eye and constructive criticisms of the manuscript have certainly helped me to compose one of my most accessible books to date. I would like to formally thank Michael and, my publisher, Julie Kirsch for the promptness and professionalism with which they have handled my book projects, and for their patience with my extremely erratic (if not a bit eccentric) research and writing regimen, which in this instance took me to dozens of university and public libraries, archives, and research centers. I am not by any means the easiest person to correspond with when I am working, but throughout the entire research and writing process they calmly fielded my inquiries and coolly encouraged me to complete my book.

This book is offered as an emblem of my deep and abiding admiration for the artists, activists, and insurgent intelligentsia of the Harlem Renaissance, Black Arts movement, and Feminist Art movement. It is also intended as a humble token of my gratitude and eternal indebtedness to the faculty, staff, and students of Booker T. Washington High School for the Performing and Visual Arts (i.e., "Arts Magnet") and the University of the Arts. Even more, however, *Hip Hop's Inheritance* will hopefully register as a contribution to the wider world's comprehension of that generation of Americans born in the aftermath of the Civil Rights, Black Power, Black Arts, Women's Liberation, and Feminist Art movements. My profound respect for each of the aforementioned can be found in each and every word to follow: *A luta continua.*

If, then, my most respected readers, any inspiration or insights are gathered from my journey through the concrete jungles of rap music and hip hop culture, I pray you will attribute them to each of the aforementioned. However, if (and when) you find foibles and intellectual idiosyncrasies, I humbly hope you will neither associate them with any of the forenamed nor, most especially, the hip hop generation. I, and I alone, am responsible for what herein is written. As is my custom, then, I begin by softly saying, almost silently singing my earnest and eternal prayer: *Nkosi Sikelel' iAfrika.*

Chapter One

"It's Bigger Than Hip Hop!": Toward a Critical Theory of Hip Hop Culture and Contemporary Society

The challenge to critical theorists to rethink their presuppositions according to the realities of non-European cultures and technologies remains the most underthematized aspect of critical theories new and old. —William Wilkerson and Jeffrey Paris, *New Critical Theory: Essays on Liberation*, p. 8

INTRODUCTION TO *HIP HOP'S INHERITANCE* AND HISTORICAL AMNESIA

I have long thought of hip hop culture as embodying both the best and the worst that my generation has to offer: the "best," insofar as it innovatively builds on and goes beyond several previous cultural aesthetic movements, and, the "worst," in light of the fact that it is often very difficult to determine whether hip hop is highlighting the ongoing harshness of the African American experience at the turn of the twenty-first century or simply glamorizing and glorifying the vices and vulgarities of ghetto life and culture. Admittedly, then, as with so many other Hip Hop studies scholars, I have my own unique love/hate relationship with hip hop culture, especially what has come to be its most visible aesthetic expressions: rap music and videos. Born into both the so-called Soul Babies and Hip Hop generations, I have come to think that part of my love/hate relationship with hip hop culture might have something to do with my still-lingering "soul baby" generation sensibilities. In *Soul Babies: Black Popular Culture and the Post-Soul Aesthetic*, my colleague Mark Anthony Neal (2002) contends that the "children of soul" (i.e., the "Soul Babies") are those folk "born between the 1963 March on Washington and the *Bakke* case," which was an unprecedented 1978 challenge to affirmative action (p. 3).[1]

According to Neal, those of us born between 1963 and 1978 are distinguished from previous generations of African Americans on account of the fact that we are the first generation of black folk "who came to maturity in the age of Reaganomics and experienced the change from urban industrialism to deindustrialism, from segregation to desegregation, from essential notions of blackness to metanarratives on blackness," and we experienced all of this "without any nostalgic allegiance to the past (back in the days of Harlem, or the thirteenth-century motherland, for that matter), but firmly in grasp of the existential concerns of this brave new world" (p. 3). The "Soul Babies" Generation, therefore, radically re-imagines contemporary African American identity and experience from simultaneously post–Civil Rights and post–Black Power movement perspectives, and in doing so they free contemporary interpretations of black identity and experience from the trappings of antiquated traditions that may very well have served a pivotal purpose in black folk's tragic and triumphant past but presently, to put it plainly, seem like a fish out of water. As with the hip hop generation, and as will be critically discussed in detail in chapter 3, the "Soul Babies" Generation might also be called the *post–Black Arts movement* and *post-blaxploitation films* generation in that many of its major motifs are derivative of the discursive formations and discursive practices of the Black Arts movement and blaxploitation films. Already, then, we witness here that, similar to the hip hop generation, the Soul Babies Generation contradictorily draws from both progressive and retrogressive aspects of 1960s and 1970s African American identity and experience.

What Neal conceived of as the "Soul Babies" Generation, others have argued might more properly be called the "hip hop" generation. For instance, in *The Hip Hop Generation: Young Blacks and the Crisis in African American Culture*, my colleague Bakari Kitwana (2002) contends that those African Americans born between 1965 and 1984 have a distinct worldview when compared with the views and values of previous generations of black folk. He cites not simply the achievements, but also the perceived failures of both the Civil Rights and Black Power movements as significant factors that have shaped and molded the hip hop generation's views and values. Obviously desegregation, the Civil Rights Act of 1964, and the Voting Rights Act of 1965, among other 1960s breakthroughs, significantly impacted the life-chances and lived-experiences of the hip hop generation. To this we might also add the influence that the unabashed embrace of "blackness" and emphasis on African Americans' "African roots" during the Black Power period has had on the hip hop generation.[2]

Among what the hip hop generation understands to be some of the failures of the Civil Rights and Black Power generations were their inability to curtail institutional racism and combat ongoing structural inequality. Even after Martin Luther King, Jr., articulated African Americans' sincere wish to live in peace, in Christian brotherhood and sisterhood, with the descendants of the folk who had enslaved their ancestors in his famous "I Have a Dream" speech, much (if not seemingly most) of white America rejected black America's plea for reconciliation and racial equality.[3] This, of course, led to the Black Power movement, which many hip hop cultural critics believe often confused discussions about social and political power with the business of actually *empowering* black people.

From many hip hoppers' points of view, after more than 350 years of anti-black racism, specifically the seething white supremacy that African American enslavement and post-Emancipation racial segregation (i.e., American apartheid) represented, much more than state-sanctioned bills, pious marches, and radical Black Power rhetoric was needed. Many hip hop cultural critics connect the increasingly high black unemployment, incarceration, and high school drop-out rates to America's ongoing institutional racism and structural inequality. However, and rather ironically I might add, as more and more of the hip hop generation comes to social and political maturity they are seeing firsthand that eradicating institutional racism and structural inequality, even under the auspices of the first African American president, Barack Obama, is problem-laden and protracted despite the dire urgency the situation demands. It would seem that we can already anticipate the kinds of criticisms that the post–hip hop generation is liable to level against the hip hop generation in light of the fact that the hip hop generation has before it an opportunity unprecedented in the annals of black America: never before have such seemingly favorable conditions for African Americans to eradicate institutional racism and structural inequality existed than during the administration of the first African American president. But, the hip hoppers bemoan, "looks are deceiving" and "everything that glitters ain't gold!" If it took more than 350 years for America to become entrenched in its own homespun apartheid and anti-black racism, then it could take about as long for it to radically transform and redeem itself.

Side-stepping the finger-pointing and blame-games that have long plagued black America and caused successive "generation gaps," *Hip Hop's Inheritance* seeks to analyze and criticize what the hip hop generation has, literally, *inherited* from previous generations of African Americans and allied others: from the Blackface Minstrel and Black Women's Club movements to the New Negro movement and Harlem Renaissance, from the Civil Rights and Black Power movements to the Black Arts and Feminist Art movements. Moreover, *Hip Hop's Inheritance* will also be concerned with what the hip hop generation has not inherited. In other words, it critically calls into question why hip hoppers have accepted, embraced, and celebrated certain elements from the past and not others. This, as can already be imagined, will reveal a great deal about the hip hop generation's politics and enable us to highlight what is progressive and what is retrogressive in hip hop culture.

By bringing contemporary hip hop aesthetics into critical dialogue with classical African American (among other) cultural aesthetic traditions and movements we will be able to better decipher many of the double-meanings and deeper messages of hip hop culture (and, by default, contemporary black popular culture), not only for the hip hop generation, but for those of the previous generations who comprehend hip hop to be much more than cursing over booty-shaking beats and senseless celebrations of licentiousness, hypermasculinism, heterosexism, materialism, alcoholism, drug-dealing, and gang-banging. This critical comparative approach to hip hop culture will also provide post–hip hop generations with a series of critiques of hip hop culture from the point of view of someone, a hip hop critical theorist, who has a dialectical relationship and critical rapport with hip hop and a healthy (albeit critical) respect for past African American cultural aesthetic traditions and movements. Insofar as I am concerned, hip hop culture is virtually incomprehensible without a working knowledge of, at the very least, the cultural aesthetics of the Harlem Renaissance and the Black Arts movement. Moreover, when the Harlem Renaissance and the Black Arts movement are connected to the corollary social and political movements from which they emerged (i.e., the New Negro and Black Power movements, respectively), then, hip hop's inheritance is discovered to be much more than cultural aesthetics. Which is also to say, hip hoppers, however unwittingly, have inherited both cultural aesthetics *and* conservative/liberal/radical politics from previous African American cultural aesthetic and sociopolitical movements. Similar to past African American cultural aesthetic and sociopolitical movements, the hip hop generation has inherited African Americans' longstanding emphasis on eloquence, rhetoric, and the spiritual dimensions of the spoken word, especially as conceived of, and articulated during the Civil Rights and Black Power movements. Therefore, is it any wonder that rap music ultimately eclipsed DJing, break-dancing, and graffiti to become the major and most visible aspect of hip hop culture?

One of the ironies of *Hip Hop's Inheritance* is that it is not a book about rap music, even though rap music is widely considered the major and most visible aspect of hip hop culture and, still further, even though most folk in the modern moment make little or no distinction between rap music and hip hop culture. On the contrary, *Hip Hop's Inheritance* is actually concerned with hip hop's history of ideas or, rather, hip hop's world of ideas, and how those ideas have been, whether consciously or unconsciously, influenced and inspired by previous African American cultural aesthetic traditions and sociopolitical movements. This means, then, that throughout this book the term the "hip hop generation" is *employed to conceptually capture not only black popular culture and black popular music after the Black Arts and Feminist Art movements, but also African American sociopolitical traditions and movements after the Civil Rights, Black Power, Women's Liberation, and Homophile movements of the 1960s and 1970s.* Although black popular music in many instances will provide the main motifs and major points of departure for *Hip Hop's Inheritance,* yet and still it is important to strongly stress that the subsequent studies are primarily preoccupied with what the origins and evolution of black popular culture and black popular music reveal to us about "the strange meaning of being [both] black" *and* a hip hopper in America, to play on W. E. B. Du Bois's apt phrase from *The Souls of Black Folk* discussed in the preface (see also Rabaka, forthcoming).

Interestingly enough, this brings us to Amiri Baraka's dictum in his classic work on black music, *Blues People* (1963), where he asserted, "it seems to me that if the Negro represents, or is symbolic of, something in and about the nature of American culture, this certainly should be revealed by his characteristic music" (p. ix). In other words, he continued, "I am saying that if the music of the Negro in America, in all its permutations, is subjected to a socio-anthropological as well as musical scrutiny, something about the essential nature of the Negro's existence in this country ought to be revealed, as well as something about the essential nature of this country, *i.e.*, society as a whole" (pp. ix–x, emphasis in original).

Obviously rap music is the latest in the long line of historic soundtracks that African Americans have created to capture their both particular and peculiar lived-experiences and lived-endurances at the turn of the twenty-first century. As Baraka's work suggests, and as *Hip Hop's Inheritance* emphasizes: *black music has always been much more than music.* It is the music of the outcast and oppressed, the "blue notes" and break-beats, the dark rhythms and rhymes emerging from the underbelly of and exiles in America, and as such it has historically and currently continues to serve sociopolitical purposes. This means, then, that rap music, as the major soundtrack of hip hop culture, as the premier soundtrack of contemporary black popular culture, is like a litmus test indicating and accenting many of the urgent issues and ills of black America, as well as those of mainstream America and, as quiet as it has been kept, many of those that have come to define our entire epoch. By shifting—in the most Foucaultian fashion imaginable—the focus from rap music to the historical evolution of hip hop culture as a whole, we will be able to better comprehend not only what the hip hop generation has inherited from previous African American cultural aesthetic traditions and movements beyond musical contributions, but also what it has or potentially could contribute to post–hip hop generation cultural aesthetic traditions and sociopolitical movements beyond musical contributions.[4] It is important to emphasize this last point, as it explicitly indicates that *Hip Hop's Inheritance* is ironically about much more than, well, hip hop's inheritance, or previous generations' contributions to the hip hop generation. It is also about hip hop's contributions to posterity, to future generations—something very few folk, even the most astute hip hop cultural critics among us, have rarely ventured to critically comment on. *Hip Hop's Inheritance*, then, is simultaneously an intellectual history of hip hop's past, a critical theory of hip hop's present, and an unpretentious forecast of its possible future.

When Baraka asserts that "if the music of the Negro in America, in all its permutations, is subjected to a socio-anthropological as well as musical scrutiny, something about the essential nature of the Negro's existence in this country ought to be revealed, as well as something about the essential nature of this country, *i.e.*, society as a whole," this is precisely where *Hip Hop's Inheritance* is conceptually situated. Here, at the intersections of contemporary ethnomusicology, sociology of music, social anthropology, feminist theory, critical race theory, and cultural studies, this is where *Hip Hop's Inheritance* updates, alters, and solemnly searches for answers to Baraka's still relevant queries—many of which were raised not only in *Blues People*, but in his other volumes of music criticism, such as *Black Music* (1967), *The Music: Reflections on Jazz and Blues* (1987), and *Digging: The Afro-American Soul of American Classical Music* (2009), as well. Consequently, building on and seeking to go beyond Baraka's assertion that black music speaks in a special way about black America in particular, the United States in general, and our age as a whole, *Hip Hop's Inheritance* will be primarily preoccupied with answering the following questions: What does hip hop culture tell us about contemporary African American culture? What does hip hop culture tell us about contemporary American culture? What does hip hop culture tell us about contemporary race relations in the United States, especially ongoing anti-black and other forms of racism? What does hip hop culture tell us about the contemporary conditions of women and homosexuals in the United States, especially considering its infamous expressions of hypermasculinism, misogyny, homophobia, and heterosexism? Lastly, what does hip hop culture tell us about the constantly changing character of contemporary capitalism, nationally and internationally, especially considering the ever-increasing chasm between the haves and the have-nots?

For those who would argue that "music is music, plain and simple," and that music should not be subjected to ideological critique or summoned for the purposes of radical politics and critical social theory. I would gently remind them that above I explicitly stated that this is not a book about rap music, but one concerned with offering an intellectual history and critical theory of hip hop culture—again, the culture from whence rap music sprang. I have long believed that although we now have a wide range of work on rap music and videos, there has been little or no scholarly attention turned to the ways in which hip hop culture is connected to, and, in many senses, represents the ongoing evolution of African American cultural aesthetic traditions and movements. For instance, by beginning his history of hip hop in the late 1960s, and by only mentioning the Black Arts movement in passing (actually on only one page), although Jeff Chang's *Can't Stop, Won't Stop: A History of the Hip Hop Generation* (2005) is certainly one of the most comprehensive works on the history of hip hop we have to date, yet and still, it leaves much to be desired and actually downplays, or erases altogether, the origins and evolution of African American intellectual and cultural history. How will his readers be able to really and truly comprehend hip hop culture without, at the very least, a working knowledge of the classical cultural aesthetic traditions and movements that hip hop, even if unwittingly, has been and continues to be in dialogue with, deconstructing and reconstructing to speak to the special needs and novel challenges of contemporary culture and society?

Too often contemporary African American history, culture, and struggle is approached as though it is not in any way connected to classical African American history, culture, and struggle. This is problematic for a plethora of reasons, although none more than the fact that it indicates that well past the first decade of the twenty-first century African Americans continue to be viewed as either subhumans or nonhumans. Allow me to briefly explain by way of W. E. B. Du Bois's "gift theory." Du Bois's gift theory is part and parcel of his overarching sociological discourse and, although often overlooked, it evolved a great deal: from his early work at the end of the nineteenth century through to his most sustained discussion of the theory in his 1924 classic *The Gift of Black Folk*. For instance, in "The Conservation of Races," which was published in 1897, it will be recalled that Du Bois (1897) declared: "We believe that the Negro people, as a race, have a contribution to make to civilization and humanity, which no other race can make" (p. 15). He held this belief primarily for two reasons.

First, his belief was based on Africa's past, "one of the richest and most intriguing which the world has known." Most race and/or racist scientists at the turn of the twentieth century either had no knowledge of Africa's past, or they were aware of it and developed their racist theories to counter claims of the greatness of African antiquity. As Du Bois (1995b) put it in "The Superior Race," which was originally published in 1923: "Lions have no historians" (p. 474). By which he wished to convey that even though the lion is universally revered as the "king of the jungle," it is nonetheless an animal and, therefore, has no history and thus no need of historians. It is only human beings who can make history and create culture, and in a white supremacist world blacks are not authentically human but, as observed above, more or less subhuman at best, or nonhuman at worst. Therefore, the history and culture that Africans did in fact produce in ancient epochs, or in the "precolonial" period, as it were, is viewed as either influenced by or derivative of

European culture, or a "primitive" attempt to imitate and emulate European culture, usually Greco-Roman culture.

The second reason Du Bois believed that Pan-African people had a significant contribution to make to human culture and civilization was because their endurance and experience of holocaust, enslavement, colonization, segregation, and so on, had "gifted" them with "second-sight," as he put it in *The Souls of Black Folk.* In this instance, "second-sight" enabled black folk to see things that others could not on account of the specificities of African and African American historicity. That is to say, Du Bois believed that blacks' contemporary "gifts" to human culture and civilization had to do with their particular and peculiar position in and struggle(s) against one of the major systems of exploitation, oppression, and violence plaguing the large majority of humanity in the modern moment: racial colonialism and, more specifically, what could more properly be called *white supremacy* (C. W. Mills, 1997, 1998, 2003b). Consequently, by continuing to disconnect contemporary African American culture from classical African and African American culture most hip hop cultural critics, however surreptitiously, are participating in, and perpetuating a form of anti-black racist historical rupture, all the while critiquing and celebrating contemporary black popular culture (i.e., rap music and hip hop culture).[5]

When hip hop culture is placed within the streams of cultural aesthetics and radical politics flowing from the Harlem Renaissance, Black Arts movement, and Feminist Art movement, new, more historically rooted and culturally relevant interpretations of hip hop culture emerge that enable us to make sense of much of what has previously appeared to be nonsense. In point of fact, and in no way condoning or apologizing for its falterings, the hip hop generation is not the first generation of virulent homophobes and heterosexists. Heterosexism has historical roots that span U.S. history and culture. The hip hop generation is not the first generation of vocal hypermasculinists and misogynists. These sentiments can be found as far back in U.S. history as the patriarchal thought and practices of the so-called founding fathers.[6] Lastly, the hip hop generation is not the first generation of young folk seemingly obsessed with obtaining bourgeois culture, values, and social status, especially the mega-materialism currently running rampant in the United States. Truth be told, at its heart the "American dream" is a bourgeois materialist or carpetbagger capitalist dream, one as deeply "American" as apple pie, baseball, and a McDonald's Big Mac. This means, then, that when hip hop culture is placed within the streams of cultural aesthetics and radical politics flowing from the Harlem Renaissance, Black Arts movement, and Feminist Art movement it is seen to embody many of the contradictions, controversies, and avant-garde inclinations of its major ancestral aesthetic movements. However, because most of the hip hop generation, as with previous generations, have so little knowledge of past African American, feminist, and queer cultural aesthetic traditions and movements, when and where hip hop culture is contradictory and controversial it appears as though it is somehow completely breaking away from classical black popular culture instead of, as is so often the case, merely synthesizing, recycling, and recreating past African American, feminist, and queer cultural aesthetic thought and traditions.

Returning to the notion that for black America *music is much more than music*, which will be a recurring theme throughout this book, it is important here to bear in mind Ralph Ellison's contention in *Shadow and Act* (1964), where he eloquently argued that African American popular music constitutes an indispensable element and cultural indicator of African Americans' lifeworlds and life-struggles. African American popular music, then, is much more than the soundtrack to black popular culture. It is more akin to a musical map and cultural compass that provides us with a window into black folk's world, and also a window into the ways in which African Americans' aforementioned "second-sight" shapes and shades their worldview. Ellison (1964) went so far as to argue that instead of "social or political freedom . . . the art—the blues, the spirituals, the jazz, the dance—was what we had in place of freedom" (pp. 247–48; see also Ellison, 1995a, 1995b, 2001).[7] In other words, black folk have long had aesthetic freedom instead of social and political freedom, linguistic wealth instead of monetary wealth. *Hip Hop's Inheritance*, therefore,will not in any way attempt to come to terms with the complexity of the ever-evolving forms and content of African American popular music, especially rap. Rather, it aims to offer an intellectual history and critical theory of hip hop culture in light of the *extramusical influences* that led to the rise of rap music and the reign of hip hop culture. In a nutshell, then, *Hip Hop's Inheritance* is essentially about hip hop culture's extramusical influences (specifically its intellectual and sociopolitical antecedents), and the ways in which the embrace or rejection of these influences sometimes simultaneously conceptually incarcerates and laudably liberates the hip hop generation.

In the final analysis, however, the hip hop generation is ultimately responsible for its own decolonization and liberation. Which is also to say, *Hip Hop's Inheritance* does not intend to contribute to, or continue the blame-game that has ruined the relationships and caused so much "bad blood" between generation after generation of African Americans since the issuing of the Emancipation Proclamation. More cultural criticism and critical theory than music criticism and ethnomusicology, the studies that constitute *Hip Hop's Inheritance* are intended as "cognitive maps" of the origins and evolution of hip hop culture. In his classic essay entitled "Cognitive Mapping," the noted Marxist literary theorist Fredric Jameson (1988) contends that the "incapacity to map socially is as crippling to political experience as the analogous incapacity to map spatially is for urban experience. It follows that an aesthetic of cognitive mapping in this sense is an integral part of any socialist political project" (p. 353). Now, whether or not my readers agree or disagree with Jameson's democratic socialist politics, the reality of the matter is that hip hop cultural critics have been bemoaning hip hop's depoliticization and embourgeoisement for more than a decade—that is, since the end of the so-called Golden Age of Rap, 1987–1999, the time period when "conscious rap" and a more progressive hip hop culture reigned.[8]

I am, as I am certain my work has already indicated, an advocate of radical humanism and democratic socialism, but, yet and still, I have issues with Jameson's conception of "cognitive mapping." Indeed, I take exception to Jameson's assertion that "anyone who believes that the profit motive and the logic of capital accumulation are not the fundamental laws of this world, who believes that these do not set absolute barriers and limits to social changes and transformation undertaken in it—such a person is living in an alternative universe; or, to put it more politely, in this universe such a person—assuming he or she is progressive—is doomed to social democracy, with its now abundantly documented treadmill of failures and capitulations" (p. 354). Here, I agree *and* disagree with Jameson: I agree that capitalism most certainly "set[s] absolute barriers and limits to social changes and trans-formation," and that social democracy is "doomed" to repeat the now "abun-dantly documented treadmill of failures and capitulations" that have come to characterize contemporary capitalist democracies. However, I strongly dis-agree with Jameson when and where he rattles off the vices and vulgarities of capitalism as though "the profit motive and the logic of capital accumulation are . . . the fundamental laws of this world." The question begs, which world? Even more, whose world? Where on earth does Jameson live (I, of course, know full well that Professor Jameson teaches at Duke University and, there-fore, must live in the vicinity of Durham, North Carolina)?

Capitalism certainly isn't singularly the most pressing sociopolitical prob-lem for women in the twenty-first century. Patriarchy seems to have lost none of its insidious power, and need I remind my readers that patriarchy preceded the emergence of capitalism? Capitalism certainly isn't singularly the most pressing sociopolitical problem for nonwhites in the twenty-first century. White supremacy, although still an offensive term to most whites, especially wealthy and politically powerful whites, remains the best term to conceptually capture the racial colonialism, racial exploitation, racial oppres-sion, and often outright racial violence that most nonwhites—which is to say the majority of humanity—historically have been and currently continue to be forced to endure at the hands of both ill-will conservative and well-meaning liberal whites. Finally, capitalism certainly isn't singularly the most pressing sociopolitical problem for homosexuals in the twenty-first century. Homophobia and heterosexism continue to plague our homosexual brothers and sisters within both capitalist and socialist democracies. All of this is to say, although *Hip Hop's Inheritance* is intended as a critical theory of hip hop culture, Marxism is merely one of many major theories that will be employed to "cognitively map" the world of hip hop beyond rap music and videos. Critical race theory, feminist theory, queer theory, and postcolonial theory, among others, will all be brought into play when and where applicable. It is here, then, that I wish to openly acknowledge *Hip Hop's Inheritance* as a continuation of my expatiation and ongoing articulation of *the Africana tradition of critical theory* and, even more importantly in this instance, *Africana critical theory of contemporary society.*[9]

To quell confusion, it will be important for me to, once again, unambiguously explain what Africana critical theory is and is not. In addition, since I have previously only applied Africana critical theory to the past, and specifically classical critical theorists (e.g., W. E. B. Du Bois, C. L. R. James, Negritude, Frantz Fanon, and Amilcar Cabral), it will be equally important here to emphasize its utility for critically engaging the present and its promise for the future. To begin, it should be said that Africana critical theory is certainly not anti-Marxist, as anyone who has closely read my previous work will surely agree. The above critique of Jameson's cultural Marxism should not be taken as an unequivocal rejection of Marxism, but more as an open and honest admission of what I understand to be some of the major limitations and discursive deficiencies of Marxist theory, and especially what has come to be called "cultural Marxism" (see Jameson, 1998, 2007). Admittedly, Africana critical theory is intellectually attracted to Jameson's conception of "cognitive mapping" because of its emphasis on the connections between social and spatial mapping and how the inability to do either ultimately leads to all sorts of postmodern apolitical and ahistorical theories and praxes that ignore the nature of neo-imperialism. However, when and where Jameson, like a good little nostalgic New Left white Marxist male, paternalistically points to "the profit motive and the logic of capital accumulation" as "the fundamental laws of this world," this is precisely when and where Africana critical theory takes issue with his conception of "cognitive mapping" and the theories of other Marxists of his ilk.

What has long intellectually attracted Africana critical theory to Marxist theory is the latter's longstanding efforts to account for determination, which helps to accent the multileveled interaction between historically situated subjects who act and materially rooted institutions and structures that colonize and circumscribe—which is to say, inimically influence and incarcerate—such action. The aforementioned human action is tantamount to what we in contemporary critical theory call "social praxis," and this praxis can be neither reduced to free-floating or neutrally discrete acts of individuals nor to impartial institutions and structures immune to the frequent sloppiness of human agency and ambition. What truly distinguishes the Marxian dialectic is its unrepentant methodological effort to critically comprehend the relationship between individuals and institutions in light of dynamic social, political, and economic practices during a particular time and in a specific space. Therefore, the overarching aim of Marxist theory is to apprehend each and every historical moment, political movement, and social phenomenon as a dynamic and multidimensional transaction between, on the one hand, individuals influenced by antecedent institutions and traditions, and, on the other hand, the institutions and social conventions of the established order in the process of being transformed by insurgent individuals. Marxist theory insists that historical and sociological explanations must perceive, in some recognizable manner, the economic arena as the fundamental determining element in accounting for the *synchronicity* (i.e., internal dynamics) and *diachronicity* (i.e., historical change) of human culture and societies in general, and capitalist culture and societies in particular (Best, 1995; Carver, 1982, 1991; Gottlieb, 1992; Jay, 1984; McLennan, 1981).

Obviously Africana critical theory cannot be considered (at least not in any narrow-minded sense) a form of Marxist critical theory, as it does not view the economic sphere as the fundamental factor in accounting for historical, cultural, social, and political change. For Africana critical theory, along with capitalism and class struggle, race and racism, gender and sexism, colonialism and neocolonialism, and sexuality and heterosexism are also fundamental factors that determine the synchronicity and diachronicity of contemporary human cultures and societies. In other words, Africana critical theory is not anti-Marxist, but it is also certainly not solely Marxist, because it quite simply does not privilege Marxist theory's critique of capitalism and class struggle over feminist theory's critique of patriarchy and misogyny, or queer theory's critique of homophobia and heterosexism, or postcolonial theory's critique of classical and contemporary colonialism (i.e., neo-colonialism), or, finally, critical race theory's critique of white supremacy and cultural racism.

Perhaps Cornel West's contentions in *Keeping Faith: Philosophy and Race in America* (1993) best captures the critical relationship and dialectical rapport between Africana critical theory and Marxist theory: "I hold that Marxist theory as a methodological orientation remains indispensable—although ultimately inadequate—in grasping distinctive features of African American oppression . . . Marxist theory still may provide the best explanatory account for certain phenomena, but it also may remain inadequate for other phenomena—notably here, the complex of racism in the modern West" (pp. 258, 267). West's view has been consistently echoed throughout African American intellectual and cultural history, although not without reservations and serious criticism. Africana critical theory, being both unapologetically interdisciplinary and intersectional, decidedly moves beyond the race/class conception of radical political and social thought frequently put forward by towering black male insurgent intellectual-activists, such as A. Philip Randolph, C. L. R. James, Oliver C. Cox, Martin Luther King, Jr., Malcolm X, Robert F. Williams, and Stokely Carmichael (Kwame Ture), and it emphasizes an *epistemic openness* to, not simply critical race theory and Marxist theory, but also to feminist theory, queer theory, and postcolonial theory, among many others. Hence, at the heart of Africana critical theory is an intense emphasis on radical humanism, one that openly acknowledges that all theories have strengths and weaknesses, and that "pristine" and "perfect" theories only exist in "mad scientists'" minds. It is important to discursively distinguish between Africana critical theory and Marxist critical theory insofar as over the years many Marxists have given lip service to "broadening the base" of their conception of critical theory, but very few have actually attempted or, even more, achieved it. This has led to what could be characterized as a serious "crisis" in contemporary critical social theory.

THE CRISIS OF CONTEMPORARY CRITICAL SOCIAL THEORY: THE BLACK RADICAL POLITICS AND CRITICAL RACE THEORY REMIX

For over a decade critical social theorists have been issuing calls for "a more multicultural, race and gender focused, and broad[er]-based" critical theory (Kellner, 1995, p. 20). Unfortunately, however, few of their fellow critical theorists have taken their summons seriously. One of the glaring ironies and intellectual injustices of contemporary critical theory is that even with the increasing academic popularity of feminist theory, postcolonial theory, queer theory and, more recently, critical race theory, the white- and male-dominated discourse(s) of critical theory have yet to develop meaningful and in-depth dialogues with these discursive communities. As a matter of fact, in the introduction to their groundbreaking volume, *New Critical Theory*, William Wilkerson and Jeffrey Paris (2001) openly admit that the "challenge to critical theorists to rethink their presuppositions according to the realities of non-European cultures and technologies remains the most underthematized aspect of critical theories new and old" (p. 8).

Part of the current crisis of critical theory has to do with its often uncritical reliance on classical Marxist concepts and categories without sufficiently revising and synthesizing them with new, especially non-Marxian and non-European, critical theoretical and radical political developments. Classical Marxism privileged class struggle and the proletariat as the agents of revolutionary social transformation, while unwittingly neglecting the overlapping, interlocking, and intersecting nature of racism and sexism in capitalist and colonialist societies. Moreover, in "The Obsolescence of Marxism?," one of the leading European American critical theorists, Douglas Kellner (1995), argues that it is "widely accepted that classical Marxism exaggerates the primacy of class and downplays the salience of gender and race. Clearly, oppression takes place in many more spheres than just the economic and the workplace, so a radical politics of the future should take account of gender and race as well as class" (p. 20). Notice that Kellner is not calling for a discursive disavowal of Marxism and/or critical class theory but coupling them, revising and synthesizing them with cutting-edge race and feminist theory. Many black radicals and multicultural Marxists, I believe, would partially agree with Kellner when he writes further:

> [W]e need to build on viable political and theoretical perspectives and resources of the past, and I would argue that Marxism continues to provide vital resources for radical theory and politics today. . . . In sum, I believe that we need new theoretical and political syntheses, drawing on the best of classical Enlightenment theory, Marxian theory, feminism, and other progressive theoretical and political currents of the present. Key aspects for such new syntheses, however, are found in the Marxian tradition, and those who prematurely abandon it are turning away from a tradition that has been valuable since Marx's day and will continue to be so in the foreseeable future. Consequently, Marxism is not yet obsolete. Rather, the Marxian theory continues to provide resources and stimulus for critical theory and radical politics in the present age. (pp. 25–26)[10]

Kellner and Africana critical theory, however, part company when and where he gives a detailed discussion of the relevance of European derived and developed theories or, rather, *Eurocentric* theories—Enlightenment theory, Marxism, and feminism—and only alludes to the work of non-European theorists or, as he put it, "*other* progressive theoretical and political currents" for renewing radical politics and critical social theory in the present (my emphasis). To his credit, Kellner states, "radical politics today should be more multicultural, race and gender focused, and broad-based than the original Marxian theory" (p. 20). But, he does not identify or critically engage the "other progressive theoretical and political currents" the way, nor to the discursive depth and detail to which he does a plethora of white male radical thinkers whose thought, he believes, contributes indelibly to the reconstruction of critical social theory.

Kellner is not alone in arguing for the continued importance of Marxism for contemporary radical politics and the reconstruction of critical social theory. In "Toward a New Critical Theory," another leading European American critical theorist, James Marsh (2001), audaciously asserts that "a critical theory without Marx" is a "critical theory that is insufficiently critical" (p. 57). He further contends:

> I think we need a much fuller appropriation and use of Marx than is going on in either postmodernism or Habermasian critical theory. If capitalism is deeply pathological and unjust, as I think it is and as I have argued in all of my works, then we need the resources of what still remains the deepest and most comprehensive critique of capitalist political economy, that which occurs in the late Marx in the pages

of the *Grundrisse, Capital,* and *Theories of Surplus Value,* a total of seven volumes that are more relevant than ever. For these reasons, I draw on Marx's theory of exploited labor in the workplace, his theory of tyranny, in which the economy and money impinge on noneconomic aspects of the lifeworld in a way that is absurd, his theory of a marginalized industrial reserve army, his theory of value and surplus value, and his account of substantive socialism. Capitalist pathology is not just colonization of lifeworld by system, although that is certainly an important part of such pathology, but includes exploitation, tyranny, domination, and marginalization as well. (p. 57)

As with Kellner's claims, Marsh is on point when he asserts the comprehensive character of Marx's critique of capitalism. Similar to Kellner, he warns contemporary critical theorists about the intellectual insularity and epistemic exclusiveness of their discourse and even goes so far as to say that "both modern and postmodern critical theory runs the risk of being idealistic in a bad sense, that is, insufficiently attentive to the task of interpreting, criticizing, and overcoming late capitalism in its racist, sexist, classist, and heterosexist aspects. We, modernists and postmodernists alike, need to get down to the job of social transformation" (p. 53). Now, after taking all of this in, one of the first critical thoughts that passes through the mind of an anti-racist and anti-sexist critical social theorist is: How will radical politics and critical social theory become "more multicultural, and race and gender focused," as Kellner and Marsh contend, if it does not turn to the thought and texts of the most progressive and, even further, *critical* race and gender theorists; some of whom happen to be nonwhite radical theorists and revolutionary intellectual-activists, particularly folk of African origin or descent, and some of whom, of course, are women, and nonwhite women in specific?

According to the Caribbean radical political theorist, Anthony Bogues (2003), who wrote in *Black Heretics, Black Prophets: Radical Political Intellectuals,* "in radical historical studies, when one excavates a different archive, alternative categories are opened up" (p. 86). To be sure, black radical theorists, such as W. E. B. Du Bois, C. L. R. James, Claudia Jones, Frantz Fanon, Amilcar Cabral, and Angela Davis, "deployed Marxism, but in [their] hands the categories used to describe historical processes were wrought into something else" (p. 81). That "something else" which Marxian categories were shaped and molded into by these theorists was based on their critical understanding of continental and diasporan African history, culture, and struggle.

Africana history, culture, and struggle are the deeply disregarded "different archives" that black radicals work with and operate from. These archives are not only in many senses distinctly divergent from the archives of most white Marxists, but embedded in them are recurring racial motifs that shade and color black radical politics and critical social theory. White Marxists' efforts to diminish and downplay racial domination and discrimination have made black radicals' marriage to Marxism a turbulent and very unhappy one. For example, in *From Class to Race: Essays in White Marxism and Black Radicalism*, the Caribbean philosopher Charles W. Mills (2003a) maintains:

> Throughout the twentieth century, many people of color were attracted to Marxism because of its far-ranging historical perspective, its theoretical centering of oppression, and its promise of liberation. But many of these recruits would later become disillusioned, both with Marxist theory and the practice of actual (white) Marxist parties. The historical vision turned out to be Eurocentric; the specificities of their racial oppression were often not recognized but were dissolved into supposedly all encompassing class categories; and the liberation envisaged did not include as a necessary goal the dismantling of white supremacy in all its aspects. Cedric Robinson's pioneering *Black Marxism* (2000), first published in 1983, recounts the long-troubled history of left-wing black diasporic intellectuals (W. E. B. Du Bois, C. L. R. James, George Padmore, Richard Wright, Aimé Césaire) with "white Marxism," and it argues for the existence of a distinct "black radical political tradition" whose historic foci and concerns cannot be simply assimilated to mainstream white Marxist theory. So even if the origin of white supremacy is most plausibly explained within a historical materialist framework that locates it in imperialist European expansionism—as the product, ultimately, of class forces and bourgeois class interests—race as an international global structure then achieves an intersubjective reality whose dialectic cannot simply be reduced to a class dynamic. (p. xvi; see also C. W. Mills, 1997, 1998, 1999, 2003b)

In other words, black radicals' issues with white Marxism often stem from the fact that they understand racism to be both economic *and* experiential. Racial oppression has more than merely an economic exploitative or class conflict dimension that can coolly and calmly be conjectured by well-meaning white Marxist social scientists (see Goldberg, 1993, 1997, 2001, 2008; Marable, 1995, 1996, 1997; Outlaw, 1996, 2005; C. J. Robinson, 2000, 2001). As I discussed in detail in *W. E. B. Du Bois and the Problems of the Twenty-First Century*, *Du Bois's Dialectics*, *Africana Critical Theory*, *Forms of Fanonism*, and *Against Epistemic Apartheid*, racism is malleable and motive, and white Marxists' insensitive attempts to reduce it to an outgrowth or offshoot of class struggle, or something internal to class conflict, robs the economically exploited *and* racially oppressed of an opportunity to critically theorize their lived-reality and a major determinant of their historical, cultural, social, and political identities (Rabaka, 2007, 2008a, 2009, 2010a, 2010b).

Many black radicals, especially black Marxists, are at pains to point out that their criticisms "should not be taken in the spirit of a complete repudiation of Marxism," since, they maintain, "a *modified* historical materialism might be able to carry out an adequate conceptualization of the significance of race" (C. W. Mills, 2003a, pp. xvi–xvii, emphasis in original). But, the longstanding problem has been and remains white Marxists' inconsideration of and unwillingness to critically grasp and grapple with the political economy of race and racism, in both capitalist and colonialist societies, in their extension and expansion of Marxian concepts and categories. Black Marxists have historically exhibited an epistemic openness, one quite characteristic of the Africana tradition of critical theory, to critical class theory in a way brazenly counter to white Marxists' almost universal unreceptiveness to, intellectual disinterestedness in, and gnarly neglect of, critical race theory.

Contemporary critical race theory, which could be defined as *anti-racist praxis-promoting theory critical of the ways in which white supremacy impacts institutions and individuals*, has its origins in the work of several civil rights lawyers in the early 1980s. Often associated with the Critical Legal Studies (CLS) movement, which demonstrated in dizzying ways that law is neither neutral nor apolitical, critical race theory began by challenging the racial neutrality of the law (Crenshaw et al., 1995; Delgado, 1995; Delgado and Stefancic 2001; Essed and Goldberg 2001; Goldberg, Musheno, and Bower, 2001; Valdes, Culp, and Harris, 2002). Nonwhite legal scholars, in complete agreement with the argument that law is non-neutral, criticized the mostly white male leaders of the CLS movement for failing to recognize and critically theorize the crucial role and continued relevance of *race* in social and political interactions and institutions. Their work was quickly recognized as *critical race theory*, and they themselves as *critical race theorists*. However, in recent years the term "critical race theory" has become what the Palestinian intellectual-activist Edward Said (1999, 2000) referred to as a "traveling theory," moving in and out of intellectual and political discursive communities far from its theoretical and intellectual origins, and with each move taking on new or multiple meanings and losing some of its original intent and logic.

In this sense, then, I argue that critical race theory should not be thought of as an uncritical coupling of anti-racism with Marxism/critical class theory, or limited to the work of the last twenty-five years explicitly identified under the rubric of "critical race theory." Its intellectual history and political journey, like that of the Africana tradition of critical theory, has been much more complicated than previously noted, especially when read against the backdrop of Africana intellectual history, black radical theory, and black revolutionary praxis. Within the Africana world of ideas and Africana intellectual history there has been and remains radical anti-racist thought on racial domination and discrimination, and specifically white supremacy, that prefigures and provides a black radical point of departure for contemporary critical race theory, and also, if truth be told, critical White studies (Rabaka, 2007, 2010a, 2010b, 2010c). Here I am hinting at what could be called *classical critical race theory*, which is not now and has never been an outgrowth of white Marxism or the Frankfurt School tradition of critical theory and, in fact, was underway long before the birth of Karl Marx in 1818.

Well ahead of Marxism and the Frankfurt School, as W. E. B. Du Bois's
Black Reconstruction and C. L. R. James's *The Black Jacobins* eloquently
illustrate, enslaved Africans developed critical anti-racist thought-traditions
in their efforts to topple white supremacy and cut capitalism and colonialism
off at their knees (Du Bois, 1995a; C. L. R. James, 1963). Enslaved African
intellectual-activists sought solutions to social and political problems as passionately and radically as—indeed, even more passionately and radically
than—the white working class, who, as the Caribbean historian and leader
Eric Williams (1966) observed in *Capitalism and Slavery*, profited from,
were complicit in, and racially privileged as a result of the very white supremacist and enslaving system dominating and discriminating against
blacks and other nonwhites. Usually critical theory is linked to modernity
and the European Enlightenment, and "modernity" is only thought of from a
Eurocentric point of view—that is, in the aftermath of European imperial
expansion around the globe what it means to be "modern" translates into how
well Europeans and non-Europeans emulate European *imperial* thought, culture, politics, etc. But, if one were to critically call into question Eurocentric
and imperial conceptions of what it means to be "modern," then, the very
"alternative categories" that Bogues discussed above "are opened up," and
contemporary critical theorists are able to observe, perhaps for the first time:
first, that it was on the fringes of Europe's imperial free-for-all, in the imperial outposts in the nonwhite world where racism and colonialism were naturalized, where modernity was conceived, and in some senses aborted; and,
second, that many of modernity's most perplexing problems were initially
put forward and keenly considered by non-European, racialized and colonized, indigenous and enslaved intellectual-activists. Charles W. Mills
(2003a) writes poignantly of this paradox and oft-ignored predicament, and
his penetrating words are worth quoting at length:

All the issues we now think of as defining critical theory's concerns were brought
home to the racially subordinated, the colonized and enslaved, in the most intimate
and brutal way: the human alienation, the instrumentalization and deformation of
reason in the service of power, the critique of abstract individualism, the paradox of
reconciling proclamations of humanism with mass murder, the need to harness
normative theory to the practical task of human liberation. So if Marx's proletariat
too often had to have proletarian consciousness "imputed" (in Georg Lukács infamous phrase) to them, and if the relation between Marxism and the actual working-
class outlook was often more a matter of faith and hopeful counterfactuals than
actuality (what the workers *would* think if only . . .), then oppositional ideas on race
have shaped the consciousness of the racially subordinated for centuries. If white
workers have been alienated from their product, then people of color, especially
black slaves, have been alienated from their personhood; if Enlightenment reason
has been complicit with bourgeois projects, then it has been even more thoroughly
corrupted by its accommodation to white supremacy; if liberal individualism has not
always taken white workers fully into account, then it has often excluded nonwhites

altogether; if it was a post–World War II challenge to explain how the "civilized" Germany of Goethe and Beethoven could have carried out the Jewish and Romani Holocausts, then it is a far older challenge to explain how "civilized" Europe as a whole could have carried out the savage genocide of indigenous populations and the barbaric enslavement of millions; and finally, if Marx's proletarians have been called upon to see and lose their chains (and have often seemed quite well-adjusted to them), then people of color (Native American populations, enslaved and later Jim Crowed Africans in the New World, the colonized) have historically had little difficulty in recognizing their oppression—after all, the chains were often literal!—and in seeking to throw it off. So if the ideal of fusing intellectual history with political practice has been the long-term goal of critical class theory, it has been far more frequently realized in the nascent critical race theory of the racially subordinated, whose oppression has been more blatant and unmediated and for whom the urgency of their situation has necessitated a direct connection between the normative and practical emancipation. (p. xviii)

Critical theories are not simply a synthesis of radical politics and social theory, but they are also a combination of cultural criticism and historical narrative. Each version of critical theory, whether critical race theory or critical class theory, seeks to radically reinterpret and revise history in light of, for example, race and racism for critical race theorists, or capitalism and class struggle for critical class theorists. In order to thoroughly comprehend a given phenomenon, critical theorists believe that one must contextualize it within its historical context, testing and teasing-out tensions between the phenomenon in question and the cultural, social, political, economic, scientific, aesthetic and religious, among other, institutions and major issues of its epoch.

Mills makes the point that although white Marxists/critical class theorists have repeatedly revisited the connection(s) between theory and praxis, more often than not the "revolutions" their works spawned have been more or less theoretical and one-dimensional (i.e., obsessively focused on the critique of capitalism) as opposed to practical and multidimensional (i.e., simultaneously critiquing capitalism *and* racism *and* colonialism). Black radicals/critical race theorists, he observes, have frequently been more successful at linking radical (anti-racist and anti-capitalist) theory to liberation struggles and social movements because their "oppression has been more blatant and unmediated," and because "their situation has necessitated a direct connection between the normative and practical emancipation." The "situation" that Mills is referring to is simultaneously historical, social, political, and economic, not to mention deeply raced and gendered. So, although critical race theorists and critical class theorists both have macro-sociohistorical concerns, in the end it all comes down to, not necessarily *how* they shift and bend the critical theoretical method for their particular purposes, but *what* they shift and bend the critical theoretical method to address. For most white Marxists race and racism are superfluous nonentities, but for many black

Marxists capitalism and class struggle are utterly incomprehensible without connecting them to the rise of race, racism, racial colonialism, racial violence, and white supremacy. Hence, black radicals' constant creation of timelines and topographies of the political economy of race and racism in capitalist and colonialist contexts, and their emphasis on revising and advancing alternatives to Eurocentric historiography and Marxist historical materialism in light of white supremacist and European imperialist concepts and ruling race narratives that render race and racism historically invisible, obsolete, or nonexistent.

Where white Marxists/critical class theorists have a longstanding history of neglecting not only the political economy of race and racism, but also the distinct radical thought-traditions, life-worlds, and life-struggles of continental and diasporan Africans in capitalist and colonialist contexts, primarily utilizing the black radical tradition, Africana critical theory endeavors to accent the overlapping, interlocking, and intersecting character of capitalism, colonialism, racism, and sexism, among other forms of domination, oppression, and exploitation. This means, then, that Africana critical theory transgresses and transcends the white Marxist tradition of critical theory in light of its epistemic openness and emphasis on continuously deepening and developing the basic concepts and categories of its socio-theoretical framework and synthesizing disparate discourses into its own original *anti-racist, anti-sexist, anti-capitalist, anti-colonialist, and sexual orientation-sensitive critical theory of contemporary society.* Just as Africana critical theory simultaneously finds much of value in *and* takes issue with many aspects of Marxist critical theory, it has a similar critical relationship with Eurocentric feminist theory.

Contemporary critical social theory clearly extends well beyond the critique of race and class, and feminists have long argued that gender domination and discrimination inform and often deform modern human identity, culture, and society. Here, then, let us critically examine some of the major movements in contemporary critical gender theory and, particularly, cutting-edge work on the radical socialist-feminist scene. This will aid us in our endeavor to further distinguish the Africana tradition of critical theory from the insights and advances of those working in the Frankfurt School tradition of critical theory. Moreover, by engaging the work of those theorists operating from a simultaneously Marxist and feminist perspective we will be able to further identify and deepen our understanding of the issues that conceptually confront and pose pivotal conceptual pitfalls for the future development of Africana critical theory, and specifically its ongoing efforts to emphasize the importance of racism and sexism, as well as other issues, with regard to any theory that claims to be a theory "critical" of the established order's ideologies and institutions. A brief but critical examination of Frankfurt School–derived feminism will, therefore, provide us with an opportunity to take a serious look at one of the most provocative theoretical productions in recent radical thought history: Nancy Fraser's (1989) articulation of a "feminist critical theory" of contemporary society.

CRITICAL RACE FEMINIST THEORY: TOWARD A CRITICAL RACE THEORY OF FRANKFURT SCHOOL–DERIVED FEMINISM

In "What's Critical About Critical Theory?: The Case of Habermas and Gender," the noted feminist and critical social theorist Nancy Fraser (1991) asserts that "a critical social theory of capitalist societies needs gender-sensitive categories," which is to say that critical theory should move away from the "usual androcentric understanding" and ordering of things commonplace in orthodox Marxian theory (p. 371). It should, contrary to the critical theories of many members of the Frankfurt School (and their discursive descendants), seriously engage the particularities of, and distinct differences between, female and male oppression and exploitation. For instance, as Jürgen Habermas says, "virtually nothing about gender" in *Theory of Communicative Action*, his much-touted magnum opus, Fraser finds his critical theory seriously deficient (p. 358; see also Balbus, 1984; Habermas, 1984, 1987b; P. Johnson, 2001; Meehan, 1995, 2000). By conducting a "gender-sensitive reading" of his social theory, Fraser reveals that "there are some major lacunae in Habermas's otherwise powerful and sophisticated model of the relations between public and private institutions in classical capitalism" (p. 370). For Fraser, when Habermas writes of the worker-citizen-soldier in his critique of the public and private spheres under capitalism, he lays bare some of the major weaknesses of his—and, in my opinion, many of the other members of the Frankfurt School's—critical theory: his failure to come to critical terms with "the gender subtext of the relations and arrangements he describes," and the fact that "feminine and masculine identity run like pink and blue threads through the areas of paid work, state administration and citizenship as well as through the domain of familial and sexual relations. This is to say that gender identity is lived out in all arenas of life" (pp. 367, 370).[11]

In complete agreement with Fraser, I believe that "gender-sensitive readings" of, and radical changes in, "the very concepts of citizenship, childrearing and unpaid work," as well as "changes in the relationships among the domestic, official-economic, state and political-public spheres" are necessary (p. 371). However, as illustrated above, my conception of critical theory also takes into consideration the *racial subtext(s)* and argues for *race-sensitive readings* of power relations in the modern and "postmodern" moments. I am very excited about the prospects of developing "feminist," "gender sensitive," and/or, as I prefer, *critical women's liberation theory*. Which is to say, in other words, I am deeply devoted to developing critical social theory and cultural criticism that acknowledges, in Fraser's words, that: "We are, therefore, struggling for women's autonomy in the following special sense: a measure of collective control over the means of interpretation and communication sufficient to permit us to participate on par with men in all types of social interaction, including political deliberation and decision-making" (p. 378).

What intellectually irks me about Fraser's articulation of a feminist critical theory, however, is the limited scope and lacuna of her social-theoretical framework. While she correctly takes Habermas—and, in many senses, the whole of the Frankfurt School tradition of critical theory—to task for the "gender-blindness" or, what I am wont to call, the *gender insensitivity* of his social-theoretical framework, like Habermas, Fraser fails to theorize some of the ways in which racism and racial colonialism add a different, perhaps even deeper dimension to domination and discrimination in contemporary culture and society. Put another way, I am highly perplexed by the *racial myopia*, that is, the racial blindness of a sophisticated feminist social theorist such as Nancy Fraser who, perhaps utilizing the Frankfurt School critical theoretical framework and philosophically following many of its male members, treats race, racism, anti-racist struggle, and critical race theory as incidental and, more to the point, tertiary to the critique of sexism (and particularly patriarchy) and capitalism.[12]

Admittedly, many theorists have explored sexism, and many theorists have explored racism, and a multitude of theorists (especially Marxists!) have critiqued capitalism. However, racism *and* sexism *and* capitalism (*and* colonialism *and* heterosexism, I might add), treated in a critical conjunctive manner—perhaps of the sort advocated by the "black lesbian feminist socialist mother of two, including one boy," Audre Lorde (1984, p. 114), and the kind of analysis that the black feminist sociologist Deborah King (1988) writes of in her classic essay, "Multiple Jeopardy, Multiple Consciousness: The Context of Black Feminist Ideology"—calls for a critical and unrepentant engagement of the Africana tradition of critical theory and its distinct contributions to radical politics and critical social theory.

What do we find when we turn to the Africana tradition of critical theory? In this often overlooked critical thought-tradition we are undoubtedly, and perhaps unexpectedly for some, exposed to an arsenal of critical constructs, a wide range of theoretical weapons that challenge and seek to provide solutions to several of the major social and political problems of the nineteenth, twentieth, and—I should like to be one of the first to add—twenty-first centuries. This assertion is all the more evident when we critically engage W. E. B. Du Bois's contributions to radical politics and critical social theory. Although his thought covers a wide range of intellectual terrain and ducks and dips into and out of various academic disciplines (history, sociology, philosophy, political science, economics, religion, education, and literature, among others), Du Bois, it can be said at this point with little or no fanfare, laid a foundation and provides a critical theoretical framework for the systematic study of the four key forms of domination and discrimination that have shaped the modern world for several centuries: racism, sexism, capitalism, and colonialism. All of his work, whether we turn to his novels, volumes of poetry, plays, autobiographies, cultural criticisms, histories, social studies, political treatises, or economic analyses, emanates from the critique of the four aforementioned forms of exploitation and oppression. Further, when Du Bois's thought is placed into critical dialogue with the work of other classical contributors to Africana critical theory, such as those examined in my book *Africana Critical Theory*, as well as contemporary contributors to Africana critical theory—such as Angela Davis, Lucius Outlaw, Cornel West, bell hooks, Audre Lorde, Manning Marable, Patricia Hill Collins, Cedric Robinson, Robin D. G. Kelley, Lewis Gordon, and Joy James, among others—an undeniable and distinct Africana tradition of critical theory emerges; a radical thought-tradition that does not simply represent a deconstructive critique of Eurocentric Marxist and feminist critical theory, but also a reconstructive challenge to all contemporary or "new" critical theorists.

This means, then, that Africana critical theory might also be characterized as a form of, and forum for *critical race feminist theory*, in that it discursively dovetails with radical feminist theory and critical race theory. However, as was witnessed above, Africana critical theory's discursive domain extends far beyond feminist theory and critical race theory and includes an epistemic openness to, and deep dialogue with Marxist theory, postcolonial theory, and queer theory, among others. In addition, where most critical race feminists primarily utilize socio-legal discourse as their point of departure, Africana critical theory employs its own unique overhauled conception of Africana studies as a *transdisciplinary human science* as its primary point of departure (see Rabaka, 2010a, pp. 11–38, 2010b, pp. 9–29).

Returning to Fraser and feminist critical theory, again, I feel compelled to reiterate that I utterly agree with her project when and where she argues that the worker-citizen-soldier in classical and contemporary Marxian traditions (of which Frankfurt School critical theory is a provocative and extremely important twentieth century strand) is not androgynous or gender neutral but, in fact, dreadfully gendered, and malevolently masculinist and male-centered at that. Fraser's (1991) radical socialist-feminist theory resonates deeply with my articulation of an Africana critical theory of contemporary society when she accents some of the ways in which basic Marxist categories, such as "worker," "wage," "consumer," and "citizen"—in her own words

are not, in fact, strictly economic concepts. Rather, they have an implicit gender subtext and thus are "gender-economic" concepts. Likewise, the relevant concept of citizenship is not strictly a political concept; it has an implicit gender subtext and so, rather, is a "gender-political" concept. Thus, this analysis reveals the inadequacy of those critical theories that treat gender as incidental to politics and political economy. It highlights the need for a critical-theoretical categorical framework in which gender, politics, and political economy are internally integrated. (p. 371)

For Fraser, there are few, if any, gender-neutral concepts in Marxian theory. In fact, much of Marxism, as she avers above, is rather gender-specific and often only speaks to male struggles against economic exploitation and political oppression. This is also to say that Marxism, as it was originally conceived and propagated, from Karl Marx through to Herbert Marcuse and the Western or Hegelian Marxist tradition, is, quite literally, one long theorization of working-class men's experience of, and class struggles against, the evils of capitalism (Barrett, 1980; Eisenstein, 1979; Guettel, 1974). The trick, though, and one that has not gone unnoticed by Marxist feminists and socialist feminists, is that for a very long time many Marxists (and, many female Marxists notwithstanding) did not realize or critically take into consideration the simple fact when they wrote or spoke of "workers," "wages," "citizens," and the like, their ideas and arguments were premised on a false gender neutrality that more often than not signified males and their (i.e., the males') gender-specific sociopolitical whims and wishes (see Di Stephano, 1991, 2011; A. Ferguson, 1998; Hearn, 1987, 1991; Sargent, 1981). In a patriarchal society, it is "normal," utterly "universal" for theorizing men to exclude the plight of women from their so-called radical social theory, theories of social change, and/or their dialectical discourses on domination and liberation (see Benhabib and Cornell, 1987; Essed, Goldberg, and Kobayashi, 2005). For male theorists to identify themselves and their discourses as "patriarchal," "male-supremacist" or "masculinist," or to make mention of gender at all, is—from their patriarchal vantage point—superfluous because of the superstructural and supra-structural dynamics of patriarchy and the ways it plays itself out in society. Fraser is, indeed, on point when she suggests that what is needed is a closer, more critical "gender-sensitive reading" of classical and contemporary radical theory and praxis in order to develop a critical theory of contemporary society.

Africana critical theory of contemporary society, however, parts company with Fraser's feminist critical theory when it calls for "a critical-theoretical categorical framework in which gender, politics, and political economy are internally integrated" without so much as mentioning, let alone seriously engaging, the socio-historical fact that race and racism have indelibly shaped and molded the modern world as well, and, therefore, should be included on the agenda of any authentic critical theory of *contemporary* society. Contemporary society, as several self-described "feminists" and/or "womanists" of African origin or descent have argued, is simultaneously sexist, racist, and economically exploitive—one need not think long about the various vicissitudes of contemporary capitalism and colonialism.[13] The task, then, of contemporary critical theory is to seek solutions to these four fundamental social and political problems, among others, as they arise.

In the classical Marxist tradition, and in most of the contemporary Marxist tradition, when Marxists theorize the plight of the "worker," they are not only writing about gender-specific workers, *male workers*, but also racially specific workers, *white workers*. The terms that the Marxists use are neither gender nor race neutral terms. For instance, just as males are normative in a patriarchal society, so too are whites in a socio-historically white supremacist society. Again, it is superfluous to make mention of such matters as race and gender in a white *and* male supremacist society, because the white male worldview is always and ever thought and taught to be "neutral" and "universal." To put it plainly: In a white *and* male supremacist society, all are indoctrinated with the dominant ideology, which is inherently a hegemonic white male worldview. Moreover, the appeal of purportedly gender and race neutral terms—such as, *worker, consumer,* and *citizen*—is that they often silently signify white males without actually overtly saying so. What this means, then, is that there are actually invisible pre-reflexive parenthetical adjectives clandestinely attached to these supposedly gender and race neutral terms: (white male) *worker*, (white male) *consumer*, and (white male) *citizen*.[14]

Hence, had Fraser turned to the Africana tradition of critical theory, and especially the work of Angela Davis (1981, 1989, 1998a), Audre Lorde (1984, 1988, 1996, 2004), bell hooks (1981, 1984, 1991, 1995b), Patricia Hill Collins (1998, 2000, 2005, 2006), and Joy James (1996, 1997, 1999), she would have found not only a critical and analytical engagement of capitalism and sexism, but also some of the most sustained and sophisticated theorizations of race and racism, as well as the ways in which racism, sexism and capitalism overlap, interlock and intersect, in recent human history. She would, further, have been able to observe not simply the gendered subtext(s) of the Marxian tradition, but also its racial (and, oft-times, racist) subtext(s), ultimately positing, as I intend to, the need for Marxists to critically note that their basic concepts and categories are race and gender specific (and supremacist), as well as political and economic. In other words, I am arguing, following the Eritrean philosopher Tsenay Serequeberhan (1994), that "political 'neutrality' in philosophy, as in most other things, is at best a 'harmless' naiveté, and at worst a pernicious subterfuge for hidden agendas" (p. 4). It is not enough, from the Africana critical theoretical perspective, for Fraser to highlight gender's import for radical political and economic analysis without, in the spirit of the Africana tradition of critical theory, stretching it to encompass the study of race, racism, critical race theory, and contemporary anti-racist struggle. Finally, in the Africana tradition of critical theory, had Fraser turned to it, she would have also found an anti-colonialist theory and discourse on revolutionary decolonization that could have possibly helped her extend and expand her concepts of the "inner colonization of the life-world," which she borrowed from Habermas, and "decolonization," which she—similar to almost the entire Frankfurt School tradition of critical theory—limits to life-worlds and life-struggles in capitalist cultures and societies (Fraser, 1989, pp. 129–43, 161–87).[15]

Capitalism, it should be stated outright, indeed does marginalize, exploit, and oppress women in ways markedly different from men, and especially in patriarchal capitalist cultures and societies. However, and equally important, capitalism also perpetuates and exacerbates racial colonialism, racial exploitation, racial oppression, and racial violence, as anyone even vaguely familiar with Native American, Asian American, Mexican American, and African American history and culture will surely concur. This is a socio-historical fact that many Marxist feminists and socialist feminists have long neglected, as will be witnessed in chapter 4 of the present volume, and it is also a fact to which the Africana tradition of critical theory, and especially radical black feminists and womanists, have devoted a great deal of time and intellectual energy. Although there is much more in Fraser's sociopolitical theory and the feminist critiques of Frankfurt School critical theory that I find philosophically fascinating, for the purposes of the discussion at hand I have briefly accentuated those aspects of Fraser's arguments that help to highlight the distinctive features of Africana critical theory of contemporary society. Let us now take a deeper, perhaps, more dialectical look at the contour(s) and character of this new conception of critical social theory that utilizes Africana studies, and the black radical tradition in particular, as its primary point of departure.

AFRICANA CRITICAL THEORY: AFRICANA STUDIES, CULTURAL CRITICISM, RADICAL POLITICS, AND CRITICAL SOCIAL THEORY

Much more than neo-black radicalism or critical race theory, *Africana critical theory* is a twenty-first century outgrowth and synthesis of a wide range of efforts aimed at accenting *the dialectics of deconstruction and reconstruction* and *the dialectics of domination and liberation* in classical and contemporary, continental and diasporan African life-worlds and life-struggles. Its major preoccupation has been and remains synthesizing classical and contemporary black radical theory with black revolutionary praxis. Consequently, Africana studies provides Africana critical theory with its philosophical foundation(s) and primary point(s) of departure, as it, Africana studies, decidedly moves beyond Eurocentric and monodisciplinary approaches to Africana phenomena. As stated in almost all of my previous work, one of the reasons I was initially and remain intellectually attracted to Africana studies is because of its *epistemic openness* and complete disregard for conventional conceptions of disciplinary development. At this point, then, it will be helpful to briefly operationalize my (new or, rather, more current) conception of Africana studies for the specific discursive purposes of *Hip Hop's Inheritance*: from an Africana critical theoretical frame of reference, Africana studies is the body of knowledge based on and built around critically and systematically studying a specific human group—that is, continental and diasporan Africans—and their particular and peculiar life-worlds and life-struggles. It is the field of critical inquiry which is most modeled on or, at the very least, seems to perfectly parallel W. E. B. Du Bois and Frantz Fanon's extensive and diverse insurgent intellectual activity and revolutionary praxis, because at its conceptual core Africana studies is a *transdisciplinary human science*.[16]

Here, I should like to take this line of logic one step further and more concretely synthesize Du Bois and Fanon's respective classical critical theories of the human sciences with contemporary Africana studies, which in this instance roughly translates into *a form of human studies incorrigibly obsessed with eradicating the blight on the souls of black folk, the wretchedness of the wretched of the earth, and indefatigably geared toward the ultimate goal of deepening and developing the Africana tradition of critical theory.* That being said, then, Africana studies is unequivocally the area of investigation, as opposed to the "academic discipline," that has most inspired Africana critical theory's unique research methods and modes of analysis—"unique" especially when compared to other forms of critical theory that emerge from traditional, single subject-focused disciplines—because Africana studies is a *transdisciplinary human science*—that is, *an area of critical inquiry that transgresses, transverses, and ultimately transcends the arbitrary and artificial academic and disciplinary borders and boundaries, the conflicted color-lines and yawning racial chasms, and the jingoism and gender injustice of traditional single phenomenon-focused, monodisciplinary disciplines, owing to the fact that at its best it poses problems and incessantly seeks solutions on behalf of the souls of black folk and the other wretched of the earth employing the theoretic innovations of both the social sciences and the humanities, as well as the political breakthroughs of grassroots radical and revolutionary social movements.* It should also be said here as well: *Hip Hop's Inheritance*, therefore, is just as much about what hip hop culture (i.e., a contemporary grassroots movement with undeniable sociopolitical sensibilities and inclinations) has bequeathed to Africana studies as it is about what previous generations have bequeathed to the hip hop generation. The hip hop generation has not simply "inherited" from previous generations, but, after more

than thirty years of seemingly carefully orchestrated controversy and contradiction, I honestly believe that it is time to identify, acknowledge, and con-
structively critique some of its major contributions to the present and future
of cultural criticism, radical politics, and critical social theory. This last point
is one that I would implore my readers to bear in mind as we venture still
further into this expatiation of the Africana tradition of critical theory, and
how the said tradition can be utilized by both Africana studies scholars and
hip hoppers to develop cultural criticism, radical politics, and critical theory
of contemporary society that speaks to the special needs and challenges of
our epoch.

To speak more generally here, from a methodological point of view critical social theory seeks to simultaneously: (1) comprehend the established
society; (2) criticize its contradictions and conflicts; and, (3) create ethical
and egalitarian (most often radical/revolutionary democratic socialist) alternatives.[17] The ultimate emphasis on the creation and offering of ethical and
egalitarian alternatives brings to the fore another core concept of critical
social theory: its *theory of human liberation and radical/revolutionary democratic socialist transformation*. The paradigms and points of departure for
critical theorists vary depending on the theorists' race, gender, class, sexual
orientation, religious affiliation, and nation of origin, among other intellectual interests and political persuasions. For instance, many European critical
theorists turn to Hegel, Marx, Weber, Freud, and/or the Frankfurt School
(e.g., Adorno, Benjamin, Fromm, Habermas, Horkheimer, and Marcuse),
among others, because they understand these thinkers' thoughts and texts to
speak in special ways to European modern and/or "postmodern" life-worlds
and life-struggles (see Drake, 2009; Held, 1980; Jay, 1996; Kellner, 1989;
Nealon and Irr, 2002; Wiggerhaus, 1995).

My conception of critical theory, *Africana critical theory*, utilizes the
thought and texts of Africana intellectual-activist ancestors as critical theoretical paradigms and radical political points of departure because so much of
their thought is not simply *problem-posing* but *solution-providing* where the
specific life-struggles of persons of African origin or descent (or, if I must,
"black people") are concerned—humble human life-struggles, it should be
said with no hyperbole and high-sounding words, which European critical
theorists (who are usually Eurocentric and often unwittingly white supremacist) have, for the most part, woefully neglected in their classical and contemporary critical theoretical discourse; a discourse, as mentioned above,
that ironically has consistently congratulated itself on the universality of its
interests, all the while (again, for the most part) side-stepping the centrality
of racism, sexism, colonialism, and heterosexism within its own discursive
communities and out in the wider social, political, and cultural world(s).
Moreover, my conception of critical theory is critically preoccupied with
classical Africana intellectual-activists and the thought-traditions they inau-

gurated, not only because of the long unlearned lessons they have to teach contemporary critical theorists about the dialectics of being simultaneously radically humanist and morally committed agents of a specific continent, nation, or cultural groups' liberation and democratic social transformation, but also because the ideas and ideals of continental and diasporan African intellectual-activists of the past indisputably prefigure and provide a foundation for contemporary Africana studies, and Africana philosophy in particular. In fact, in many ways, Africana critical theory, besides being grounded in and growing of out the interdisciplinary and intersectional discourse(s) of Africana studies in general, can be said to be a critical theoretical offshoot of Africana philosophy, which according to the acclaimed African American philosopher, Lucius Outlaw (1997a), is

a "gathering" notion under which to situate the articulations (writings, speeches, etc.), and traditions of the same, of Africans and peoples of African descent collectively, as well as the sub-discipline or field-forming, tradition-defining, tradition-organizing reconstructive efforts which are (to be) regarded as philosophy. However, "Africana philosophy" is to include, as well, the work of those persons who are neither African nor of African descent but who recognize the legitimacy and importance of the issues and endeavors that constitute the disciplinary activities of African or [African Caribbean or] African American philosophy and contribute to the efforts—persons whose work justifies their being called "Africanists." Use of the qualifier "Africana" is consistent with the practice of naming intellectual traditions and practices in terms of the national, geographic, cultural, racial, and/or ethnic descriptor or identity of the persons who initiated and were/are the primary practitioners—and/or are the subjects and objects—of the practices and traditions in question (e.g., "American," "British," "French," "German," or "continental" philosophy). (p. 64)

Africana critical theory is distinguished from Africana philosophy by the fact that critical theory cannot be situated within the world of conventional academic disciplines and disciplinary divisions of labor. It transverses and transgresses the boundaries between traditional disciplines and accents the interconnections and intersections of, for example, philosophy, history, politics, economics, psychology, sociology, anthropology, and the humanities, among other disciplines and/or areas of critical inquiry. Critical theory is contrasted with mainstream, monodisciplinary social theory through its mixed and multidisciplinary methodology and its efforts to develop a comprehensive dialectical theory of domination and liberation specific to the special needs of contemporary society. Truth be told, Africana philosophy has a very different agenda, one that seems to me more meta-philosophical than philosophical at this point, because it entails theorizing-on-tradition and tradition-reconstruction more than tradition extension and expansion through the production of normative theory and critical pedagogical praxis aimed at earnest *application* (i.e., immediate radical/revolutionary self- and social transformation).

The primary purpose of critical theory is to relate radical thought to revolutionary practice, which is to say that its focus—philosophical, social, and political—is always and ever the search for ethical alternatives and viable moral solutions to the most pressing problems of our present age. Critical theory is not about, or rather *should not* be about, allegiance to intellectual ancestors and/or ancient schools of thought, but about using *all* (without regard to race, gender, class, sexual orientation, and/or religious affiliation) accumulated radical thought and revolutionary practices in the interest of human liberation and democratic social transformation. With this in mind, Cornel West's (1982) classic contentions concerning "Afro-American critical thought" offer an outline for the type of theorizing that Africana critical theory endeavors:

> The object of inquiry for Afro-American critical thought is the past and present, the doings and the sufferings of African people in the United States. Rather than a new scientific discipline or field of study, it is a genre of writing, a textuality, a mode of discourse that interprets, describes, and evaluates Afro-American life in order comprehensively to understand and effectively to transform it. It is not concerned with "foundations" or transcendental "grounds" but with how to build its language in such a way that the configuration of sentences and the constellation of paragraphs themselves create a textuality and distinctive discourse which are a material force for Afro-American freedom. (p. 15)

Although Africana critical theory encompasses and is concerned with much more than the life-worlds and life-struggles of "African people in the United States," West's comments here are helpful, as they give us a glimpse at the kinds of transdisciplinary connections critical theorists make or, rather, *should* make in terms of their ideas having a radical political impact and significant influence on society. Africana critical theory is not thought-for-thought's sake (as it often seems is the case with so much contemporary philosophy—Africana philosophy notwithstanding), but *critical thought-for-life-and-liberation's sake*. It is not only a style of writing which focuses on radicalism and revolution but, even more, it (re)presents a new way of *thinking* about and *doing* revolution that is based and constantly being built on the best of the radicalisms and revolutions of the past, and the black radical and black revolutionary past in particular.

From West's frame of reference, "Afro-American philosophy expresses the particular American variation of European modernity that Afro-Americans helped shape in this country and must contend with in the future. While it might be possible to articulate a competing Afro-American philosophy based principally on African norms and notions, it is likely that the result would be theoretically thin" (p. 24). Quite contrary to West's comments,

Africana critical theory intrepidly represents and registers as that "possible articulat[ion] of a competing [Africana] philosophy based principally on African norms and notions," and although he thinks that the results will be "theoretically thin," Africana critical theory—faithfully following Frantz Fanon (1965, 1967, 1968, 1969) and Amilcar Cabral (1972, 1973, 1979)— understands this risk to be part of the price the wretched of the earth must be willing to pay for their (intellectual, political, psychological, and physical) freedom.[18] Intellectually audacious, especially considering the widespread Eurocentrism of contemporary conceptual generation, Africana critical theory does not acquiesce or give priority and special privilege to European history, culture, and thought. It turns to the long overlooked thought and texts of women and men of African origin or descent who have developed and contributed radical thought and revolutionary practices that could possibly aid us in our endeavors to continuously create an *anti-racist, anti-sexist, anti-capitalist, anti-colonialist, and sexual orientation-sensitive critical theory of contemporary society.*

Above and beyond all of the aforementioned, Africana critical theory is about offering alternatives to *what is* (domination and discrimination), by projecting possibilities of *what ought to be* and/or *what could be* (human liberation and radical/revolutionary democratic social transformation). To reiterate, Africana critical theory is not afraid, to put it as plainly as possible, to critically engage and dialogue deeply with European and/or other cultural groups' thought-traditions. In fact, it often finds critical cross-cultural dialogue and astute appropriation (i.e., *Africanization*) necessary considering the historical conundrums and current shared conditions and shared crises of the modern or "postmodern," transnational, and almost completely multicultural world. Africana critical theory, quite simply, does not privilege or give priority to European and/or other cultural groups' thought-traditions since its philosophical foci and primary purpose revolves around the search for solutions to the most pressing social and political problems in continental and diasporan African life-worlds and life-struggles in the present age.

"EACH GENERATION MUST OUT OF RELATIVE OBSCURITY DISCOVER ITS MISSION, FULFILL IT, OR BETRAY IT!": APPLYING AFRICANA CRITICAL THEORY OF CONTEMPORARY SOCIETY TO CONTEMPORARY CULTURE AND SOCIETY

Africana critical theory navigates many theoretic spaces that extend well beyond the established intellectual borders and boundaries of Africana studies as it is conventionally conceived. At this point, it is clearly characterized by an *epistemic openness* to theories and methodologies usually understood to be incompatible with one another, and often with Africana studies. Besides providing it with a simultaneously creative and critical tension, Africana critical theory's *antithetical conceptual contraction* (i.e., its utilization of concepts perceived to be contradictory to, and/or in conflict and competing with one another) also gives it its theoretic rebelliousness and untamable academic quality. Which is to say, Africana critical theory exists or, rather, is able to exist well beyond the borders and boundaries of the academy and academic disciplines, because the bulk of its theoretic base, that is, its primary points of departure, are the ideas and actions of Africana (among other wretched of the earth) intellectual-activists entrenched in radical political practices and revolutionary social movements. The word "theory," then, in the appellation "Africana critical theory" is being defined and, perhaps, radically refined, for specific *transdisciplinary human scientific* discursive purposes and practices. This is extremely important to point out because there has been a long intellectual history of chaos concerning the nature and tasks of "theory" in Africana studies.

To an Africana critical theorist it seems highly questionable, if not simply downright silly at this juncture in the history of Africana thought, to seek a theoretical "Holy Grail" that will serve as some sort of panacea to our search for the secrets to being, culture, politics, society or, even more, liberation. Taking our cue from W. E. B. Du Bois and C. L. R. James, it may be better to conceive of theory as an "instrument" or, as Frantz Fanon and Amilcar Cabral would have it, a "weapon" used to attack certain targets of exploitation, oppression, and violence. Theories are, among many other things, optics, ways of seeing; they are perspectives that illuminate specific phenomena. However, as with any perspective, position, or standpoint, each theory has its blind spots and lens limitations, what we call in the contemporary discourse of Africana philosophy, *theoretical myopia.*

Recent theoretical debates in Africana studies have made us painfully aware of the fact that most theories emerging from academe are almost invariably discipline-specific constructs and products, created in particular intellectual contexts, for particular intellectual purposes (see Aldridge and James, 2007; Aldridge and Young, 2000; Anderson and Stewart, 2007; Asante and Karenga, 2006; Bobo and Michel, 2000; Bobo, Hudley, and Michel, 2004; Conyers, 2005; Gordon and Gordon, 2006a, 2006b; Marable, 2000, 2005). Contemporary Africana thought has also enabled us see that theories are always grounded in and grow out of specific social discourses, political practices, and national and international institutions. Here, then, we have come back to Serequeberhan's (1994) contention that "political 'neutrality' in philosophy, as in most other things, is at best a 'harmless' naïveté, and at worst a pernicious subterfuge for hidden agendas" (p. 4). Truth be told, each discipline has an academic agenda. Therefore, the theories and methodologies of a discipline promote the development of that particular discipline. Theories emerging from traditional disciplines that claim to provide an eternal philosophical foundation or universal and neutral knowledge transcendent of historical horizons, cultural conditions, and social struggles, or a metatheory (i.e., a theory about theorizing) that purports absolute truth that transcends the interests of specific theorists and their theories, have been and are being vigorously rejected by Africana studies scholars and students (see Azevedo, 2005; BaNikongo, 1997; Norment, 2007a, 2007b).

Theory, then, as Serequeberhan (1994) says of philosophy, is a "critical and explorative engagement of one's own cultural specificity and lived historicalness. It is a critically aware explorative appropriation of our cultural, political, and historical existence" (p. 23).[19] This conception of theory really resonates with me, because in offering *Hip Hop's Inheritance* I am, literally, exploring and critically engaging my own "cultural specificity and lived historicalness," and appropriating my own "cultural, political, and historical existence" in the interest of deepening and developing cultural criticism, radical politics, and critical theory of contemporary society. In a sense, then, *Hip Hop's Inheritance* symbolizes Africana critical theory's shift from identifying and analyzing continental and diasporan Africans' creation of, and contributions to critical theory emerging from the past, to an exploration of African Americans' creation of, and contributions to critical theory emerging from both the past *and* the present. All of this is to say that *Hip Hop's Inheritance* is a book about and for my generation, whether one prefers either the "Soul Babies" or "Hip Hop" generation labels, or neither. What is more, *Hip Hop's Inheritance* represents an earnest effort to bring classical black radical politics and critical social theory into discursive dialogue with contemporary black radical politics and critical social theory, which ultimately means that this is an unprecedented project considering that prior to *Hip Hop's Inheritance* there has been no work aimed at developing a *critical theory of hip hop culture*.

In *The Wretched of the Earth*, when Fanon (1968, p. 206) forcefully asserts that "[e]ach generation must out of relative obscurity discover its mission, fulfill it, or betray it," it would seem that he is saying that each generation has to come to *critical consciousness*—what he famously referred to in *Black Skins, White Mask* as "conscienciser" (i.e., "to bring or be brought to consciousness") and what Paulo Freire in *Pedagogy of the Oppressed* and *Education for Critical Consciousness*, closely following Fanon, called "conscientization," or *conscientização* in Portuguese—and develop its own forms of cultural criticism, radical politics, and critical social theory to speak to the special needs and novel challenges of its unique "cultural, political, and historical existence" (see Fanon, 1967; Freire, 1993, 1994, 1996). Indeed, *Hip Hop's Inheritance* offers a critical theory of hip hop culture, but in order to really and truly understand hip hop culture one must grasp and seriously grapple with African American intellectual and cultural history, the history and sociology of African American social and political movements, and, most especially, the evolution of African American cultural aesthetic theory and praxis. Here, we have come back to *Hip Hop's Inheritance*'s emphasis on the importance of theory in its efforts to combat the hip hop generations' historical and cultural amnesia and its efforts to highlight the hip hop generations' contributions to cultural criticism, radical politics, and critical theory of contemporary society.

Theoretic discourse does not simply fall from the sky like windblown rain, leaving no traces of the direction from which it came and its initial point of departure. On the contrary, it registers as, and often radically represents, critical concerns interior to epistemologies and experiences arising out of a specific cultural condition and historical horizon within which it is located and discursively situated. In other words, similar to a finely crafted wood-carving or handwoven garment, theories retain the intellectual and cultural markings of their makers, and although they can and do "travel" and "cross borders," they are optimal in their original settings and when applied to the original phenomena that inspired their creation (Giroux, 1992; Said, 1999, 2000).

A more modest conception of theory sees it, then, as an instrument (or, as Michel Foucault would have it, a "tool") to help us illuminate and navigate specific social spaces, pointing to present and potential problems, interpreting and criticizing them, and ultimately offering ethical and egalitarian alternatives to them.[20] At their best, theories not only illuminate sociopolitical realities, but they *should* help individuals make sense of their life-worlds and life-struggles. To do this effectively, theories usually utilize metaphor, allegory, images, symbols, discursive concepts, counter-arguments, conversational language, rhetorical devices, and narratives. Modern metatheory often accents the interesting fact that theories have literary components and qualities: they narrate or tell stories, employ rhetoric and semiotics and, similar to literature, often offer accessible interpretations of classical and contemporary life. However, theories also have cognitive and kinship components that allow them to connect with other theories' concepts and common critical features, as when a variety of disparate theories in the Africana studies arena raise questions concerning race and racism, or questions concerning domination and liberation.

There are many different types of theory, from literary theory to linguistic theory, cultural theory to aesthetic theory, and political theory to postmodern theory. Africana critical theory is a critical conceptual framework that seeks an ongoing synthesis of the most emancipatory elements of a wide range of *social and political theory* in the anti-imperialist interests of continental and diasporan Africans in particular, and the other wretched of the earth in general. This means that Africana critical theory often identifies and isolates the social and political implications of various theories, some of which were not created to have any concrete connections with the social and political world (and certainly not the Africana world), but currently do as a consequence of the ways they have been appropriated, (re)articulated and, in terms of Africana critical theory, *decolonized* and *Africanized.*

Here, it is extremely important to recall the often hidden history of theory. Theories are instruments and, therefore, they can be put to use in a multiplicity of manners. Historically, theories have always traveled outside of their original contexts, but two points of importance should be made here. The first point has to do with something the Palestinian literary theorist and political activist Edward Said (1999, 2000) said long ago, and that is that theories lose some of their original power when taken out of their original intellectual and cultural contexts, because the sociopolitical situation is different, the suffering and/or struggling people are different, and the aims and objectives of their movements are different. The second point is reflexive and has to do with the present moment in the history of theory: Never before have so many theories traveled so many mental miles away from their intellectual milieux. This speaks to the new and novel theoretical times that we are passing through. Part of what we have to do, then, is identify those theories ("instruments" and/or "weapons," if you prefer) that will aid us most in our struggles against racism, sexism, capitalism, colonialism, and heterosexism, among other (neo)imperial epochal issues.

The turn toward and emphasis on social and political theory suggests several of Africana critical theory's key concerns, such as the development of a synthetic sociopolitical discourse that earnestly and accessibly addresses issues arising from: everyday black life and experiences in white supremacist societies; women's daily lives in male supremacist (or, if you prefer, "patriarchal") societies; and, the commonalities of, and the distinct differences between black life in racial colonialist and racial capitalist countries, among other issues. Social and political *theoretical* discourse is important because it provides individuals and groups with topographies of their social and political terrains. This discourse, especially when it is "critical," also often offers crucial concepts and categories that aid individuals and groups in critically engaging and radically altering their social and political worlds.

Social and political theories, in a general sense, are simultaneously heuristic and discursive devices for exploring and explaining the social and political dimensions of the human experience. They accent social conditions and can often provoke social action and political praxis. Social and political theories endeavor to provide a panoramic picture that enables individuals to conceptualize and contextualize their life-worlds and life-struggles within the wider field of social and political, as well as historical and cultural relations and institutions. Additionally, social and political theories can aid individuals in their efforts to understand and alter particular sociopolitical events and artifacts by analyzing their receptions, relations, and residual effects.

In addition to sociopolitical theoretical discourse, Africana critical theory draws directly from the discourse on *dialectics* because it seeks to understand and, if necessary, alter society as a whole, not simply some isolated or culturally confined series of phenomena. The emphasis on dialectics also sends a signal to those sociopolitical theorists and others who are easily intellectually intimidated by efforts to grasp and grapple with the whole of human history, culture, and our current crises, that Africana critical theory is not in any sense a "conventional" critical social theory but, unapologetically, *a social activist and political praxis-promoting theory* that seriously seeks the radical redistribution of cultural capital, social wealth, and political power. The dialectical dimension of Africana critical theory enables it to make connections between seemingly isolated and unrelated parts of society, demonstrating how, for instance, supposedly neutral social terrain, such as the education industries, the entertainment industries, the prison industrial complex, mainstream politics, or the realm of religion are sites and sources of ruling race, ruling gender, and/or ruling class privilege, prestige, and power.

Dialectics, the art of discursively demonstrating the interconnectedness of parts to each other and to the overarching system or framework as a whole, distinguishes Africana critical theory from other theories in Africana studies because it simultaneously searches for progressive and retrogressive aspects of Africana, Eurocentric, and/or other racio-cultural groups' epistemologies, methodologies, and praxeologies. This means, then, that Africana critical theory offers an external *and* internal critique, which is also to say that it is unrepentantly *a self-reflexive social and political theory*: a social and political theory that relentlessly reexamines and refines or, rather, deconstructs and reconstructs its own philosophical foundations, methods, positions, presuppositions, and praxes. Africana critical theory's dialectical dimension also distinguishes it from other traditions and versions of critical theory because the connections it makes between social and political parts and the social and political whole are those that directly and profoundly affect continental and diasporan Africans in particular, and the other racially colonized wretched of the earth in general. No other tradition or version of radical politics or critical social theory has historically or currently claims to highlight and accent *sites of domination* and *sources of liberation* in the anti-imperialist interests of the wretched of the earth in general, and, in this specific instance, the hip hop generation in particular. All of this brings us to the intricacies of applying Africana critical theory—in this incarnation under the guise of a *critical theory of hip hop culture*—to the intellectual history, discursive formations, and discursive practices of the hip hop generation.

REINTERPRETING AND REWRITING HIP HOP'S INTELLECTUAL AND CULTURAL HISTORY: FOUCAULT, ARCHAEOLOGY, GENEALOGY, AND CRITICAL SOCIAL THEORY

As mentioned above, where most of my previous work has focused on classical continental and diasporan African contributions to radical politics and critical social theory, *Hip Hop's Inheritance* is a work preoccupied with the present and the future. Obviously critical analysis of the past will play a pivotal role in the studies to follow—how else could we connect the discursive dots, the labyrinthic lines of continuity and discontinuity between the Harlem Renaissance, the Black Arts movement, the Feminist Art movement, and the hip hop generation? However, hip hop's ancestral movements will be engaged in a more or less instrumental manner, one aimed at emphasizing hip hop's evolution and unique intellectual and cultural history. In others words, *Hip Hop's Inheritance* could be just as easily characterized as an "archaeology" and/or "genealogy" of hip hop culture as much as a critical theory of hip hop culture.

Continuing with this line of logic leads us to an open admission and brief discussion of the fact that the present critical theory of hip hop culture is conceptually connected to and was conceptually conceived in the aftermath of Michel Foucault's articulation of an archaeology of various discursive formations and discursive practices. For instance, my critical theory of hip hop culture critically follows Foucault's philosophical histories and/or historicist philosophies: from his critique of psychiatry in *The History of Madness in the Classical Age*, to his critique of the evolution of the medical industry in *The Birth of the Clinic: An Archaeology of Medical Perception*; from his critique of the evolution of the human sciences in *The Order of Things: An Archaeology of the Human Sciences*, to his critique of the historical-situatedness of truth, meaning, and reason (i.e., the *epistēmē* of an epoch), and the very methodologies through which they are arrived at or comprehended in his extremely innovative *The Archaeology of Knowledge* (see Foucault, 1971, 1973, 1974, 1994, 2009).[21]

According to Foucault (1994), archaeology is distinguished from "the confused, under-structured, and ill-structured domain of the history of ideas" (p. 195). He, therefore, rejects the history of ideas as an idealist and liberal humanist, purely academic or ivory tower mode of writing that traces an uninterrupted evolution of thought in terms of the conscious construction of a tradition or the conscious production of subjects and objects. Against the bourgeois liberalism of the history of ideas approach, Foucaultian archaeology endeavors to identify the states and stages for the creation and critique of ongoing and open-ended or, rather, more nuanced knowledge, as well as the hidden rules and regulations (re)structuring and ultimately determining the form and focus of discursive rationality that are deeply embedded within and often obfuscatingly operate below the perceived borders and boundaries of disciplinary development, methodological maneuvers, or interpretive intention. At the outset of *The Order of Things*, Foucault (1971) contended: "It is these rules of formation, which were never formulated in their own right, but are to be found only in widely differing theories, concepts, and objects of study, that I have tried to reveal, by isolating, as their specific locus, a level that I have called . . . archaeological" (p. xi).

Moreover, this critical theory of hip hop culture also draws from Foucault's more mature materialist genealogies, such as *Discipline and Punish: The Birth of the Prison*, *The History of Sexuality, Vol. 1: The Will to Knowledge*, *The History of Sexuality, Vol. 2: The Use of Pleasure*, and *The History of Sexuality, Vol. 3: The Care of the Self*, where he deepened and developed his articulation of archaeology and evolved it into a unique conception of genealogy, which signaled an intensification of his critical theorization of power relations, social institutions, and social practices (see Foucault, 1979, 1990a, 1990b, 1990c). However, my critical theory of hip hop culture does not understand Foucault's later focus on genealogy to be a break with his earlier archaeological studies as much as it is taken to represent a shift of discursive direction and, even more, an extension and expansion of his discursive domain. Similar to his archaeologies, Foucault characterized his later genealogical studies as a new method of investigation, a new means of interpretation, and a new mode of historical writing.

Truth be told, then, both of these Foucaultian methodologies endeavor to radically reinterpret the social world from a micrological standpoint that allows one to identify discursive discontinuity and discursive dispersion instead of what has been commonly understood to be continuity and uninterrupted identity evolution and, as a consequence, Foucault's methodologies enable us to grapple with and, in many instances, firmly grasp historical happenings, cultural crises, political power-plays, and social situations in their complete and concrete complexity. Furthermore, both Foucaultian methodologies also attempt to invalidate and offer more nuanced narratives to commonly held conceptions of master narratives and great chains of historical continuity and their teleological destinations, as well as to hyperhistoricize what has been long-thought to be indelibly etched into the heart of human history. In other words, and more meta-methodologically speaking, in discursively deploying archaeology and/or genealogy Foucault sought to disrupt and eventually destroy hard and fast bourgeois humanist historical identities, power relations, and imperial institutions by critically complicating, by profoundly problematizing and pluralizing the entire arena of discursive formations and discursive practices—hence, freeing historical research and writing from its hidden bourgeois humanist social and political hierarchies, by disavowing and displacing the bourgeois humanist (and, therefore, "socially acceptable") subject, and critically theorizing modern reason and increasing rationalization through reinterpreting and rewriting the history of the human sciences.

Here, my intentions are admittedly less ambitious than those of Foucault, although, I honestly believe, they are just as relevant considering the state of contemporary culture, politics, and society. In *Hip Hop's Inheritance*, therefore, I seek to reinterpret and rewrite the history of contemporary cultural criticism, radical politics, and critical social theory in light of the hip hop generation's inheritance from past sociopolitical and cultural aesthetic movements, as well as the hip hop generation's contributions to future sociopolitical and cultural aesthetic movements. By identifying and critically analyzing the three major antecedent cultural aesthetic movements that have indelibly influenced the evolution of hip hop culture (as opposed to merely rap music), *Hip Hop's Inheritance* reinterprets and rewrites the conventionally conceived relationship between African American radical politics and cultural aesthetics, ultimately revealing that black radical politics and cultural aesthetics historically have been and currently continue to be inextricable—constantly overlapping, interlocking, and intersecting, intensely infusing and informing each other. African American art and cultural aesthetic movements are not now and never have been created in a vacuum, but within the historical, cultural, social, political, and economic context of the United States. This means, then, that like previous African American cultural aesthetic traditions and movements, hip hop culture is emblematic not only of contemporary black America, but also eerily indicative of the state of the "American dream" (or, for many U.S. citizens, the "American nightmare") at the turn of the twenty-first century.

SCHIZOPHRENIA, HISTORICAL AMNESIA, AND HIP HOP'S INHERITANCE: CHALLENGES TO HIP HOP CULTURE AND CHAPTER SUMMARIES

Hip hop means many things to many different people. For some folk, say your everyday average youth in the United States (if such persons still or ever existed), hip hop is a way of life, a worldview which informs and impacts their life-worlds and life-struggles in ways that many adults and other authority figures can hardly fathom. For others, let's say the so-called adults and other authority figures, hip hop is a cultural virus infecting everything from their children to their church life with its cancerous conundrums and contradictions. And yet and still, there are others, much like myself, who, on the one hand, have a longstanding and still lingering love of hip hop and see its potential as a vehicle for radical social and political change but who, on the other hand, harbor deep and often perplexing concerns about hip hop's seemingly schizophrenic social and political mission and message. *Hip Hop's Inheritance*, therefore, will take a critical and dialectical (or, rather, a *critical theoretical*) look at hip hop culture—which is also to say that this book provides a series of studies that sojourn through and search for the good *and* the bad, the beautiful *and* the ugly, the sacred *and* the secular, and, yes, the divine *and* the demonic in contemporary popular culture, especially African American popular culture. Special emphasis will be placed on the intellectual, cultural, social, and political history of hip hop and its often overlooked roots in and rise from minstrelism, the Harlem Renaissance, the Black Arts movement, and the Feminist Art movement, to its current place at the center of U.S. popular culture, entertainment, and athletics, or what I would more generally call—following the Frankfurt School critical theorists Max Horkheimer and Theodor Adorno (1995) in *Dialectic of Enlightenment*—the contemporary "culture industries."

The premise that guides *Hip Hop's Inheritance* is that hip hop culture represents a set of aesthetic, economic, social, political, and cultural relationships that simultaneously reflect and contradict the dominant social arrangements and institutions of contemporary U.S. society. Issues of power and powerlessness are central to this book, as they illuminate how social arrangements and institutions are imagined, constructed, and challenged. Following Du Bois, Fanon, and Foucault, among others, we pay particular attention to those communities and individuals who are part of the periphery—those outside "official" spheres of power, as opposed to those wielding power. We consider questions such as who is part of the periphery, and why? How does one become part of the periphery? What is the impact of center/periphery relations, among other barbarous binary oppositions, in a so-called civilized, developed, technologically advanced, and democratic society such as the United States of America? Also, how has African Americans' longstanding marginalization in U.S. history, culture, and society influenced, not simply their sociopolitical movements, but also their cultural aesthetic movements? And, lastly, how does the hip hop generation's cultural aesthetic movement measure up against past African American cultural aesthetic movements?

In order to effectively engage each of these questions *Hip Hop's Inheritance* will treat the major cultural aesthetic movements that have indelibly influenced hip hop culture in a series of studies carried out over the course of the following chapters. Hence, the next chapter, "Civil Rights by Copyright (Da ReMix!): From the Harlem Renaissance to the Hip Hop Generation," critically examines the "real" roots of the hip hop aesthetic and calls into question whether the roots of contemporary black popular culture ironically lie in blackface minstrelism, not simply the Harlem Renaissance or the Black Arts movement. Intentionally courting controversy, the chapter shifts from exploring hip hop culture's possible roots in blackface minstrelism to its often unwitting utilization of the cultural aesthetic contributions and motifs of the Harlem Renaissance. As the cultural aesthetic outgrowth of the New Negro and Black Women's Club movements, the Harlem Renaissance's contributions are demonstrated to be the major point of departure and paradigm for the evolution of African American aesthetic culture from the turn of the twentieth century through to the turn of the twenty-first century—which is also to say, up to the emergence of hip hop culture.

Chapter 3, "'Say It Loud!—I'm Black and I'm Proud!': From the Black Arts Movement and Blaxploitation Films to the Conscious and Commercial Rap of the Hip Hop Generation," critically engages the notion that the hip hop generation seems to have inherited its own unique historical amnesia with regard to the Harlem Renaissance and a distinctly schizophrenic relationship with respect to the Black Power and Black Arts movements—one moment repudiating its origins in the Black Arts movement, and at other times celebrating the radical politics (and radical rhetoric) of the Black Power period. The chapter explores the intellectual and artistic interrelation between the Black Arts movement and the hip hop generation by addressing several key questions: How did Black Arts movement members perceive the aesthetic radicalism of the Harlem Renaissance? What, if anything, did they inherit from the Harlem Renaissance? Likewise, what did the Black Arts movement bequeath to the hip hop generation? And, how has the hip hop generation interpreted its inheritance—whether understood to be social and political, or cultural and aesthetic, or each of the aforementioned—from the Black Power and Black Arts movements?

The fourth chapter, "'The Personal Is Political!' (Da Hip Hop Feminist ReMix): From the Black Women's Liberation and Feminist Art Movements to the Hip Hop Feminist Movement," focuses on what the Black Women's Liberation movement bequeathed to the Hip Hop Feminist movement in particular, and the hip hop generation in general. To engage hip hop's inheritance in this instance it will be important to, first, briefly discuss some of the major organizations and theorists of the 1960s and 1970s Black Women's Liberation movement and their relationship to the more mainstream (white) Women's Liberation movement. Next, the chapter explores the often overlooked relationship between the black Women's Liberation, Black Arts, and Feminist Art movements. Although not as readily recognized, the Women's Liberation movement had a significant impact on late twentieth-century women's artistry, and even though the Feminist Art movement is not as widely known its influence arguably extends to the hip hop feminist movement. The chapter closes with a discussion of the ways in which hip hop feminists have controversially remixed or synthesized their own homespun feminism with the contributions of black and other nonwhite feminists of previous generations and, consequently, they have come to create a feminism and neo-Women's Liberation movement that speaks to the special needs of the women of the hip hop generation.

The final chapter, "Is Hip Hop Dead? or, At the Very Least, Dying?: On the Pitfalls of Postmodernism, the Riddles of Contemporary Rap Music, and the Continuing Conundrums of Hip Hop Culture," reassesses hip hop's inheritance in light of the foregoing studies and suggests that if hip hop culture is to continue, and to represent something more than the current generation's party culture and/or contributions to sexism, heterosexism, and materialism, much more emphasis will need to be placed on cultural criticism, radical politics, and critical theory of contemporary society. This chapter brings the disparate discourses from the previous chapters together in the interest of highlighting how the aesthetic advances and political breakthroughs of the past have impacted hip hop's aesthetics and politics in the present, especially the origins and evolution of rap music. We begin by exploring the interrelation between hip hop culture and postmodernism. The next section critically engages what I have termed the "hyper-corporate colonization of hip hop culture," especially the "conscious" versus "commercial" rap dichotomy, intensely exploring how late 1970s and early 1980s African American underclass and other working-poor youth culture, which was initially thought to be nothing more than a mere passing ghetto fad and poor young folks' foolishness, evolved into an artistic and sociopolitical force of great significance, not only nationally but internationally. The last section of this chapter brings *Hip Hop's Inheritance* to a close by building on and going beyond the critique of the "conscious" versus "commercial" rap dichotomy, solemnly emphasizing that what should really matter with regard to rap music, and hip hop culture more generally, is not whether a hip hopper's artistry falls within the corporate America-created categories of "commercial" or "conscious" rap but, even more, whether the messages in the hip hopper's work reflect the "real" issues and ills, as well as the hopes, dreams, and deep-seated desires, of the hip hop generation. Let us, then, begin our exploration of hip hop's inheritance by turning to minstrelism and the Harlem Renaissance, and engaging how hip hop culture's roots can be said to teeter-totter between the two.

NOTES

1. The impact of 1960s and 1970s soul music on the hip hop generation will be discussed in detail in chapter 4. For more thorough discussions of the *Bakke* case, please see Ball (2000), Cahn (2002), and Dreyfuss and Lawrence (1979).

2. The Black Power movement's emphasis on African American's "African roots" will be discussed in detail in chapter 3, which is devoted to what the Black Arts movement bequeathed to the hip hop generation.

3. For those who are skeptical of my assertion that "much (if not seemingly most) of white America rejected black America's plea for reconciliation and racial equality" even after Martin Luther King, Jr., delivered his impassioned "I Have a Dream" speech, please see the work of the award-winning King scholars Taylor Branch (1988, 1998, 2006), Adam Fairclough (1987, 1995), and David Garrow (1981, 1986), each of whom happen to be persons of European origin or descent. Without understanding African Americans' continued suffering and social misery even after the 1963 March on Washington and the passage of the Civil Rights Act of 1964 and the Voting Rights Act of 1965, the emergence of both the Black Power and Black Arts movements are virtually incomprehensible. This incomprehension will ultimately make it impossible to grasp the "Golden Age of Rap," 1987–1999, with its emphasis on "conscious" rap music and progressive hip hop culture. For further discussion, see chapter 3.

4. My utilization of Michel Foucault's "archaeological" and "genealogical" methods in the interest of developing an intellectual history and critical theory of hip hop culture will be discussed in critical detail below.

5. For further discussion of Du Bois's "gift theory," concept of "second-sight," sociology of race, and critique of white supremacy, please see my book *Against Epistemic Apartheid: W. E. B. Du Bois and the Disciplinary Decadence of Sociology* (2010), especially chapter 2, "Du Bois and the Sociology of Race: The Sociology of the Souls of Black and White (Among Other) Folk" (pp. 107–74).

6. My interpretation of the "founding fathers'" patriarchal thought and practices has been informed by Kann (1999) and Schloesser (2002), especially Schloesser's brilliant conception of "racial patriarchy."

7. It is interesting here to observe how Ellison's assessment of the instrumentality and functionality of African American music mirrors Du Bois's turn of the twentieth-century music criticism in *The Souls of Black Folk* (1903), where he declared: "Little of beauty has America given the world save the rude grandeur God himself stamped on her bosom; the human spirit in this new world has expressed itself in vigor and ingenuity rather than in beauty. And so by fateful chance the Negro folk-song—the rhythmic cry of the slave—stands to-day not simply as the sole American music, but as the most beautiful expression of human experience born this side the seas. It has been neglected, it has been, and is, half despised, and above all it has been persistently mistaken and misunderstood; but notwithstanding, it still remains as the singular spiritual heritage of the nation and the greatest gift of the Negro people" (p. 251). What is truly amazing here is that Du Bois's age-old words could conceivably be applied to the soundtrack of hip hop culture, rap music—"the Negro folk-song—the rhythmic cry of the slave—" of the twenty-first century. Certainly, rap music "has been neglected, it has been, and is, half despised, and above all it has been persistently mistaken and misunderstood," but none of this negates the fact that in its own way rap music and hip hop culture are recreating and currently represent African American popular culture. Therefore, if it is conceded that for black America *music is much more than music*, then, the framework and major foci of *Hip Hop's Inheritance* can be said to have been dictated by the longstanding instrumentality and functionality of African American music, as asserted above by Du Bois, Ellison, and Baraka, among others.

8. For further discussion of Jameson's Marxist literary theory and socialist politics, see Jameson (1971, 1981, 1990, 1991, 1998, 2000, 2007). And for the major secondary sources that have informed my interpretation and critique of Jameson's cultural Marxism and "cognitive mapping" project, see Buchanan (2006), Homer (1998), Kellner and Homer (2004), and Roberts (2000). More detailed discussion of the "Golden Age of Rap" and "conscious rap" is provided in chapters 3 and 5.

9. The Africana Critical Theory (ACT) intellectual archaeology project, which includes my previous works *W. E. B. Du Bois and the Problems of the Twenty-First Century*, *Du Bois's Dialectics*, *Africana Critical Theory*, *Forms of Fanonism*, and *Against Epistemic Apartheid*, will be discussed in detail below.

10. Truth be told, since its inception Marxism has been in crisis, but this does not negate the fact that it has historically and continues currently to provide one of, if not *the* most penetrating and provocative critiques of capitalism and class struggle. In response to constant criticisms that Marxism had been falsified, Frankfurt School critical theorist Herbert Marcuse (1978) may have put it best when he asserted in a classic 1978 BBC interview:

[I] do not believe that the theory [Marxism], as such, has been falsified. What has happened is that some of the concepts of Marxian theory, as I said before, have had to be re-examined; but this is not something from outside brought into Marxist theory, it is something which Marxist theory itself, as an historical and dialectical theory, demands. It would be relatively easy for me to enumerate, or give you a catalogue of, those decisive concepts of Marx which have been corroborated by the development of capitalism; the concentration of economic power, the fusion of economic and political power, the increasing intervention of the state into the economy, the decline in the rate of profit, the need for engaging in a neo-imperialist policy in order to create markets and opportunity of enlarged accumulation of capital, and so on. This is a formidable catalogue—and it speaks a lot for Marxian theory . . . Marxian theory would be falsified when the conflict between our ever-increasing social wealth and its destructive use were to be solved within the framework of Capitalism; when the poisoning of the life environment were to be eliminated; when capital could expand in a peaceful way; when the gap between rich and poor were being continuously reduced; when technical progress were to be made to serve the growth of human freedom—and all this, I repeat, within the framework of Capitalism. (pp. 72–73; see also Marcuse, 1967)

Many black radicals, especially black Marxists, concede with their white Marxist counterparts that capitalism does not enhance but, in fact, inhibits human life and liberation. However, in contradistinction to most white Marxists, black Marxists also emphasize the political economy of race and racism and, often employing a deconstructed and reconstructed race-conscious and racism-critical historical materialist framework, point to the interconnections and parallel historical evolution of racism and capitalism. As early as his 1907 essays, "Socialist of the Path" and "The Negro and Socialism," for instance, W. E. B. Du Bois (1985c) detected and detailed deficiencies in the Marxist tradition which included, among other things, a silence on and/or an inattention to: race, racism, and anti-racist struggle; colonialism and anti-colonialist struggle; and the ways in which *both* capitalism and colonialism exacerbate not simply the economic exploitation of non-Europeans, but continues (both physical and psychological) colonization beyond the realm of political economy. Du Bois, therefore, laboring long and critically with Marxian theory and methodology, deconstructed it and developed his own original radical democratic socialist theory that: simultaneously built on his pioneering work as a (classical) critical race theorist and anti-colonialist; called for the radical transformation of U.S. society and the power relations of the world; was deeply concerned about and committed to world peace and demanded disarmament; and, advocated the liberation of all colonized, politically oppressed, and economically exploited persons (see Rabaka, 2007, 2008a, 2010a, 2010c).

11. With regard to Frankfurt School critical theory, Erich Fromm and Herbert Marcuse incorporated aspects of what could loosely be termed "feminist theory" into their articulations of a critical theory of contemporary society. However, neither theorist was consistent nor ever fully developed a feminist and/or anti-sexist dimension in their respective theories of social change. Although Fromm's inchoate socialist-feminist thinking by far surpasses that of Marcuse prior to the 1960s, it is important to observe Marcuse's efforts in the last decade of his life to take a "feminist turn," if you will, and to merge Marxism with feminism, among other elements of 1960s radical social thought and political practice. See, for example, Fromm's "The Theory of Mother Right and Its Relevance for Social Psychology," "Sex and Character," "Man-Woman," and "The Significance of Mother Right for Today," and Marcuse's "Dear Angela,"*Counterrevolution and Revolt*, and "Marxism and Feminism" (Fromm, 1947, 1955, 1970; Marcuse, 1971, 1972, 1974). For critical commentary on these thinkers' pro-feminist thought, see Funk (1982), Kellner (1984, 1989, 1992), and P. J. Mills (1987). And, for further feminist critiques of classical and contemporary Frankfurt School-based critical theory, see Benhabib (1986, 1992), W. Brown (2006), Fraser (1989, 1991), and Heberle (2006).

12. Once again the innovative work of Lucius Outlaw weighs in. Here and throughout the remainder of this section his work in philosophy of race and critical race theory are juxtaposed with Fraser's feminist philosophy and feminist critical theory. In particular, Outlaw's essays, "Toward a Critical Theory of Race," "Critical Theory in a Period of Radical Transformation," and "Critical Social Thought in the Interests of Black Folk," have been employed as decon-

structive and reconstructive paradigms (see Outlaw, 2005). Where I find Fraser's conception of critical theory weak in terms of grasping and grappling with race, racism, and racial colonialism, I believe that one of the major weaknesses of Outlaw's conception of critical theory is that it, in most instances, either does not adequately acknowledge gender, sexism or patriarchy, or it inadequately engages them when and where it does. My conception of critical theory, Africana critical theory, seeks to salvage and synthesize the most radical, if not revolutionary, aspects of Fraser and Outlaw's conceptions of critical theory, along with a wide range of new critical theory, to create and humbly contribute a simultaneously anti-racist, anti-sexist, anti-capitalist, anti-colonialist, and sexual orientation-sensitive critical theory of contemporary society (see Rabaka, 2006, 2007, 2008a, 2009, 2010a, 2010b).

13. A more detailed discussion of the distinct differences between black and white feminist theory and praxis, as well as the convergences and divergences of their respective Women's Liberation movements, will be offered in chapter 4.

14. In terms of my argument here, the influence of the Caribbean philosopher Charles Mills (1997, 1998, 2003a, 2003b) simply cannot be overstated, and specifically his work in *Blackness Visible: Essays on Philosophy and Race* (1998), where he innovatively asserted:

Suppose we place race at the center rather than in the wings of theory. The idea is to follow the example of those feminists of the 1970s once characterized as radical (as against liberal or Marxist), who, inspired by the U.S. black liberation movement, decided to put gender at the center of their theorizing and appropriated the term *patriarchy* to describe a system of male domination. So rather than starting with some other theory and then smuggling in gender, one begins with the fact of gender subordination. . . . The important point—as "race men" [and "race women"] have always appreciated—is that a racial perspective on society can provide insights to be found in neither a white liberalism nor a white Marxism [nor a white feminism], and when suitably modified and reconstructed, such a perspective need not imply biological generalizations about whites or commit the obvious moral error of holding people responsible for something (genealogy, phenotype) they cannot help. (pp. 98, 104, emphasis in original)

Deeply indebted to Mills's work, Africana critical theory advocates a *conjunctive* approach to critical theory; an approach which places race *and* gender *and* class *and* sexuality at the center of, not only critical analyses of contemporary society, but at the center of the creation, deconstruction, and reconstruction of the radical theories and revolutionary praxes aimed at transforming contemporary society. Africana critical theory, therefore, does not argue that race and racism are the most pressing social and political problems confronting the critical theorists of the twenty-first century, and it does not claim that class should be replaced with race or gender as the central problematic of critical theory. However, it does audaciously assert that critical theory stands in need of discursive deconstruction and radical reconstruction, and that critical race theory, feminist theory, postcolonial theory, and queer theory, among other emerging radical political perspectives, should be critically utilized to *supplement* conventional critical theory's critiques of capitalist class struggle and political economy. The main idea here is to correct the methodological omissions and strengthen the epistemic weaknesses of classical and contemporary critical theory, not prescribe yet another intellectually insular and/or myopic methodology.

15. I think it most fitting to conclude here by noting that since she published "What's Critical About Critical Theory?: The Case of Habermas and Gender" (which was originally published in 1985), Fraser (1998) has critically engaged the discourse of critical race theory, especially in her breathtakingly brilliant essay, "Another Pragmatism: Alain Locke, Critical 'Race' Theory, and the Politics of Culture." Therefore, I want to make it clear that my criticisms of her conception of critical theory are specific to "What's Critical About Critical Theory?" and are not in any way indicative of my, otherwise, profound intellectual admiration for and affinity to her work. Truth be told, she, too, has made her own unique contribution to my conception of Africana critical theory. Here, then, I have only raised my concerns about how her omission of critical race theory and the Africana tradition of critical theory weakened

her otherwise extremely erudite and astute articulation of a new critical theory of contemporary society.

16. The literature on Africana studies, which in its most comprehensive sense includes African, African American, Afro-American, Afro-Asian, Afro-European, Afro-Latino (a.k.a. Latino Negro), Afro-Native American, Caribbean, Pan-African, Black British and, of course, Black studies, is diverse and extensive. However, for quick comprehensive overviews, see Asante and Karenga (2006), Gordon and Gordon (2006a, 2006b), Rabaka (2009, 2010a, 2010b), F. Rojas (2007), and Rooks (2006).

17. Along with Africana studies and more general critical social scientific research methods (see the in-text citations), Africana critical theory has also been deeply influenced by the monumental meta-methodological studies of Bonilla-Silva and Zuberi (2008), Bulmer and Solomos (2004), Dei and Johal (2005), Fong (2008), Gunaratnam (2003), Ramji (2009), Sandoval (2000), L. T. Smith (1999), and Twine and Warren (2000), which collectively seek to decolonize research methods and emphasize their importance for developing *critical theories of white supremacist patriarchal colonial capitalist societies*. The influence of these works on Africana critical theory's mixed- or multi-methodological orientation cannot be overstated. For further discussion, see my previous work *Africana Critical Theory* (Rabaka, 2009).

18. Africana critical theory is not alone in its critique of West's lack of faith in the conceptual generation capacities of black folk in particular, and the other wretched of the earth in general. Several scholars, many working within Africana studies, have advanced constructive criticisms of his work. See, for example, Cowan (2003), Gilyard (2008), C. S. Johnson (2003), Wood (2000), and Yancy (2001).

19. Here, and throughout the remainder of this section of the introduction, I draw heavily from the discourse on Africana hermeneutics or, rather, Africana philosophy of interpretation in an effort to emphasize the importance of culturally grounded inquiry and interpretation in Africana critical theory. As Okonda Okolo (1991) observed in his classic essay, "Tradition and Destiny: Horizons of an African Philosophical Hermeneutics," Africana hermeneutics, as with almost all hermeneutical endeavors, centers on the ideas of "Tradition" and "Destiny" and how successive generations interpret, explain, and embrace their historical, cultural, and intellectual heritage(s). In his own words:

> For our part, we want to test the resources but also the limits of our hermeneutical models and practices, by examining the two notions that encompass our interpretative efforts in an unconquerable circle—the notions of Tradition and Destiny. These notions simultaneously define the object, the subject, the horizons, and the limits of interpretation. To interpret is always to close the circle of the subject and the object. We cannot, however, make this circle our own if we do not lay it out beyond the thought of the subject and the object, toward a thinking of our horizons and the limits of our interpretation defined by the reality of our traditions and the ideality of our destiny. (p. 202)

Okolo, among other Africana hermeneuticists, highlights the abstruse issues that arise in interpretative theory and praxis in our present sociopolitical world and world of ideas. Historical and cultural experiences and struggles determine and, often subtly, define *what* and *how* we interpret. If, for instance, Africana thought-traditions are not known to, and are not shared with, theorists and philosophers of African origin or descent and other interested scholars (i.e., Africanists), then they will assume there is no history of theory or philosophy in the African world. These would-be Africana theorists will draw from another cultural group's thought-traditions, because human existence, as the Africana philosophers of existence have pointed out, is nothing other than our constant confrontation with ontological issues and existential questions. What is more, the nature of theory, especially in the current postmodern/postcolonial period, is such that it incessantly links with and builds on other theories. In other words, a competent theorist must not only be familiar with the history and evolutionary character of theory, but with the intellectual origins of theories—that is, with *who*, *where*, and *why* specific theories were created to describe and explain and, even more, *alter* a particular subject and/or object. For further discussion of Africana hermeneutics, see Okere (1971, 1991) and Serequeberhan (1991, 2000, 2007).

20. I offer a more in-depth discussion of Africana critical theory's appropriation of certain aspects of Foucault's critical theories of power, knowledge, domination, and discourse below.

21. As is well known, *epistēmē* is a Greek word for knowledge. However, because it was taken up by Kant, Foucault went out of his way to distinguish his conception of *epistēmē* from the Kantian conception. In *Foucault Live*, for instance, he made it clear that he was employing the term to simply denote "all those relationships which existed between the various sectors of science during a given epoch" (Foucault, 1996, p. 76). Therefore, anything labeled with the adjective "epistemic," which is closely connected to the corollary term "epistemological," has some relation to knowledge, or to a general theory of knowledge (hence, "epistemological") (see also Rabaka, 2010a, pp. 1–45).

Chapter Two

"Civil Rights by Copyright" (Da ReMix!): From the Harlem Renaissance to the Hip Hop Generation

In an accurate, if humorous, sense, blacks have felt the need to attempt to "reconstruct" their image probably since that dreadful day in 1619, when the first boatload of Africans disembarked in Virginia. Africans and their descendants commenced their cultural lives in this hemisphere as veritable deconstructions of all that the West so ardently wished itself to be. Almost as soon as blacks could write, it seems, they set out to redefine—against already received racist stereotypes—who and what a black person was, and how unlike the racist stereotype the black original actually could be. To counter these racist stereotypes, white and black writers erred on the side of nobility, and posited equally fictitious black archetypes, from Oroonoko in 1688 to Kunte Kinte in more recent times. If various Western cultures constructed blackness as an absence, then various generations of black authors have attempted to reconstruct blackness as a presence. —Henry Louis Gates and Gene Andrew Jarrett, *The New Negro: Readings on Race, Representation, and African American Culture, 1892–1938*, p. 3

BLACK FACES, WHITE BODIES: FROM MODERNISM AND MINSTRELISM TO POSTMODERNISM AND POSTMILLENNIAL MINSTRELISM

Although hip hop did not emerge until the last quarter of the twentieth century, it is extremely important to acknowledge its cultural and aesthetic antecedents. Hip hop's artistic ancestors extend well beyond the aesthetes and activists of the Black Arts movement. Quiet as it has been kept, the hip hop generation's social, political, cultural, and aesthetic consciousness is actually linked to much earlier forms of African American expressive culture, some reaching all the way back to the era of minstrelsy. Minstrelsy, or the minstrel show, was one of the earliest authentically "American" forms of entertainment. It incorporated comedy routines, dancing, singing, and variety acts performed by whites in blackface or, especially during the Reconstruction and post-Reconstruction periods, blacks in blackface (Cockrell, 1997; Mahar, 1999; Springhall, 2008; Toll, 1974).

Minstrel shows arose as a counter to the efforts of the abolitionists, both black and white, who argued that enslaved Africans should be set free. In essence, minstrel shows caricatured enslaved Africans as ignorant, lazy, dirty, buffoonish, superstitious, ever-joyous, and ever-musical. In many senses, materializing as a response to the Haitian Revolution (1791–1804) and the consecutive revolts of Gabriel Prosser, Chatham Manor, George Boxley, Denmark Vessey, Nat Turner, and *La Amistad* rebellion in the 1830s, the minstrel show grew out of brief burlesques and comic *entr'actes*, and evolved and eventually took shape as a fully formed musical review by the beginning of the 1840s.[1] From the 1830s and well into the first decade of the twentieth century minstrel shows were utilized for every propagandistic or, rather, every anti-black racist purpose imaginable. To be sure, several stock characters manifested themselves in minstrel shows, such as the "happy slave," the "dandy," the "coon," the "mammy," the "old darky," the "mulatto wench," and the buffoonish black soldier (Browder, 2000). Minstrels, again, mostly whites until about the last quarter of the nineteenth century, insistently asserted that their characters, songs, and dances were based on "real" black folkways and culture, but the extent of the exact influence of authentic African American culture on minstrelsy has long remained a point of contention. What has been historically documented, however, is that when the spirituals began to be sung in minstrel shows in the 1870s, it marked the first time that unmistakably African American music entered into the minstrel show's musical repertoire (Abbott and Seroff, 2002; Lhamon, 2003).

No matter what the hip hop generation may make of all of this, one thing is for certain, and that is that blackface minstrelsy was undeniably the first distinctly "American" theatrical form (R. M. Lewis, 2003; C. J. Robinson, 2007; Sotiropoulos, 2006). What is more, blackface minstrelsy was the motor inside the machine that not only led to the emergence of, but also consistently powered the American music industry during its most formative phase of development (R. Crawford, 2005; Shaw, 1986; Werner, 2006). Although often downplayed, it should be emphasized that American popular culture came into being by mercilessly mocking blacks and their blackness. The minstrel shows' spread from the South to the North in the early 1840s marked a significant turning point in the marketing of minstrelsy and opened up an entirely new age that saw the rise, commercial appeal, and institutionalization of blackface minstrelsy.

With its caricatures of African American singing, dancing, and speaking styles, blackface minstrelsy ensured that the most popular image of blacks in the white social imagination was one of them (i.e., blacks) as infantile and pathological brutes (Strausbaugh, 2006). Hence, even in so-called freedom (i.e., even in the post-Emancipation period), African Americans were frequently referred to and reproached as the "Negro Problem."[2] They were seen as a social menace, in many senses, because their life-worlds and life-struggles impugned the longstanding lie of lily-white democracy in America. And, even more, they were a constant reminder that race and its corollary racism has always been, and will remain for the foreseeable future, part and parcel of American citizenship and democracy. Beginning in the Jacksonian era, an age which extended voting rights to all white men by eliminating property laws and other qualifications, the omnipresent image of the blackface minstrel incessantly announced that black men (white and nonwhite women would not gain the right to vote until 1920) were utterly unqualified to contribute to or participate in American democracy in any meaningful way (R. L. Jackson, 2006; Tucker, 2007). What, pray tell, many whites asked, did ignorant, infantile, and indolent "slaves" and "former slaves" have to do with American citizenship and democracy?

Whites, to put it unpretentiously, were mesmerized by blackface minstrelsy. It was as though they were on safari, journeying through a jungle world filled with black (among other nonwhite) half-human and half-animal-like creatures who were as "savage" as they were sad. And, it was this white supremacist and anti-black racist construction of blacks that was celebrated and sold to whites and, truth be told, other nonwhites, nationally and internationally, as "authentic blackness." It is extremely interesting to observe that a wide range of whites, from Abraham Lincoln and Mark Twain to "ethnic" European immigrants in northern ghettoes and poor whites in the southern states, were among the most ardent admirers of the minstrel show. In this sense, then, the impact of blackface minstrelsy was, and covertly continues to be, both profound and pervasive. For instance, in *The Rise and Fall of the White Republic: Class, Politics, and Mass Culture in Nineteenth-Century America*, Alexander Saxton (1990) observed, "[p]aced by the extraordinary popularity of blackface minstrelsy, theater expanded into an industry of mass entertainment" (p. 109). Furthermore, whites' fascination with, combined with the widespread popularity of, blackface minstrelsy served as a recurring anti-black racist reference point for whites of seemingly all social classes. Ironically, blackface minstrelsy, both wittingly and unwittingly, aided and abetted the spread of the "whiteness as property" ethos and white racial egalitarianism, irrespective of social, political, regional, and religious differences (Du Bois, 1920; C. I. Harris, 1993; Roediger, 2005). Whiteness, in and of itself, was henceforth and seemingly forevermore the only qualification to be met to make one an authentic citizen and beneficiary of all that American citizenship and democracy had to offer (Delgado and Stefancic, 1997; Lott, 1995; Meer, 2005; Olson, 2004; Roediger, 2007).

Additional emphasis should be placed on the foregoing contention that the anti-black racist representations of blacks and blackness propagated in blackface minstrelsy aided and abetted the creation of previously nonexistent alliances between the national white bourgeoisie and both northern and southern white workers by affirming a nationwide "racial contract" and sociopolitical commitment to *the diabolical dialectic of white superiority and black inferiority.*[3] In essence, blackface minstrelsy was the public theater space where whites' private fears and misunderstandings, not only of blacks, but also, on an even deeper level, of each other, were played out. For example, by embracing blackface minstrelsy northern whites proved to southern whites that they too could be just as unsympathetic to black suffering and black social misery, while white southerners demonstrated to white northerners that they still had a sense of humor after the devastating defeat they suffered in the Civil War. After all, both sides seemed to be saying to each other with their participation in, and perpetuation of the fiendish dehumanizing and recolonizing free-for-all that was blackface minstrelsy, what still matters most with respect to American citizenship and democracy is not one's wealth or status as a worker, but one's "God-given" whiteness; hence, here we return to Cheryl Harris's (1993) groundbreaking discourse on "whiteness as property."

As Saxton observed above, the meteoric rise of blackface minstrelsy facilitated the popularization of theater throughout the United States, while also widening theater patronage beyond the bourgeoisie. In other words, to reiterate, blackface minstrelsy was the first authentically "American" popular culture. It was a simultaneously trans-class, trans-occupation, trans-education, trans-ethnic, and trans-regional space, which—for the first time—allowed whites to commingle on *their* hard won "American" common ground—that is, the common ground of their whiteness and all of its prickly proprietary rights. Although blacks did participate in blackface minstrelsy from the late 1870s through to the 1910s, it is important to emphasize that whites constituted the overwhelming majority of blackface minstrel performers and patrons. Considering the fact that more than 90 percent of African Americans were enslaved and the few emancipated African Americans in the United States were not allowed to attend white theaters, during its more than a century of existence the minstrel show was an almost exclusively white cultural aesthetic arena where whites' commodified and consumed anti-black racist representations of blackness and black performance. In fact, one of the distinguishing factors of authentically "American" music, theater, dance, children's stories, and literature by the late nineteenth century was its recurring and increasing reliance on anti-black racist representations of blackness and black performance (i.e., black caricatures).

Various genres of "American" performing arts provided whites with myriad mediums through which to commodify and consume black caricatures, ironically enabling whites to feel as though they really and truly had been exposed to, and knew firsthand authentic African American culture. In reality, of course, they were consuming figments of other whites' imaginations and not authentic African American culture in any way whatsoever. White blackface minstrels' anti-black racist representations of blackness and black performance was as close as most whites, generation after jostling generation, would ever come to blacks and black culture. Which is also to say, the minstrel show was nothing other than a century-spanning public discourse on *the diabolical dialectic of white superiority and black inferiority*. In *The Hip Hop Revolution: The Culture and Politics of Rap*, the acclaimed African American historian Jeffrey Ogbar (2007) observed:

> The purpose of the minstrel was twofold. Minstrels provided easy and immediate entertainment to whites who simultaneously enjoyed the construction and dissemination of an ostensibly white American character by being the antithesis of the minstrel. The minstrel, or coon, was, in effect, an inversion of the white man. While white America prided itself on its scientific and technological achievements at world fairs, in government, in scholarship, and in other arenas, the carefree, happy, and irresponsible Negro offered a sharp contrast to articulations of whiteness and national identity. Additionally, the minstrel justified the sociopolitical and economic structure in the United States. The most important function of the minstrel was its role in rationalizing white supremacy. The enduring image of the happy, docile, cowardly, and shiftless coon insisted that black people were fundamentally ill equipped to compete with white people in any meaningful way. Blacks were barred from equal access to jobs, education, housing, military service, and democracy. The coon, therefore, assuaged the conscience of many whites who reasoned that things could not be too terrible if blacks were always happy. (p. 14)

There is a sense in which Ogbar's comments help to unambiguously accent the ways in which *the diabolical dialectic of white superiority and black inferiority* played itself out in the ubiquitous figure of the minstrel—a figure, he highlights, which existed long before and long after the Civil War, the Emancipation Proclamation, and Reconstruction. The blackface minstrel has been hidden from the hip hop generation, just as have most of the pertinent details of the African holocaust, African American enslavement, and the emergence of American apartheid during the post-Reconstruction period. Exposing the hip hop generation to the minstrel show will hopefully help them to critically comprehend that it is possible for blacks to suffer and experience a great deal of social misery even though hip hoppers and the moguls of the music, movie, and fashion industries are commodifying and advocating increasing consumption of hip hop culture, which is unequivocally rooted in and rose out of African American popular culture. The main point here is that simply because black performers are socially visible or high-profile does not mean that black suffering and black social misery is actually being critically engaged or, even more, consciously eradicated.

In his groundbreaking book, *Raising Cain: Blackface Performance from Jim Crow to Hip Hop*, W. T. Lhamon (1998) argues that blackface minstrelsy was not an invariable or monolithic mode of expression: "It seems most important to notice how blackface performance can work . . . against racial stereotyping" (p. 6). Similar to many rap songs, many songs sung by blackface minstrels frequently entailed double entendre when they were performed by black rather than white blackface minstrels. For instance, the nineteenth century minstrel song "De New York Nigger" clandestinely critiqued white supremacy, but one would have to have a working knowledge of authentic African American life-worlds and life-struggles in order to catch the innuendo at work in the songs' lyrics. Lhamon went on to suggest that blackface minstrelsy also represented a repudiation of white America's socially sanctioned codes of convention and respectability. He argued that their popularity was due, at least in part, to young white workers identification with the hardships of the "coon" characters: "The black figure appealed across the Atlantic as an organized emblem for workers and the unemployed. Hated everywhere, he could be championed everywhere alike" (pp. 44–45, 118). It would seem that here, however, Lhamon is exaggerating the white workers' relationship with the coon characters of the minstrel shows because he is overlooking the fact that white workers' whiteness in and of itself makes their situations comparably different from the situations of black workers and the black unemployed in a white supremacist society that was built on the blood, sweat, and tears of the African holocaust, African American enslavement, and the rise of American apartheid in the post-Reconstruction period (Richardson, 2001; McDermott, 2006; Roediger, 2005, 2007).

Lhamon's slightly lopsided argument here raises an important issue that seems to have been handed down to contemporary Hip Hop studies, and that issue entails the nature of whites', especially white youths', affinity with authentic African American history, culture, and struggle, as opposed to anti-black racist representations of blackness and black performance (Kitwana, 2005; Raphael-Hernandez, 2004; Tanz, 2007). To be sure, the coon character could be interpreted as an archetypical outsider and exile who rebuffed the white supremacist world that has so long rejected him. However, as much as this is an extremely attractive argument attempting to introduce a new angle on the agency of the wretched of the earth in America, it seems to almost utterly ignore the historical reality that very often the very same white workers who found blackface minstrelsy so entertaining were very often the same folk who committed unspeakable acts of anti-black racist violence against black workers and the black unemployed. For example, white workers often provided American apartheid with its infantry. From the white enslavers who went to the African continent and the white overseers on antebellum plantations, to the klansmen and klanswomen of the Ku Klux Klan, white workers have been rather consistent in their complicity in anti-black racist violence (e.g., lynchings, anti-black racist rapes, and race riots) (see Ifill, 2007; Markovitz, 2004; Nevels, 2007; Pfeifer, 2004; H. Shapiro, 1988; Waldrep, 2006). The most serious weakness of Lhamon's argument, therefore, lies in the fact that it attempts to whitewash black workers and the black masses' troublesome historical relationship with white workers, as well as white youths' willingness to be entertained by and embrace "black performance" while they, whether consciously or unconsciously, participate in physical, psychological, sexual, and verbal anti-black racist violence (Choi, Callaghan, and Murphy, 1995; Karcher, 1980; Mixon, 2005; O'Brien, 1999; Williams-Myers, 1995).

The foregoing brings us to a discussion of the ways in which stereotypical images, what black feminist sociologist Patricia Hill Collins in *Black Feminist Thought* called "controlling images," of blacks speaks to both the white bourgeoisie and the white proletariat's embrace of white supremacy and, most especially, "whiteness as property." Collins (2000) contends that "[p]ortraying African American women as stereotypical mammies, matriarchs, welfare recipients, and hot mommas helps justify U.S. black women's oppression. Challenging these controlling images has been a core theme in black feminist thought" (p. 69). Taking Collins's concept and critique of the "controlling images" of African American women that function to reify *anti-black racist relations of race, gender, and class power* and extending it to include stereotypical images of African American men as "happy slaves," "coons," "dandies," "old darkies," "bumbling black rapists," and "buffoonish black soldiers" as well, here we are able to highlight how white supremacy surreptitiously racially colonizes blacks across the chasms of both gender and class, ultimately presenting figments of white folks' imaginations of who blacks are and what "real" blackness is. Lhamon's analysis above overlooks the ways in which white workers' embrace of anti-black racist representations of blackness and black performance in minstrel shows actually enabled them to further distinguish themselves from blacks and insidiously increase the value of their (i.e., white workers') most prized possession—their whiteness and, therefore, their humanness when compared with blacks' nonwhiteness and, therefore, their nonhumanness.

As the entertainment industries and mass media rapidly evolved from the turn of the twentieth century to the mid-twentieth century, so too did the "controlling image" of the minstrel. Minstrelism, often covertly, morphed and moved from the nineteenth into the twentieth century, going undetected except by the most vigilant observers who were often amazed by its ability to infiltrate almost every major new mode of expression American popular culture had to offer. From vaudeville and silent movies to children's stories and cartoons, from novels and plays to poems and song lyrics, blackface minstrelsy was part and parcel of early twentieth-century race relations and racial politics in the United States (Riggs, 1986, 1991, 1995). In several senses, African American aesthetics, from the late nineteenth century to the early twenty-first century, has been and remains both defined and deformed by the "controlling images" that were first propagated during *the century of minstrelsy*. Protesting the blackface minstrel as anti-black racist propaganda, African Americans' major cultural aesthetic movements—that is, the Harlem Renaissance, the Black Arts movement, and the hip hop generation—have both consciously and unconsciously, and often schizophrenically, embraced and rejected aspects of the "controlling image" of the blackface minstrel (Heaggans, 2009).

In light of the New Negro movement and its aesthetic arm, the Harlem Renaissance, by the time of the Black Power movement and its artistic outlet, the Black Arts movement, the "controlling image" of the blackface minstrel was seemingly not as powerful or pervasive as it was at the turn of the twentieth century. This was partly due to the fact that the New Negro, Civil Rights, and Black Power movements each altered the way in which race was publicly perceived and performed in the United States. To be sure, anti-black racism and blackface minstrelism are still here with us in the rap music and hip hop culture of the twenty-first century, but the chameleonic character of *postmodern minstrelism* has become so subtle and so sophisticated, so "freaky" and so fragmentary that it makes it extremely difficult to decipher which aspects of contemporary African American popular culture (specifically, hip hop culture) are linked to the legacy of blackface minstrelism and which are authentic aesthetic expressions of African Americans as they transition from the twentieth into the twenty-first century. No matter what, however, it is important for Hip Hop studies scholars and students to come to terms with the fact that blackface minstrelism has indeed had an indelible impact on rap music and hip hop culture, just as it left the imprint of its legacy on the Harlem Renaissance and the Black Arts movement. Of course, most African American artists, from the Harlem Renaissance through to the Black Arts movement, responded to the historical figure of the blackface minstrel by producing work after work of resistive art grounded in black pride and black radical political recurring themes, which unequivocally rejected the anti-black racist, crude, and vicious portrayals of African Americans propagated by blackface minstrelism. However, truth be told, there have been many African American artists, whether consciously or unconsciously, in both the Harlem Renaissance and the Black Arts movement, who have embraced elements of the "controlling image" of the blackface minstrel. The hip hop generation unwittingly inherited and, however covertly, have continued the schizophrenic relationship most African American artists have had with the menace of blackface minstrelism since the early 1830s.

It is important for us now, then, to turn our attention to the real roots of the hip hop aesthetic, not blackface minstrelsy but, as quiet as it has been kept, the aesthetic radicalism of the Harlem Renaissance. As mentioned above, however, the Harlem Renaissance evolved out of the New Negro movement, an often overlooked sociopolitical movement which arguably laid the foundation for the Civil Rights movement of the 1950s and 1960s. Almost all of the major issues confronting the hip hop generation, from race and gender to class and sexuality, were prefigured in the discursive formations and discursive practices of the insurgent intellectuals and aesthetic radicals of the Harlem Renaissance. And, similar to the hip hop generation, they too understood themselves to be rupturing their relationships with what they found to be the constricting public image and conservative politics of the late nineteenth and early twentieth century "New Negro." What, then, was the New Negro movement? What were its goals? What was it moving away from, and what was it moving toward?

ON THE ORIGINS AND EVOLUTION OF NEW NEGRO CRITICAL SOCIAL THEORY AND COUNTER-IDEOLOGY: FROM THE NEW NEGRO MOVEMENT TO THE HARLEM RENAISSANCE

It would be extremely difficult to understand the aesthetic radicalism of the Harlem Renaissance without critically comprehending turn-of-the-twentieth-century "New Negroes." The New Negro movement, of which the Harlem Renaissance was its artistic apogee, is commonly understood to have taken place between the mid-1890s and the late 1930s, or 1940 at the latest. Ironically, considering the incessant celebrations of, and expatiations on black masculinity and "race men" throughout both the New Negro movement, and especially the Harlem Renaissance, it was the womanism of the Black Women's Club movement that helped to sparked what ultimately came to be known as the New Negro movement. Although the term "New Negro" had been used prior to the mid-1890s, it is interesting to note some of the major historical (and *herstorical*) events that signaled, quite literally, a *new* "Negro" consciousness and presence in the United States.[4]

First, the evolution of the Black Women's Club movement, specifically the National Association of Colored Women (NACW), from the Woman's Era Club of Boston and the various Dorcas societies of Philadelphia in the early 1890s to the National Federation of Afro-American Women (NFAAW) in the mid-1890s, black women established the first nationally networked "racial uplift" organization among African Americans. This is a point that should be emphasized because time and time again black women's contributions to both the New Negro movement and, especially, the Harlem Renaissance have been either downplayed or erased altogether—that is, of course, with the exception of a few notable "race women" here and there (e.g., Ida B. Wells, Amy Jacques Garvey, Zora Neale Hurston, Bessie Smith, and Josephine Baker) (see Mitchell and Taylor, 2009; Patton and Honey, 2001; Sherrard-Johnson, 2007; Wall, 1995). We will witness below the continued colonization or complete erasure of black women's life-worlds and life-struggles in hip hop culture.[5]

Frederick Douglass's death on February 20, 1895 marked the second significant event influencing the emergence of the New Negro. In the wake of Douglass's death two of the major male figures of the New Negro movement began their ascent to national prominence: W. E. B. Du Bois and Booker T. Washington. An avowed admirer of Douglass, Du Bois had long-aspired to liberate and lead his beloved black folk. He wanted nothing more than to use what he had gained from his studies at Fisk, Harvard, and the University of Berlin in the best interest of black liberation. As the first African American to earn a Ph.D. from Harvard in May of 1895, he believed that he was the ideal candidate to fill the leadership void left as a result of Douglass's death, but Washington's accommodationism quickly dashed Du Bois's ambitious dream (D. L. Lewis, 1993, 2000; Rabaka, 2007, 2008, 2010a, 2010c).

In September of 1895 Booker T. Washington delivered what has been infamously referred to as "The Atlanta Compromise Address," where, in so many words, he told wealthy white capitalists that black workers would accommodate their (i.e., wealthy whites') interests. In the same speech he told blacks that they should focus their energies on manual labor and leave mental labor to wealthy whites and their minions. His rhetoric of accommodation simultaneously won him many wealthy white friends and alienated him from many black leaders, especially turn-of-the-twentieth-century black liberals and black radicals. However, because Washington's associations with rich whites increased his national influence and political power, many of his critics, both black and white, were silenced in one way or another (Harlan, 1972, 1982, 1983; Meier, 1963; Rabaka, 2008; M. R. West, 2005).

The New Negro movement, then, meant many things to many different people, and from its inception there were, at the least, two distinct conceptions. On the one hand, there was *the Washingtonian conservative conception*, which advocated that African Americans turn their attention to the employment and economic aspects of what was then referred to as the "Negro Problem." On the other hand, there was *the Du Boisian liberal-radical conception*, which exhorted African Americans to not only attend to the employment and economic aspects, but also the myriad social, political, legal, intellectual, and cultural issues inherent in the "Negro Problem" and, even more, authentic African American and Pan-African liberation.

Washington, Du Bois, and the leaders of the Black Women's Club movement, most of whom held conceptions of the New Negro or "race woman" somewhere between Washington and Du Bois's articulations of the New Negro, represented the first generation of African Americans to collectively express the social, political, and educational aspirations of black folk, indeed, of the *New* Negroes (Dublin, Arias, and Carreras, 2003). From the time of Washington's rise to national prominence in 1895 to his death in 1915, the New Negro movement's main focus was on securing African Americans' civil rights. But, Washington's accommodationism and railroading of seemingly all blacks into the realm of manual labor increasingly rubbed more and more New Negroes the wrong way. Hence, in response to the growing disdain for Washington's accommodationist politics, Du Bois co-founded, first, the Niagara movement and, then, the National Association for the Advancement of Colored People (NAACP), which unambiguously laid the foundation for the subsequent black radicalism of the twentieth century. Paralleling the phenomenal rise of the Black Women's Club movement, the New Negro movement sought to dialectically rupture African Americans' relationship with the bondage of their past and provide a bridge to the freedom of their future. In this sense, Washington, Du Bois, and the members of the Black Women's Club movement all understood themselves to be breaking away from the stereotypical image of the "Old Negro" and/or blackface minstrel that had long dominated mainstream American discourse on black folk.

It was almost as if even in "freedom" African Americans remained chained and bound, freeze-framed as perpetual "slaves" and minstrels. This kind of "freedom," truth be told, was a farce. *New* Negroes would have none of it. After centuries of the most excruciating and unforgiving enslavement and blackface minstrel mockery imaginable they put forward their own homespun critical social theory and counter-ideology. In other words, to offset the fictions and fantasies of white supremacy and the anti-black racist ideology of the "Old Negro" archetype, turn-of-the-twentieth-century African Americans discursively developed *New Negro critical social theory and counter-ideology.*[6] Writing on this very issue in their groundbreaking volume, *The New Negro: Readings on Race, Representation, and African American Culture, 1892–1938*, Henry Louis Gates and Gene Andrew Jarrett (2007) declared:

In an accurate, if humorous, sense, blacks have felt the need to attempt to "reconstruct" their image probably since that dreadful day in 1619, when the first boatload of Africans disembarked in Virginia. Africans and their descendants commenced their cultural lives in this hemisphere as veritable deconstructions of all that the West so ardently wished itself to be. Almost as soon as blacks could write, it seems, they set out to redefine—against already received racist stereotypes—who and what a black person was, and how unlike the racist stereotype the black original actually could be. To counter these racist stereotypes, white and black writers erred on the

side of nobility, and posited equally fictitious black archetypes, from Oroonoko in
1688 to Kunte Kinte in more recent times. If various Western cultures constructed
blackness as an absence, then various generations of black authors have attempted to
reconstruct blackness as a presence. (p. 3)

After two decades dominated by Washington's seemingly schizophrenic embrace and rejection of the "Old Negro" archetype, and also in light of the
increase in lynchings and other anti-black racist violence, the years leading
up to World War I and immediately following Washington's death in 1915
proved to be an unprecedented turning point in African American history,
culture, and struggle. Years and years of New Negro acquiescence (à la
Washington) and New Negro agitation and activism (à la Du Bois) gave way
to an innovative and distinctly *African American* expressive culture: the aesthetic radicalism of the Harlem Renaissance. Washington's death ended the
bitter ideological battle between he and Du Bois over the best leadership
strategy for black liberation. But, even before Washington's death Du Bois
had begun to dabble in the arts, writing short stories, poems, and publishing
his first novel, *The Quest of the Silver Fleece*, in 1911. Challenging white
constructions of "blackness as an absence," Du Bois was among the first
generation of African American authors to consciously attempt to "reconstruct blackness as a presence." Unlike any of the other major African
American post-Reconstruction writers, such as Charles Chesnutt, Pauline
Hopkins, Sutton E. Griggs, and Paul Laurence Dunbar, Du Bois's work had
an impact on the overall New Negro movement *and* its radical aesthetic
explosion under the guise of the Harlem Renaissance (D. L. Lewis, 1993,
2000; Moses, 1978, 1990, 1993, 1998, 2004; Wintz, 1996a).

According to David Levering Lewis (1989) in *When Harlem Was in
Vogue*, the social and political focus of the New Negro movement gradually
shifted from an accommodationism-cum-civil rights initiative (à la Washington) and an activism-cum-civil rights initiative (à la Du Bois) to an "arts-
cum-civil rights" initiative (à la the intellectuals and artists of the Harlem
Renaissance) (p. xvi). In other words, the Harlem Renaissance represents the
New Negro movement modified or "remixed," if you will. The social and
political focus of the movement remained on securing African Americans'
civil rights, but newfound cultural and aesthetic avenues were utilized in
ongoing efforts to achieve, not simply civil rights, but to contribute to the
deconstruction and reconstruction of "citizenship" and "democracy" in the
United States. Lewis, perhaps, put it best when he argued that the Harlem
Renaissance's main motto could be paraphrased as: "civil rights by copyright" (p. xvi). This apt phrase, it seems to me, best summarizes the ways in
which the New Negro movement and Harlem Renaissance critically converge and diverge.

This means, then, that here the Harlem Renaissance is not seen as a completely separate movement when compared with the New Negro movement. Following many of the major Harlem Renaissance studies scholars, I understand the Harlem Renaissance to be indicative of the evolution or, even more, the cultural aesthetic maturation of the New Negro movement, just as most Black Power studies scholars understand the Black Arts movement to be the cultural aesthetic outlet of the Black Power movement (Huggins, 1971; D. L. Lewis, 1989; R. E. Washington, 2001; Wintz, 1996a, 1996d, 1996g). Part of the confusion surrounding interpreting the connections between the New Negro movement and the Harlem Renaissance may have to do with the fact that Black studies was not established within the American academy until a quarter of a century after both the New Negro movement and Harlem Renaissance had ended. Therefore, the abundance of theory and methodology currently utilized to critique and/or appreciate African American intellectual and cultural history was not available to the early advocates of what has come to be called "African American studies" and, with greater and greater frequency in the twenty-first century, "Africana studies" (i.e., continental and diasporan African studies). In a sense, the Black Power and Black Arts movements, being the most recent sociopolitical and cultural aesthetic paradigms offered by the generation that immediately preceded the hip hop generation, represent more "modern" and "concrete" models of black radical politics and cultural aesthetics.

It should also be observed that generation after generation of African Americans have, whether consciously or unconsciously, followed in the footsteps of the New Negroes, who in forming their movement understood themselves to be breaking with the "Old Negro" and/or blackface minstrel archetype. The intellectuals and artists of the Harlem Renaissance conceived of themselves, initially, as breaking with the Washingtonian New Negro, and then eventually the Du Boisian New Negro. The young, insurgent intellectuals and aesthetic radicals of the Harlem Renaissance sought to deconstruct and reconstruct not simply American "citizenship" and "democracy," but the very notion of what it meant to be an "American Negro" (or, rather, a "Negro American"). The radicals of the Harlem Renaissance were yet and still "New Negroes," but they were decidedly "New Negroes" with a twist; in a word, they were *neo-New Negroes*. As Jeffrey Stewart (2007) stated in "The New Negro as Citizen," for neo-New Negroes being "New Negroes" was "never simply" about "racial identities, but new, more complex personalities, black individuals, sparkling in their multifarious talents, inclinations, and aspirations, modern black people" (p. 18).

Stewart goes on to offer a stunning description of the neo-New Negroes of the Harlem Renaissance that subtly sounds as though he could be describing twenty-first-century hip hop generation intellectuals, artists, and activists: "Here was an outstanding group of intellectuals as well as artists, men and women as comfortable in the white intellectual world as the black, yet grounded by a commitment to try and find in the black experience a new voice of America. A new kind of enlightened American citizen had emerged—the race cosmopolitan, who was able to discuss the national literary and intellectual heritage in black and white, exhibit a worldliness and breadth of influences less evident in the black nationalisms of the 1960s, yet remain committed to the race and the transformation of America through the culture of the black community" (p. 19). Clearly, again, whether consciously or unconsciously, the intellectuals, artists, and activists of the hip hop generation have been influenced by the neo-New Negroes of the Harlem Renaissance, if not the New Negro movement in general. In fact, one of the major distinguishing factors between the Black Arts movement and the hip hop generation may very well be the hip hoppers' emphasis on "race cosmopolitan[ism]."

As the first generation of African Americans to come of age after the Civil Rights and Black Power movements, the hip hop generation appears to be deeply "committed to the race and the transformation of America through the culture of the black community." However, as with other social, political, cultural, and aesthetic movements that emerged in the midst of postmodernism, the hip hop generation's politics are often muted and masked. Young black folk are not shouting "Black Power!" in the streets the way they did during the turbulent 1960s and 1970s. But, make no mistake about it, the hip hop generation *is* political. In fact, considering the wide range of 1960s and 1970s multi-issue movements that advocated for authentic multiracial and multicultural democracy in America it is not at all surprising that the hip hop generation's major cultural and aesthetic motifs have provided the multiracial and multicultural foundation upon which most twenty-first-century popular culture, national and international, has been based.[7]

COUNTER-HERSTORIES OF HIP HOP'S (HETERO)SEXISM: ON THE NIGGERATI OF THE HARLEM RENAISSANCE, RAP MUSIC'S FEMINIST ROOTS, AND THE HOMO-HOPPERS OF THE HIP HOP GENERATION

What is particularly troubling about the bulk of the hip hop generation's politics, although their multiculturalism is quite commendable, is their often unapologetic embrace of several of the "isms" and ideologies of the past. Where most hip hoppers seem willing, at least musically, to cross the "color-line," to employ Du Bois's apt phrase from *The Souls of Black Folk* here, they do not appear to be eager to cross the *gender-line*—which is to say, they appear to be completely reluctant to engage the ways in which racism is almost always inextricable from, and intensely intertwined with sexism (e.g., patriarchy and misogyny). What is more, where many hip hoppers seem to have some semblance of sensitivity to poor and poverty-stricken people's struggles, they appear to be almost utterly insensitive to the struggles of homosexuals in a world decidedly dominated by heterosexuals and hetero-normativity (e.g., both covert and overt homophobia and heterosexism).

Returning to the critique of the hip hop generation's historical amnesia, there is a sense in which the revolt of the neo-New Negroes of the Harlem Renaissance, those whom Zora Neale Hurston and Wallace Thurman dubbed the "Niggerati," might be able to provide progressive hip hoppers with models for the kinds of contemporary, not simply "race cosmopolitans" but, even more, *race, gender, class, and sexuality cosmopolitans* who are so desperately needed now—especially in hip hop communities in the United States.[8] Once again, Stewart offers insight, observing: "Despite the legitimate criticisms of the New Negro as largely a male and heterosexist cultural icon, it should be remembered that many talented women, gay, and lesbian intellectuals and artists found themselves in the New Negro Movement" (p. 19). Accordingly, a couple of questions quickly beg: Aren't hip hoppers frequently criticized for being "largely . . . male and heterosexist cultural icon[s]?" And, more importantly, how many "talented women, gay, and lesbian intellectuals and artists [have] found themselves" silenced or rendered utterly invisible within the world of hip hop?

The revolt of the "Niggerati" of the Harlem Renaissance was not only a rebellion against the "Old Negro" and/or blackface minstrel archetype, the Washingtonian New Negro, and the Du Boisian New Negro. It was also a revolt against turn-of-the-twentieth-century New Negroes' increasing embrace of white middle-class culture and morality, specifically its simultaneously Eurocentric and thoroughly bourgeois obsession with genteelism and Victorianism. For the neo-New Negroes of the Harlem Renaissance what it meant to really and truly be both "New" *and* "Negro" entailed not simply a break with the "Old Negro" and/or blackface minstrel archetype, but also a rupture with past gender and sexual relations. Stewart importantly asserted:

> To be New Negro [for the neo-New Negroes or, rather, the "Niggerati"] meant to live in the present with echoes of past crimes and silenced communities echoing in one's head, regardless of what the rest of the nation thought of it. And it meant dreaming in the 1920s of a new kind of citizenship, of at-homeness, grounded in a capacious black urban community that was far more advanced in its foregrounding of feminist and homosexual identities than the rest of the nation. It meant the courage to resist not only 100 percent Americanism, but also gender bias and homophobia within a black community in transition. (p. 19)

When we survey the current Hip Hop studies scene it appears as though the Harlem Renaissance has had little or no impact on the hip hop generation.

However, as will be discussed in the next chapter, if several Hip Hop studies scholars are correct when they connect hip hop's aesthetics to the cultural aesthetics of the Black Arts movement, then it should also be acknowledged that the members of the Black Arts movement were influenced by—even as they sought to radically rupture their relationships with—the artistic legacies of the "Niggerati" of the Harlem Renaissance. Why is it that so many other aspects of the artistic legacy of the neo-New Negroes of the Harlem Renaissance have been, however surreptitiously, handed down to the hip hop generation, but not their distinct conceptions of American citizenship and democracy? Is it because their conceptions of American citizenship and democracy were unequivocally anti-sexist and anti-heterosexist or, as Stewart stated above, utterly open to "feminist and homosexual identities"? How many hip hoppers, especially African American hip hoppers, can relate to the "Niggerati's" definition above of what it meant to be a "New Negro"? How many, truth be told, would much rather start and stop with the first sentence, "[t]o be [a hip hopper] mean[s] to live in the present with echoes of past crimes and silenced communities echoing in one's head, regardless of what the rest of the nation [thinks] of it," ultimately excising any and all references to "feminist and homosexual identities"?

In her watershed work, *Gay Voices of the Harlem Renaissance*, A. B. Christa Schwarz (2003) has emphasized the centrality of bisexuality, homosexuality, and transgressive sexuality within the world of the Harlem Renaissance. Her expert analysis highlights the double-meanings (i.e., the homoeroticism) of much of the artistry of several of the major neo-New Negroes of the Harlem Renaissance. In her explorative essay, "Transgressive Sexuality and the Literature of the Harlem Renaissance," Schwarz (2007) contends that "[m]any Renaissance participants were indeed same-sex interested. Most of them were covertly gay (for example Alain Locke and Countee Cullen) or bisexual (for example Claude McKay and Wallace Thurman)" (p. 142). This means, then, that most of the bisexuality, homosexuality, and transgressive sexuality of the Harlem Renaissance was masked, except in the case of Richard Bruce Nugent. Schwarz candidly continued, "[o]nly the bohemian Richard Bruce Nugent dared to openly display his same-sex desire" (p. 142; see also Holcomb, 2007; Nugent, 2002; Somerville, 2000; Woods, 1998).

The bisexual and homosexual women of the Harlem Renaissance could be said to have muted and masked their same-sex desire even more than the males of the Renaissance on account of both the sexism and heterosexism of the white and black bourgeoisies, who were the primary patrons of the Renaissance. Schwarz (2007) shared, "faced with gender discrimination and often burdened with family obligations, female Renaissance authors in general experienced more repressive living and writing conditions than their male counterparts" (p. 142). Same-sex interested Renaissance women such as Angelina Weld Grimké and Alice Dunbar-Nelson's homoeroticism was also hampered by longstanding myths surrounding black women's lasciviousness and promiscuousness, which was propagated during and after African American enslavement. From the point of view of the black bourgeoisie, African American women who embraced transgressive sexuality, especially lesbianism, were, in essence, exacerbating and perpetuating the myth of black women's lasciviousness and promiscuousness. By publicly announcing or "parading" their same-sex desire African American bisexual and homosexual women artists were aiding and abetting anti-black racism and fueling fictions about black women, or so the black bourgeoisie believed. "The black bourgeoisie strove to control black women's sexual image," Schwarz stated, and Grimké, Dunbar-Nelson, Zora Neale Hurston, Nella Larsen, Ma Rainey, Bessie Smith, and Josephine Baker, among others, challenged the colonization of black women's sexuality by either the white or black bourgeoisie (p. 143; see also A. Y. Davis, 1998c; Egar, 2003; Honey, 2006; Hull, 1987; Roses and Randolph, 1996; Wall, 1995).

It is interesting to observe the ways in which homosexuality and homoeroticism was hidden during the Harlem Renaissance, similar to the ways they are frequently hidden in rap music and contemporary hip hop culture. For instance, in "It's All One: A Conversation," Homo-Hop movement founders Juba Kalamka and Tim'm West (2006) argue that the history of hip hop "is incomplete until the presence of Queerness within is acknowledged" (p. 198). Contesting the notion that hip hop is somehow incompatible with Queerness, Kalamka and West touch on what I have termed "hip hop's historical amnesia," asserting that the "hip hop-is-incompatible-with-being-Queer" contention "springs from a very typical romanticism and nostalgia and lack of memory that's a component of most pop-cultural pop discourse, especially around music" (p. 199). Consequently, many, if not most, so-called hip hop purists have long pandered to extremely heteronormative and hypermasculine conceptions of hip hop culture without critically coming to terms with how hip hop has been and remains profoundly influenced by homosexual culture (Amani, 2007; Stephens, 2005; T. T. West, 2005).

Homosexual hip hoppers were a part of hip hop culture long before the recent Homo-Hop movement. As a matter of fact, one of the problematics of the more recent discourse surrounding "the gay rapper" is that it negates the significance of "closeted" versus "out" hip hoppers, not to mention the importance of the entire "coming out" and unapologetic-embrace-of-Queerness process (Rodriguez, 2006; Tan, 2006). Kalamka and West argue that "[w]hile we too are men on the mic, it is taken for granted that this man with a mic is straight, urban, masculine, and any other number of adjectives that fall in the lazy categorical imperatives associated with the MC" (p. 199).[9] However, critical questions concerning sexuality, especially transgressive sexuality, in hip hop culture extend well beyond MCs ("the dudes holding phallic symbols at their mouths") and help to complicate and provide coun-

ter-histories of hip hop producers, DJs, graffiti artists, b-boys, b-girls, jour-
nalists, and activists. The truth is, hip hop has always had transgressive
sexualities, it is just that most heterosexuals have refused to acknowledge the
diversity of hip hop sexualities. In other words, a hard-line *heterosexualiza-
tion and hypermasculinization of hip hop* has taken place, and this heterosex-
ualization and hypermasculinization of hip hop hinges on a distinctly heteronormative and hypermasculine historical amnesia that completely downplays
and diminishes how flamboyant, feminist, and queer musical forms, such as
funk, punk, new wave, disco, and house music, directly contributed to the
development of rap music and hip hop culture. Kalamka and West offer
weighted words:

> If you want to get even deeper—what kind of conversation about authenticity and
> maleness/masculinity, and by extension the absence of women and Queers, would
> we have if we talked about the Sugarhill Gang being the brainchild of soul singer
> and label owner Sylvia Robinson? How do we talk about the place of said maleness
> when the same woman is responsible for bringing Grandmaster Flash and the Furi-
> ous Five to international attention? Or what about Blondie and lead singer Deborah
> Harry's contribution to hip hop's mainstreaming with the single "Rapture"? Or
> Talking Heads bassist Tina Weymouth and her Tom Tom Club's "Genius of Love"
> being the basis for the Furious Five's "It's Nasty"? Who "belongs" in hip hop then?
> Who's "real"? Are straight black men who sample records by white women "real"
> b-boys? The line is clearly arbitrary and glaringly ahistorical. (p. 200)

To complicate matters even more, the overt sexism and heterosexism exhibited by most mainstream (or, rather, *male*stream) hip hoppers, no matter how
"progressive" they claim to be, actually resembles nothing more than an
unrefined "remixed" version of the conservatism of both the white and black
bourgeoisies of the turn of the twentieth century. Here we witness where hip
hop's historical amnesia is not simply cultural and aesthetic, but also ad-
versely gendered and *hyperheterosexual.* How might being exposed to the
fact that the first rap record and rap group was the "brainchild" of an African
American woman, Sylvia Robinson, have altered our current relationships
with hip hop culture? What about the fact that the same Sylvia Robinson not
only produced the world's first rap record, "Rapper's Delight" by the Sugarhill Gang in 1979, but also prefigured what is commonly referred to as the
"Golden Age of Rap" (i.e., "conscious" or "message" rap music, from 1987
to 1999) by masterminding "The Message" by Grandmaster Flash and the
Furious Five in 1982? What about being aware of white women's unique
contributions to the early development and popularization of rap music as
well? How many postmillennial hip hoppers "big up" or give long-overdue
"props" (i.e., respect) to Deborah Harry or Tina Weymouth? The history *and*
"herstory" of hip hop is much more complicated than previously imagined
when we look at it through the illuminating lenses of feminism, womanism,

and the ongoing Women's Liberation movement, as will be witnessed in chapter 4.

Acknowledging these "herstorical" and musical facts will only help hip hop culture return to its *real* roots, which it must do if it intends to recreate itself and contribute more than corporatized/colonized song after song singing sexism and heterosexism's praises. To speak freely here, I have often wondered about how Sylvia Robinson, Deborah Harry, and Tina Weymouth, among other hip hop foremothers, might feel about the sexism they hear spewing from their children or, perhaps, their grandchildren's iPod speakers (i.e., assuming they have children or grandchildren). It is, to say the least, a bit ironic, if not outright absurd, that although hip hop's real roots are undeniably feminist/womanist it has evolved into one of the most hypermasculinist and misogynistic musics in national and international history/herstory (Babb, 2002; R. N. Brown, 2008; Morgan, 1999; Osayande, 2008). This is an issue that all hip hoppers, not just hip hop feminists, must raise everywhere and every time hypermasculinist histories of rap music and hip hop culture are put forward. What I am humbly calling for here could be called *counter-herstories* of hip hop culture—that is, *unapologetically woman-centered or womanist histories of hip hop culture which highlight women's distinct contributions to the discourse and ongoing development of rap music and every other aspect of hip hop culture.*

For Kalamka and West, the conversation around hip hop's sexual diversity "is not just about the reclamation of hip hop by Queers, as is seen in the budding gay hip hop and Homo-Hop Movement in the U.S., but a reexamination of how we've imagined hip hop in ways that have de-emphasized and discounted Queer presence. Similar counter-histories are being explored with the military and professional sports, but I think that hip hop, like these others I've mentioned, is the last stubborn bastion of self-congratulating homophobia" (p. 200). Here, we could also speak of hip hop as one of "the last stubborn bastion[s] of self-congratulating [sexism, and specifically patriarchy]." The issue I am raising here centers around the following questions; questions I intend to raise with recurrence throughout this book: Are the currently accepted histories of hip hop, however sometimes surreptitiously, hypermasculinist? Do they, in fact, render invisible and utterly erase the "Queer presence" in, and the "Queer elements" of hip hop? How do the women and homosexuals of the hip hop generation feel about hip hop's homespun sexism and heterosexism? And, what can we all—i.e., women and men, homosexuals and heterosexuals—*do* to deconstruct and reconstruct hip hop culture to reflect the dreams and realities, as well as the ecstasy and agony of what it means to be the first generation to come into adulthood in the "postmodern," "postcolonial," "post-feminist," "post-Marxist," "post-Civil Rights," "post-AIDS," etc., poverty-stricken and war-torn world of the twenty-first century?

One of the many reasons I believe that more connections need to be made between the Harlem Renaissance and the hip hop generation is because, for all of its faults (e.g., its sometimes subtle embrace of blackface minstrelism, internalized black primitivism, and often intense Eurocentrism), the Harlem Renaissance represents one of the first times in U.S. history where black and white, male and female, heterosexuals and homosexuals created an alliance. Of course, as discussed below, much of the homosexuality of the Harlem Renaissance was "covert" and couched in "coded language," but, yet and still, I honestly believe that the *heterosexual-homosexual alliance* of the Harlem Renaissance provides the truly progressive of the hip hop generation with much to build on. Both the black radicals and the authentic white anti-racist allies of the Harlem Renaissance offer examples, however imperfect, of what an authentic male-female/heterosexual-homosexual alliance is capable of producing. Tellingly, I write all of this solemnly bearing in mind pioneering Harlem Renaissance scholar Nathan Huggins's heartfelt words in *Voices from the Harlem Renaissance* (1976):

> Symbolically, then, the Harlem Renaissance stands for something more than the actual works of art it produced. Like all symbols, its primary significance is the deep emotional force it embodies, both for those whose experience it was and for those of us who find in it an important moment in our past. It is for us a principal emotional source, verifying our manliness and womanliness. Through the impact of it, we re-experience the triumph of that time and emerge as sensitive, sophisticated, compli-cated, and resourceful human beings who are capable of tolerance, cooperation, and love, but who also have ample capacity for anger, hatred, resentment, and retalia-tion. The experience of the Harlem Renaissance tell us that we are to be taken seriously—by ourselves as well as by others. (p. 4)

Huggins's words help to highlight the fact that moral outrage and, even more, anger directed at sexism and/or heterosexism is nothing new in African American cultural aesthetic movements. As was mentioned above, feminist and homosexual contributions frequently have been either completely erased or co-opted as male contributions in the hypermasculine and heteronormative narratives of generation after generation of historians. Huggins's words also emphasize movement member's capacity for "tolerance, cooperation, and love." Indeed, the Harlem Renaissance is much more than the works of art that have become its calling card. It is also "an important moment in our past" that, if earnestly engaged from radical humanist as opposed to hyper-masculinist and/or heteronormative perspectives, has the potential to funda-mentally alter contemporary hip hop culture. This reclamation of the Harlem Renaissance is not advocated only to highlight its "Queer elements," but also to reclaim its history-making heterosexual-homosexual alliances, its open-ness to feminist/womanist artistry and culture, and its receptiveness to au-thentic white anti-racist civil rights radicalism.

Here, the Harlem Renaissance is offered up as a model movement that provides important paradigmatic perspectives for the progressives of the hip hop generation. Admittedly, the alliances between the blacks and whites, men and women, as well as the heterosexuals and homosexuals of the Harlem Renaissance were fraught with great difficulties and disappointments. However, as a hip hop intellectual-activist deeply influenced by critical theory, I understand these "great difficulties and disappointments" to be indicative of the radicals of the Harlem Renaissance "keeping it real" with one another and "being true to the game" of their time. Authenticity has always been important in African American cultural aesthetic movements, which is one of the reasons so many hip hoppers have no respect for folk who "fake the funk!"—that is, people who are hip hop posers, and who really only embrace certain elements of hip hop culture because they are in vogue (i.e., commercial or mainstream rap music and other commercial hip hop trends). "Keeping it real" when and where we come to the setbacks that the radicals of the Renaissance suffered means that we are bringing the dialectic to bear and consciously seeking to develop both an appreciative and critical relationship with the radicalism of the Renaissance, which is also something we must do with regard to our relationships with every aspect of hip hop culture (and, again, this includes hip hop's sexism and heterosexism).

What I seek to do here is offer tangible, more concrete examples of the kinds of work we must endeavor if we are to truly deconstruct and reconstruct hip hop culture, and extend and expand it to include *all* hip hoppers, and not simply those who are male and heterosexual. At the heart of critical theory is an emphasis on the critique of the ideologies of the established order. Ironically, even though hip hop began as a critique of the ideologies of the established order, over the years, especially since its so-called Golden Age (1987–1999), it has increasingly backslid and retreated to the lame logic of the U.S. status quo, which has long been, however sometimes subtly, simultaneously racist, sexist, capitalist, colonialist, and heterosexist (P. H. Collins, 1998, 2000, 2003, 2005, 2006, 2007). At its inception, hip hop was decidedly critical of each of these *interlocking ideologies*, which have long constituted *overlapping and incessantly intersecting systems of exploitation, oppression, and violence.*

In the postmillennial moment it would appear as though hip hop has been co-opted and corporatized/colonized. At least in the most popular and socially visible manifestation of hip hop culture, commercial or mainstream rap music, hip hop seems to have morphed and moved away from being the polyvocal voice of the voiceless, the mouthpiece of the oppressed "minorities," and the neo-sorrow songs of human suffering and postmodern social misery, to the unrepentant representative of the cultural voyeurism of corporate America, the soundtrack to suburban America's ghetto safari, and the crude cultural and musical accompaniment to the seemingly never-ending postmillennial neo-minstrel show.

Returning to the emphasis on the seminal nature of the Harlem Renaissance for the hip hop generation, it is important to accent the ways in which the radicals of Renaissance sought to consciously go against the status quo of their epoch. Of course, much has been written about the anti-racist, anti-capitalist, and anti-colonialist artistry and activism of the radicals of the Renaissance. However, those Renaissance radicals who embraced explicitly feminist/womanist and homosexual identities have very rarely been revered for their heroism and key contributions to the Renaissance and the wider struggle for civil rights and social justice. What is more, several Renaissance radicals were simultaneously committed to the struggles for civil rights, women's rights, *and* homosexual rights. What is even more amazing are the myriad issues that the homosexual rebels of the Harlem Renaissance raised that have recently come to haunt the hip hop generation. For instance, Schwarz (2007) writes of how many Renaissance radicals were "covertly gay," wrote in "coded language," and whose corpuses are strewn with "camouflaged gay reference[s]" (pp. 142, 150–51). After screening *Pick Up the Mic! The (R)Evolution of the Homo-Hop Movement* by Alex Hinton (2006) I have no doubt that there are many bisexual and homosexual hip hoppers out there who feel forced to choose between their queer identity or their hip hop identity (see also Ajalon, 1993; Brack, 2008; Frilot, 1995; Phipps, 1992, 1993; Welbon, 1993). Here it is important for us to turn to Audre Lorde's *Sister Outsider* (1984), where she revealingly wrote:

> As a black lesbian feminist comfortable with many different ingredients of my identity, and a woman committed to racial and sexual freedom from oppression, I find I am constantly being encouraged to pluck out some one aspect of myself and present this as the meaningful whole, eclipsing or denying the other parts of self. But this is a destructive and fragmenting way to live. My fullest concentration of energy is available to me only when I integrate all the parts of who I am, openly, allowing power from particular sources of my living to flow back and forth freely through all my different selves, without the restrictions of externally imposed definition. Only then can I bring myself and my energies as a whole to the service of those struggles which I embrace as part of my living. (pp. 120–21; see also Abod, 1990; DeVeaux, 2004; Griffin and Parkerson, 1996; Lorde, 1988, 1996, 2004, 2009)

The "Niggerati" of the Harlem Renaissance rejected the "restrictions of externally imposed definition[s]," as put forward by the black bourgeoisie, of who and what a "New Negro" was and how they should live, love, and express themselves. Additionally, Audre Lorde, among others, audaciously challenged the sexism and heterosexism of both the Black Power and Black Arts movements. Therefore, the homosexuals of the hip hop generation have models and need not feel like political and/or aesthetic orphans. The radicals of the Harlem Renaissance have bequeathed much to the hip hop generation, and part of hip hop's inheritance hinges on an unfettered and principled expression of sexuality: bisexuality, homosexuality, heterosexuality, and transgressive sexuality. Lorde's words help to capture a vision of the kind of *transfigured selves* (i.e., *homosexual rights* and *sexual orientation sensitive selves*) that all so-called progressive hip hoppers should be striving towards. Her words also help to highlight the activist dimension that needs to be brought back to the heart of hip hop, and not just activism on behalf of the issues that effect us personally but, on the most hallowed humanist principles, activism on behalf of those who might have very different issues than our own, or, rather, the heteronormative and hypermasculine majority of hip hop.[10]

Although much has been made of it as of late, it is also interesting to note that the "Niggerati" of the Harlem Renaissance were the first to touch on black bisexuality, especially black male bisexuality (Dean, 2009). In fact, the entire "on the down low" phenomenon seems to have been prefigured by several Renaissance writers, especially Claude McKay in *Home to Harlem*, *Banjo*, and "Romance in Marseilles," where he depicted "manly" black men's "[c]asual sexual involvement with pansies" and "painted boys" (Schwarz, 2007, p. 147; see also Holcomb, 2007). As *Pick Up the Mic!* demonstrates with the controversy surrounding the bisexual white rapper and producer Dutchboy, bisexuality (not to mention "bi-curious," "homoflexible," and "heteroflexible") continues to be a contentious topic in the homosexual hip hop community. Similar to the politics of the truly "progressive" (as opposed to the *rhetorically radical*) of the hip hop generation, the radicalism of the Harlem Renaissance was not simply centered around anti-racism, class struggle, and cultural aesthetics, but also deeply entrenched in women's and homosexual liberation. As a matter of fact, in "The Black Man's Burden" (1993), no less a savant than Henry Louis Gates, Jr., went so far as to say that, as quiet as it has been kept, the Harlem Renaissance "was surely as gay as it was black" (p. 233). Moreover, in *When Harlem Was in Vogue*, the ever-scrupulous and cool-penned David Levering Lewis (1989) observed the "aesthetic straight-jacketing" of the younger New Negroes who eventually formed the "Niggerati" and published *Fire!!!* and *Harlem*, which simultaneously lamented Harlem being turned into the "white man's house of assignations" and warmly welcomed authentic "Negrotarians" (i.e., whites who supported not simply the cultural aesthetics of the Harlem Renaissance, but also the New Negro movement's quest for civil rights and social justice) (pp. 141, 165; see also S. Watson, 1995, pp. 95–103). *Fire!!!* and *Harlem* contained pieces that were more or less "pointillistic soft pornography," Lewis (1989) nervously noted, which unrepentantly celebrated the increasingly common "transvestite floor shows, sex circuses, and marijuana parlors along 140th Street" (pp. 197, 211). Undoubtedly, then, sexuality and, as Lorde said above, "sexual freedom" was at the heart of the aesthetic radicalism of the Harlem Renaissance, and homosexuals and their distinct expressions of their homosexuality played a pivotal role which should not be downplayed or diminished. As Lorde (1984) insightfully exclaimed:

> By ignoring the past, we are encouraged to repeat its mistakes. The "generation gap" is an important social tool for any repressive society. If younger members of a community view older members as contemptible or suspect or excess, they will never be able to join hands and examine the living memories of the community, nor ask the all important question, "Why?" This gives rise to a historical amnesia that keeps us working to invent the wheel every time we have to go to the store for bread. (p. 117)

THE HEGEMONY OF HETERONORMATIVITY AND HYPERMASCULINITY: ON CRITICAL QUEER THEORY, PATRIARCHAL HOMOSEXUALITY, AND HIP HOP RADICAL HUMANISM

Feminist and homosexual radicals were at the heart of the revolt of the "Niggerati" of the Harlem Renaissance, just as many feminist and homosexual radicals have and continue to contribute to hip hop culture or, what Jeffrey Ogbar (2007) has termed, the "Hip Hop Revolution." To put it plainly, if indeed hip hop constitutes a culture, instead of a group of "largely . . . male and heterosexist cultural icon[s]" or, rather, a sexist and heterosexist cult, then, progressive male and heterosexual hip hoppers must honestly open themselves to the discourses and life-struggles of female and homosexual hip hoppers. Once they open themselves, then it is important to solemnly open others, especially their friends and family members, to the life-worlds and life-struggles of the women and homosexuals of the hip hop generation. It is not, and never will be, enough for male and heterosexual hip hoppers to critique the myriad ways in which racism and capitalism are corroding American citizenship, democracy, and society. Similar to the radicals of the Harlem Renaissance, progressive hip hoppers must be willing to extend and expand what it means to be a hip hopper. Men do not have a monopoly on what it means to be a hip hopper anymore than heterosexuals have a monopoly on love, marriage, or religion. Where the "Niggerati" of the Harlem Renaissance deconstructed and reconstructed the moniker "New Negro" to include women and homosexuals, as well as "the low-down folks, the so-called common element," as Langston Hughes (1997) roared in his classic "The Negro Artist and the Racial Mountain," *it is time for hip hoppers to radically embrace humanism* (p. 53). Moreover, it is time for *hip hop radical humanists* to either deconstruct and reconstruct hip hop culture to make it inclusive of hip hop feminists and hip hop homosexuals or, and I say this quite solemnly, leave the world of hip hop altogether and create a new, authentically humanist *post–hip hop culture*.[11]

There are many lessons that hip hop radical humanists can learn from the revolt of the "Niggerati" of the Harlem Renaissance, especially Langston Hughes's "The Negro Artist and the Racial Mountain," where he audaciously asserted:

> We younger Negro artists who create now intend to express our individual dark-skinned selves without fear or shame. If white people are pleased we are glad. If they are not, it doesn't matter. We know we are beautiful. And ugly too. The tom-tom cries and the tom-tom laughs. If colored people are pleased we are glad. If they are not, their displeasure doesn't matter either. We build our temples for tomorrow, strong as we know how, and we stand on top of the mountain, free within ourselves. (p. 56; see also Rampersad, 2002a, 2002b)

Faithfully following, and to paraphrase, Hughes, hip hop radical humanists should say, in so many words: "We [hip hop radical humanists] who create now intend to express our individual [feminist, homosexual, etc.] selves without fear or shame. If [male hip hoppers] are pleased we are glad. If they are not, it doesn't matter. We know we are beautiful. And ugly too. . . . If [heterosexual hip hoppers] are pleased we are glad. If they are not, their displeasure doesn't matter either. We build our temples for tomorrow, strong as we know how, and we stand on top of the mountain, free within ourselves." The best of hip hop is about being "free within ourselves" and standing in solidarity with others, especially others whose life-struggles might be or, in fact, are very different from our own. This is so because "real" hip hop has always been about daringly breaking down barriers and consciously crossing-borders.

Radical humanist hip hoppers, both heterosexual and homosexual, must end hip hop's "don't ask, don't tell" policy. It is time to acknowledge our full *inheritance* from our cultural aesthetic ancestors, especially the radicals of the Harlem Renaissance. How is it that the radicals of the Harlem Renaissance could develop an anti-sexist and anti-heterosexist cultural aesthetic nearly six decades prior to the birth of hip hop, but yet postmillennial hip hop culture remains as misogynistic and homophobic as the sky is blue and water is wet? This is a serious issue, one that demands that those of us who identify as both hip hoppers *and* radical humanists interrogate immediately. I write all of this consciously bearing in mind that I/we have been socialized in *sanitized or user-friendly sexist and heterosexist settings*: from the black church to black colleges and universities, from the expressions of black entertainers to the acrobatics of black athletes. But, as I have illustrated above, in the midst of every major modern black social and political movement there have been women and homosexuals, as well as heterosexual radical humanists, who were willing to go against *the hegemony of heteronormativity* and consciously contribute to heterosexual-homosexual alliances (Brandt, 1999; Johnson and Henderson, 2005; Sears and Williams, 1997).

As it was with the Harlem Renaissance, within the world of the Homo-Hop movement (i.e., again, the Homosexual Hip Hop movement), the artistry and activism of homosexual men have almost always eclipsed the artistry and activism of homosexual women. The conception of hip hop radical humanism articulated here, then, does not give the *patriarchal homosexuality* and *internalized (hetero)sexism* promoted and practiced by many gay male rappers a pass (Halberstam, 1997, 1998, 2005; Piontek, 2006; Wilton, 1995). As with white supremacy and anti-black racism, patriarchy and misogyny are utterly evil, no matter who the culprit is, whether black or white, male or female, heterosexual or homosexual (R. A. Ferguson, 2004; Stockton, 2006; Stokes, 2001). In their groundbreaking article, "Sista Outsider: Queer Women of Color and Hip Hop," Eric Pritchard and Maria Bibbs (2007) interrogate the patriarchal homosexuality and internalized (hetero)sexism of many gay male rappers, writing:

> In the advent of the movement called "Homo-Hop," which serves to frame gay hip hop within a term acknowledging the larger LGBT community that is a part of the culture, males benefit from being the center of this "gay rapper" discourse while bisexual and lesbian women of color in the hip hop game remain maligned and subsequently ignored in media coverage and opportunities. In the popular news media, criticisms of homophobic rhetoric, the potential for "gay hip hop" to be a viable genre of hip hop culture, and even the homophobic rhetoric itself are all gendered male. We wish to stress here that this does not mean queer men are not marginalized in the hypermasculine, heteronormative and homophobic discourse of hip hop, however, in order to present the collective and diverse voices of queer women of color in hip hop, it is necessary to critique the male privilege and sexism existing for queer men as well and how that affects women in the LGBT and hip hop communities. (p. 22)[12]

Bisexual and lesbian nonwhite women are faced with a set of serious problems within the world of hip hop. On the one hand, they must confront the sexism and heterosexism of mainstream hypermasculinist and heteronormative hip hop. On the other hand, they have to contest the patriarchal homosexuality of many gay male hip hoppers and critique the gender hierarchy within the Homo-Hop movement. It is this double- (or triple-) bind that makes bisexual and lesbian women's relationship with rap music and hip hop culture qualitatively different than any of the other members of the hip hop community. Few dispute rap music's misogyny, or hip hop's sexism in general. However, it is a rare (a very rare) Hip Hop studies scholar and/or activist who will break the longstanding silence surrounding hip hop's heterosexism and homophobia. Admittedly, considering my lack of intimate knowledge with regard to homosexuals' lived-experiences, I am not the ideal Hip Hop studies scholar-activist to break the silence and broach this subject. But, as someone who identifies as both a hip hopper *and* a radical humanist, my conscience compels me to speak truth to power by using my male and heterosexual privilege in the interest of women's and homosexual liberation. As a hip hop radical humanist who also happens to be a critical social theorist, there is also a sense in which I want to utilize my evolving interdisciplinary studies and ongoing emphasis on intersectionality to reach an audience who might not otherwise be aware of, or care for what has come to be called "critical queer theory."[13]

Truth be told, I have gone back and forth over whether I should raise the issue of the hegemony of heteronormativity in hip hop. I kept telling myself that there are so many other well-established Hip Hop studies scholars who are certainly much more qualified than I to speak on the hegemony of heteronormativity in hip hop. But, as I surveyed the postmillennial hip hop scene I became increasingly aware of the excruciating pain and suffering that many homosexual hip hoppers, some of whom are close brother- and sister-comrades of mine, have experienced during the more than three decades of the hip hop generation's existence. It is not simply the silence surrounding homosexuality within the world of hip hop but, even more, the near erasure and/or invisibility of homosexuals as a result of the hegemony of heteronormativity within U.S. society as a whole.

Recently one of my homosexual colleagues told me that she could not wait for me to complete my book on hip hop. I earnestly asked her why. Next she said something that has stuck with me since then. She patiently explained to me that I will be able to reach heterosexuals in ways that most homosexuals cannot. She, of course, was referring to me reaching African American heterosexuals and the ways in which African American homosexuals are silenced and, frequently, physically, psychologically, and verbally violated (e.g., Sakia Gunn, Rashawn Brazell, Duanna Johnson, Roger English, and Roberto Duncanson) in the black community and wider world. I told her that I know many black heterosexuals who love (or, at the least, appreciate) Langston Hughes, James Baldwin, Audre Lorde, Essex Hemphill, and Angela Davis. Then, she solemnly checked me with impunity. She said: "Listen, Rabaka, I ain't never heard no straight black person talk about how Baldwin's gayness factored into his books, or how Angela Davis's lesbianism is linked to her political activism—especially, her post-Black Panther and post-George Jackson activism." I sat there silent for a moment, staring into the distance, thinking things over. She was on point. She was right and, not that she needed to hear it from me, I told her so. Her weighted words helped me to think about how the various identities we either reject or embrace influence our ability to appreciate aspects of others' identities, and develop deep sensitivities to their distinct identity formation processes and ongoing identity politics.

Bisexual and lesbian nonwhite women in the world of hip hop are regularly asked to choose between being homosexuals or hip hoppers, as well as homosexuals or members of their specific racio-cultural groups. The work of hip hop lesbian feminists has documented how gay men often play prominent roles in coercing bisexual and lesbian women to choose between their queer identities and their identities as hip hoppers. In other words, this is what might be termed "gay-on-gay violence" (Lundy and Leventhal, 1999; Renzetti and Miley, 1996). Clearly, then, a gay man's sexual orientation does not automatically preclude him from practicing patriarchy anymore than a woman's gender somehow automatically precludes her from perpetuating patriarchy. For the record: Nonwhites can, and often do, internalize white supremacy and racism. Women can, and frequently have, internalized patriarchy and misogyny. And, homosexuals can, and historically have, internalized heterosexism and homophobia. This is precisely why anti-racism, in and of itself, solves only part of the problem; feminism, in and of itself, solves only part of the problem; and, anti-heterosexism, in and of itself, solves only part of the problem. Without emphasizing that racism, sexism, classism, and heterosexism are all extremely important interlocking systems of exploitation, oppression, and violence that must be collectively combated, then all we are left with are drive-by, hit or miss movements meandering from one pressing issue to the next with no concrete or coherent radical humanist and authentically "universal" end-goal (Herek, 1998; Jung and Smith, 1993; Sears and Williams, 1997; Wehbi, 2004).

The Homo-Hop movement gives us an almost ideal opportunity to explore the reasons why anti-racism, anti-sexism, anti-classism, and anti-heterosexism divorced from authentic radical humanism often yields little more than empty rhetoric and the continued social segregation of so-called "progressive" communities. How truly progressive are male anti-racists if they, whether consciously or unconsciously, dehumanize women? How truly progressive are white feminists if they, whether consciously or unconsciously, dehumanize non-white people, especially nonwhite women? How truly progressive are anti-heterosexist gay male activists if they, whether consciously or unconsciously, dehumanize and marginalize bisexual and lesbian women? What about the ways in which white homosexuals, whether consciously or unconsciously, dehumanize and marginalize nonwhite homosexuals' life-worlds and life-struggles (Brandt, 1999; Johnson and Henderson, 2005; E. S. Nelson, 1993; Somerville, 2000; Stockton, 2006; Stokes, 2001)?

In her eye-opening essay, "'I Used to Be Scared of the Dick': Queer Women of Color and Hip Hop Masculinity," Andreana Clay (2007) critically discusses white and male supremacy in the ways in which homosexuality is depicted in the United States and some of the reasons that nonwhite (especially black and brown) bisexual and lesbian women continue to identify with hip hop culture. She rhetorically and revealingly asks, "[s]o, who and why do queer women identify with this culture that is known for its homophobia and sexism? And, how do we continue to maintain queer feminist ideology and practice in this groove" (p. 151)? First, she asserts that as of late often when black homosexuality is discussed the conversation almost immediately turns "on the down low" phenomenon, which centers on bisexual black men's closeted sex lives. Consequently, bisexual and gay black men's "promiscuity" and "unhealthy sexual practices" dominate the discourse on black homosexuality. Secondly, she writes, even though "the larger gay community has pushed a national debate about same-sex marriage into the public eye . . . [m]ost of the poster children for the same-sex marriage debate are white: gay neighborhoods or scenes, like the Castro district in San Francisco, is predominantly white, male, and middle class. In both of these contexts, queer black desire and identity has been erased, especially for women" (pp. 152–53). Clay continues, "[b]ecause we are absent from a discussion of black same-sex sex on the one hand and one of gay and lesbian identity on the other, it's no surprise that young, queer women of color find reprieve anywhere we can—including the often sexist, homophobic, and hypermasculine genre of hip hop" (p. 153).

Clay claims that "queer engagement with hip hop masculinity is mad full of complexity and contradiction" (p. 160). This is so because, as Todd Boyd (1997) argued in *Am I Black Enough for You?: Popular Culture from the 'Hood and Beyond*, many black men have embraced the "nigga" identity, and "the nigga is not interested with anything that has to do with the mainstream, though his cultural products are clearly an integral part of mainstream popular culture" (p. 33). In a sense, the "nigga" is mainstream America's unacknowledged alter ego, its "bastard" brother, sister, or—from mainstream America's paternalistic perspective—its "bastard" child. Therefore, ironically, "[t]he nigga rejects the mainstream even though he has already been absorbed by it" (p. 33; see also Judy, 2004; Kelley, 1997; Quinn, 2005; V. A. Young, 2007).

In U.S. culture and society African American masculinity, as with African American sexuality, is situated in a sociocultural context that is simultaneously within and without, inside and outside of mainstream heteronormativity, because black men and their blackness is always being psychopathically and schizophrenically rejected *and* absorbed by mainstream American heteronormativity (Byrd and Guy-Sheftall, 2001; Carbado, 1999; P. H. Collins, 2005; Hine and Jenkins, 1999, 2001; Lemelle, 2010). Hip hop masculinity has been expressed through the guises of the nigga, the playa, the hustla, the thug, the prisoner, and the ex-con, among others. Each of these expressions of hip hop masculinity has been much maligned by mainstream America. Therefore, one can comprehend why the bisexual and lesbian "sista outsiders" of the hip hop generation could come to selectively embrace certain elements of rap music and hip hop culture, because rap music and hip hop culture, despite its mainstream absorption, continues to provide a, however "underground," polyvocal voice for the voiceless, a culture for the supposedly cultureless, and a sense of belonging for those who have been told in no uncertain terms that they do not belong, especially in mainstream America.

Similar to many of the homosexuals of the Harlem Renaissance, the homosexuals of the hip hop generation have long demonstrated their ability to appreciate and contribute to "mainstream" hip hop culture. However, similar to many of their heterosexist antecedents, very few of the heterosexuals of the hip hop generation have challenged the hegemony of hip hop's heteronormativity. As with the New Negro movement at the turn of the twentieth century, either hip hop culture will consciously extend and expand itself to include the life-worlds and life-struggles of homosexuals, completely freeing itself from heteronormativity, or else homosexual and radical humanist heterosexual hip hoppers are justified in leaving the world of hip hop and creating a new, radically humanist post-hip hop culture. Neither homosexuals, females and males, nor heterosexual women should have to tolerate hip hop's sexism and heterosexism one minute longer. It is time for hip hop to clean its house. Out with the old, and in with the new, as the saying goes.

The expression, "out with the old, and in with the new" is apropos here, as it could be said to perfectly capture most Black Arts movement members' relationship with the Harlem Renaissance. From the Black Arts aesthetes' point of view, the Renaissance represented a kind of pre–Civil Rights movement cultural primitivism that was too closely associated with African American enslavement and blackface minstrelism. Consequently, the historical context and complexities of Renaissance radicalism were flattened and ultimately ironed into nothing more than uncultivated contradictions. This is to say, then, that similar to so much of hip hop's inheritance from the Harlem Renaissance, the Black Arts movement's inheritance from the Harlem Renaissance was ironically repudiated even as it surreptitiously and subtly informed the frameworks and foci of the artistry and aesthetics of the Black Arts movement. We will now turn our attention to hip hop's inheritance from the Black Arts movement, but not before we critically engage what the Black Arts movement inherited from the Harlem Renaissance.

NOTES

1. Historically there has been a great deal of discussion concerning whether or not the revolts of enslaved Africans had any significant impact on bringing African American enslavement to an end. Often more attention is paid to the "white abolitionists" without also noting the

"black abolitionists" (Quarles, 1969). To get a sense of the significance of the revolts of the enslaved and their impact on toppling African American enslavement, see Aptheker (1983), D. B. Davis (2006), Gaspar and Hine (1996), Genovese (1992), H. Jones (1987), Rucker (2006), Sale (1997), and E. R. Taylor (2006).

2. It may be difficult for many of my readers to comprehend the complexities and contradictions of what was commonly called the "Negro Problem" between the waning years of the Civil War through to the increased militancy of the Civil Rights movement, a period roughly running from 1855 to 1965. However, it is extremely important to highlight this often overlooked discourse within mainstream American and, especially, African American intellectual history and culture because it helped to shape and define the intellectual, artistic, and activist cultures of every major African American social and political movement from the turn of the twentieth century all the way through to the turn of the twenty-first century. Furthermore, the "Negro Problem" discourse, however surreptitiously, also influenced every major post-Emancipation African American cultural and aesthetic movement, from the Harlem Renaissance through to the hip hop generation. For further discussion, please see chapter 1 of my book *Against Epistemic Apartheid*, where I engaged arguably one of the loudest and longest critics of the "Negro Problem" discourse, W. E. B. Du Bois, and most of his major works regarding the "Negro Problem" and its solution (see Rabaka, 2010a).

3. Here I am, of course, drawing from the pioneering work of the Jamaican political philosopher, Charles Mills (1997), who, in *The Racial Contract*, famously contended:

> The Racial Contract is that set of formal or informal agreements or meta-agreements (higher-level contracts *about* contracts, which set the limits of the contracts' validity) between the members of one subset of humans, henceforth designated by (shifting) 'racial' (phenotypical/genealogical/cultural) criteria . . . as 'white,' and coextensive (making due allowance for gender differentiation) with the class of full persons, to categorize the remaining subset of humans as 'nonwhite' and of a different and inferior moral status, subpersons, so that they have a subordinate civil standing in the white or white-ruled politics the whites either already inhabit or establish or in transactions as aliens with these polities, and the moral and juridical rules normally regulating the behavior of whites in the dealings with nonwhites or apply only in a qualified form (depending in part on changing historical circumstances and what particular variety of nonwhite is involved), but in any case the general purpose of the Contract is always the differential privileging of whites as a group with respect to nonwhites as a group, the exploitation of their bodies, land, and resources, and the denial of equal socioeconomic opportunities to them. All whites are *beneficiaries* of the Contract, though some whites are not *signatories* to it. (p. 11, emphasis in original)

In other words, Mills's work accents the surreptitious nature of white supremacy within the contemporary world. The "racial contract" is not a thing of the past, but continues to *racially colonize* almost each and every interaction in the (post)modern moment. Clearly, blackface minstrelism speaks volumes about the ways in which whites were considered human in juxtaposition to black and other nonwhite nonhumans. Additionally, it is important to emphasize that *the diabolical dialectic of white superiority and black inferiority* did not end with the Emancipation Proclamation or the Civil War. It continued through Reconstruction, Post-Reconstruction, the New Negro movement, the Harlem Renaissance, World War I, World War II, the Civil Rights movement, the Black Power movement, and stubbornly remains here with us in the post-millennial moment of the hip hop generation. In order for the hip hop generation to really and truly disrupt its historical amnesia, it will be necessary to engage white supremacy and anti-black racism, even though most white and, truth be told, many nonwhite hip hoppers believe that racism no longer exists or only flares-up every now and then. For further discussion of the "racial contract" and the "racial polity," see Mills (1998, 1999, 2003a, 2003b). And, for a more detailed discussion of *the diabolical dialectic of white superiority and black inferiority*, see my previously mentioned *Against Epistemic Apartheid: W. E. B. Du Bois and the Disciplinary Decadence of Sociology*, as well *Forms of Fanonism: Frantz Fanon's Critical Theory and the Dialectics of Decolonization* (Rabaka, 2010a, 2010b).

4. The rising racial consciousness of the "New Negroes" was sparked by the infamous Hayes-Tilden compromise of 1877, which subsequently led to the 1896 Supreme Court "separate but equal" verdict in the *Plessy v. Ferguson* case. Between 1895 and 1940, African Americans experienced an intense period of social transformation, which had an enormous impact on their social and political consciousness, and it is this evolution of African Americans' cultural, social, and political consciousness during the period ending the nineteenth century and beginning the twentieth century that is commonly called the New Negro movement. African American historian Rayford Logan (1954) famously referred to the decade closing the nineteenth century as the "nadir" of African American history, and his work, along with the work of several other scholars, has brought to light more than three thousand documented lynchings during this unfortunate era (see Brundage, 1993, 1997; Gonzales-Day, 2006; Ifill, 2007; Nevels, 2007; Pfeifer, 2004; Waldrep, 2006; Zangrando, 1980). The New Negro movement culminated with the wide and varied cultural and aesthetic innovations of the Harlem Renaissance. In essence, "New Negroes" were distinguished from "Old Negroes" by their resistance to African American re-enslavement and American apartheid. They rejected the *minstrelesque mischaracterizations* of African Americans and the whitewashed revisionist interpretations of the African holocaust and African American enslavement, which made white enslavers appear as though they were patently pious, benevolent Christians who "civilized" and "Christianized" the "heathen," "barbarous," and "irreligious" Africans they ruled over on their palatial antebellum plantations. New Negro studies, then, is an extremely important area of inquiry within African American studies, even though it is frequently folded into Harlem Renaissance studies. Undoubtedly New Negro studies and Harlem Renaissance studies discursively dovetail but, yet and still, it is important to distinguish between the two because, to put it plainly, the cultural and aesthetic innovations of the Harlem Renaissance are virtually incomprehensible without first engaging the historical, cultural, social, and political coming-to-critical consciousness that the New Negro movement fostered. For my (re)interpretation of the New Negro movement, I have drawn from: A. E. Carroll (2005), Favor (1999), Foley (2003), Gates and Jarrett (2007), Hutchinson (1995, 2007), Lamothe (2008), D. L. Lewis (1989), Locke (1968), W. J. Maxwell (1999), Peplow and Davis (1975), and Wintz (1996g).

5. For further discussion of the origins and evolution of the Black Women's Club movement, from the National Federation of Afro-American Women to the National Association of Colored Women, see Cash (2001), E. L. Davis (1996), Higginbotham (1993), Salem (1990), S. Shaw (1991), C. H. Wesley (1984), and D. G. White (1999).

6. The body of research on the radicalism of the intellectuals and artists of the Harlem Renaissance has grown greatly over the last decade. This work helps to highlight why it is important to grasp and seriously grapple with the social and political influence of the New Negro movement on the Harlem Renaissance prior to exploring its aesthetic innovations. Most members of the Renaissance, in one way or another, had connections to, or, at the least, affinities with, leftist, working-class, and/or mass movements. However, what distinguished the radicalism of the Renaissance from both the turn-of-the-twentieth-century New Negroes and the white socialists, communists, and unionists of their epoch was their unapologetic critique of racism *and* capitalism. In this sense, then, it is both the political *and* aesthetic radicalism of the Harlem Renaissance that proves unprecedented in African American history and culture. Hence, here we are given grounds to point to what could be called *New Negro critical social theory and counter-ideology*. For the most noteworthy works which have informed my interpretation of *New Negro critical social theory and counter-ideology*, see: Baldwin (2002), Foley (2003), W. James (1998), W. J. Maxwell (1999), Mullen and Smethurst (2003), Naison (2005), Smethurst (1999), and Solomon (1998).

7. For detailed discussions of the various 1960s and 1970s multi-issue movements that advocated for authentic multiracial and multicultural democracy in America which the hip hop generation, whether consciously or unconsciously, has drawn from, see: Anner (1996), Breines (2006), Churchill and Wall (1988), Haney-López (2003), D. A. Harris (1995), Maeda (2009), Mariscal (2005), Ogbar (2004), Rosales (1996), Roth (2004), and Springer (2005).

8. In *When Harlem Was in Vogue*, David Levering Lewis (1989) discussed the growing disdain that younger New Negroes developed in relation to the New Negro civil rights establishment:

"Wallie" Thurman had become increasingly distressed by party-line art. Temporarily replacing [George] Schuyler in 1926 as editor of *The Messenger*, he lashed out repeatedly against the Victorian aesthetics of civil rights grandees—those whom he and novelist Zora Hurston later ridiculed as the "Niggerati." Before the end of the year, he decided to recruit younger artists and launch a magazine [i.e., *Fire!!!*] devoted to art for the artist's sake—and for the sake of the folk. His rent-free place on 136th Street—the infamous "267 House" . . . was the cradle of revolt against establishment arts. Thurman and Hurston also mocked themselves by calling 267 House "Niggerati Manor," and all the younger artists called Thurman their "leader"—the fullest embodiment of outrageous, amoral independence among them. Thurman never doubted that, freed from the prim guidance of the leading civil rights organizations, the artists would recognize the need "for a truly Negroid note" and would go to the proletariat rather than to the bourgeoisie for characters and material. (p. 193)

Although the "Niggerati" neologism took form as a rebuke of the Victorianism and conservatism of the New Negro civil rights establishment, observe how—similar to the artists and activists of both the Black Arts movement and the hip hop generation—a controversial new name and movement moniker was eventually embraced by the young radicals of the Harlem Renaissance. As the unrepentant "Niggerati" of the Harlem Renaissance, Hurston, Thurman, Langston Hughes, Helene Johnson, Richard Bruce Nugent, Gwendolyn Bennett, and Aaron Douglass, among others, sought not only civil rights, but also socialist and sexual revolution. For further discussion of the "Niggerati" of the Harlem Renaissance, see: Gates and Jarrett (2007), Hurston (1979), Marks and Edkins (1999), and Thurman (2003).

9. Kalamka and West's critique of the ways in which black masculinity, as publicly perceived and performed, is connected to a growing body of scholarly research that challenges black heterosexual males supposed monopoly on black maleness and black masculinity. For example, see: Alexander (2006), Blount and Cunningham (1996), Byrd and Guy-Sheftall (2001), Carbado (1999), R. A. Ferguson (2004), Hine and Jenkins (1999, 2001), hooks (2004a, 2004b), E. P. Johnson (2003), Lemelle (2010), and Mutua (2006). More specifically, Kalamka and West's words here help to highlight and critically turn us toward a counter-history of *hip hop masculinity*, which is primarily based on black male speaking, singing, rapping, dancing, and other styles, but which has become absorbed by the nonblack males, both white and nonwhite, of the hip hop generation. It is not simply suburban young white males who have embraced the mutilating machismo and often brutal braggadocio of hip hop masculinity, but also poor white, Mexican American, Latin American, Asian American, Native American, and Caribbean, among other, "postmodern" and/or postmillennial males. Accenting homosexual or "queer" masculinities within global, national, and local hip hop communities will only bring us one step closer to bridging the yawning chasm between hip hop's radical rhetoric concerning "freedom," "liberation," "peace," and "justice," and its actual prickly practices toward homosexuals—which is to say, its infamous homophobia and heterosexism. What we must do, I honestly believe, is expand the range and meaning of "manhood," "maleness," and "masculinity" for the hip hop generation by deconstructing and reconstructing it, making it more multidimensional and inclusive of what bell hooks (2004b), in *The Will to Change: Men, Masculinity, and Love*, has famously referred to as "alternative masculinities" (see "Feminist Manhood" in hooks [2004b], pp. 107–24; see also, "Reconstructing Black Masculinity" in hooks [1991], pp. 87–114 and "Feminist Masculinity" in hooks [2000a], pp. 67–71). For further discussion, and for the most noteworthy works which have influence my interpretation of hip hop masculinity, see: T. J. Brown (2006), Greene (2008), Hagedorn (2008), K. M. Harris (2006), Hopkinson and Moore (2006), R. L. Jackson (2006), Powell (2003), Rodriguez (2009), E. Watson (2009), and V. A. Young (2007).

10. It is important here to remind my readers that at the conceptual core of critical social theory is a commitment to justice, especially what has come to be called "social justice." My specific conception of critical social theory, "Africana critical theory," entails theorizing about the "social," "political," and "cultural" in the interest of racial, gender, economic, sexual, educational, and religious justice. What makes critical social theory "critical" is its unconditional commitment to justice, not simply for one's own group, but also for other oppressed and

struggling groups. Hence, my conception of critical social theory is humanist or, rather, *radically humanist* in that it extends beyond black folk, heterosexuals, and males—in other words, allegedly my "own group(s)." When confronted with a situation where group differences result in one group being privileged while others are oppressed, the radical humanism at the heart of my conception of critical social theory demands an unflinching and principled rejection of exploitation, oppression, and/or violence and an earnest embrace of justice and fairness. This means, then, that while individuals' human rights matter, my critical theory emphasizes justice and fairness in broader—communal, national, and international—terms, as a collective- or group-based phenomenon. Usually questions of justice and fairness fall outside of the orbit of conventional social theory, but they are conspicuously at the conceptual core of critical social theory. For further discussion of my conception of critical social theory, see chapter 1 and Rabaka (2007, 2008, 2009, 2010a, 2010b).

11. For further discussion of my conception of "radical humanism" (as well as "revolutionary humanism"), which has been indelibly influenced by the insurgent intellectual and radical political legacies of W. E. B. Du Bois, Frantz Fanon, Amilcar Cabral, Audre Lorde, James Baldwin, Angela Davis, and bell hooks, among others, see Rabaka (2008, 2009, 2010a, 2010b).

12. My analysis throughout this section has greatly benefited from systemic readings of several noteworthy works in Lesbian, Gay, Bisexual, and Transgender (LGBT) studies. For example: Abelove, Barale, and Halperin (1993), Beemyn and Eliason (1996), Haggerty and McGarry (2007), Piontek (2006), Richardson and Seidman (2002), and Wilton (1995).

13. The discourse on "critical queer theory" or "queer critical theory" has been developing since the mid-1990s, and some of the earliest articulations can be found in Steven Seidman's "Deconstructing Queer Theory, or the Under-Theorization of the Social and the Ethical" (1995), *Queer Theory/Sociology* (1996), and *Difference Troubles: Queering Social Theory and Sexual Politics* (1997). Major postmillennial contributions to critical queer theory include: K. Floyd (2009), Foucault (1990a, 1990b, 1990c), Hames-Garcia (2001), Morton (1996), E. S. Nelson (1993), Plummer (2005), and Seidman, Fischer, and Meeks (2006). Critical queer theory constitutes theorizing about queerness in the interest of justice and fairness for homosexuals. It accents and criticizes homophobia and heterosexism in social, political, and cultural thought, practices, and institutions.

Chapter Three

"Say It Loud!—I'm Black and I'm Proud!": From the Black Arts Movement and Blaxploitation Films to the Conscious and Commercial Rap of the Hip Hop Generation

The serious black artist of today is at war with the American society as few have been throughout American history. . . . The question for the black critic today is not how beautiful is a melody, a play, a poem, or a novel, but how much more beautiful has the poem, melody, play, or novel made the life of a single black man? How far has the work gone in transforming an American Negro into an African American or black man? The Black Aesthetic, then, as conceived by this writer, is a corrective—a means of helping black people out of the polluted mainstream of Americanism, and offering logical, reasoned arguments as to why he should not desire to join the ranks of a Norman Mailer or a William Styron. To be an American writer is to be an American, and, for black people, there should no longer be honor attached to either position. —Addison Gayle, Jr., *The Black Aesthetic*, p. xxiii

BLACKENING AESTHETICS: FROM THE NEW NEGRO AESTHETIC OF THE HARLEM RENAISSANCE TO THE BLACK AESTHETIC OF THE BLACK ARTS MOVEMENT

In his 1971 essay, "Renaissance I to Renaissance III?: An Introduction," acclaimed Black Arts movement poet Haki Madhubuti (1971a) infamously asserted: "The black arts movement in the twenties [i.e., the Harlem Renaissance] was of minimal influence and virtually went unnoticed by the majority of black people in the country. More whites knew about what was happening than brothers and sisters. One of the main reasons for the short life of renaissance I is that no black people, other than the artists themselves, were involved in it. No lasting institutions were established" (p. 12). With all due respect, perhaps Madhubuti missed Langston Hughes's "The Negro Artist and the Racial Mountain," or Wallace Thurman's *Fire!!!* and *Harlem*, but it would seem that the aesthetic radicals of the Harlem Renaissance themselves were the first to critique both the white *and* black bourgeois bohemian-conservatism that came to dominate Harlem Renaissance creativity and culture. However, to be fair to Madhubuti, whom I have long intellectually admired, I must admit that his criticism has some credence, especially when we focus on his statement that the Harlem Renaissance offered future generations of African American artists "[n]o lasting institutions." In light of the African Commune of Bad Relevant Artists, Association for the Advancement of Creative Musicians, Black Arts Repertory Theatre and School, Black Artists Group, Black Arts/South, Black Arts/West, Broadside Press, Congress of African People, Institute of the Black World, Organization of Black American Culture, Third World Press, and Jihad Productions, all established by Black Arts movement members (Third World Press by Madhubuti himself), elements of Madhubuti's assertion strike one as incontrovertible. But, yet and still, there are other aspects of Madhubuti's 1971 assessment of the Harlem Renaissance that are clearly intellectually and aesthetically disingenuous.

Directly contradicting Madhubuti's contention, Jeffrey Stewart (2007) stated, "[i]nterestingly, after the major victories of the Civil Rights movement of the mid-1960s, another intellectual and cultural rebellion surfaced, sometimes called the Black Power movement, other times the Black Arts movement, which looked back to the Harlem Renaissance for inspiration to reinvigorate a New Negro in the 1960s" (p. 25). Continuing, he importantly emphasized, "[w]hile the Black Arts Movement tended to cleave off the interracial cosmopolitanism of the earlier movement, the later movement rediscovered and republished such canonical New Negro texts as Alain Locke's *The New Negro: An Interpretation*" (p. 25). As will be recalled, in the preceding chapter I argued that one of the major contributions the Harlem Renaissance bequeathed to the hip hop generation was its history-making black and white, male and female, heterosexual and homosexual alliances. If, indeed, Black Arts movement members "tended to cleave off the interracial cosmopolitanism of the earlier movement," we must ask, why? Even more, the question of whether each and every interracial alliance is somehow automatically detrimental to black self-determination and black liberation should also be earnestly raised.

Taking Madhubuti's assertion as indicative of most (though certainly not all) Black Arts movement members' relationship with the Harlem Renaissance, we have here once again evidence of younger African American artists and intellectuals attempting to dissociate and distance themselves from the politics and aesthetics of previous generations of black artists and intellectuals. As it was with the young radicals of the Harlem Renaissance and their efforts to break with the "old Negro" archetype and the black bourgeoisie of the New Negro movement, the artist-activists of the Black Arts movement endeavored to rupture their relationships not only with the Harlem Renaissance but with the Civil Rights movement as well. Directly discussing successive generations of African American artists' reception of the Harlem Renaissance in "'The Aftermath': The Reputation of the Harlem Renaissance Twenty Years Later," literary critic Lawrence Jackson (2007) opined:

> This phenomenon, the repudiation of a group of socially marginalized black creative writers by a subsequent and similarly marginalized generation of black critics, is doubly curious because the critics of the 1930s, 1940s, and 1950s were fairly conspicuous in their devotion to and appreciation of vernacular black culture. But for more than a score of years following the 1920s, these writers and critics expressed mainly the utmost impatience with the achievements of African American writers during the 1920s. It was an impatience and disregard that would not really be reversed until the success of the modern Civil Rights Movement and the creation of Black studies academic programs in the late 1960s and early 1970s. (p. 240; see also Flowers, 1996; A. Mitchell, 1994; Napier, 2000; R. E. Washington, 2001)

The "utmost impatience" and often outright disdain that many Black Arts movement members expressed with regard to the Harlem Renaissance and its allegedly excessive white patronage appears slightly ironic considering the fact that several of the major literary works of the Black Arts movement, including Amiri Baraka and Larry Neal's *Black Fire: An Anthology of Afro-American Writing*, were published under the auspices of white presses—hence, with white patronage (see J. K. Young, 2006). Black Arts aestheticians dismissive critiques of the Harlem Renaissance appear even more paradoxical when one considers that one of the first items on the early Black studies movement's agenda was to critically reevaluate African American history, culture, and struggle from a black perspective (Blassingame, 1973; Karenga, 2010; Marable, 2000; F. Rojas, 2007; Rooks, 2006). This leads us to larger questions, questions of whether the artists and activists of the Black Arts movement actually engaged the Harlem Renaissance on its own terms (and/or from an authentically *African American* perspective), taking into critical consideration the milieu of the New Negro movement from the turn of the twentieth century through to 1940 and its impact on the aesthetics, politics, and economics of the Harlem Renaissance.

In other words, by either not having access to, or willfully ignoring the more complex history of the Harlem Renaissance, many Black Arts movement members failed to see that what they were really repudiating was not the Harlem Renaissance at all, but rather some aspect of it—if not, truth be told, the more commercial, racially colonized, or whitewashed aspects of it. This might seem like a delicate distinction to make to some of my readers, but it is absolutely necessary in order to critically comprehend the ways in which hip hop's inheritance has been recurringly masked and muted genera- tion after generation, and not simply by the political economy of anti-black racism within the white world but within the black world as well. This *ritual of repudiation*, if you will, is indisputably part and parcel of hip hop culture, but what I wish to demonstrate here is that it is not exclusive to the hip hop generation and that the entire spectrum of this "ritual of repudiation" (from the Harlem Renaissance through to the hip hop generation) appears to reek of historical amnesia. As was witnessed in the previous chapter, the Harlem Renaissance generation renounced most of the sociopolitical and sexual eti- quette of the black embourgeoisement of the New Negro movement and, as will be seen below, the Black Arts movement impertinently rejected many of the artistic achievements of the Harlem Renaissance. In a similar fashion, the hip hop generation seems to have inherited its own unique historical amnesia with regard to the Harlem Renaissance and a distinctly schizophrenic rela- tionship with respect to the Black Power and Black Arts movements, one moment repudiating its origins in the Black Arts movement, and at other times celebrating the radical politics (and radical rhetoric) of the Black Pow- er period.

This chapter, therefore, will explore the intellectual and artistic interrela- tion between the Black Arts movement and the hip hop generation by ad- dressing several key questions: How did Black Arts movement members perceive the aesthetic radicalism of the Harlem Renaissance? What, if any- thing, did they inherit from the Harlem Renaissance? Likewise, what did the Black Arts movement bequeath to the hip hop generation? And, how has the hip hop generation interpreted its inheritance, whether understood to be so- cial and political or cultural and aesthetic, from the Black Power and Black Arts movements?

Clearly part of the Black Arts aesthetes' interpretation of the Harlem Renaissance revolves around the undeniable white presence within and white patronage of the Renaissance. However, most Black Arts critics of the Ren- aissance failed to acknowledge the ways in which the black intellectuals and artists of the 1920s and 1930s resisted the racial colonization of African American aesthetic culture in ways that were specific to their pre–Civil Rights movement (i.e., New Negro movement) milieu and, consequently, should not be judged solely in light of their associations with white patrons but rather on the basis of their insurgent intellectual and artistic legacies. Every intellectual and artist has their own enigmatic and eclectic process(es) through which they create and contribute their work, and it seems strikingly strange to me that less than a hundred years after the issuing of the Emancipation Proclamation and less than fifty years after the end of Reconstruction Harlem Renaissance intellectuals and artists are criticized because of white patronage. It is, insofar as I am concerned, akin to blaming victims for their victimization. Besides, what if Langston Hughes, Zora Neale Hurston, and Claude McKay, among many others, secretly thought of white patronage as a subtle form of reparation? Why isn't more critical focus placed on the white patrons' perpetuation and practices of the racial colonization of African American aesthetic culture instead of exclusively on Renaissance artists and intellectuals' racially colonized cultural productions? At what point do we grasp and critically grapple with the fact that, whether we like it or not, blackness is inextricable from whiteness, and whiteness is inextricable from blackness (Entman and Rojecki, 2000; Fredrickson, 1987; Jordan, 1974, 1977; Roediger, 1998; Yancy, 2004, 2005, 2008).

I am asserting here, then, that black intellectuals and artists' internalization of Eurocentrism and anti-black racism should always be identified and critiqued. However, I am also saying that black intellectuals and artists' internalization of Eurocentrism and anti-black racism is incomprehensible without first critically engaging the milieu in which they were living and working, and whether that milieu was subtly white supremacist, outright anti-black racist, or what have you. The racial colonization of the Harlem Renaissance is often glaringly obvious in hindsight. However, what is less apparent are the ways in which the Black Arts critics' knee-jerk reactions against the politics and aesthetics of the Renaissance interrupted 1960s and 1970s artists and intellectuals' inheritance of potentially positive and innovative elements of the Harlem Renaissance legacy.

Even with the white presence in and white patronage of the Harlem Renaissance, surely the black radical intellectuals and artists of the 1920s and 1930s handed down something of value to the black radical intellectuals and artists of the 1960s and 1970s. If nothing else, we might look to the models they developed for creating and critiquing black art. For instance, as is well known in Harlem Renaissance studies, in 1926 W. E. B. Du Bois organized a symposium in *The Crisis* exclusively devoted to "The Negro in Art: How Shall He Be Portrayed?," which featured essays by prominent Renaissance radicals, such as: Charles W. Chesnutt, Langston Hughes, Jessie Fauset, Countee Cullen, Georgia Douglass Johnson, Benjamin Brawley, Carl Van Vechten, and Walter White, among others (Kirschke, 2007; S. M. Smith, 2004; S. K. Wilson, 1999). In other words, here I am highlighting what Cary Wintz (1996d, 1996g) has termed: the emerging "New Negro aesthetic" of the Harlem Renaissance. Black Arts critics' complete disregard for the New Negro aesthetic of the Harlem Renaissance demonstrates not only the "divide and conquer" nature of racial colonization, but also the often overlooked fact that many of the more narrow-minded forms of black nationalism of the 1960s and 1970s unwittingly exacerbated and perpetuated African

Americans' historical amnesia by, in the most Manichaean manner imaginable, rudely rejecting the cultural aesthetic radicalism of the Harlem Renaissance (Wintz, 1996b, 1996c, 1996e, 1996f).

Also at issue here are the ways in which Black Arts movement members' contemptuous critiques of the Harlem Renaissance mask the ways in which both movements were critical of white supremacy *and* its black agents, which is to say, its racially colonized "Negro" compradors. No one who has really read W. E. B. Du Bois's "Criteria of Negro Art," or James Weldon Johnson's "Race Prejudice and the Negro Artist," or Langston Hughes's "The Negro Artist and the Racial Mountain," or Sterling Brown's "The Negro Character as Seen by White Authors" can claim that the radicals of the Renaissance were soft on white supremacy or, even more, as eminent Black Arts poet Kalamu ya Salaam (2002) recently asserted, Renaissance artists "were always on the leash of white patrons and publishing houses" (p. 40). Indeed, it is a bit ironic that a similar *rhetoric of condemnation* aimed at white supremacy and its racially colonized "Negro" compradors runs through both the Harlem Renaissance and Black Arts movement. This means, then, that both interracial *and* intraracial conflict is a recurring theme in African American cultural aesthetic movements—a theme, as will be discussed later, which continues to haunt the hip hop generation. It was not only black struggles against white power, but also the deep social divisions within black communities that shaded and shaped the emergence of an inchoate New Negro aesthetic in the 1920s and 1930s, as well as the more sophisticated articulations of a Black Aesthetic in the 1960s and 1970s.

Consequently, sociopolitical factors simultaneously external *and* internal to black communities influenced the origins and evolution of the Black Aesthetic, and those who privilege the external (white) factors over the internal (black) factors—especially without even acknowledging the internal factors—advance arguments that seem to smack of a certain, extremely subtle kind of Eurocentrism and racial essentialism that has long hinged on contentions concerning the homogeneous nature of black folk and their culture.[1] The reality of the matter is, both the Harlem Renaissance and Black Arts movement advocated that *authentic African American art can only be produced when black artists transcend the diabolical dialectic of white superiority and black inferiority*—which is to say, *real black art can only be created by black artists who have freed themselves from Eurocentric illusions and influences.* Howard University professor of philosophy Alain Locke (1925) opened arguably the most influential anthology of the Harlem Renaissance, *The New Negro*, emphasizing that the time had come "to document the New Negro culturally and socially,—to register the transformations of the inner and outer life of the Negro in America that have so significantly taken place in the last few years" (p. xv). We witness here firsthand, then, that much like the members of the Black Arts movement many of the Renaissance artists understood themselves to be a part of a New Negro or Black Aesthetic movement, one that was preoccupied with black "folk-spirit," black "folk expression," and black "folk interpretation."

Then, with language that seems to directly challenge Salaam's above contention that Renaissance writers "were always on the leash of white patrons and publishing houses," Locke declared, "[s]o far as he is culturally articulate, we shall let the Negro speak for himself" (p. xv). This sounds like a very subtle articulation of black "self-determination" (Locke's words) to my ears, as well as an unrepentantly "radical" statement for the times (p. xvii). However, Locke did not stop there, he went on to audaciously assert:

> Of all the voluminous literature on the Negro, so much is mere external view and commentary that we may warrantably say that nine-tenths of it is *about* the Negro rather than of him, so that it is the Negro Problem rather than the Negro that is known and mooted in the general mind. We turn therefore in the other direction to the elements of truest social portraiture, and discover in the artistic self-expression of the Negro today a new figure on the national canvas and a new force in the foreground of affairs. Whoever wishes to see the Negro in his essential traits, in the full perspective of his achievement and possibilities, must seek the enlightenment of the self-portraiture which the present developments of Negro culture are offering. (p. xv, emphasis in original)

Here, Locke clearly contrasts whites' discourse on the "Negro Problem" with blacks' "self-portraiture," blacks' "social portraiture" and, above all else, blacks' "artistic self-expression." This is extremely telling, as it appears to fly in the face of most Black Arts movement critics' conception of the Harlem Renaissance as little more than a twentieth-century form of blackface minstrelsy. When Locke accents blacks' "self-portraiture" and "artistic self-expression" it is almost as if he is speaking directly and unambiguously to those Black Arts critics of the Harlem Renaissance who misinterpreted it as little more than early twentieth-century minstrelsy. Foreshadowing many of the major motifs of the Black Arts movement by noting the new "race literature" and new "race journalism," Locke argued that the Harlem Renaissance represented a "racial awakening on a national and perhaps even a world scale" (pp. xvi–xvii). Undoubtedly something very similar could be said about the Black Arts movement, but in characteristic fashion, Locke went even further with his foreshadowing:

> The galvanizing shocks and reactions of the last few years are making by subtle processes of internal reorganization a race out of its own disunited and apathetic elements. A race experience penetrated in this way invariably flowers . . . Negro life is not only establishing new contacts and founding new centers, it is finding a new soul. There is a fresh spiritual and cultural focusing. We have, as the heralding sign, an unusual outburst of creative expression. There is a renewed race-spirit that consciously and proudly sets itself apart. (p. xvii)

The connections between the rationale behind the Harlem Renaissance and the ethos of the Black Arts movement are obvious: both movements sought the "internal reorganization [of] a race out of its own disunited and apathetic elements"; both movements sought to discover a "new soul" and "a fresh spiritual and cultural focusing" for black folk; and, both movements sought to document and develop "a renewed race-spirit that consciously and proudly set [. . .] itself apart" from white America.[2] As discussed in the previous chapter, the New Negroes of the Harlem Renaissance sought to sever their relationship with the "Old Negro" archetype but, ironically, no matter how doggedly they attempted to distance themselves from the "Old Negro" they seemingly could not because the birth and life of the New Negro was predicated on the death and incessant eulogizing of the "Old Negro." New Negro comparisons with the "Old Negro" were never-ending, which means that the "Old Negro" archetype was unwittingly and recurringly resuscitated throughout the Harlem Renaissance in particular, and the New Negro movement in general. This was so because in order to evoke an authentically *New* Negro they had to repeatedly remind themselves of precisely who the "Old Negro" was, how the "Old Negro" came into being, and how far they had vauntingly ventured from that sadistic symbol.

Part of the contradictory character of the Harlem Renaissance revolves around 1920s and 1930s black intellectuals and artists' perceived need to constantly celebrate the symbolic death of the Old Negro, and the incessant angst this constant celebration caused. How has this seemingly early form of *figurative black-on-black violence* influenced African American aesthetics? How has anti-black racist psychological violence—to invoke Frantz Fanon's discourse on revolutionary decolonization—affected black artists and the development of the Black Aesthetic? What might black art have been like if black artists did not have to contend with racial colonization, white supremacy, and anti-black racism? The deep desire to document distinctions between the Old Negro ideology (firmly grounded in white supremacist fictions) and the New Negro philosophy (supposedly free from the influence of the diabolical dialectic of white superiority and black inferiority) ultimately led the radicals of the Harlem Renaissance to a compulsion that essentially invented antagonisms that would internally play themselves out in every major African American cultural aesthetic movement from the Harlem Renaissance through to the hip hop generation.

Coming back to the connections between the Harlem Renaissance and the Black Arts movement, in "A Familiar Strangeness: The Spectre of Whiteness in the Harlem Renaissance and the Black Arts Movement" literary theorist Emily Bernard (2006) wrote:

African American arts of the 1920s was intoxicated with the idea that it had invented itself, not only in terms of its creative ambitions, but as a locus of a new black identity. A version of the same fantasy characterizes the Black Arts Movement. "We advocate a cultural revolution in art and ideas," Larry Neal echoed in 1966. In his introduction to *The Black Aesthetic*, Addison Gayle, Jr., summarized the objectives of the Black Arts Movement: "Speaking honestly is a fundamental principle of today's black artist. He has given up the futile practice of speaking to whites, and has begun to speak to his brothers." Gayle posits the Black Arts strategy as histori-cally unique, but his gesture itself is actually redundant, Alain Locke and Langston Hughes being among those Harlem Renaissance artists and intellectuals who pre-ceded him. Like the Harlem Renaissance, the Black Arts Movement articulated its objectives in powerful but pointedly abstract language that was finally more confus-ing than illuminating. How a black artist "could speak to his brothers" without any white mediation proved more confounding than Black Arts leaders were willing to concede. But if the Black Arts Movement wasn't clear on how it would get where it was going, it was very clear on where it was *not* going, and that was in the direction taken by the movement against which it continuously measured itself: the Harlem Renaissance. (pp. 260–61, emphasis in original)[3]

When Bernard claims that the Harlem Renaissance was "the movement against which [the Black Arts movement] continuously measured itself," we have here more evidence to corroborate my above contention that the Harlem Renaissance was more influential on the Black Arts movement than previ-ously acknowledged by Black Arts artists and activists. Even if Black Arts critics of the Harlem Renaissance interpreted it negatively, still it stands to reason that the Renaissance figured into Black Arts aesthetes' conception and articulation of a Black Aesthetic. Moreover, it seems highly improbable that Black Arts aesthetes found absolutely nothing of cultural or aesthetic value in the artistry and legacy of Renaissance radicals, many of whom were grap-pling with similar issues, especially those centered around the political econ-omy of anti-black racism in a white supremacist capitalist society, the politi-cal economy of racially gendered black/non-white women's life-worlds and life-struggles in a white supremacist patriarchal capitalist society, and the political economy of the racial colonization of art and aesthetics in a white supremacist patriarchal clandestinely colonial capitalist society.

The intellectuals, artists, and activists of the Black Arts movement under-stood part of their task to be to correct the damage done to the African American image by the Harlem Renaissance, just as the New Negroes of the Harlem Renaissance sought to deconstruct the Old Negro archetype and ideology. Critique and the offering of cultural correctives was a major preoc-cupation for Black Arts theorists, artists, and activists. "The Black Aesthet-ic," according to Black Arts impresario Addison Gayle (1971), "is a correc-tive—a means of helping black people out of the polluted mainstream of Americanism, and offering logical, reasoned arguments as to why they should not desire to join the ranks of a Norman Mailer or a William Styron" (p. xxiii). Therefore, it is important here to emphasize that Black Arts critics were critical of "the polluted mainstream of Americanism" as well as what they understood to be the "interracial cosmopolitanism" of the Harlem Renaissance. However, even in light of its "interracial cosmopolitanism," there is a sense in which the Black Arts movement was inextricably connected to the Harlem Renaissance. Even in their most outlandish efforts to discursively distance and dissociate themselves from the politics and aesthetics of the Harlem Renaissance, Black Arts critics inadvertently acknowledged the seminal influence of Renaissance radicalism. Take, for instance, Larry Neal's (1989) assertions in his pioneering 1968 essay, "The Black Arts Movement," where he sternly stated:

> The Black Arts Movement represents the flowering of a cultural nationalism that has been suppressed since the 1920s. I mean the "Harlem Renaissance"—which was essentially a failure. It did not address itself to the mythology and the life-styles of the black community. It failed to take root, to link itself concretely to the struggles of that community, to become its voice and spirit. Implicit in the Black Arts Movement is the idea that black people, however dispersed, constitute a *nation* within the belly of white America. This is not a new idea. Garvey said it and the Honorable Elijah Muhammad says it now. And it is on this idea that the concept of Black Power is predicated. (p. 78, emphasis in original; see also Neal, 1989)[4]

Here, Neal clearly makes his contribution to the "ritual of repudiation" in African American cultural aesthetic movements by audaciously asserting that the Harlem Renaissance "was essentially a failure." However, his comments here also seem to place the Black Power and Black Arts movements within a continuum that reaches back to "a cultural nationalism that has been suppressed since the 1920s," which is to say, since the heyday of the Harlem Renaissance. Neal admitted that the Black Power and Black Arts generation did not invent black cultural nationalism, going so far to say, "[t]his is not a new idea. Garvey said it and the Honorable Elijah Muhammad says it now." Notice that Neal was willing to acknowledge the Black Power and Black Arts movements' *cultural nationalist* influences from the Harlem Renaissance era, but unwilling to recognize its *cultural aesthetic* influences from the same time period. This, indeed, is a curious kind of Black Arts cultural criticism—one that accepts and celebrates Renaissance social and political inspirations, but rejects and denigrates cultural and aesthetic antecedents.

By invoking Marcus Garvey (and his Universal Negro Improvement Association), undoubtedly representing the most popular expression of cultural nationalism during the Renaissance years, Neal appears to inadvertently problematize his own claim that the Harlem Renaissance "was essentially a failure." How much of a "failure" could the Harlem Renaissance have been if it, however surreptitiously, sowed the seeds that enabled the emergence and awe-inspiring achievements of the Black Arts movement, not to mention the hip hop generation? Was the Renaissance really a "failure" when we move away from Madhubuti's critique of its lack of "lasting institutions" (which is a very valid critique) and turn our attention to its inchoate articulation of a New Negro aesthetic, which irrefutably informed Black Arts intellectuals and artists' articulation of a Black Aesthetic? Since black folk in the twenty-first century are still struggling against anti-black racism, white supremacy, colonialism, and capitalism—all major issues that the Black Power and Black Arts movements sought to eradicate—are we (i.e., hip hop intellectuals and artists) now given credence to claim that the Black Power and Black Arts movements were "essentially failure[s]?"

Hip hop artists and intellectuals should, on principle, refuse to contribute to the "ritual of repudiation" by openly acknowledging the influence of both the Harlem Renaissance *and* the Black Arts movement, but this, of course, will mean developing a real relationship with classical and contemporary African American studies (if not African and African Diasporan studies—i.e., *Africana studies*). It is time for us to see the "ritual of repudiation" for what it always has been and remains: nothing other than racial colonialism's ever-evolving "divide and conquer" program willfully at work in *African* America. To be sure, some criticism of the Harlem Renaissance's embrace of Eurocentrism, "black primitivism," "black eroticism," and "black exoticism," among other issues, is undoubtedly warranted. However, such criticism is unwarranted when and where it is not connected to the myriad ways in which Renaissance radicals, such as Wallace Thurman, Zora Neale Hurston, Langston Hughes, Claude McKay, and Richard Bruce Nugent, among others, contested both the New Negro embourgeoisement *and* the white supremacist racial colonization of black folk and black art.

It is important here to bear in mind something one of the leading hip hop historians, Robin D. G. Kelley (2002), wrote in *Freedom Dreams: The Black Radical Imagination*: "the desires, hopes, and intentions of the people who fought for change cannot be easily categorized, contained, or explained" (p. ix). Hip hop cultural critics should bear this in mind as we begin to seriously, and hopefully systematically, assess the impact and influence of the Harlem Renaissance and the Black Arts movement on the hip hop generation. This caveat carries even more weight when we acknowledge that already there is a growing post–hip hop generation emerging who will more than likely continue the "ritual of repudiation" if we, the hip hop generation, do not discursively disrupt it and identify it for what it really is: again, part and parcel of racial colonialism's ever-evolving "divide and conquer" program willfully at work in *African* America. In so many words, Madhubuti, Salaam, and Neal, among others, collectively argue that the Harlem Renaissance "was essentially a failure." However, I would like to caution against this kind of one-dimensional/"all or nothing at all!" criticism, which, when critically engaged from an authentic African American studies perspective, looks like nothing more than a weak version of Eurocentric or Manichaean thought in blackface. Instead of an *either/or* analysis of African American cultural aesthetic movements, I would like to offer up a *both/and* Africana critical theoretical approach to these movements.[5]

An Africana critical theoretical approach to the Harlem Renaissance and the Black Arts movement assesses them, not in terms of their "success" or "failure," but in terms of their incessant offering of sources of inspiration to successive generations of intellectuals, artists, and activists. Moreover, as mentioned above, Madhubuti may have a valid criticism when he asserted that the Harlem Renaissance contributed "[n]o lasting institutions" to its political and aesthetic heirs, but his criticism flagrantly fails to acknowledge what the Harlem Renaissance indeed *did* hand down to its heirs. For instance, whether Black Arts movement members acknowledged it or not, the Harlem Renaissance in fact provided several seminal radical political paradigms, social movement models, and aesthetic innovations to generation after generation of their dark (and often damned) descendants. As argued above, it is ironic how closely 1960s and 1970s discussions of the "Black Aesthetic" mirror 1920s and 1930s discourse on the New Negro aesthetic. At what point are we willing to concede that many (if not most) members of the Black Arts movement may have missed an ideal opportunity to deepen and develop the Black Aesthetic by refusing to openly acknowledge or critically compare and contrast their work as part of a cultural aesthetic continuum that reached back to the incendiary artistry of their enslaved ancestors? In addition, and most importantly to me, how can we keep the hip hop generation from making the same mistake, that is if we hip hoppers have not already made it?[6]

Part of the solution to this problem, I honestly believe, is offered up by Robin D. G. Kelley when he cautions us against judging whether a movement was a "success" or a "failure" based on whether or not it was able to achieve *all* of its goals. To speak candidly here, serious social and political movements, as well as insurgent cultural aesthetic movements, are often not so much about eradicating each and every ill on their respective agendas as much as they are about critical consciousness-raising and radicalizing others, inspiring them to begin their processes of self-transformation and social transformation. Kelley contends:

> Unfortunately, too often our standards for evaluating social movements pivot around whether or not they "succeeded" in realizing their vision rather than on the merits or power of the visions themselves. By such a measure, virtually every radical movement failed because the basic power relations they sought to change remain pretty much intact. And yet it is precisely these alternative visions and dreams that inspire new generations to continue to struggle for change. (p. ix)

Here we are given grounds to ask whether or not "the basic power relations" Madhubuti, Salaam, Neal, and the Black Arts movement "sought to change remain pretty much intact"? Drawing my understanding of "the basic power relations" from Africana critical theorists—such as W. E. B. Du Bois, Angela Davis, C. L. R. James, bell hooks, Frantz Fanon, James Baldwin, Patricia Hill Collins, Amilcar Cabral, and Audre Lorde—black folk historically have and currently continue to struggle against the ideologies and political economies of white supremacy, patriarchy, colonialism, capitalism, and heterosexism, among other issues. Consequently, we can quickly conclude that both the Black Power and Black Arts movements were "essentially failure[s]." But, as Kelley commented above, such an assessment negates the glaring fact that both the Black Power and Black Arts movements' articulations of "alternative visions and dreams" undeniably "inspire[d] new generations to continue to struggle for change"—most especially, the hip hop generation.

It is not necessary for us to agree with each and every aspect of a previous sociopolitical or cultural aesthetic movement in order for us to be able to acknowledge, appreciate, and/or critique the vision of that movement. Moreover, it will be extremely difficult for anyone to deny that the Harlem Renaissance had its own unique vision, one that transports those of us who seriously engage it to another time and place, urging us to remember the happiness and horrors of the 1920s and 1930s and, even more importantly, enabling twenty-first-century souls to build on and go beyond the Renaissance radicals' vision of a new humanity and a new society. We twenty-first-century souls must bear in mind that the environments and the pressing issues that brought the Harlem Renaissance and the Black Arts movement into being compelled their respective intellectuals and artists to dream and intensely imagine something different, and ultimately to realize that life need not always be the way it was. It is the continuity of this collective *freedom dream*, as Kelley put it, that connects the Harlem Renaissance to the Black Arts movement, and the Black Arts movement to the hip hop generation, and, we can only conjecture, the hip hop generation to the post–hip hop generation.

"BLACK IS BEAUTIFUL!": THE BLACK POWER MOVEMENT, THE BLACK ARTS MOVEMENT, AND THE EMERGENCE OF THE BLACK AESTHETIC OF THE 1960S AND 1970S

In order to critically understand the Black Arts movement, it is important, first and foremost, to engage the myriad meanings of the Black Power movement, its central message and mission. However, identifying the essential message and mission of the Black Power movement has proved to be extremely difficult in light of the fact that "Black Power" actually meant many different things to many different individuals and institutions. As a matter of fact, one could go so far as to say that there was no such thing as the Black Power movement, singular, but rather something more akin to Black Power movements, plural. *Black Power studies* is an emerging, discursively diverse, and conceptually contentious arena within Africana studies that seeks to document and develop a critical reevaluation of the Black Power period, 1965 to 1975. Because of the wide range of issues Black Power movement members and organizations addressed, Black Power studies is a highly heterogeneous field, one that, much like the Black Power movement itself, challenges the homogenization of the interpretation and appreciation of black history, culture, and struggles in general, and Black Power histories, cultures, and struggles in particular. Needless to say, even with all of its discursive diversity, several central questions and concerns, recurring themes and theories emerge that have enabled Black Power studies scholars and students to capture the contours of the movement (Collier-Thomas and Franklin, 2001; Glaude, 2002; Jeffries, 2002; C. Johnson, 2007; P. E. Joseph, 2001, 2002, 2006a, 2010; Ogbar, 2004).

In *New Day in Babylon: The Black Power Movement and American Culture, 1965–1975*, the acclaimed cultural historian William Van Deburg (1992) declared: "Black Power was a revolutionary cultural concept that demanded important changes in extant patterns of American cultural hegemony. Its advocates hoped that this revolution eventually would reach the very core of the nation's value system and serve to alter the social behavior of white Americans" (p. 27). In order to challenge and change "American cultural hegemony," however, Black Power advocates—faithfully following Malcolm X and Frantz Fanon—argued that African Americans needed *psychological liberation* and to undergo a *protracted process of decolonization and reeducation*—what I have termed elsewhere, *revolutionary re-Africanization* (Rabaka, 2008b, 2009, 2010b). Before they could "alter the social behavior of white Americans," Black Power advocates asserted, black folk "had to be awakened, unified, and made to see that if they were to succeed they must define and establish their own values while rejecting the cultural prescriptions of their oppressors" (Van Deburg, 1992, p. 27). This is also to say that *self-discovery, self-definition, self-determination,* and *self-defense* were at the heart of the Black Power movement, its central message and mission. In fact, we could go so far as to say that the Black Power movement might more properly be called *the Black Empowerment movement,* because it was not a movement that had as its end-goal black supremacy but a bona fide multiracial and multicultural democracy. For example, in arguably one of the most widely read works of the movement, *Black Power: The Politics of Liberation in America,* Stokely Carmichael and Charles V. Hamilton (1967) strongly stressed that the "ultimate values and goals" of the Black Power movement "are not domination or exploitation of other groups, but rather an effective share in the total power of society" (p. 47; see also Carmichael, 2003, 2007; P. E. Joseph, 2008).

Twenty-first century discussions of the Black Power movement often degenerate into debates revolving around "Malcolm X's advocacy of black rage and violence," or Frantz Fanon as "the prophet of Third World violence," or "the Black Panther Party's glorification of senseless violence" without in any way attempting to understand that each of the aforementioned made undeniable distinctions between *counter-revolutionary violence, state-sanctioned violence*, and *self-defensive violence*—in other words, *the violence of domination* and *the violence of liberation* or, rather, *the violence of the oppressor* and *the violence of the oppressed.*[7] It is not as though black folk just woke up one morning and said, "It's time to go out there and get whitey!" That, quite simply, is not what happened. Truth be told, many of the gross misinterpretations of the Black Power movement are actually symptomatic of most people's (including many black people's) general lack of knowledge concerning African American history, culture, and struggle, especially during the 1960s and 1970s.

The early advocates of Black Power came to the conclusion that the *nonviolence, civil disobedience*, and *passive resistance* strategies and tactics of the Civil Rights movement had been exhausted, and that the time for masking and muting ongoing black suffering and black social misery, as well as black anger and black outrage aimed at racial and economic injustice, had long passed. After centuries of anti-black racist oppression, exploitation, and violence, Black Power advocates decided it was time for *black solidarity, black self-love*, and *black self-defense*. "They proclaimed that," Van Deburg writes, "blacks were indeed beautiful. Also claimed was the right to define whites" (p. 27). It is difficult at this point to determine what caused white America of the 1960s and 1970s more angst: blacks' radical redefinition of themselves and their blackness, or blacks' radical redefinition of whites and their whiteness.

In *Waiting 'Til the Midnight Hour: A Narrative History of Black Power in America*, acclaimed Haitian American historian Peniel Joseph (2006b) wrote that Stokely Carmichael's "calls for blacks to organize a national Black Panther political party . . . placed racial solidarity ahead of interracial alliances—he dared white and black liberals to 'prove that coalition and integration are better alternatives'" (p. 163). Carmichael's critique of the increasing obsolescence of civil rights strategies and tactics had a resounding—indeed, *black radicalizing*—effect on Black Power political culture. After all, Carmichael not only issued the call for the formation of "a national Black Panther political party," but he and his Student Nonviolent Coordinating Committee comrades also provided the Black Power movement with its name; as is well known, he popularized the "Black Power" slogan during an impassioned speech delivered in the course of the 1966 "March Against Fear" in Mississippi (pp. 142–62). However, as Joseph's judicious research highlights, throughout the Black Power period Carmichael went through great pains to explain that "Black Power" was not about hating white people, but about loving black people.

Whites, to put it plainly, were not the focus of Black Power, and most Black Power proponents believed that whites' narrow-minded and knee-jerk reactions to the movement had more to do with their own, whether conscious or unconscious, deep-seated hatred of and historical amnesia about black people, their history, culture, and ongoing struggles. What is more, Black Power radicals averred, whites' histrionic and hypernegative reactions to the Black Power movement also seemed to be symptomatic of their unacknowledged uneasiness about the epoch-making calls for *black solidarity, black self-love,* and *black self-defense* coming from black folk coast to coast. With respect to Carmichael's conception of Black Power, Joseph astutely observed:

> For Carmichael, Black Power did indeed promote universalism, but it did so in black. That is to say Black Power recognized power's ability to shape politics, identity, and civilization, and sought to extend these privileges to African Americans—a group that was too often excluded from even the broadest interpretations of whose interests constituted those of humanity. While critics feared that Black Power hinted at a perverse inversion of America's racial hierarchies, Carmichael envisioned something both more and less dangerous—a black community with the resources, will, and imagination to define the past, present, and future on its own terms. (p. 172)

When one takes a long and hard look at the history of the Black Power movement it is easy to see it as the logical evolution of the Civil Rights movement's efforts to attain liberty, dignity, and equality for black folk in America. To be sure, Black Power militants greatly differed in semantics and tactics when compared with the civil rights moderates, but it must be borne in mind that in the final analysis the core concerns of the two movements were more congruous and complementary than conflictual and contradictory. Where the Civil Rights movement was reformist and moderate, the Black Power movement was radical and militant. In fact, the Black Power movement ushered in a whole new age of unprecedented *black radicalism* in the wake of the woes of the Civil Rights movement. Its goals extended well beyond Civil Rights movement conceptions of "integration" and "assimilation," and it was not preoccupied with the reaffirmation of African Americans' civil rights and the U.S. government's public admission that it had a legal and ethical obligation to protect the constitutional rights of its black citizens.

Black Power proponents daringly demanded access to the fundamental operative force in U.S. history, culture, society, and politics: *power*—physical and psychological, social and political, economic and educational, cultural and aesthetic, etc. Following Malcolm X, they argued that they would gain *power* "by any means necessary." Moreover, Malcolm X admonished blacks to focus their energies and resources on improving their own conditions rather than exhorting whites to allow them to integrate into mainstream America. He also preached black self-defense, repeatedly reminding his audiences that blacks have a constitutional right to retaliate against anti-black racist violence (Malcolm X, 1989, 1990, 1991a, 1991b, 1992a, 1992b, 1992c; see also Marable, 2011; Terrill, 2010). Black Power radicals challenged whites' constant claims that they (i.e., Black Power radicals) had essentially reversed America's racial hierarchy by deconstructing the "myth of black racism." From Malcolm X to Stokely Carmichael, from Maulana Karenga to Amiri Baraka, and from the Black Panther Party to the Republic of New Afrika, the Black Power period offered up innumerable contestations of the "myth of black racism," and William Van Deburg's (1992) weighted words continue to capture this quandary best:

> To the militant mind, white racism had no valid black analogue. By definition, racism involved not only exclusion on the basis of race, but exclusion for the purpose of instituting and maintaining a system of arbitrary subjugation. Throughout American history, whites, not blacks, had been the chief supporters of this corrupt ideology. Black people had not lynched whites, murdered their children, bombed their churches, or manipulated the nation's laws to maintain racial hegemony. Nor would they. To adopt the ways of the white racist as their own would be counterproductive and, for a minority group, self-destructive. What whites called black racism was only a healthy defense reflex on the part of Afro-Americans attempting to survive and advance in an aggressively hostile environment. (p. 21)

It is important here to emphasize, once again, that Black Power was not about *hating* white people, but about *loving* black people, and defending them against anti-black racist assaults (again, both physical and psychological). When the history of anti-black racist violence in the United States is taken into serious consideration then, and perhaps only then, does Van Deburg's contention that Black Power proponents' stance on self-defensive violence as "a healthy defense reflex on the part of Afro-Americans attempting to survive and advance in an aggressively hostile environment" make any sense. Even though Malcolm X's words on black self-love and black self-defensive violence were held as prophecy by most Black Power radicals, more often than not, in practice the activist expressions of their movement followed more carefully defined and, for the most part, more familiar African American sociopolitical movement methods (e.g., direct-action protests, street rallies, marches, demonstrations, conferences, concerts, etc.). In fact, according to Van Deburg, although the Black Power movement "was not exclusively cultural . . . it was essentially cultural. It was a revolt in and of culture that was manifested in a variety of forms and intensities" (p. 9).[8]

In so many words, it could be said that at its core the Black Power movement was essentially an *African American cultural revolution*. This, of course, is where the cultural aesthetic radicalism of the Black Arts movement comes into play. Here it would seem that we have stumbled upon a pattern with respect to African American cultural aesthetic movements: recall that the Harlem Renaissance only emerged when the younger New Negroes of the New Negro movement believed that an embourgeoisement of the movement had taken place and that Washingtonian and Du Boisian articulations of New Negro politics had run their course. There was, indeed, a discernable shift away from politics in the traditional civil rights sense and greater emphasis placed on New Negro culture and aesthetics. This is extremely telling insofar as the emphasis on cultural aesthetics appears to arise only after what is perceived to be a political impasse in the more mainstream African American civil rights and social justice struggle. Clearly something very similar occurred when we consider that the young militants of the Black Arts movement were extremely frustrated with the Civil Rights movement's strategies and tactics of *non-violence, civil disobedience*, and *passive resistance* in light of seemingly ever-increasing displays of white supremacy and anti-black racist exploitation, oppression, and violence by the mid-1960s.

Although in Africana studies it is generally accepted that the Black Arts movement represented the cultural aesthetic arm of the Black Power movement, it is important to observe that unlike the Harlem Renaissance, which is widely considered the cultural aesthetic outlet of the New Negro movement, and much like the hip hop generation that arose in its aftermath, the Black Arts movement blossomed in a wide range of locations. In fact, virtually every community and college campus with a substantial African American presence between 1965 and 1975 offered up its own unique Black Arts movement–inspired organizations and theaters, with neo-black nationalist writers, actors, dancers, musicians, and visual artists. For instance, noted Black Arts movement organizations and institutions of the era included: the Umbra Poets Workshop, the New Lafayette Theater, and the Black Arts Repertory Theater and School, in New York, New York; BLKARTSOUTH, the Free Southern Theater, and the Southern Black Cultural Alliance, in New Orleans, Louisiana; the Sudan Arts South/West, in Houston, Texas; the Theater of Afro-Arts, in Miami, Florida; the Black Arts Workshop, in Little Rock, Arkansas; the Black Belt Cultural Center and the Children of Selma Theater, in Selma, Alabama; the Blues Repertory Theater, in Memphis, Tennessee; the Last Messengers, in Greenville, Mississippi; the Kuumba Theater, the Association for the Advancement of Creative Musicians, the Organization of Black American Culture, and the African Commune of Bad Relevant Artists, in Chicago, Illinois; the Committee for a Unified Newark and the Spirit House, in Newark, New Jersey; the Black Arts Group, in Saint Louis, Missouri; Black Arts/West and the Black House, in San Francisco, California; the Watts Writers Workshop, the Underground Musicians Association, the Union of God's Musicians and Artists Ascension, and the Pan-

Afrikan Peoples Arkestra, in Los Angeles, California; and Broadside Press, in Detroit, Michigan.

Where many Black Power radicals conceived of it as a movement for black political and economic independence, others understood it to be more of a revolutionary political struggle against racism, capitalism, and other forms of imperialism in the United States and throughout the wider world. However, yet another wing of the Black Power movement interpreted it as a black consciousness-raising and cultural nationalist movement, emphasizing *African roots* and *African American fruits*. It is this latter group of Black Power proponents who created and crusaded on behalf of the Black Arts movement. Similar to the Black Power movement, Black Arts intellectuals, artists, and activists embraced a wide range of political and cultural ideologies: from precolonial or indigenous African worldviews and religions to revolutionary Marxist-Leninism; from Malcolm X–styled radical Islam to Frantz Fanon–inspired revolutionary decolonization; and, from Maulana Karenga's articulation of Kawaida philosophy to the Black Panther Party's emphasis on black folk wisdom and black popular culture. As Van Deburg (1992) perceptively put it:

> Despite an observable tendency for differing factions to claim the entire movement as their own, the multifaceted nature of Black Power was one of its most significant characteristics. One important mode of Black Power expression was cultural. Playwrights, novelists, songwriters, and artists all had their chance to forward a personalized vision of the militant protest sentiment. They used cultural forms as weapons in the struggle for liberation and, in doing so, provided a much needed structural underpinning for the movement's more widely trumpeted political and economic tendencies. (p. 9)

This means, then, that despite the jaw-dropping range of what would otherwise be considered conflicting ideological positions, Black Arts advocates generally held a collective belief in African American liberation and African Americans' right to self-definition and self-determination. However, in order to really and truly define or, rather, *redefine* themselves, ironically, 1960s and 1970s black cultural aesthetes came to the startling conclusion that blacks would have to radically deconstruct whites and their whiteness. Here, we have come back to the diabolical dialectic of white superiority and black inferiority, and the precise reason why Black Arts advocates, almost as a rule, employed their "cultural forms as weapons in the struggle for liberation." In *The Wretched of the Earth*, which has long been said to have been the "handbook" of the Black Power movement, Frantz Fanon (1968) famously argued: "Decolonization is the veritable creation of new men. But this creation owes nothing of its legitimacy to any supernatural power; the 'thing' which has been colonized becomes man during the same process by which it frees itself" (pp. 36–37). In other words, the racially colonized could only rescue and reclaim their long-denied humanity by "a complete calling into question of the colonial situation," which had been created and administered by whites, for the benefit of whites, and to the detriment of nonwhites, and we are speaking here especially of blacks (p. 37).

Black Arts radicals sought to either recover or discover an authentic national African American culture free from white capitalist commodification and consumer culture. This authentic national African American culture was believed to be buried in African American folk philosophy and popular culture because the masses of black folk were understood to have had little or no lasting contact with white bourgeois culture and values.[9] Hence, although discussing revolutionary decolonization in Africa, Fanon's words deeply resonated with Black Power and Black Arts radicals, especially when he wrote: "While at the beginning the native intellectual used to produce his work to be read exclusively by the oppressor, whether with the intention of charming him or of denouncing him through ethnic or subjectivist means, now the native writer progressively takes on the habit of addressing his own people. . . . This may be properly called a literature of combat, in the sense that it calls on the whole people to fight for their existence as a nation" (p. 240). Fanon's words here capture the evolution of many Black Arts intellectuals and artists as they shifted from the moderatism of the Civil Rights movement to the militancy of the Black Power movement.

Obviously from the point of view of people who are critically conscious of their oppression, politics and aesthetics are frequently combined, searingly synthesized in ways often unimaginable and/or incomprehensible to people, particularly politicians, artists, and critics, who know nothing of the lived-experiences and lived-endurances of oppression. This is precisely why the discourse on the development of a Black Aesthetic specific to the special needs of black folk during the 1960s and 1970s was such a major preoccupation for the Black Arts movement. It could be argued that at the conceptual core of the Black Arts movement was an incendiary effort to, literally, *decolonize* every aspect of African American expressive culture or, rather, *the art of black expression*. When Fanon wrote of the creation of a decolonized and/ or decolonizing "literature of combat" that "calls on the whole people to fight for their existence as a nation," Black Arts insurgents solemnly took his words to heart because they too were waging a war on behalf of "a nation," a *black nation*.

As Larry Neal's (1968) classic essay "The Black Arts Movement" reveals, Fanon's critical theory was a key contribution to Black Arts aesthetes' conceptualization and articulation of a Black Aesthetic, and it is not difficult to understand why when we turn to *The Wretched of the Earth* (pp. 29, 34, 37). For Fanon, the art of an oppressed or colonized people is always already political, and his conception of a "literature of combat" strongly stressed that anti-colonial intellectuals and artists' "combat" must be more than merely intellectual warfare or radical rhetoric; it had to connect ideas with action or, rather, radical political theory with revolutionary social praxis. In his own weighted words:

> The colonized man who writes for his people ought use the past with the intention of opening the future, as an invitation to action and a basis for hope. But to ensure that hope and give it form, he must take part in action and throw himself body and soul into the national struggle. You may speak about everything under the sun; but when you decide to speak of that unique thing in man's life that is represented by the fact of opening up new horizons, by bringing light to your own country, and by raising yourself and your people to their feet, then you must collaborate on the physical plane. (Fanon, 1968, p. 232)

It is not a blind hatred of the colonizer that motivates the anti-colonial intellectual, artist, and activist, but instead a deep desire to provide their colonized comrades with "an invitation to action and a basis for hope." Fanon understood the colonizer's literature and art to be nothing but so many subtle, or not so subtle, contributions to the continuance of colonization, and a lame literature and art that was/is neither created for, nor in the anti-imperial interests of the colonized. This is also to say that Fanon viewed the colonizer's literature and art as, quite literally, *the art of imperialism*. That is why he contended that intellectuals and artists actively involved in the decolonization process, to reiterate, "ought use the past with the intention of opening the future, as an invitation to action and a basis for hope." In other words, the art of the oppressed, which at its best is *the art of social transformation and human liberation*, must have a solid sense of history that heuristically brings the oppressed from the periphery to the center. Additionally, anti-colonial intellectuals and artists' "histories," if you will, must do much more than rattle off tragedy after tragedy, they must also point to triumphs and astutely inspire the oppressed to continue to struggle. Hence, the literature and art of the oppressed, in some senses, serves as *counter-histories* and *critical theories* that challenge dominant discourse and ideological arrangements (see Smethurst, 2005, pp. 76–84).

Equally emphasized and expatiated by Fanon in *The Wretched of the Earth* (1968) was his heartfelt belief that anti-colonial intellectuals, artists, and activists' work (or "combat," as he aptly put it above) must provide "political education" to the colonized people. His words to anti-colonial intellectuals, artists, and activists were unequivocal; with respect to revolutionary decolonization, authentic human liberation, and truly democratic social transformation, he sternly stated: "You will not be able to do all this unless you give the people some political education" (p. 180). He went even further, exhorting anti-colonial intellectuals, artists, and activists to always bear in mind that "[e]verything can be explained to the people, on the single condition that you really want them to understand" (p. 189). Here it is important to take this one step further and critically engage Fanon's distinct definition of "political education," because it had a profound impact on the radicals and radicalism of both the Black Power and the Black Arts movements. He intrepidly announced:

> Now, political education means opening their minds, awakening them, and allowing the birth of their intelligence; as [Aimé] Cesaire said, it is "to invent souls." To educate the masses politically does not mean, cannot mean, making a political speech. What it means is to try, relentlessly and passionately, to teach the masses that everything depends on them; that if we stagnate it is their responsibility, and that if we go forward it is due to them too, that there is no such thing as a demiurge, that there is no famous man who will take responsibility for everything, but that the demiurge is the people themselves and the magic hands are finally only the hands of the people. (p. 197)[10]

It is easy to see why so many Black Power and Black Arts advocates were attracted to Fanonian philosophy. When he wrote of "opening their [i.e., 'the masses'] minds, awakening them, and allowing the birth of their intelligence," one does not have to go far to understand how such an assertion would resonate with Black Power and Black Arts radicals, especially those who became major players in the Black studies movement.[11] Fanon's philosophy of education is one that centers Africa and its diaspora and unapologetically emphasizes Africana agency, transhistorically and globally. When he wrote, "[t]o educate the masses politically does not mean, cannot mean, making a political speech," it takes us right back to Black Power and Black Arts proponents' critiques of the Civil Rights movement as little more than a bunch of political pandering and religious rhetoric, as opposed to "real" or revolutionary struggle, for African American civil rights and social justice. This last point also enables us to see that when Black Power and Black Arts radicals read "there is no famous man who will take responsibility for everything," their critiques of Martin Luther King, and his leadership of the Civil Rights movement in specific, were grounded in a growing frustration with what they perceived to be the demiurgical discourse in which the Civil Rights movement was then caught. Black Power and Black Arts insurgents' politics and aesthetics were preoccupied with providing the black masses with counter-histories, critical theories, and radical political education that decidedly demonstrated, in Fanon's weighted words, that "the demiurge is the people themselves and the magic hands are finally only the hands of the people." In other words, Black Power and Black Arts activists desired nothing more than to prove that there was, quite simply, no social justice or civil rights "Wizard of Oz."

In a nutshell, this is what the discourse surrounding the Black Aesthetic was about. Although a heatedly debated concept between 1965 and 1975, with often widely differing definitions, the Black Aesthetic could be said to collectively include: a corpus of oral and written fiction and nonfiction that proclaimed the distinctiveness, beauty, and sometimes superiority of African American thought, culture, and aesthetics; an assemblage of radical political principles openly opposed to white supremacy and anti-black racism which promoted black unity and solemn solidarity with other oppressed nonwhites, such as Native Americans, Asian Americans, Mexican Americans, and other Latinos; and, an ethical exemplar and aesthetic criteria outlining "authentic" and "inauthentic" African American literature and art. Above all else, the Black Aesthetic strongly stressed that "authentic" black art was always *historically grounded, politically engaged, socially uplifting,* and *consciousness-raising* (H. A. Baker, 1980, 1988; Bodunde, 2001; Gayle, 1971; Wright, 1997).

It could be said that the Black Aesthetic provided the major theoretical thrust of the Black Arts movement. The unrelenting searching for, and definition and redefinition of the Black Aesthetic gave way to a set of distinctive discursive formations and discursive practices that continue to reverberate through conscious rap music and hip hop culture (e.g., see the work of Public Enemy, KRS-ONE, X Clan, Paris, the Jungle Brothers, Tribe Called Quest, De La Soul, Brand Nubian, Arrested Development, Outkast, Goodie Mob, Lauryn Hill, Wyclef Jean, Spearhead, Erykah Badu, Nas, Common, Mos Def, Talib Kweli, Jill Scott, the Roots, India.Arie, and Dead Prez). In fact, one of the more innovative aspects of the discourse on the Black Aesthetic revolved around its unambiguous critique of "Western cultural aesthetics." For instance, in "The Black Arts Movement," Larry Neal (1968) articulated the collective ambitions of the advocates of the Black Aesthetic:

> The Black Arts Movement is radically opposed to any concept of the artist that alienates him from his community. This movement is the aesthetic and spiritual sister of the Black Power concept. As such, it envisions an art that speaks directly to the needs and aspirations of black America. In order to perform this task, the Black Arts Movement proposes a radical reordering of the Western cultural aesthetic. It proposes a separate symbolism, mythology, critique, and iconology. The Black Arts and the Black Power concepts both relate broadly to the Afro-American's desire for self-determination and nationhood. Both concepts are nationalistic. One is concerned with the relationship between art and politics; the other with the art of politics. (p. 29; see also Karenga, 1968, 1972, 1997)

Emphasis should be placed on the fact that the Black Arts activists understood their movement to be "the aesthetic and spiritual sister of the Black Power concept." Which is also to say, there was a deliberate division of labor between those who were primarily "concerned with the relationship between art and politics" (i.e., the Black Arts movement) and those who were preoccupied with "the art of politics" (i.e., the Black Power movement). This is an extremely important point, not simply because it reveals the sophistication of

1960s and 1970s African American aesthetic and political culture but, even more, because it highlights one of the major differences between the Black Arts movement and the Harlem Renaissance: Black Arts movement members' artistry was not a reaction to the nadir of "Negro" life or leadership between 1965 and 1975, but an audacious call to action that was inextricable from the radical politics of the larger Black Power movement—a social and political movement that arose in the aftermath of the Civil Rights movement, which many consider, in light of the signing of the Civil Rights Act of 1964 and the Voting Rights Act of 1965, the most successful social justice movement in African American history. In fact, James Smethurst (2005) has eloquently argued in his award-winning book, *The Black Arts Movement: Literary Nationalism in the 1960s and 1970s*: "It is a relative commonplace to briefly define Black Arts as the cultural wing of the Black Power Movement. However, one could just as easily say that Black Power was the political wing of the Black Arts movement" (p. 14).

As discussed in chapter 2, in some senses it could be said that most of the radicals of the Harlem Renaissance felt that their aspirations were increasingly out of sync with those of the wider New Negro movement of the 1920s and 1930s. If this is conceded, then, we are given grounds to argue that the Black Arts movement may very well have been *the first national African American cultural aesthetic movement to have consciously mirrored a national African American social and political movement*. At no other point in African American history, culture, and struggle have so many black writers and artists collectively responded to the call of black radical politics and a black revolutionary social movement—save perhaps, and this is said quite solemnly, the innumerable "slave narratives" and radical abolitionist writings contributed by African Americans to the Abolitionist movement (e.g., Olaudah Equiano, Phillis Wheatley, David Walker, Nat Turner, George Moses Horton, Sojourner Truth, Maria Stewart, Harriet Jacobs, William Wells Brown, Henry Bibb, Sarah Forten, Henry Highland Garnet, Victor Séjour, Frederick Douglass, James Whitfield, Frances Harper, and Harriet Wilson) (Andrews and Gates, 1999, 2000; Fisch, 2007; Y. Taylor, 1999a, 1999b). However, my more critical readers might observe, neither the Abolitionist movement nor the Harlem Renaissance were exclusively or distinctively *for black folk* and *in the interest of black folk* in the ways in which the Black Arts movement unequivocally was. [12]

Here it is equally important to understand that when Neal wrote that the Black Arts movement was "the aesthetic and spiritual sister of the Black Power concept," he was also hinting at the ways in which the two movements discursively dovetailed virtually from their inceptions. This is to say, going back to Smethurst's comment, that during the Black Power period "black radical politics" was not automatically privileged over "black art," but that black politics and black art were understood to be complementary. As a matter of fact, between 1965 and 1975 there was a kind of symmetry between "art and politics" and "the art of politics" that had not been achieved before or since the Black Power and Black Arts movements. Directly commenting on what I have termed the "discursive dovetailing" between the Black Power and Black Arts movements, Neal (1968) shared:

> Recently, these two movements have begun to merge: the political values inherent in the Black Power concept are now finding concrete expression in the aesthetics of Afro-American dramatists, poets, choreographers, musicians, and novelists. A main tenet of Black Power is the necessity for black people to define the world in their own terms. The black artist has made the same point in the context of aesthetics. The two movements postulate that there are in fact and in spirit two Americas—one black, one white. The black artist takes this to mean that his primary duty is to speak to the spiritual and cultural needs of black people. Therefore, the main thrust of this new breed of contemporary writers is to confront the contradictions arising out of the black man's experience in the racist West. Currently, these writers are reevaluating Western aesthetics, the traditional role of the writer, and the social function of art. Implicit in this reevaluation is the need to develop a "Black Aesthetic." It is the opinion of many black writers, I among them, that the Western aesthetic has run its course: it is impossible to construct anything meaningful within its decaying structure. We advocate a cultural revolution in art and ideas. The cultural values inherent in Western history must either be radicalized or destroyed, and we will probably find that even radicalization is impossible. In fact, what is needed is a whole new system of ideas. (p. 29)

The Black Arts movement sought to offer "a whole new system of ideas" that would complement the radical politics of the Black Power movement. It was, as Neal explicitly stated, a "cultural revolution in art and ideas" that took very seriously the notion that *black artists' work should be historically rooted, socially relevant, politically radical, and reflect the ongoing struggles of the black community (or, rather, the black nation)*. In fact, it could be said that the Black Arts movement in several senses represented the 1960s and 1970s blossoming of the aspirations of the Niggerati of the Harlem Renaissance of the 1920s and 1930s insofar as the Niggerati was more or less the African American avant-garde of its era. It is relatively easy to see, as the work of Aldon Nielsen (1997) and Fred Moten (2003) emphasize, that the Black Arts movement was the Black Power movement's avant-garde.

Above when Neal wrote that the Black Arts advocates believed that "the Western aesthetic has run its course: it is impossible to construct anything meaningful within its decaying structure," his words simultaneously connected the Black Arts movement to many of the aesthetic ambitions of the Niggerati of the Harlem Renaissance and more mainstream American avant-gardism (Arthur, 2005; Hobbs, 1997; Nel, 2002; Yu, 2009). With respect to its connection to the Niggerati of the Harlem Renaissance, when Neal asserted that the Black Arts movement is "radically opposed to any concept of the artist that alienates him from his community" and we observe the myriad ways in which Black Arts activists frequently connected their work to and/or took their aesthetic cues from black popular culture, and when we recall that one of the major missions of the Niggerati was to document and celebrate the life and culture of the "low-down folks" (as Langston Hughes put it in 1926) as opposed to simply black bourgeois life and culture during the Renaissance years, we are presented with ample evidence of the "low-down folk culture" link between the Black Arts movement and the Niggerati of the Harlem Renaissance. Both cultural aesthetic movements sought to document and celebrate the life-struggles and life-lessons of the "low-down folks," which is something that has consistently distinguished African American cultural aesthetic movements (including hip hop culture) from most other cultural aesthetic movements in the United States.[13]

In terms of the ways in which the Black Arts movement simultaneously converges with and decidedly diverges from more mainstream avant-gardism in the United States, it is important to observe what could be interpreted as Neal's proto-postmodern critique of the Western cultural aesthetic. When he wrote that the Black Arts movement "proposes a radical reordering of the Western cultural aesthetic. It proposes a separate symbolism, mythology, critique, and iconology," his words undoubtedly prefigured both postmodern and postcolonial critiques of European modernity's cultural aesthetics. Moreover, when Neal wrote "the Western aesthetic has run its course: it is impossible to construct anything meaningful within its decaying structure," his critique further prefigured and innovatively invokes more mainstream American avant-gardist critiques associated with the postmodern and postcolonial critics of the 1980s and 1990s. Let me be clear here: it is not my intention here to argue that the Black Arts movement was a "postmodern" or "postcolonial" movement, which it most certainly was not, but instead to emphasize the ways in which even when placed within the continuum of more mainstream avant-gardism in the United States the Black Arts movement is decidedly distinguished in light of its unrelenting and unrepentant critique of white supremacy and anti-black racism, combined with its critiques of U.S. capitalism, militarism, and hedonism, among other issues and ills. In fact, it would be difficult, if not impossible, to find U.S. cultural aesthetic movements besides the Harlem Renaissance, the Black Arts movement, and the hip hop generation that have sincerely documented and celebrated black "low-down folks'" life, culture, and struggles.

Neal's above assertion that Black Arts intellectuals and artists were "reevaluating Western aesthetics, the traditional role of the writer, and the social function of art," not only illustrates that the Black Arts movement was an avant-garde movement, but also that the inner-workings of the aesthetic wing of the Black Power movement was much more complicated and complex than previously acknowledged. His contention that "[i]mplicit in this reevaluation is the need to develop a 'Black Aesthetic,'" directly contradicts long-standing claims that the Black Arts movement was essentially anti-intellectual or, what is more, a movement predicated on *black anti-intellectualism.* Such claims not only negate the glaring fact that the Black studies movement evolved out of the Black Power and Black Arts movements, but they also fail to fully engage Black Arts aesthetes' almost obsessive preoccupation with intensely interrogating and critically theorizing "the traditional role of the writer" and "the social function of art" and their relationship with African American history, culture, and ongoing struggle. From an Africana studies perspective, and especially from the point of view of Africana critical theory, this is undoubtedly one of the most distinctive features of the movement when compared with either the Harlem Renaissance or, if truth be told, the hip hop generation.

"IT'S A MAN'S MAN'S MAN'S WORLD!" OR "GOTTA LET A WOMAN BE A WOMAN/AND LET A MAN BE A MAN!": ON THE BLACK ARTS MOVEMENT'S HYPERMASCULINITY, MISOGYNY, MALE SUPREMACY, AND OTHER CONTRADICTORY CONTRIBUTIONS TO HIP HOP CULTURE

Hegemonic expressions of gender and sexual identity undoubtedly played a pivotal role in the "radical" politics of both the Black Power and Black Arts movements. Usually when this subject is broached the bulk of the blame is placed on the "profoundly problematic masculinist ethic" of 1960s and 1970s black nationalism, as Phillip Brian Harper (1996) emphasized in *Are We Not Men?: Masculine Desire and the Problem of African American Identity* (p. 53). At the heart of Black Arts movement expressions of black nationalism, as was witnessed above, was the conceptualization and articulation of a "black nation." According to John Bracey, August Meier, and Elliott Rudwick (1970) in *Black Nationalism in America,* "[t]he concept of racial solidarity . . . is essential to all forms of black nationalism," but calls for "racial solidarity" were often ironically coupled with the quest for *black male supremacy* during the Black Power period (p. xxvi). And, there is a sense in which more contemporary calls for the rise of a (however multicultural) "hip hop nation" eerily echo past summons for ("Third World") solidarity and continued quests for (nonwhite) male supremacy.

However, Harper's work advocates that we interrogate black masculinism and black nationalism without sacrificing "one for the other," which is to say *black masculinism is not always and everywhere nationalist, and black nationalism is not always and everywhere masculinist.* Considering that both black masculinism and what could be loosely termed "black nationalism" are evident in both "conscious" and "commercial" hip hop culture, we would do well to critically engage hip hop's inheritance here as well. Harper (1996) helps to drive the point home:

> While Black Arts politics—the most recent fully theorized version of African American nationalism—is not a quarter-century old, its continuing import can be discerned in a range of rather more current phenomena, from the interest in accounts of the Black Power era by such authors as Elaine Brown, David Hilliard, and Hugh Pearson, to Afrocentric educational movements and certain aspects of hip hop culture. It is as crucial as ever, then, to offer a cogent critique of black masculinism and the nationalist impulse. The point, of course, as is already clear, is not to sacrifice the one for the other—a practical impossibility in any event—but, by fully analyzing the workings of both, to expose and abolish the limits they present in promising liberation for "all black people," but not, evidently, for "you." (p. 53)

The "you" that Harper invokes at the close of the above quotation conceivably encompasses not simply the "bourgeois," whitewashed, and mild-mannered "Negroes" of the 1960s and 1970s, but also black women, whether "bourgeois," "proletariat," or "lumpenproletariat" (to use the terms of the times). If, in fact, black women as a whole were excluded from Black Power projects aimed at "liberation for 'all black people,'" and if it is conceded that hip hop culture seems to have inherited, at the very least, certain aspects of black masculinism and black nationalism from the Black Power and Black Arts movements, then Harper's contention that "a cogent critique of black masculinism and the nationalist impulse" is needed is as relevant with respect to hip hop culture as it is in terms of Black Power politics and aesthetics. It is obvious that the Black Power and Black Arts movements embraced and articulated their own unique "black" version of American sexism grounded in the rhetoric of 1960s and 1970s black nationalism. However, what is less obvious are the ways in which the hip hop generation has inherited and built on a lot of the sexism and heterosexism of the Black Power and Black Arts movements. Even in emphasizing all of this, however, it is extremely important to avoid one-dimensional interpretations of extremely multidimensional movements such as the Black Power and Black Arts movements. Therefore, here critique must be coupled with caution, so as not to lose sight, not simply of what hip hop has inherited from the Black Power and Black Arts movements, but also in order to steer clear of the caricatures of black culture which have long-plagued black people and their search(es) for social justice.

In *The Black Arts Movement*, James Smethurst (2005) observed that "a commonplace about the Black Arts Movement is that it was characterized, almost defined, by an extremely misogynist and homophobic masculinism," which, needless to say, is the very kind of masculinism that has come to characterize or, rather, define and deform rap music and hip hop culture (p.

84). In fact, Smethurst continued, "one might say that certain branches of Black Arts (and post–Black Arts) thought are locked in a sort of death embrace with some schools of feminist criticism, with the result that the Black Arts Movement is often projected as hopelessly masculinist and homophobic in the worst ways, and feminism is equally often portrayed as an alien interloper in the African American community" (p. 84). It is interesting to note that almost the exact same relationship continues to exist between hip hop culture and "third wave feminism" (i.e., feminism from 1990 to the present), except for the fact that contemporary black feminism and hip hop feminism have complicated not only what it means to be a "feminist," but also what it means to be a "hip hopper."[14]

Smethurst's (2005) groundbreaking research and interviews revealed that several members of the Black Arts movement "deny bitterly that the movement was particularly homophobic and misogynist" (pp. 84–85). Instead they argue that although their thought and behavior illustrate their embrace of patriarchy and heterosexism, as well as their inattention and insensitivity to black women and black homosexuals' life-worlds and life-struggles, the same could be said of almost every sector of American society at the time. In fact, Black Arts elders have pointed out, women in particular were extremely active in the movement. The range and reach of Black Arts women's contributions frequently went beyond local or regional African American enclaves and landed them in the national Black Arts limelight. Moreover, it is extremely important for us to observe, like hip hop feminists in the twenty-first century, many of the Black Arts women indeed did develop internal critiques of the movement's hypermasculinity, misogyny, and male supremacy. However, here we come back to Smethurst's contention that "feminism is . . . often portrayed as an alien interloper in the African American community": because the women of the Black Arts movement did not label themselves "feminist" in the 1960s "second wave" feminist sense, and because their critiques of the hypermasculinity, misogyny, and male supremacy of the Black Arts movement grew out of their distinct lived-experiences and lived-endurances as black women intellectuals, artists, and activists within the black male-dominated world of the Black Power period, their critiques seem to have fallen through the cracks and crevices of the great bulk of Black Power, Black Arts, and Women's studies.[15]

Black Arts women, such as Sonia Sanchez, Nikki Giovanni, Gwendolyn Brooks, Jayne Cortez, Johari Amini (Jewel Lattimore), Abena Joan Brown, Margaret Danner, Sarah Fabio, Val Gray Ward, Carolyn Rodgers, Elma Lewis, Barbara Ann Teer, and Nayo Watkins, frequently critiqued the hypermasculinist, misogynist, and male supremacist thought and practices of Black Arts men. However, because their critiques differed from both "second wave" white bourgeois feminists, who for the most part failed to contest racism and capitalism, and white Marxist feminists, who frequently failed to contest the political economy of racism to the depth and detail they critiqued sexism and capitalism, Black Arts womanists' politics and aesthetics seem to fall outside of the orbit of what is conventionally accepted as "feminist politics" and "feminist aesthetics." This is all to say that Black Arts womanists seem to have been shunned by both the black men of the Black Arts movement and the white women of the Women's Liberation movement. Yet and still, Black Arts womanists work was influential on both movements (see chapter 4; see also Breines, 2002, 2006; Clarke, 2005; P. H. Collins, 2006; Gore, Theoharis, and Woodard, 2009; Leonard, 2009; Roth, 2004; Vaz, 1995).

Even a cursory content analysis of, for instance, Haki Madhubuti's (1971b) *Dynamite Voices: Black Poets of the 1960s* demonstrates that at least some of the males of the Black Arts movement were open to, and respected the contributions of Black Arts women. As a matter of fact, six of the fourteen poets included in *Dynamite Voices* were women (i.e., Mari Evans, Margaret Danner, Sonia Sanchez, Carolyn Rodgers, and Nikki Giovanni). It would be difficult to locate another critical anthology focused on a transgender, national artistic movement during the 1960s and 1970s that prominently featured the work of women (especially African American women) as did *Dynamite Voices*. However, even in including the work of Black Arts womanists Madhubuti made, according to Nikki Giovanni, condescending comments that, for all intents and purposes, continued *the parade of patriarchy* within the Black Arts movement (Clarke, 2005; Mance, 2007; R. J. Patterson, 2009).

Madhubuti was certainly not the only male member of the Black Arts movement to make condescending hypermasculinist comments, if not outright misogynist and male supremacist remarks. For example, in his infamous essay "Black Women," which was published in *Black World*, major Black Arts movement leader Amiri Baraka (1970) went so far as to say:

> We talk about the black woman and the black man like we were separate because we have been separated. . . . We were separated by the deed and process of slavery. We internalized the process, permitting it to create an alien geography in our skulls. . . . And so this separation is the cause of our need for self-consciousness by providing ourselves with healthy African identities. By embracing a value system that knows of no separation but only of the divine complement the black woman is for her man. For instance, we do not believe in the "equality" of men and women. We cannot understand what the devils and the devilishly influenced mean when they say equality for women. We could never be equals . . . nature has not provided thus. The brother says, "Let a woman be a woman . . . and let a man be a man." (pp. 7–8)

Notice here Baraka's coded language: "the divine complement the black woman is for her man." He does not come right out and say terms like "patriarchy" or "male supremacy" but, make no mistake about it, this is *black patriarchy* or, rather, *black male supremacy*, pure and simple. After historicizing his comments by invoking "the deed and process of slavery" that separated African American women and men, Baraka argued that what was needed was an embrace of "healthy African identities." Of course, from a black patriarchal point of view, those "African identities" that are truly "healthy" are the ones that provide paradigms for the continuation of black patriarchy in the United States. The "deed and process of slavery" in so many words, Baraka and others of his ilk seemed to be saying, emasculated black men; white males' domination of politics and economics (i.e., capitalist political economy) emasculated black men; and, white males' legal and illegal prevention of black men from being the "protectors and providers" of black women and children was yet another way in which black men were emasculated. No thought was given to the fact that each of the aforementioned impacted the life-worlds and life-struggles of black women. As James Brown's famous 1966 classic said, "It's a Man's Man's Man's World!," and black women's lot in life was/is to silently suffer hypermasculinity, misogyny, and male supremacy.

Not only was Baraka's conception of a "new" black nation hypermasculinist, misogynist, and male supremacist, but also it was equally (and ironically) preoccupied with duplicating white middle-class sex roles and family structures within the "new" black nation. As strange as it may seem, many Black Arts movement men absorbed the views and values of white middle-class patriarchs, and they, therefore, were overly eager to accept theories of black men's emasculation (i.e., *The Moynihan Report*), which posited that black manhood had long been deformed as a result of the racial hierarchy of the United States that had historically denied them unconditional access to *power*, especially *patriarchal power* (see S. C. Watkins, 1998, pp. 218–19). Hence, here we witness firsthand that many black males' articulation of "Black Power" during the 1960s and 1970s was actually a plea for *black patriarchal power*. Baraka's own words indict him; recall, above he austerely stated: "we do not believe in the 'equality' of men and women. . . . We could never be equals . . . nature has not provided thus," which is the exact same male supremacist rhetorical rubbish that most white men in America were ranting and raving, along with anti-black racist rhetoric, during the 1960s and 1970s.

Moreover, many of the male members of the Black Power and Black Arts movements who were the most vocal and vituperative in their condemnations of "the white man" and his abuse of power, it would seem, secretly admired and desired access to "the white man's" power. Their hatred of, and hostility toward the "white power structure" was less a critique of white supremacist patriarchal capitalism and more of a small-minded reaction against the fact that they had not been allowed to share in the spoils of patriarchal capitalism because of white supremacy and anti-black racism. It would be difficult to deny a continuum of black patriarchal thought and practices throughout African American history and culture, and by advocating black male subjugation of black women most male proponents of the Black Power and Black Arts movements sought to connect with this continuum and parade black patriarchy in order to receive (white male) public recognition of their distinct *black* manhood. What is more, their parade of black patriarchy was meant to illustrate unequivocally that black men were, in the most hypermasculine, misogynistic, and male supremacist manner imaginable, the "real" heads of black households and the undisputed rulers of the black family—in other words, the kings of their kingdom, the "black nation."

Based on the foregoing, one of the questions that immediately arises, at least from a black feminist perspective, is: If the males of the Black Power and Black Arts movements earnestly thought they were articulating visions of a "new" black nation, then, how was the "new" black nation going to be distinctly different from the "white man's" world if patriarchy continued to plague black women (not to mention black children)? Furthermore, we are given grounds to ask: How can a "new" black nation be based on an "old" patriarchy profoundly influenced by white middle-class patriarchal customs and culture? It would seem that the "new" black nation, as articulated by Baraka, among many others, merely swapped white patriarch for black patriarch. The "new" black nation would provide the white world with proof-positive that black men were "real" men because at the very moment "the white man's" woman (i.e., "the white woman") was "talking out of turn" and "getting out of line" with her Women's Liberation movement, black men would have "their" women "in check." Consequently, Baraka and other black men would finally be able to call "the white man's" manhood into question and return centuries of insult and "black emasculation" by labeling white men effeminate and emasculated.

A black feminist or womanist interpretation of the Black Arts movement critically moves past the tired tendency to concentrate on the more male-dominated organizations and institutions, such as the Umbra Poets Workshop, the Black Arts Repertory Theater and School, and *Liberator*, and instead turns attention to the pivotal role women played in establishing several pillars of the Black Arts movement. African American women coast to coast made indelible contributions to the Black Arts movement. For instance, Elma Lewis in Boston; Jayne Cortez in Los Angeles; Sonia Sanchez and Sarah Webster Fabio in the Bay Area; Margaret Danner, Naomi Long Madgett, Gloria House, and Melba Joyce Boyd in Detroit; Johari Amini, Gwendolyn Brooks, Carolyn Rodgers, Margaret Burroughs, and Val Gray Ward in Chicago; and Lorraine Hansberry, Rosa Guy, Esther Cooper Jackson, Sonia Sanchez, Abbey Lincoln, Barbara Ann Teer, and Sarah Wright in New York. As Smethurst (2005) correctly contends: "One would have to go back to the early New Negro Renaissance to find a major black cultural movement in which women played such leading roles prior to the 1970s" (p. 85). This means, then, that even with all of the hypermasculinism, misogyny, and male supremacy within the Black Arts movement, black women not only developed their own distinct brand of womanist criticism aimed at black patriarchy, but they did so while also leaving a lasting legacy with their *feminist activist-oriented artistry.*

Smethurst's work takes this line of logic one step further and cautions the critics of the Black Arts movement not to "mistakenly generalize" a particular misogynistic piece of writing (or set of writings) by a Black Arts movement member and take it to "encompass all of the movement" (p. 86; see also D. L. Smith, 1991). As I have attempted to demonstrate above, the Black Arts movement is much more heterogeneous than most critics have been willing to concede, and I solemnly say all of this without in any way apologizing for the hypermasculinism, misogyny, and male supremacy within the movement, which, to be perfectly honest, I find morally repugnant to the utmost and reject on revolutionary humanist principles. In addition, it must be emphasized, critics' caricatured, one-dimensional critiques of the Black Arts movement's hypermasculinism, misogyny, and male supremacy that refuse to acknowledge Black Arts womanists' distinct politics and aesthetics, which is to say their innovative critiques of white supremacist patriarchal capitalism, not only render these black women's voices silent and their agency invisible, but these one-dimensional critiques also rob hip hop feminists, and perhaps even post–hip hop feminists, of arguably some of the best examples and models of black feminism and/or womanism black women have ever created and contributed (Christian, 1985, 1988; M. Evans, 1983; Hernton, 1990; G. A. Jarrett, 2005; Tate, 1983; Traylor, 2009).

When the Black Arts movement is placed in historical and cultural context, several significant facts quickly come to the fore. First, as Smethurst (2005) strongly stressed, to contend that the Black Arts movement "as a whole was particularly male supremacist and particularly homophobic, as opposed to, say, the abstract expressionist painters, the early high modernists, or the bohemian arts community of the Lower East Side in the 1950s and 1960s, is in fact problematic" (p. 86). Which is to say that it seems that Black Arts proponents' work is often held up as especially egregious examples of sexism and/or heterosexism without at the same time bringing critique to bear on the sexism and heterosexism of the participants of more mainstream or white American movements. This is not only "problematic," as Smethurst has correctly contended, but it also seems to smack of the white supremacist double-standard that blacks and other nonwhites have long been held to in U.S. art, culture, politics, and society. For instance, a white person's—especially a white male's—morally reprehensible, whether sexist or racist or what have you, thought and behavior is often excused (or awkwardly accepted) in a white supremacist patriarchal capitalist society such as the United States in a way that the exact same thought and behavior on the part of a nonwhite person disqualifies, denounces, and condemns them and their lifework forever and ever, Amen! This prickly practice is nothing more than *the dialectic of white preferential treatment and nonwhite differential treatment.*

Lopsided and, to a certain extent, lame (because they reek of anti-black racism) critiques of the Black Arts movement's male supremacy also downplays and diminishes the myriad ways in which Black Arts womanists created spaces within the movement to come to voice and speak their special truths, not just to black men, but to the wider world. "In fact," Smethurst announced, "the Black Arts and Black Power Movements were among the few intellectual spaces in the United States in the 1960s where it was comparatively easy to raise the issue of male supremacy as opposed to, say, the institutions of mainstream academia. (The proportion of women in the leadership of the Black Arts Movement measures up well against that of tenured women faculty in the overwhelming majority of college and university English departments in the 1960s and early 1970s)" (p. 86). Whether one turns to Toni Cade Bambara's pioneering anthology *The Black Woman* (1970) or Barbara Sizemore's "Sexism and the Black Male" (1973), it is extremely important to acknowledge the ways in which Black Power and Black Arts womanists critiqued hypermasculinism and sexism from inside as opposed to outside of these movements, which to my mind makes their criticism all the more hard-hitting. Again, one-dimensional and caricatured critiques of both the Black Power and Black Arts movements as fundamentally and unusually male supremacist masks and mutes the other positive (from a black point of view) contributions emerging from them and, even more importantly here, the political legacy and radical artistry of Black Power and Black Arts womanists who contributed not only to these movements but also, as quiet as it has been kept, to the ascent of second wave feminism and the wider Women's Liberation movement.

ON CIVIL RIGHTS AND CIVIL WRONGS: BLAXPLOITATION, BLACK AESTHETICS, AND THE ONGOING BLACK ANGST OF THE HIP HOP GENERATION

By the early 1970s there were clear signs that the Black Power and Black Arts movements were beginning to wane. However, the distinct politics and aesthetics of these movements continue to inform and influence not only hip hop politics, aesthetics, and culture but, even more broadly, national and global discourse on race, gender, class, and sexuality. For instance, to take the most obvious example, contemporary conceptions and articulations of race and anti-racism are so commonly based on Black Power and Black Arts conceptions and articulations of race and anti-racism that they are frequently unnamed and, consequently, unnoticed. In fact, there is a sense in which the hip hop generation's prolonged preoccupation with African American vernacular culture can be said to be nothing other than a continuation of a cultural aesthetic continuum that reaches back to Harlem Renaissance radicals' early emphasis on "low-down folk" culture and Black Arts advocates' stress on black "street" culture. Hence, here we have come back to the *"low-down folk culture"* link accented above.

Black Arts conceptions and articulations of what constitutes "authentic" black culture continue to offer the major modes for interpreting African American identity and culture in the twenty-first century and, in their own newfangled way, rap music and hip hop culture revisit and revise many of the (both progressive and regressive) motifs of the Black Arts movement. From "urban" fiction and poetry to "urban" fashion and films, the Black Arts movement's influence on hip hop culture is seemingly ubiquitous. Even if we were to limit our discussion to a couple of the more popular expressions of hip hop culture—let's say, movies, music, and poetry—it is fairly easy to make connections between the Black Arts movement and the hip hop generation.

Let us first take the "blaxploitation" films (i.e., the black exploitation films) of the 1960s and 1970s into quick consideration. In her groundbreaking book, *Spectacular Blackness: The Cultural Politics of the Black Power Movement and the Search for a Black Aesthetic*, Amy Abugo Ongiri (2010) stated: "Between 1966 and 1975 approximately seventy feature-length black action films were created as part of this genre, either by Hollywood studios making extensive, first-time use of African American production and distribution staff or by newly formed independent African American production companies. The films that fall within the genre category of Blaxploitation are in some senses as varied and uneven as the conditions of their production" (pp. 159–60).

Blaxploitation films opened up a new arena within black popular culture that seemed to almost schizophrenically reject and embrace Hollywood cinematic (mis)representations of black people, black history, and black culture. Films such as *Uptight!* (1968), *Cotton Comes to Harlem* (1970), *Shaft* (1971), *Sweet Sweetback's Baadasssss Song!* (1971), *Super Fly* (1972), *Coffy* (1973), *The Mack* (1973), *Cleopatra Jones* (1973), *The Spook Who Sat By the Door* (1973), *Foxy Brown* (1974), *Three the Hard Way* (1974), *Mandingo* (1975), and *Dolemite* (1975) provided African American audiences with many of their first experiences of *visual fantasy*—which is to say, cinematic worlds where black was good and white was bad, worlds where blacks were heroes and whites were outlaws. Many African American film critics have argued that Blaxploitation films, if looked at objectively, actually offered blacks critiques of, and counter-narratives to their racially colonized lived-experiences in the white dominated world of the 1960s and 1970s (J. Howard, 2007; Lawrence, 2008; Sévéon, 2008; Walker, Rausch, and Watson, 2009). However, other African American film critics have observed the ways in which Blaxploitation films perpetuated and exacerbated anti-black racist myths and stereotypes about blacks, in essence, making African American audience members complicit in the continued racial colonization of black folk (Dunn, 2008; Guerrero, 1993; Quinn, 2001; Rome, 2004; Sims, 2006; Van Deburg, 2004). As a matter of fact, there was such a strong and seemingly ever-growing groundswell against Blaxploitation films within the black community in the 1970s that constant critiques were issued by Amiri Baraka on the east coast and the Coalition Against Blaxploitation was established on the west coast.

Whether one agrees or disagrees that Blaxploitation films had either a positive or negative impact on African Americans during the late 1960s and 1970s, their influence on hip hop culture is almost undeniable. Similar to the ways in which the Black Arts movement surreptitiously inherited its emphasis on "street" culture from Harlem Renaissance radicals' accentuation of "low-down folk" culture, hip hoppers have put their special spin on the celebration of black vernacular culture (Dorsey, 1997; George, 1994; Massood, 2003). Although, a major difference between the Harlem Renaissance, on the one hand, and the Black Arts movement and the hip hop generation, on the other hand, is the fact that the Harlem Renaissance radicals were really celebrating Southern black vernacular culture's survival and re-creation in a Northern urban environment (i.e., Harlem specifically, and New York City more generally), as was discussed in the previous chapter. Black Arts advocates were, and hip hop aesthetes are, for the most part, preoccupied with African American identity and culture in urban environments. Even when they hail from the South, the point of reference for most hip hoppers is usually a Southern city (i.e., an urban environment). This means, then, that hip hop seems to have inherited an emphasis on a "ghetto-fabulous" or "street-savvy" inner-city identity and culture rather than African American identity and culture emerging from rural regions (Adjaye and Andrews, 1997; F. P. Brown, 1999; Campbell, 2005; Gundaker, 1998).

The Blaxploitation/ghetto-fabulous inner-city identity and culture emphasis in hip hop culture is fairly easy to observe, whether we turn to Snoop Doggy Dogg's assertion that he can "clock a grip like my name Dolemite," to the often overlooked fact that the Notorious B.I.G./Biggie Smalls' stage name was taken from an ill-fated gangster named Hiawatha "Biggie" Smalls featured in the 1975 Blaxploitation film *Let's Do It Again*. Here, we should also observe Tupac Shakur's almost incessant references and tributes to the Black Panther Party, which, according to Amy Ongiri (2010), had its own unique relationship with Blaxploitation films, especially Melvin Van Peebles's highly controversial *Sweet Sweetback's Baadasssss Song!* (pp. 171–75).

As is well known, Shakur's parents, Afeni Shakur and Billy Garland, were active members of the New York chapter of the Black Panther Party. At this point it is almost common knowledge that Shakur grew up grounded in the Panthers' conception and articulation of the "bad nigger" and, according to some critics, the Panther's "glorification" of "the brothers on the block" (Alkebulan, 2007; Austin, 2006; Cleaver and Katsiaficas, 2001; Dyson, 2002; C. E. Jones, 1998; Lazerow and Williams, 2006, 2008; Pearson, 1994; Rhodes, 2007). Considering that as of early 2010 Tupac Shakur has reportedly sold more than 85 million albums, making him one of the best-selling musical artists of all time, it is not at all far-fetched to assert that his very real relationship with the Black Power and Black Arts movements (i.e., via his concrete connections to the Black Panther Party) has indelibly informed both the politics and aesthetics of the hip hop generation. What is more, through the influence of Shakur, among others, the insurgent inner-city identity and culture emphasis and the championing of "the brothers on the block" explicitly articulated in both the Black Arts movement and blaxploitation films has become the criteria with which authentic blackness and "real" hip hop is demarcated.

In terms of the influence of the Black Arts movement, and the Black Aesthetic in particular, on the poetry, spoken-word, and rap music of the hip hop generation, we need look no further than Kevin Powell and Ras Baraka's groundbreaking *In the Tradition: An Anthology of Young Black Writers* (1992). In the introduction to their anthology, Powell and Baraka wrote of the hip hop generation's excruciating feelings of abandonment by their parents' generation. Their words are all the more poignant considering the fact that Ras Baraka, as is well known, is the son of Black Arts activists Amina and Amiri Baraka. Seeming to direct their critical comments to the Civil Rights movement more than the Black Power and Black Arts movements, Powell and Baraka's (1992) words are weighted with a sense of frustration and repulsion: "We are children of the post-integration (nightmare!), post–Civil Rights era, abandoned to find our way in a pot bent on melting our culture into mainstream oblivion" (p. xi). However, even as they critique the pitfalls of the past their work and, quite literally, *their words* reveal political and aesthetic alliances with both the Black Power and Black Arts movements. Their connections to the Black Power and Black Arts movements manifest themselves in, at the very least, two significant ways.

First, it would seem that when Powell and Baraka's anthology is placed alongside similar volumes, such as Miguel Algarín and Bob Holman's *Aloud: Voices from the Nuyorican Poets Café* (1994), Keith Gilyard's *Spirit and Flame: An Anthology of Contemporary African American Poetry* (1997), Derrick I. M. Gilbert's *Catch the Fire!!!: A Cross-Generational Anthology of Contemporary African American Poetry* (1998), Tony Medina and Louis Rivera's *Bum Rush the Page!: A Def Poetry Jam* (2001), Tony Medina,

Samiya Bashir, and Quraysh Ali Lansana's *Roll Call: A Generational Anthology of Social and Political Black Art and Literature* (2002), and Carla Cooks and Antonia Garner's *Lyrical Madness: An Anthology of Contemporary African American Poetry by African American Poets* (2004), what we are really witnessing is the deconstruction and reconstruction of the Black Arts/Black Aesthetic tradition at the turn of the twenty-first century. Moreover, Powell and Baraka went so far as to unequivocally call for a "new Black Consciousness Movement," which, based on the work that followed in the wake of their volume, it would seem that many of the poets and political activists of their generation (i.e., the hip hop generation) heeded and seriously took to heart. For instance, although writing directly of the multi-issue, multicultural, and transethnic spoken-word and slam poetry movement underway in New York City in the early 1990s, Algarín and Holman's (1994) conception and articulation of "the poet" and poetry for the hip hop generation discursively dovetails with Black Arts articulations of "the poet" and poetry during the Black Power period: "The poet of the nineties is involved in the politics of the movement. There need be no separation between politics and poetry. The aesthetic that informs the poet is of necessity involved in the social conditions the people of the world are in" (p. 11). Recall Larry Neal opened his classic essay "The Black Arts Movement" with the following sentence: "The Black Arts Movement is radically opposed to any concept of the artist that alienates him from his community." The connections between Black Arts movement and hip hop generation conceptions and articulations of the artist and her or his artistry are apparent. Whether we critically engage the work of hip hop poets, dancers, filmmakers, musicians, or visual artists, it would seem that each of the aforementioned in one way or another creates art and, often literally, "use[s] the past with the intention of opening the future, as an invitation to action and a basis for hope," to employ Fanon's apt phrase again.

In "Black Arts to Def Jam: Performing Black 'Spirit Work' Across Generations," Lorrie Smith (2006) not only acknowledges the influence of the Black Arts movement on the poets of the hip hop generation, but she goes even further to accent the special issues surrounding the deconstruction and reconstruction of the Black Arts/Black Aesthetic tradition, asserting "the reclamation of a usable Black Arts past is fraught with challenges particular to our age" (p. 352). Going on to discursively detail the "challenges particular to our age," she candidly continued, they are:

(1) a vacuum caused by the critical neglect, disparagement, and suppression of Black Arts writing since the late 1970s until very recently in African American as well as mainstream literary criticism; (2) the fear that black identity is being melted down in the kettle of a bland multiculturalism, globalized monoculture, and disingenuous color-blindness; (3) the concomitant and paradoxical "high visibility" com-

modification of "blackness" and the commercialization of hyper-black modes of rap and hip hop; (4) postmodern and new Black Aesthetic forms of pastiche and parody that undercut a visionary political tradition; (5) a generation gap within the larger black community that, according to journalist Bakari Kitwana, divides the Hip Hop generation from the Civil Rights/Black Power generation; and (6) economic and political conditions that fuel rage and nihilism in the urban communities. (p. 352)

It is important here to acknowledge the ways in which many hip hop poets, spoken-word performers, and rappers disrupt historical amnesia within African American culture by utilizing Black Arts poetics and politics as paradigms and points of departure. Indeed, here we have an almost incontrovertible instance where hip hoppers are not only conscious of but, even more, seem to openly accept and celebrate their inheritance from the Black Arts movement. However, it is the specific aspects of the Black Power and Black Arts legacies that are being acknowledged and celebrated by the hip hop generation that need to be incessantly interrogated. It would seem that many of the more commercial, "cross-over," or mainstream elements of the Black Power and Black Arts movements are the ones that have long enthralled the hip hop generation and their handlers. Consequently, hip hoppers frequently leave the more nationalist, womanist, and anti-imperialist aspects of the Black Power and Black Arts movements in the lurch in favor of engagements of blaxploitation films and folklore.

The second significant way that hip hop seems to be connected to the Black Power and Black Art movements revolves around the excruciating feelings of abandonment, frustration, and repulsion mentioned earlier. Clearly, Black Power proponents felt that the Civil Rights movement did not go far enough in its efforts to eradicate anti-black racism and black exploitation at the hands of capitalism. As was witnessed above with the words of Powell and Baraka, the hip hop generation has articulated almost identical sentiments concerning the advances of the Civil Rights movement. According to my colleague, Bakari Kitwana (2002), hip hoppers' frustrations with the Civil Rights movement stem from what they understand to be "America's unfulfilled promise of equality and inclusion" (p. xx). After all of the protests, marches, sit-ins, and freedom rides of the 1960s, the hip hop generation, similar to the Black Power proponents, have called into question the concrete gains of the Civil Rights movement. As a matter of fact, Kitwana contends, African Americans in the twenty-first century continue to be plagued by racism and the crude racial calculus of U.S. capitalism that the 1950s and 1960s civil rights struggle was gallantly waged against.

All too often historical amnesia seems to rear its head when and where discussions concerning the gains of the 1950s and 1960s civil rights struggle fail to acknowledge the truly troubling state of black America since the late 1960s. "Ignored is the grim reality," Kitwana cautioned, "that concrete progress within the civil rights arena has been almost nil for nearly four decades. Neither acknowledged are the ways persisting institutionalized racism has intensified for hip hop generationers despite 1950s and 1960s civil rights legislation" (pp. xx–xxi). With all due respect, then, politically conscious hip hoppers have refused to romanticize and mythologize the social gains of the Civil Rights movement because they know all too well that those advances were not the end all and be all in terms of African Americans' ultimate achievement of a truly democratic and multicultural society free from racism and the evils of capitalist political economy. In other words, it seems that the politically conscious among the hip hoppers have come to the uncomfortable conclusion that no matter how "great" and "groundbreaking" the Civil Rights movement's achievements were, African Americans' search for social justice must go on unabated in the twenty-first century—*a luta continua*, to solemnly invoke the motto of the FRELIMO movement during Mozambique's war for independence. Highlighting how the hip hoppers' struggles against racism and capitalism differs from those of both the Civil Rights and Black Power generations, Kitwana sternly stated:

> The 1950s and 1960s brought many changes in law, and the early 1970s ushered in an age of black elected officials, but the 1980s and 1990s were void of any significant movement around which young blacks could organize at the national level. For us, in part due to the previous generation's victories, today's "enemy" is not simply white supremacy or capitalism. White supremacy is a less likely target at a time when lynchings aren't commonplace (in the traditional sense) and when blacks can vote and are not required by law to sit in the back of the bus. To deem capitalism the enemy when financial success and the righteousness of the free market have become synonymous with patriotism is hardly popular. (pp. 148–49)

It is understood, then, that the hip hop generation has its own distinct versions of racism and capitalism that it must critique and contend with. What is less understood, however, is that many of the strategies and tactics of past social movements do not automatically offer viable solutions to our problems in the present. Obviously there are myriad ways in which the racism and capitalism of the twenty-first century are inextricable from the racism and capitalism of the twentieth century, but acknowledging how they are inextricable without also acknowledging their *ideological evolution* over the last fifty years does not help hip hop activists identify, critique, and contend with contemporary expressions of racism and capitalism.

This means, then, that in the final analysis the Black Power and Black Arts movements can only provide us with paradigms and points of departure that raise our awareness of *why* the preceding generation struggled and *what* they struggled against. It is up to hip hoppers to determine when and how they will struggle against the most pressing issues of their epoch. However, the main point is that there must be ongoing and increased insurgent struggle.

As Kitwana bemoaned above, "the 1980s and 1990s were void of any significant movement around which young blacks could organize at the national
level," and, sadly, something similar could be said for young folk of other
colors and cultures. How has coming of age in an era "void of any significant
[national] movement" depoliticized the hip hop generation? Or, at the very
least, how has it caused their entire approach to politics to be drastically
different from any generation of Americans, especially African Americans,
in post–Civil War history?

The foregoing questions are even more poignant when we ask them placing the young women of the hip hop generation at the discursive center. So
often within the world of hip hop women are marginalized and objectified.
What happens when we turn our attention to their life-worlds and life-struggles and earnestly ask: How has coming of age in an era "void of any
significant [Women's Liberation] movement" depoliticized the women of the
hip hop generation? Or, at the very least, how has it caused their entire
approach to politics, especially unapologetically womanist and/or feminist
politics, to be drastically different from any generation of women in U.S.
history? I wholeheartedly agree with Kitwana when he writes above, "today's 'enemy' is not simply white supremacy or capitalism." Indeed, there
are other issues the hip hop generation must engage, from religious intoler-
ance and "ethnic cleansing" to ecological devastation and animal extinction.
But, perhaps there is no greater issue confronting the hip hop generation than
its dire need to critique and unflinchingly contend with the part it has played
in the continued physical, psychological, and verbal violence against women.
Bearing this in mind, we now turn to a critical exploration of the Women's
Liberation and Feminist Art movements' (conceptual and potential) contributions to the women and men of the hip hop generation.

NOTES

1. At the end of the nineteenth century W. E. B. Du Bois declared in *The Philadelphia
Negro* (1899), "There is always a strong tendency on the part of the [white] community to
consider the Negroes as composing one practically homogenous mass. This view has of course
a certain justification," after all, he solemnly said, "the people of Negro descent in this land
have had a common history, suffer today common disabilities, and contribute to one general set
of social problems" (p. 309). But then, like a lion calmly luring his prey into his lair, he
sardonically said, "yet if the foregoing statistics have emphasized any one fact it is that wide
variations in antecedents, wealth, intelligence and general efficiency have already been differentiated within this group." Which, in other words, is to say that African American social
classes had "already been differentiated" and did not—and certainly not always and in every
instance—quickly coincide with European or European American social classes or class struggles. Here we have broached the subject of what I have recently referred to in *Against Epistemic Apartheid* as Du Bois's *conceptual coup d'état* in the midst of Max Weber and Karl Marx's
conceptions of class (see Rabaka, 2010a, pp. 77–88).

2. According to acclaimed African American literary theorist Houston Baker in *Modernism and the Harlem Renaissance* (1987), it may not have been so much a question of blacks "'consciously and proudly set[ting] [themselves] apart' from white America" as much as it was a case where blacks' lived-experiences made them painfully aware of the fact that they were racially colonized and socially ostracized in a country that constantly claimed to be both Christian and democratic: "The world of *The New Negro* represents a unified community of national interests set in direct opposition to the general economic, political, and theological tenets of a racist land. The work is, in itself, a *communal* project, drawing on resources, talents, sounds, images, rhythms of a marooned society or nation existing on the frontiers or margins of *all* American promise, profits, and modes of production" (p. 77, all emphasis in original). Then, writing of one of many shared cultural and aesthetic motifs that connect the Harlem Renaissance to the Black Arts movement, Baker observes that the radicals of the Renaissance drew "inspiration" from "the very flight, or marronage, to the urban North of millions of black folk" (p. 77). Below it will be illustrated that many Black Arts advocates were similarly inspired by and celebrated "urban" or "inner-city" African American identity and culture close to three decades after the Renaissance's demise. However, the major difference between Renaissance and Black Arts celebrations of African American vernacular culture is that Renaissance celebrations of "urban" blackness were usually connected to the majority of early twentieth-century black folk's rural roots, where by the time of the Black Arts movement it had become customary to privilege urban African American identity and culture over rural African American identity and culture. For further discussion of Alain Locke's Renaissance and post-Renaissance philosophy of art and philosophy of culture, see Locke (1933, 1936a, 1936b, 1940, 1949, 1983, 1989, 1992).

3. In terms of Bernard's claim that, "[l]ike the Harlem Renaissance, the Black Arts movement articulated its objectives in powerful but pointedly abstract language that was finally more confusing than illuminating. How a black artist 'could speak to his brothers' without any white mediation proved more confounding than Black Arts leaders were willing to concede," I would like to refer my readers to John Young's excellent *Black Writers, White Publishers: Marketplace Politics in Twentieth-Century African American Literature* (2006), which, from what I can gather, appears to be the first extended application of editorial theory to African American literature.

4. My interpretation of Larry Neal's articulation of the Black Aesthetic has been informed by Houston Baker's *Afro-American Poetics: Revisions of Harlem and the Black Aesthetic* (1988), and specifically the chapter "Critical Change and Blues Continuity: An Essay on the Criticism of Larry Neal" (pp. 140–59). It is interesting to observe that Baker asserts that, although Neal was extremely critical of the Harlem Renaissance, arguing that it "was essentially a failure" because "[i]t did not address itself to the mythology and the life-styles of the black community. It failed to take root, to link itself concretely to the struggles of that community, to become its voice and spirit," ultimately Neal "left the Black Aesthetic, at least in part, because he began to read extensively and enthusiastically in literary criticism and theory." Baker continued, "[l]ike many of us, he began to search for viable models of black criticism and theory. Readers who were not white and male, circa 1964-65, had begun to feel that the standard story of 'American' literature told by traditional criticism was weak and weary, tired and dreary" (p. 141). We witness here, then, that Neal's claim that the Harlem Renaissance "was essentially a failure" must be contested considering the fact that after the Black Power decade between 1965 and 1975 many of the major Black Arts movement advocates and activists found themselves entering into the very same (or, at the very least, strikingly similar) "polluted mainstream of Americanism" and "interracial cosmopolitanism" that the radicals of Renaissance were so mercilessly criticized for. Baker boldly wrote in an semi-autobiographical register:

> Neal was objectively and coolly representative of transformations that led Baraka to Marxism, Sonia Sanchez to the Nation of Islam, and me to the realms of literary theory. Having commenced as avowed guerrilla theater revolutionaries, we found ourselves, suddenly, playing to respectable houses whose paying audiences eagerly awaited our next scenes. These audiences, by any objective count, were predominantly white. That is to say, only a serious fantasy could sustain the notion that the intended readers of a book

like my theoretical work *The Journey Back* (1980) were members of the black masses. (pp. 140–41)

In other words, like the Harlem Renaissance of the past and the hip hop generation of the present, the Black Arts movement indeed did ultimately give way to a species of "interracial cosmopolitanism" and, like the aforementioned movements, ironically ended up with "predominantly white" patrons and audiences. Therefore, hardcore black nationalist criticisms of African American cultural aesthetics movements must always bear in mind the fact that black art historically has been and currently continues to be created within the wider cultural context of U.S. history, culture, and political economy, which is to say within the broader world of a multiracial, multicultural, and transethnic society.

5. My analysis here has been greatly influenced by Henry Louis Gates's *Figures in Black: Words, Signs, and the "Racial" Self* (1987), and specifically his groundbreaking "Literary Theory and the Black Tradition," where he succinctly stated:

> The challenge of the critic of comparative black literature is to allow contemporary theoretical developments to inform his or her readings of discrete black texts but also to generate his or her own theories from the black idiom itself. The challenge of theorists generally is to realize that what we have for too long called "the tradition" is merely one tradition of several and that we have much to learn from the systematic exploration of new canons. That which unites those of us whose canonical texts differ is the shared concern with theory that arises from these texts. It is here that we are to find common ground; it is here that we can bridge text milieus. It is here that the hegemony of the Western tradition at last can be seen to be the arbitrary and ideological structure that it is. (p. 58)

My reading of the relationship between the Harlem Renaissance and the Black Arts movement is grounded in Gates's contention that "the critic of comparative black literature [must] allow contemporary theoretical developments to inform his or her readings of discrete black texts" and that through these new readings the critic must "generate his or her own theories from the black idiom itself." I am also in complete agreement with Gates when he asserts that "what we have for too long called 'the [black] tradition' is merely one tradition of several" and that "we have much to learn from the systematic exploration of new canons." My body of work to date has solemnly sought "the systematic exploration of new canons," specifically continental and diasporan African contributions to radical politics and critical social theory, and my conception and articulation of critical theory is directly derived "from the black idiom itself." Here, I intend to employ Africana studies–informed interdisciplinary and intersectional critical social theory—what I have elsewhere termed "Africana critical theory"—in my efforts to highlight what the Black Arts movement inherited from the Harlem Renaissance and what the Black Arts movement bequeathed to the hip hop generation. For further discussion of the Africana tradition of critical theory or, rather, Africana critical theory, see chapter 1 and Rabaka (2006, 2007, 2008a, 2009, 2010a, 2010b).

6. Here, my interpretation of the African American cultural aesthetic continuum has been enriched by Houston Baker's *The Journey Back: Issues in Black Literature and Criticism* (1980). My contention that there are cultural aesthetic connections between the art of the enslaved (e.g., "slave narratives"), the Harlem Renaissance, the Black Arts movement, and the hip hop generation is based, for the most part, on Baker's body of work, especially H. A. Baker (1983, 1984, 1987, 1988, 1990, 1993) and Baker and Redmond (1989).

7. In *Forms of Fanonism*, to use Fanon as an example of the ways in which there seems to be a double-standard when it comes to *the violence of domination* and *the violence of liberation* or, rather, *the violence of the oppressor* and *the violence of the oppressed*, I wrote:

> What is most often missing from the harangues about Fanon's views on violence are any serious discussions of *how* and *why* he advocated *self-defensive antiracist, anti-colonialist, anti-capitalist, and anti-sexist violence.* No mention is made of the intermin-

able imperialist violence that the wretched of the earth have been barbarically forced to endure at the hands of the white supremacist patriarchal colonial capitalist world. No mention is made of the holocausts, genocides, enslavements, racializations, colonizations, segregations, pogroms, and lynchings that the wretched of the earth have long had to live and labor through. No mention is made of the many millions of ways in which the white supremacist patriarchal colonial capitalists have repeatedly robbed the wretched of the earth of their human rights, civil rights, voting rights, and any other kind of "rights." This is all brushed aside with a subtle and brisk brutality which has caused a couple of European critical theorists with serious social consciences to question the ways in which Europe has narcissistically and racistly quarantined "humanism" to include "whites only" and "nonviolence" to involve "nonwhites only." (Rabaka, 2010b, p. 275)

In essence, to put it plainly, nonwhites who are not nonviolent in the face of their suffering and social misery deviate from the "model minority" model that whites have long encouraged them to embrace if they are to have a future in the United States (and the wider world). It is interesting to observe that some of this same sentiment has been handed down from the movements of the 1960s and 1970s to the hip hop generation, with contemporary "urban" nonwhite youth being seen as more violent than "suburban" white youth. In fact, there are several ways in which the motifs of minstrelism discussed in chapter 2 continue to haunt how the hip hop generation is interpreted or, more correctly, misinterpreted. For further discussion of Fanon's views on violence, as well as those of Jean-Paul Sartre and Herbert Marcuse, see "Revolutionary Humanist Fanonism" in *Forms of Fanonism* (Rabaka, 2010b, pp. 271–304).

8. Beyond Van Deburg's work, my analysis here has greatly benefited from Cedric Johnson's judicious research in *Revolutionaries to Race Leaders: Black Power and the Making of African American Politics* (2007), where he audaciously "calls into question those modes of political engagement that have become hegemonic within black public life since the late sixties" (p. xxiii). In many ways updating the work of Harold Cruse in his classic *The Crisis of the Negro Intellectual: A Historical Analysis of the Failure of Black Leadership* (1967), which critically surveyed the evolution of black political and intellectual culture from the 1920s to the 1960s, Johnson's book examines the transition from black radical to black reformist politics from the mid-1960s to the mid-1990s. Although relatively under-discussed in Africana studies circles, Johnson (2007) highlights how the "evolution of Black Power as a form of ethnic politics limited the parameters of black public action to the formal political world. Insurgent demands for black indigenous control converged with liberal reform initiatives to produce a moderate black political regime and incorporate radical dissent into conventional political channels" (p. xxiii). His narrative captures both the conceptual and political shifts along the "winding historical path from the defiant calls for systemic transformation and radical self-governance during the Civil Rights and Black Power movements toward the consolidation of a more conservative politics predicated on elite entreaty, racial self-help, and incremental social reforms" (p. xxiii). This means, then, that at the very moment that many of the Black Power proponents were, for the lack of a better word, "integrating" into mainstream American culture, politics, and society circa the mid-1970s, rap music and hip hop culture were beginning to take shape as the dominant mediums through which to express the "new" (i.e., post–Civil Rights, post–Black Power, post–Vietnam War, etc.) politics and aesthetics of the generation born between 1965 and 1990. This should be borne in mind as we explore what the Black Power and Black Arts movements bequeathed to the hip hop generation and, in turn, the hip hop generation's arguably more "mainstream" and "multicultural" politics and aesthetics compared to both the Harlem Renaissance and the Black Arts movement.

9. It is important here to observe that Black Power and Black Arts radicals' view that the masses of black folk during the 1960s and 1970s had little or no lasting contact with white bourgeois culture and values was more than likely influenced by Fanon's *The Wretched of the Earth* (1968, pp. 111–12, 129–40). For instance, calling his readers' attention to the intense inferiority complex and the burgeoning embrace of bourgeois views and values on the part of the African proletariat and, for that matter, most Africans who came into regular contact with white colonizers and their culture, Fanon pointed to the African peasantry and those who had the least direct and daily contact with racial colonialism and its political economy. However, it

should be pointed out that it was not the rural radicalism of the African peasantry alone that constituted the singular revolutionary socialist force of change in Africa for Fanon, but a creative coalition and alliance of anti-colonialist, anti-capitalist, and antiracist rural, urban and, even suburban sociopolitical classes with a shared interest in Africa's development, as well as the distinct development of their respective nations, cities, towns, and rural regions. This means, then, that Fanon did not completely reject the active and important radical political participation of the African proletariat as much as he emphasized its embourgeoisement when compared and contrasted with the lived-experiences, life-struggles, and, more importantly, the anti-imperialist and potential revolutionary consciousness (if provided with proper "political education") of the lumpenproletariat and peasantry of Africa. For further discussion, my readers are urged to see my analysis in *Forms of Fanonism*, especially in chapter 3, "Marxist Fanonism" (Rabaka, 2010b, pp. 145–216). Fanon's influence on the cultural aesthetics of the Black Arts movement is discussed in greater detail below.

10. For further discussion of Fanon's theory of radical political education and contributions to critical pedagogy, see Rabaka (2010b, pp. 161–69).

11. The Black studies movement emerged within the context of other 1960s and 1970s sociopolitical movements, such as the Civil Rights, Black Power, Women's Liberation, Third World Liberation, Free Speech, and Anti-War movements. Where the Black Arts movement is commonly conceived of as the cultural aesthetic arm of the Black Power movement, the Black studies movement may be taken as its intellectual and educational outlet. As a movement and *interdisciplinary discipline* Black studies, which is now known as *Africana studies*, evolved out of the Black Power movement's strong stress on black self-definition, black self-determination, culturally relevant education, cultural pluralism, and student activism. The first efforts to establish a Black studies department began in 1966 at San Francisco State College (now known as San Francisco State University), where black students, according to Maulana Karenga (2002), "[i]nfluenced by the writings of the African revolutionary Frantz Fanon's [*The Wretched of the Earth*] and the emphasis on Third World solidarity by Third World Liberation Movements . . . issued fifteen demands which served as a model for other Black Studies struggles" (p. 14). It is interesting to observe that other nonwhite student groups at San Francisco State joined with the Black Student Union to form the "Third World Front" of student groups who struggled for Black studies. Included among these student groups were the Mexican American Student Confederation, the Latin American Student Organization, the Asian American Political Alliance, the Intercollegiate Chinese for Social Action, and the Philippine American Collegiate Endeavor. After two years of student protest for Black studies, University of Chicago–trained sociologist Nathan Hare was appointed the coordinator of Black studies in February of 1968 and charged with the task of formulating an autonomous academic department devoted to systematically and critically studying African American history, culture, and struggle. After several delays by the board of trustees and other administrators, as well as further student protests, the first department of Black studies was established at San Francisco State College in November of 1968. Here emphasis should be placed not only on the fact that what we now know as Africana studies was inaugurated during the Black Power period, but also that it took African Americans in alliance with other oppressed and racially colonized groups to found the field. This is equally important when we bear in mind the often one-dimensional interpretations of the Black Power period as a time of "black supremacy" where African Americans advanced "reverse racism," and also the undeniable fact that rap music and hip hop culture, in its own unique way, has continued many of the coalitions and alliances established during the 1960s and 1970s student movements. The literature on Africana studies, which currently in its most comprehensive sense has come to include African, African American, Afro-American, Afro-Asian, Afro-European, Afro-Latino, Afro-Native American, Caribbean, Pan-African, Black British and, of course, Black studies, is diverse and extensive. The most noteworthy overviews and critical analyses are: Aldridge and James (2007), Aldridge and Young (2000), Anderson and Stewart (2007), Asante and Karenga (2006), Asante and Mazama (2005), Azevedo (2005), BaNikongo (1997), Bobo and Michel (2000), Bobo, Hudley, and Michel (2004), Gordon and Gordon (2006a, 2006b), Johnson and Henderson (2005), Johnson and Lyne (2002), Kopano and Williams (2004), F. Rojas (2007), Rooks (2006), and Whitten and Torres (1998).

12. As is well known, Benjamin Quarles's *Black Abolitionists* (1969) has long been regarded as a classic and one of the cornerstone texts in African American Abolitionist studies. Although not explored as often as other areas in African American history, culture, and struggle, over the years since Quarles's study a steady stream of black abolitionist research has been published. For example, Blackett (1983), Mabee (1970), McKivigan and Harrold (1999), Sanneh (1999), Stauffer (2002), Wu (2000), and Yee (1992). For further examples of, and critical commentary on the body of literature produced by enslaved Africans and now common called "slave narratives," please see Andrews and Gates (1999, 2000), Fisch (2007), and Y. Taylor (1999a, 1999b).

13. What I have termed here the *"low-down folk culture"* link between the Black Arts movement and the Niggerati of the Harlem Renaissance connects with hip hoppers' obsession with "ghetto-fabulous" life and culture and continues to have currency among Africana studies scholars. Most work in what is currently called "Black Popular Culture Studies" in one way or another engage contemporary black folk culture or, rather, black vernacular culture. For example, see Basu and Lemelle (2006), Bolden (2008), Bracey (2003), Dent (1992), Iton (2008), M. A. Neal (1999, 2002, 2003), H. B. Shaw (1990), and Tucker (2007).

14. For overviews of contemporary black feminism, see P. H. Collins (2000, 2005, 2006), A. Y. Davis (1981, 1989), Guy-Sheftall (1995), hooks (1981, 1984, 1991), Hull, Scott, and Smith (1982), and Lorde (1984, 1988, 1996, 2004). And, for surveys of hip hop feminism, see chapter 4 and Morgan (1999), Perry (2004), Pough (2002, 2004), Pough et al. (2007), and Sharpley-Whiting (2007).

15. Without placing too fine a point on it, it is interesting to observe that Black Arts movement members' contention that almost every sector of American society at the time embraced certain aspects of sexism (and heterosexism) has been, to a certain extent, corroborated by Jeffrey Ogbar in his groundbreaking study, *Black Power: Radical Politics and African American Identity* (2004). Ogbar (2004) observed that "despite myopic approaches that tend to fixate on the BPP [Black Panther Party]," and the Black Power movement in general, "as a bastion of sexism, the party made systematic challenges to patriarchy that were rare for its time" (p. 105). In fact, the Black Panther Party was "the first major black organization to publicly endorse the women's and gay liberation movements. While the major religious organizations of Christians, Jews, and Muslims advocated very rigid patriarchy, women ascended to major positions in the Black Panther Party." What is often overlooked in one-dimensional interpretations of the Black Panther Party are the ways in which women profoundly transformed the gender politics of the party, so much so that they "led chapters, edited the newspaper, wrote articles, defended offices from police attack, and fed thousands of impoverished children across the country, as had their male counterparts" (p. 105). Ultimately, then, if the Black Panther Party is taken as a cultural, social, and political barometer for the Black Power movement, as is so often the case, it could be said that their gender politics were reflective of the gender politics of the hypermasculinist, misogynist, and male supremacist society in which the party was formed and fought against. In all honesty, however, it must be admitted that the Black Panther Party was radically transformed as a result of the leadership and incalculable contributions of female panthers and, consequently, the party came to critique patriarchy in ways that most mainstream (whether reformist or radical) organizations, quite simply, did not. The Black Panther Party, Ogbar candidly concluded, "challenged themselves to transcend patriarchy and homophobia in ways the NAACP, Urban League, or the Republican or Democratic parties did not" (p. 105). For further discussion of the Black Panther Party's positions on women's and homosexual liberation, see Huey P. Newton's classics "The Women's Liberation and Gay Liberation Movements" and "Eve, the Mother of All Living," both in *Huey P. Newton Reader* (2002), and the section entitled "Black Panther Women Speak" in *The Black Panthers Speak* (2002) edited by the late Philip Foner, which includes work by Kathleen Cleaver, Linda Harrison, Connie Matthews, Joan Bird, and Tupac Shakur's mother, Afeni Shakur.

Chapter Four

"The Personal Is Political!" (Da Hip Hop Feminist ReMix): From the Black Women's Liberation and Feminist Art Movements to the Hip Hop Feminist Movement

I see this split between black women and women of color working within popular culture and those within grassroots organizations less as a generational divide than as reflecting the absence of analysis that conceptualizes these expressions of black women's activism as intersecting versus parallel spheres of activity. For example, feminism need not be central to, or even listed within, an organization's activities for feminist politics to be present. Just because an individual or an organization refuses to claim feminism does not mean that African American women's empowerment is being neglected. —Patricia Hill Collins, *From Black Power to Hip Hop*, p. 194

INTRODUCTION: ON THE POETICS, POLITICS, AND PROBLEMATICS OF HIP HOP FEMINISTS' CONCEPTION OF "THE PERSONAL IS POLITICAL!" PARADIGM

Although the field of hip hop feminist studies has grown by leaps and bounds over the last decade or so, there are as yet very few noteworthy works that critically identify what the black feminist movement of the 1960s and 1970s bequeathed to the hip hop feminist movement. Of course, Gwendolyn Pough's *Check It While I Wreck It!* (2004) and Patricia Hill Collins's *From Black Power to Hip Hop* (2006) are the most notable exceptions, but beyond these works scant scholarly attention has been devoted to the *herstorical* connections between, and the contributions to critical theory emerging from the major black Women's Liberation movements over the past four decades. As observed in Collins's epigraph above, it is important for us to analyze and explore continuity and consensus rather than merely discontinuity and discord by developing analyses that consider "expressions of black women's activism as intersecting versus parallel spheres of activity."

Similar to the sisters who participated in the black freedom movements of the 1960s and 1970s who were given the cruel ultimatum to chose between struggling for racial justice or gender justice, hip hop feminists have often felt forced to chose between hip hop and feminism. Joan Morgan's *When Chickenheads Come Home to Roost: A Hip Hop Feminist Breaks It Down* (1999) offered the first extended discussion of what it means to be both a hip hopper and a feminist. More recently she reflected on her groundbreaking book, stating: "I didn't write *Chickenheads* with a movement in mind, but I think we might of gotten one anyway" (Morgan, 2007, p. 478). Indeed, Morgan's work helped to spark a movement among the women of the hip hop generation—a new wing of the Women's Liberation movement that seems to simultaneously embrace and reject the fundamentals of feminism and the contradictions of hip hop culture. [1]

Further reflecting on *Chickenheads*, Morgan wrote of "feeling a bit invisible" within the world of 1980s and 1990s black feminist academic discourse. "[W]hile my feminist sensibilities had been forged by a vital tradition of black feminist thought," she asserted, "it was difficult to find my post–civil rights, post-soul, post–women's movement, worshipping at the temple of hip hop self reflected in the authors and scholars whose work I revered—bell hooks, Angela Davis, Audre Lorde, Pearl Cleage, Alice Walker, Toni Morrison, [and] Ntozake Shange, most of whom were not checking for hip hop" (p. 475). [2] In other words, the whole notion that one could be both a hip hopper and a feminist was not being adequately addressed by "old school feminists" (Morgan's words) in the 1980s and 1990s, at least not in any substantial way beyond compulsory (albeit extremely important) critiques of rap music's misogyny. For Morgan and the other members of the hip hop feminist movement, there is a "symbiotic relationship" between hip hop and feminism, a relationship that has eluded the acumen of most non–hip hop feminists. As she astutely explained:

I believed that hip hop, despite its obvious transgressions, had a cultural currency not seen in American popular culture since the birth of rock-n-roll. Harnessed correctly, it possessed the power to better black folks' lives. When it came to hip hop, I was invested emotionally, socially, professionally and politically, so much so that I could no more separate hip hop from feminism than I could my blackness from my femaleness. What was clearly a symbiotic relationship to me was incongruent to most, problematic to others and probably, for a few old school feminists, downright offensive. (p. 476)

What is it about hip hop culture that has made so many young women invest "emotionally, socially, professionally and politically" in it, despite the fact that most "old school feminists" find it "downright offensive"? Morgan's emphasis on her intimacy with, and lived-experience of hip hop culture provides us with some initial answers, and it would seem that hip hop feminism, taken as a whole, further answers the foregoing question. For many of the women of the hip hop generation hip hop and feminism are not completely incongruent. In fact, similar to those who have noted the "unhappy marriage of Marxism and feminism," it could be said that hip hop feminism represents the unhappy marriage of hip hop and feminism.[3] For instance, many socialist feminists have critiqued the male-centered character of most forms of Marxism's critique of capitalism, even as they appreciate the Marxist tradition for providing one of the most comprehensive critiques of capitalism and class struggle (Donovan, 2000; Hearn, 1991; Himmelweit, 1991; L. C. Johnson, 1990). Marxist feminists, therefore, do not denounce all Marxist discourse, even though Karl Marx himself and most male Marxists seem to support (however subtly) male supremacy and have very little to say about the political economy of patriarchy (Benston, 1969; McDonough and Harrison, 1978; Slaughter and Kern, 1981; Vogel, 1983). Marxist feminists generally focus on the critique of patriarchy and capitalism, where hip hop feminists usually focus on the critique of patriarchy and popular culture, especially African American popular music and African American popular culture. However, because most hip hop feminists are nonwhite women from impoverished and working-class communities hip hop feminism is also critical of white supremacy and economic exploitation. Therefore, even in its formative phase early hip hop feminists, such as Tricia Rose (1989, 1990, 1991, 1994), Lisa Jones (1994), Joan Morgan (1995), Veronica Chambers (1996), and Nancy Guevara (1996), called on the women of the hip hop generation to discursively develop their own special spin on anti-racism, feminism, womanism, women's liberation, and hip hop culture.

Perhaps one of the most remarkable features of hip hop feminist writing is its revelry in self-reflection and autobiography. However, as is well known, self-reflective and autobiographical writing have long been cornerstones of the conventional feminist canon (L. R. Anderson, 1997; L. R. Bloom, 1998; Swindells, 1995; R. Walker, 1995). In fact, we could quickly point to the 1960s and 1970s Women's Liberation movement slogan "the personal is political," as well as the corollary cottage industry of literature centered around the slogan, to succinctly settle any lingering doubts. What truly distinguishes hip hop feminist thought from other schools of feminist thought is its focus on the life-worlds and life-struggles of the women of the hip hop generation, and its openness to simultaneously critiquing and appreciating the poetics, politics, and problematics of hip hop culture. Besides Angela Davis (1998b), bell hooks (1994a), and Patricia Hill Collins (2005), one would be hard pressed to find a feminist born before 1955 who has been willing to bring the dialectic to bear on and critically dialogue with hip hop culture. This brings us to several critical questions: Is there a "generation gap" between hip hop feminists and their feminist foremothers, especially their grandmothers and mothers? How can some women who identify as "feminist" or "womanist" embrace hip hop while so many others denounce it as sexism's new "sexy" soundtrack, nothing more than mindless misogynistic music? Isn't it a bit ironic that any form of feminism or womanism has emerged from within the bowels of hip hop culture—a culture frequently, albeit one-dimensionally, interpreted as hypermasculinist, misogynist, and male supremacist? What is it that hip hop feminists, such as dream hampton, shani jamila, Cheryl Keyes, Sheena Lester, Ipeleng Kgositsile, Kierna Mayo, Imani Perry, Gwendolyn Pough, Rachel Raimist, Tara Roberts, Tricia Rose, Tracy Sharpley-Whiting, Danyel Smith, and Eisa Ulen, among others, find of value in hip hop culture that most of the feminists and womanists of the previous women's movements fail to fully comprehend? And, lastly, what has the hip hop feminist movement (whether consciously or unconsciously) inherited from previous women's movements, and how is hip hop feminism extending and expanding what it means to be both a hip hopper and a feminist?

Eerily echoing the accounts of the black feminists of the 1960s and 1970s who were often ill-advised to chose between their racial identity (via black nationalism) or their gender identity (via white feminism), Morgan (2007) audaciously announced, "I could no more separate hip hop from feminism than I could my blackness from my femaleness" (p. 476). What is more, "not only did I believe that my feminism and hip hop were not mutually exclusive," she went on, "I believed hip hop and the generation of black women who claim it could bring vital, complex, sometimes maddeningly contradictory experiences to the continuum of black feminist thought, whether we label ourselves feminist or not" (p. 477). This last point must be accented, as many of the women of the hip hop generation identify neither as feminists nor as womanists. Nomenclature is not at issue here, but rather the ways in which hip hop women's thought and practice discursively dovetails with developments in black (among other nonwhite) feminist theory and praxis over the past forty years.

It is fairly easy to see how hip hop feminists' self-reflective and autobiographical writings squarely place their work within the "personal is political" paradigm first put forward by 1960s and 1970s women's liberationists. By the same token, it is probably equally as obvious that hip hop feminists' understanding and articulation of what constitutes both the "personal" and the "political" simultaneously converges with and starkly diverges from previous feminist movements' expressions of the "personal" and the "political." In fact, recent feminist scholarship suggests that in its own controversial and/or contradictory way the hip hop feminist movement may very well be the most politically polyvocal and socially visible manifestation of the ongoing evolution of the Women's Liberation movement prevalent in contemporary U.S. society (A. Anderson, 2003; R. N. Brown, 2008; Hernández and Rehman, 2002; Pough et al., 2007). Even though the male-centered and male-dominated media has regularly ridiculed, if not outright insultingly offered the movement egregious epitaph after epitaph, the Women's Liberation movement continues to grow and develop in ways often unfathomed by "old school" feminists *and* "old school" masculinists. Drawing on the work of Verta Taylor (1989a, 1989b), Verta Taylor and Leila Rupp (2008), and Verta Taylor, Nancy Whittier, and Cynthia Pelak (2001), the Women's Liberation movement can be said to have passed through several periods: mobilization (1960s and 1970s); decline (1970s and 1980s); abeyance (1980s–present); and, as I intend to argue below, a new period of mobilization spearheaded by the women of the hip hop generation (1990s–present).

Just as the Women's Liberation movement has undergone several significant changes over the last four decades, so too has feminist theory and the feminist slogan the "personal is political." If, indeed, hip hop feminism and the hip hop feminist movement emerged at a time when the mainstream Women's Liberation movement was in abeyance, we should ask ourselves upfront what this might say about the resilience of feminist theory and the Women's Liberation movement. Because the women of the hip hop generation came of age at a time when the Women's Liberation movement was either in decline or in abeyance, according to Taylor and her colleagues, many of the hard-won sociopolitical advances, theories, and praxes of the Women's Liberation movement are utterly unknown to many of the women of the hip hop generation. Undoubtedly, then, this makes the fact that women in the hip hop generation are not only (re)finding feminism but, even more, ushering in a new period of feminist mobilization all the more remarkable. From Joan Morgan to Kierna Mayo, Imani Perry to Gwendolyn Pough, Rachel Raimist to Tricia Rose, and on and on, women in the hip hop generation have consistently deconstructed and reconstructed feminism and womanism to speak to the special needs of their life-worlds and life-struggles, their unique lived-experiences and lived-endurances. In the process they have produced an unprecedented form of feminism—a "functional feminism," according to Morgan (1999), that is "committed to 'keeping it real'" with respect to the critique of the interlocking and overlapping nature of sexism, racism, and capitalism in the lives of black and other nonwhite women (pp. 61–62). Seeming to simultaneously embrace and reject the fundamentals of feminism, the women of the hip hop generation, like the hip hop generation in general, have blurred the lines between the "personal" and the "political" by critically dialoguing with a culture that commonly renders them invisible or grossly misrepresents them when and where they are visible.

In this chapter I focus on what the black Women's Liberation movement bequeathed to the hip hop feminist movement in specific, and the hip hop generation in general. To engage hip hop's inheritance here it will be important to, first, briefly discuss some of the major organizations and theorists of the 1960s and 1970s black Women's Liberation movement and their relationship to the more mainstream (white) Women's Liberation movement. Next, I will explore the often overlooked relationship between the black Women's Liberation, Black Arts, and Feminist Art movements. Although not as readily recognized, the Women's Liberation movement had a significant impact on late twentieth-century women's artistry, and even though the Feminist Art movement is not as widely known its influence arguably extends to the hip hop feminist movement. The chapter closes with a discussion of the ways in which hip hop feminists have controversially remixed or synthesized their own homespun feminism or womanism with the contributions of black (among other nonwhite) feminists of previous generations and, consequently, they have come to create a feminism and Women's Liberation movement that speaks to the special needs of the women of the hip hop generation.

ON HIP HOP FEMINISTS' FOREMOTHERS: BLACK RADICAL FEMINISTS AND THE BLACK WOMEN'S LIBERATION MOVEMENT

As of late there has been a great deal of discussion concerning African American women's alienation and ill-treatment within the Civil Rights, Black Power, and Women's Liberation movements. Recent research has demonstrated that many black women were participants in the aforementioned widely recognized movements, as well as their own often unrecognized movement: the black Women's Liberation movement. As with any other social movement, the black Women's Liberation movement of the 1960s and 1970s had major objectives, organizations, activists, theorists, and themes. In this section I will briefly discuss the black Women's Liberation movement with an eye on its acknowledged and often unacknowledged contributions to the hip hop feminist movement.

Similar to the hip hop feminist movement, it is important to acknowledge that not all of the women who participated in the black Women's Liberation movement self-identified as feminists. However, whether they identified as black feminists, womanists, women's liberationists or not, it is important to emphasize that their collective goal was *black women's empowerment*, the liberation of all black people (which, of course, includes black men) and humanity as a whole, as well as a radical reconstruction of social relations and a radical redistribution of political power (V. V. Gordon, 1985; Radford-Hill, 2000; Solomon, 1989). Neither the Civil Rights movement, nor the Black Power movement, nor the white Women's Liberation movement, nor the New Left movement adequately focused on black women's decolonization and liberation. As the Civil Rights movement began its decline and transition into the Black Power movement in the mid-1960s, African American women witnessed the rise of an unrelenting black nationalist masculinism accompanied by a rhetoric of revolution and black liberation that, at best, quarantined black women to "traditional" gender roles and, at worst, excluded their life-worlds and life-struggles from the Black Power agenda altogether.

As the Civil Rights movement came to a close black women were increasingly being relegated to supportive roles behind the scenes, and with the rise of black nationalist masculinist rhetoric during the early years of the Black Power movement they came to understand that the black male leaders of the movement, essentially in response to the infamous 1965 Moynihan report, wanted black women to embrace "traditional" gender roles based on white middle-class conceptions of womanhood and motherhood. The Moynihan report disreputably revealed that the African American family was dominated and deformed by "black matriarchs" who, in essence, emasculated black men because they, black women, supposedly had more economic power and greater access to social resources as a result of their greater employment opportunities in mid-twentieth-century America (D. C. Carter, 2009; Herring, 1997; J. T. Patterson, 2010).

The Moynihan report blamed the "disorganization" and "pathology" of the black family on the emergence of a matriarchal culture that reached back to black life on Southern plantations during the antebellum era. Moynihan attributed the dogged continuation of black matriarchy in mid-twentieth-century America, most readily revealed in single-mother-headed households, to poverty, promiscuity, and crime because, he boldly proclaimed, it both demoralized African American men and deformed their "natural" male leadership (i.e., patriarchal) instincts. In order to relieve this "crushing burden on the Negro male" and, in so many words, to restore his patriarchal instincts, Moynihan mused, young black men needed to be quarantined to "an utterly masculine world . . . away from women," going so far as to suggest that a tour of duty in Vietnam just might suffice. As to be expected, the Moynihan report was widely criticized and heatedly debated within the black community but, as the hypermasculinism and misogyny of the Black Power movement attests, many black men heartily concurred that strong-willed and assertive African American women usurped what little authority they had within and without the black community and, therefore, black women had indeed emasculated black men.[4]

In hindsight, it is easy to see how the Moynihan report helped to deepen and further develop pretensions toward patriarchy already running rampant within the mostly male-led and male-dominated Civil Rights movement. The black nationalists of the Black Power movement, like legions of black nationalists before them, were inclined to embrace patriarchal views and values, and many frequently put their misogyny on full display. The black nationalist masculinists of the Black Power movement regularly argued that it was time for black women to help "the black man" reclaim his mangled manhood by being subordinate, supportive, and submissive helpmates. Ironically, the black masculinist reaction to the Moynihan report failed to take into consideration the fact that the study also quite clearly stated that black women were the most economically impoverished group in the United States at the time (D. Harris, 2001; Springer, 2006; R. Y. Williams, 2006). It made no matter to the black nationalist masculinists, it was "the black man's time to shine!" Needless to say, black women, especially those with womanist sensibilities, rejected both Civil Rights and Black Power male leaders' attempts to confine them to stereotypical, behind-the-scenes "female tasks," such as secretarial work, cooking, cleaning, and bearing and raising children (i.e., "young warriors" for the black revolution).

Where black women encountered issues revolving around sexism and hypermasculinism in the Civil Rights and Black Power movements, in the white Women's Liberation movement they were confronted with what social movement sociologist Steven Buechler (1990) has termed white feminists' "race and class unconsciousness" (p. 134). White feminists' "race and class unconsciousness" caused many black women to shun feminism, and others who identified as feminists to be extremely reluctant to participate in a Women's Liberation movement that was destined to liberate white middle-class women only. Black women were as constricted on account of racism and capitalism as they were on account of sexism, and they understood white feminists' "race and class unconsciousness" as yet another reminder of the yawning chasm between black and white women's life-worlds and life-struggles. Besides, many black feminists asserted, joining the white Women's Liberation movement would be another double-duty for black women in that they would have to constantly deconstruct and reconstruct white feminist issues and (re)educate white feminists about black women's lived-experiences and lived-endurances, especially as they revolve around the political economy of anti-black racism in a simultaneously white supremacist, patriarchal, and capitalist society (Giardina, 2010; Randolph, 2009; Valk, 2008).

In *The Trouble Between Us: An Uneasy History of White and Black Women in the Feminist Movement*, feminist sociologist Winifred Breines (2006) broaches the subject of "feminist racism," going so far as to say that by the late 1960s "[f]eminist racist attitudes and racial bias had led to such a narrow conception of women's discrimination and liberation, of gender, that African American women could not see themselves in the movement" (pp. 6, 8). Of course, there were some white feminist organizations that were anti-racist and who openly acknowledged the racial and class differences between black and white women. In fact, Breines herself was a member of the famed Boston socialist feminist group Bread and Roses. Yet and still, she audaciously admitted that many whites who look back on their participation in both the Civil Rights and Women's Liberation movements often do so with what she termed "white nostalgia." Revealingly reflecting of her discovery of her own "white nostalgia," Breines bravely wrote:

> It was beyond my comprehension that whites who were opposed to racism could be unconsciously racist. The idea had not yet crossed my mind that white people, members of the dominant, privileged group, including even those who want to reject their privilege, inevitably absorb their group's attitudes—which means they are arrogant and ignorant despite themselves. Because black people called it to their attention, white people learned that they live as white people—that simply by being white we are granted privileges not granted to African Americans or people of other races and ethnic backgrounds. The heart of the issue, what white radical feminists had to deal with, was that racism, or its absence, is not only a matter of personal intention. It is also a social structural system that works subconsciously in individuals. Black feminists consistently confronted their white sisters, saying, "Look at this, you have to do something about the stereotypes and prejudice at work in you whether or not you are aware of them." Although they tried mightily, movement activists in the second half of the twentieth century could not evade the history of whites' enslavement of blacks and the dreadful story of racial oppression in which white women have colluded since. (pp. 10–11)

Breines' brave words here help to drive home the point that what has frequently been referred to as black women's "ambivalence" toward feminism is not so much an ambivalence toward feminism as it is a critical rejection of *anti-black racist feminism* or, rather, "feminist racism"—and that is whether white feminist are conscious of their racism or not. This, of course, brings us right back to Buechler's conception of white feminists' "race and class unconsciousness." For black and other nonwhite women active during the 1960s and 1970s, women's liberation was inextricable from the fight for racial and economic justice, and they resented white feminists' privileging the eradication of sexism over that of racism and classism. In the late 1960s as black women began to self-identify and organize as feminists they offered a number of critiques regarding white feminists "race and class unconsciousness."

First, black feminists maintained that the white Women's Liberation movement lacked an understanding of the ways in which racism, sexism, and capitalism intersected in, and simultaneously impacted black women's life-worlds and life-struggles. That the white feminist agenda omitted the other major forms of oppression and exploitation that direly affected black women was a sure sign, from the black feminists' perspective, that the white Women's Liberation movement was as insensitive to black women's needs as were the black nationalist masculinists leading the Black Power movement. Neither white feminists' race nor class unconsciousness was excusable from black feminists' point of view (G. I. Joseph, 1981; Joseph and Lewis, 1981; D. K. King, 1988; D. K. Lewis, 1977).

Second, and deeply connected to the critique of white feminists' "race and class unconsciousness," was black feminists' critique of white feminists' liberal-reformist politics, which the black feminists believed privileged middle-class white women's more or less intra-cultural issues over the urgent economic needs of nonwhite women, especially black women. For instance, black feminists were critical of what they perceived to be white feminists' obsession with *their* body image, *their* sexual freedom, and *their* getting equal pay for equal work without in any substantial way acknowledging that black women, whether feminist or not, were still struggling to obtain bare necessities, such as food, clothing, shelter, education, and health care. Many black feminists criticized white feminists' call for abortion on demand by observing that from their point of view the larger issue was that all women's reproductive rights should be respected, and that is above and beyond the issue of abortion on demand. White feminists' racial and economic privilege was even more apparent when their call for abortion on demand was contrasted with the black feminist reproductive rights agenda that pointed to black women's long history of involuntary sterilization, the life-struggles that pressure working-poor black women to abort, and the historical fact that women on welfare have been frequently forced by the government to have abortions and get on birth control (Avery, 1990; A. Y. Davis, 1990; National Black Women's Health Project, 1990; Rutherford, 1992; Beverly Smith, 1990; A. Walker, 1990).

In addition to involuntary sterilizations and coerced abortions, as Harriet Washington astutely observed in *Medical Apartheid: The Dark History of Medical Experimentation on Black Americans from Colonial Times to the Present* (2006), it is important to raise the issue of the horrid history of medical experimentation on black and other nonwhite women.[5] Obviously the struggle for black and poor women's reproductive rights was marred by the very same racist patriarchal capitalist U.S. political economy that gender oppressed but racially and economically privileged white feminists and blinded them to the impact that the interlocking systems of racial, gender, and class oppression had on black women's reproductive rights and their ragged relationship to the medical industry. Insofar as the black feminists of the 1960s and 1970s were concerned, white feminists' calls for women's solidarity and sisterhood were nothing more than empty rhetoric until they (i.e., white feminists) were willing to struggle against racism and capitalism with the same tough-talk and tenacity with which they battled patriarchy (Amos and Parmar, 2005; Carby, 1996; Joseph and Lewis, 1981; Roth, 1999a).

Finally, black feminists' last major point of contention with white feminists revolved around their differing conceptions of, and experiences within the family. Where white feminists struggled to disrupt the nuclear family, black women felt that the black family was being assaulted from every side as a result of the Moynihan report and other forms of anti-black racism. It was as if white feminists were working to attack and destroy the family at the very same time that black feminists, and black women in general, were attempting to protect and rebuild the family—although, it should be emphasized, black feminists' vision of the black family greatly differed from the male-centered and male-dominated version of the black family as espoused by the black nationalist masculinists of the Black Power movement. On the one hand, for many white women family obligations were a major source of their oppression and exploitation (Heath and Ciscel, 1988; Holmstrom, 1982; Hooyman and Gonyea, 1995; K. B. Jones, 1988; Landes, 1977; Lloyd, Few, and Allen, 2009; E. Reed, 1975; Thorne and Yalom, 1992). On the other hand, for most black women their family settings provided one of the few spaces where they found themselves relatively free from anti-black racism, although often they still had to contend with in-house sexism. In this sense, many black women perceived of the family as an imperfect institution but, yet and still, as a sort of sanctuary where they were shielded from racism even though they continued to endure a peculiar form of "black patriarchy" (Amoo-Adare, 2006; Dill, 1994; Hane, 1999; R. L. Jarrett, 1994; Landry, 2000; Rose, 2003).

It is relatively easy to see why middle-class white feminists' desire to work outside of their homes did not connect with the bulk of black women. This was so, in part, because there has never been a time in U.S. history where black women were not working, both within and without their homes, and experiencing economic exploitation: from the period of African American enslavement all the way through to the present (Harley, 2002; J. Jones, 1985; D. G. White, 1985). What the white feminists of the 1960s and 1970s failed to comprehend was that their experience of the family, although extremely oppressive and exploitive, was still predicated on racial and economic privilege when compared with the experiences of nonwhite women and, truth be told, it is always easier to advocate reforming or destroying an institution when you have the racial and economic support of an extremely powerful social and political system (i.e., the U.S. government and the wider white society). White feminists also failed to consider that because black women historically have been and remain one of the most poverty-stricken groups in the United States, not only do they not have the kinds of institutional support (i.e., racial privilege) that white women do, they do not have the economic resources (i.e., class privilege) available to buy themselves out of family obligations by hiring other (usually poor, nonwhite) women to do their housework for them, as has been a longstanding custom among upper- and middle-class white women (Bounds, Brubaker, and Hobgood, 1999; Durr and Hill, 2006; R. Y. Williams, 2004).

Hence, here we see that black women were more or less sympathetic to certain aspects of the white feminist agenda (particularly their critique of patriarchy and misogyny), but extremely disappointed with white feminists' insensitivity toward and inattention to white women's participation in, and perpetuation of anti-black racism and nonwhite women's economic exploitation. Obviously black women's alleged "ambivalence" toward feminism and their reluctance to organizing within (or, actually, even with) the white Women's Liberation movement was based on what they perceived to be white feminists' bias toward middle-class white women's issues and the liberal-reformist feminist politics that emerged from white feminists' preoccupation with middle-class white women's issues. Black women questioned the relevance of joining white feminist groups, and a larger white Women's Liberation movement, that seemed obsessed with combating sexism but unable to critically comprehend (and confront) the interlocking and overlapping nature of racism, sexism, and capitalism in black (and other nonwhite) women's life-worlds and life-struggles. This means, then, that black feminists were critical of the middle-class bias in both the Black Power and white Women's Liberation movements, and their newfound politics, what Kimberly Springer (2001) has dubbed their "interstitial politics," drew from the Black Power movement's critique of anti-black racism and the white Women's Liberation movement's critique of sexism, as well as the New Left movement's critique of U.S. capitalism. The black Women's Liberation movement articulated a radical political theory that was arguably the first to explicitly advocate an intersectional critique of racism, sexism, and capitalism (and, later, heterosexism) (P. H. Collins, 2000; A. Y. Davis, 1981; hooks, 1981; Roth, 1999a; Springer, 1999, 2006).

It should be observed here that the foregoing analysis challenges the flat-footed notion that black women were so mesmerized and brainwashed by the radical rhetoric of the black nationalist masculinists of the Black Power movement that there was, as Joreen Freeman put it in *The Politics of Women's Liberation* (1975), an "ideological barrier" blocking black women from becoming feminists and joining the Women's Liberation movement (pp. 37–43). Even though Freeman over-simplified, her work at the very least enables us to examine how the relationship between the black men and black women of the Black Power generation impacted black women's conception(s) of feminism and their relationship with the Women's Liberation movement. Admittedly, there were definitely "ideological barriers" put into place by the black nationalist masculinists of the Black Power movement that conceptually constrained and inhibited black women from teaming up with the white Women's Liberation movement (see V. V. Gordon, 1985; Joseph and Lewis, 1981; Solomon, 1989). However, as discussed above, it is equally as important to observe that white feminists' privileging of the eradication of gender oppression over that of racial and class oppression rubbed black and other nonwhite women the wrong way and, therefore, also represented an often overlooked "ideological barrier" that helps to further highlight why black women have seemed "ambivalent" toward white feminism and the white Women's Liberation movement. What I am more interested in here is not so much how the black male leaders of the Black Power movement and the white female leaders of the Women's Liberation movement placed "ideological barriers" in black women's way, but the fact that black women developed their own distinct discursive formations and discursive practices that enabled them to deconstruct the "ideological barriers" before them and inaugurate their own insurgent intersectional forms of feminism, womanism and, even more, Women's Liberation movement.

Instead of genuflecting to white feminists' gender obsession, and rather than kowtowing to the radical rhetoric of black nationalist masculinists, black women mobilized their own insurgent intersectional movement. As Benita Roth's *Separate Roads to Feminism: Black, Chicana, and White Feminist Movements in America's Second Wave* (2004) and Kimberly Springer's *Living for the Revolution: Black Feminist Organizations, 1968–1980* (2005) reveal, between 1966 and 1980 black women established a number of autonomous black women-led and black women-centered organizations, including the Black Women's Liberation Committee of SNCC, which broke away from SNCC in 1968 to form an independent group initially named the Black Women's Alliance and later the Third World Women's Alliance (1968–1980); the National Black Feminist Organization (1973–1975); the National Alliance of Black Feminists (1976–1980); the Combahee River Collective (1975–1980); and Black Women Organized for Action (1973–1980). There were also important debates and critical discussions concerning black women's liberation that were undertaken within organizations not commonly perceived as sites for "feminist" or "womanist" mobilization, such as the Black Panther Party, the National Welfare Rights Organization, and the National Domestic Workers Union.

Along with establishing activist-oriented organizations, the black women of the 1960s and 1970s black Women's Liberation movement also discursively developed black feminist theory and praxis to speak to their special needs. For instance, the polymathic Toni Cade Bambara published her seminal edited volume, *The Black Woman*, in 1970; the Third World Women's Alliance published a newspaper, *Triple Jeopardy*, at least ten times between 1971 and 1975; Black Women Organized for Action published a monthly newsletter regularly between 1973 and 1980; in April of 1977 Barbara Smith, Beverly Smith, and Demita Frazier issued their groundbreaking "Combahee River Collective Statement"; and, evolving out of the Combahee River Collective's Black Women's Network retreats, in 1980 Barbara Smith, Audre Lorde, and Cherríe Moraga, among others, co-founded Kitchen Table Women of Color Press, which published pioneering nonwhite feminist texts, such as *All the Women Are White, All the Men Are Black, but Some of Us Are Brave* (1982) edited by Gloria Hull, Patricia Bell Scott, and Barbara Smith; *Home Girls: A Black Feminist Anthology* (1983) edited by Barbara Smith; and *This Bridge Called My Back: Writings by Radical Women of Color* (1984) edited by Cherríe Moraga and Gloria Anzaldúa.[6] Several recurring themes surfaced in the writings of black and other nonwhite feminists of the late 1960s, 1970s, and early 1980s that demonstrate their distinct deconstruction and reconstruction of the concept of consciousness-raising and the personal-as-political model: an emphasis on the intersection of race, gender, and class oppression as the only viable way to critically analyze and adequately articulate the lived-experiences and lived-endurances of black and other nonwhite women; the "feminist racism" and "race and class unconsciousness" of the white Women's Liberation movement; homophobia and heterosexism; domestic violence; rape; reproductive rights; healthcare; political prisoners; alternative and women-centered education; and, nonwhite women's leadership and activism, among others.

As stated above, the Third World Women's Alliance (TWWA) evolved out of SNCC's Black Women's Liberation Committee (Fleming, 2001; Third World Women's Alliance, 1970; S. Ward, 2006). Initially known as the Black Women's Alliance, the group shared SNCC's anti-imperialist and Pan-Africanist politics, but felt that SNCC was weak where the critique of patriarchy was concerned. Frances Beal, one of the founders of the TWWA, asserted that she and the other women who established the TWWA were accused of being "divisive" and brainwashed by white feminists. However, Beal and her black feminist comrades begged to differ, with Beal going so far as to say, "[w]e actually saw our feminism emerging from our personal lives and from our experiences in terms of taking up the struggle against racism" (quoted in Roth, 2004, p. 90). The lived-experiences and lived-endurances of the women of the TWWA led them to develop theory and praxis that clearly distinguished their "interstitial" politics from the politics of both the black nationalist masculinists leading SNCC and other black freedom organizations during the late 1960s and the white feminists leading the Women's Liberation movement of the late 1960s (Springer, 2001). Much more than merely critiquing racism à la black nationalist masculinists and sexism à la white feminists, according to Roth (2004), the TWWA was arguably the first organization to establish "the concept of black feminist organizing as intersectional" (p. 91).

In "Double Jeopardy: To Be Black and Female," undoubtedly the most influential document the TWWA published (originally published in 1970 in both Toni Cade Bambara's collection *The Black Woman* and Ruth Morgan's *Sisterhood Is Powerful* anthology), Beal (1995) articulated an early version of intersectional politics that simultaneously critiqued anti-black racism, black males' sexism, white feminists' racism, the racist and sexist character of U.S. capitalism, and both black nationalist masculinists and white feminists' adoption of "the white middle-class model" of manhood and womanhood (p. 147). She intrepidly announced, "[w]e unqualitatively [*sic*] reject these respective models." We witness here, then, that Beal's conception of consciousness-raising, rather than being exclusive to black women only, extended to white women and black men, especially critically dialoguing with white feminists and black nationalist masculinists, as will be seen below. In fact, a great deal of "Double Jeopardy" was aimed at revealing the ways in which the interlocking systems of racial, gender, and class oppression colonized all notions of femininity and masculinity in the United States. Speaking directly to black men, she asserted, it is "fallacious reasoning that in order for the black man to be strong, the black woman has to be weak" (p. 148). Beal and the TWWA called into question the black nationalist masculinists' vision of black liberation and, even more, what it meant to be a black revolutionary. With words that were surely shunned by the black nationalist masculinists of the Black Power movement, Beal boldly rebuked with words laced with a heartfelt radical humanism:

A people's revolution that engages the participation of every member of the community, including man, woman, and child, brings about a certain transformation in the participants as a result of this participation. Once you have caught a glimpse of freedom or experienced a bit of self-determination, you can't go back to old routines that were established under a racist, capitalist regime. . . . This will mean changing the traditional routines that we have established as a result of living in a totally corrupting society. . . . If we are going to liberate ourselves as a people, it must be recognized that black women have very specific problems that have to be spoken to. . . . Those who consider themselves to be revolutionary must begin to deal with other revolutionaries as equals. And so far as I know, revolutionaries are not determined by sex. (p. 154)

Here, Beal puts the premium on what it means to be a black revolutionary. In so many words, she let the black nationalist masculinists know that they did not have a monopoly on black radical politics and revolutionary social movements. Her theory of black revolution was unapologetically inclusive, welcoming the "participation of every member of the community, including man, woman, and child," where the black nationalist masculinists' oft-articulated theory of black revolution might more properly be termed "the black man's revolution" or, rather, a revolution for black men's liberation. For Beal and the TWWA, all black nationalist men were not at fault or the enemy, they understood, as Robin Kelley wrote in *Freedom Dreams: The Black Radical Imagination* (2002), "not all black nationalist men were hopelessly sexist. On the contrary, some openly challenged sexist statements, rejected talk of polygamy and mothering for the nation, and fought for real gender equality" (pp. 142–43).[7] The black revolution that Beal and the TWWA envisioned, as with any real revolution, would create a dialectical relationship between the *self-transformation* of the participant and the *social transformation* of the larger society and wider world.

Shifting her critique from black nationalist men's sexism, bourgeois notions of womanhood, and bogus theory of "the black man's revolution" to white feminists' "race and class unconsciousness" and liberal-reformist bourgeois politics, Beal (1995) further demonstrated the distinctiveness of early black feminist interstitial politics, openly acknowledging that the white Women's Liberation movement "is far from being monolithic" (p. 153). Indeed, there are "certain comparisons one can make between" the lived-experiences and lived-endurances of black and white women. However, she quickly quipped, "[a]ny white group that does not have an anti-imperialist and antiracist ideology has absolutely nothing in common with the black woman's struggle." From Beal and the TWWA's point of view, white feminists basically saw the bulk of their oppression emanating from "male chauvinism." Black and other nonwhite women had to contend with much more than "male chauvinism." There was also the issue of racism, as well as that of the extra-exploitation of nonwhite women's labor under capitalism. In fact, Beal went so far as to explicitly articulate that it was not simply the critique of racism and anti-racist struggle that distinguished the black Women's Liberation movement from the white Women's Liberation movement, but also many black and other nonwhite feminists staunch critique of the racist *and* sexist character of U.S. capitalism. In her own weighted words,

Another major differentiation is that the white Women's Liberation movement is basically middle class. Very few of these women suffer the extreme economic exploitation that most black women are subjected to day by day. This is the factor that is most crucial for us. It is not an intellectual persecution alone; it is not an intellectual outburst for us; it is quite real. We as black women have got to deal with the problems that the black masses deal with, for our problems in reality are one and the same. If the white groups do not realize that they are in fact fighting capitalism and racism, we do not have common bonds. If they do not realize that the reasons for their condition lie in the system and not simply that men get a vicarious pleasure out of "consuming their bodies for exploitative reasons" . . . , then we cannot unite with them around common grievances or even discuss these groups in a serious manner because they're completely irrelevant to the black struggle. (p. 153)

Emphasis must be placed on Beal's last point, and that is that many of the middle-class white women's issues that seemed to preoccupy so many white feminist groups were "completely irrelevant to the black struggle." Just as they challenged the black nationalist masculinists' narrow conception of black liberation, Beal and the TWWA disputed white feminists' more or less liberal racist and bourgeois theory of women's liberation. The emerging intersectional politics of the black Women's Liberation movement was aimed at the "elimination of all forms of oppression," not merely anti-black racism (à la the black nationalist masculinists) or sexism (à la the white feminists). Invoking the names and echoing the words of Harriet Tubman, Sojourner Truth, Mary McLeod Bethune, and Fannie Lou Hamer, Beal audaciously asserted that "the exploitation of black people and women works to everyone's disadvantage" and "the liberation of these two groups is a stepping-stone to the liberation of all oppressed people in this country and around the world" (p. 150). It is important here to observe the larger, radical humanist impulse at the heart of black feminist intersectional politics and the wider black Women's Liberation movement.

Beal and the TWWA did not advocate for the liberation of black and other nonwhite women only, or poor black and other nonwhite women only, or bourgeois black and other nonwhite women only, but instead they fought for the liberation of humanity as a whole. What is more, their theory of revolution and liberation, on radical humanist principle, refused to place the critique of racism over the critique of sexism or capitalism, or vice versa. Their intersectional theory of revolution and liberation—again, distinguished from those being put forward by black nationalist masculinists, white feminists, and New Left white masculinists at the time—critiqued and combated racism and capitalism, all the while incessantly arguing that "[u]nless women in any enslaved nation are completely liberated, the change cannot really be called a revolution" (p. 154). In order for an authentic revolution to be brought into being racism and capitalism must be fought right alongside of sexism (among other forms of imperialism), and this means, then, that the glaring disparities between "the white haves and the nonwhite have-nots" needs to be acknowledged, as does the "white skin privilege of the white workers" (pp. 150–51). Even at this early stage black feminist politics was insurgently intersectional insofar as it did not simply add a critique of anti-black racism to the white feminist agenda, as is so often surmised, but it developed a new multiperspectival political paradigm that went above and beyond the white feminist agenda by simultaneously critiquing and combating racism, sexism, and capitalism.

Early black feminist intersectional politics was not free from self-reflexive, constructive criticism, which significantly contributed to its ongoing evolution. As the black Women's Liberation movement blossomed in the 1970s, two national organizations were founded: the National Black Feminist

Organization (NBFO) and the National Alliance of Black Feminists (NABF). Similar to the Combahee River Collective (CRC), which will be discussed in detail below, the NABF grew out of the NBFO, therefore the centrality of the NBFO should be recognized. Emerging out of black women's consciousness-raising sessions held in New York City in 1973, similar to Beal and the TWWA, the NBFO began by exploring what feminism had to offer to black women. Early on they engaged the alleged "ideological barrier" between black women and feminism, questioning whether their embrace of feminist theory and praxis would help or harm the larger black liberation movement. Through subsequent consciousness-raising sessions, primarily led by Margaret Sloan and Eleanor Holmes Norton, they came to highlight the *racially gendered* and impoverished nature of black women's life-worlds and life-struggles, even within the Black Power and Women's Liberation movements. The discovery of their common lived-experiences and lived-endurances prompted them to organize the NBFO.

. Although the NBFO was short-lived, from 1973 to 1975, part of its significance lies in the fact that it provided a national forum for black women to (re)define feminism to speak to their special needs. The NBFO argued that far from turning their backs on confronting anti-black racism, by coming into critical dialogue with the larger Women's Liberation movement they would actually infuse it with radical anti-racist politics and expand its focus to include much more than gender oppression, middle-class white women's issues, and "male chauvinism." It is important to observe that black women who identified as feminists expended a great deal of time and energy defending themselves against attacks as a result of their commitment to combating sexism.

In the landmark work *Living for the Revolution*, Kimberly Springer (2005) reveals that both the NBFO and its Chicago-area offshoot the NABF "repeatedly revisit[ed] the argument of whether to associate with feminism while trying to establish their own organizations" (p. 80). She continued, "[t]hose against using feminist in the organization's name predicted that they would spend too much time defending their name against those who thought feminists were antimale. Proponents of feminism maintained that feminism was profemale, not antimale, and worth asserting from the outset" (p. 80). The NBFO and NABF's argument that feminism is "profemale, not antimale" not only speaks to the radical humanism at the heart of black feminism and the larger black Women's Liberation movement, but it is also an argument that has been handed down to hip hop feminists, as will be seen below.

The Boston chapter of the NBFO felt that the parent organization failed to articulate a clear critique of capitalist political economy and, therefore, the NBFO was not speaking to the economic issues effecting the majority of black women who were poor and extremely poverty-stricken. They also took issue with the NBFO's heteronormative feminist politics, which did not adequately speak to black lesbian feminist issues and experiences, not simply with black nationalist men, but with the larger black community. Consequently, in 1974 the more radical Boston branch of the NBFO broke with the national organization to form the Combahee River Collective (CRC). The name of the new organization was chosen to commemorate a military campaign that the radical black abolitionist Harriet Tubman led during the Civil War, which resulted in the emancipation of more than 750 enslaved Africans. As a matter of fact, Tubman's Combahee River campaign in South Carolina was the only one led by a woman during the Civil War (Bell-Scott, 1999; Clinton, 2004; Combahee River Movement, 1982; Lowry, 2007; Barbara Smith, 1993, 1998).

The CRC built on and went beyond the NBFO by mobilizing an even more intersectional and inclusive black feminist movement that was open to, and addressed the needs of all black women irrespective of social class or sexual orientation. In the 1977 classic "A Black Feminist Statement," CRC founding members Barbara Smith, Beverly Smith, and Demita Frazier stated that they became "an independent collective since we had serious disagreements with NBFO's bourgeois-feminist stance and their lack of a clear political focus" (Combahee River Collective, 1982, p. 20). The CRC was unapologetically socialist, although they did not believe socialism was a panacea for racism, sexism, and heterosexism. Socialism, they argued, might remedy black women's extra-exploitation as a result of capitalism, but it would not, and was not created to, eradicate other super-structural and interlocking forms of oppression, such as the racial, gender, and sexual domination and discrimination that impact black women's—especially black lesbians'—lifeworlds and life-struggles. After critically dialoguing with white socialist feminists and attending the 1976 National Socialist Feminist Conference, the CRC asserted, "despite the narrowness of the ideology that was promoted at that particular conference, we became more aware of the need for us to understand our own economic situation and to make our own economic analysis" (p. 20). They, therefore, did not uncritically accept white women's conceptions of feminism or socialist feminism. Announcing their insurgent intersectional politics, the CRC distinguished their political theory and praxis from other black feminist organizations, as well as white feminist, black nationalist masculinist, and New Left masculinist organizations:

> The most general statement of our politics at the present time would be that we are actively committed to struggling against racial, sexual, heterosexual, and class oppression and see as our particular task the development of integrated analysis and practice based upon the fact that the major systems of oppression are interlocking. The synthesis of these oppressions creates the conditions of our lives. As black women we see feminism as the logical political movement to combat the manifold and simultaneous oppressions that all women of color face. (p. 13)

We witness here, then, that the CRC's black radical feminism simultaneously critiqued capitalism, racism, sexism, and heterosexism. As illustrated by their participation in the National Socialist Feminist Conference and their subsequent commitment to "understand[ing] our own economic situation and to make our own economic analysis," their political theory was obviously elastic and open to change. Eschewing narrow-minded, ideological interpretations of feminism, the CRC's political theory was informed by their praxis and the process of entrenched intersectional struggle. They understood that open-ended struggle, and especially struggling on many different fronts, would inevitably produce new theories, new praxes, and perhaps even new identities. They were especially cognizant of their unprivileged position as black lesbian socialist feminists, contending that the "major difference in our political work is that we are not just trying to fight oppression on one front or even two, but instead to address a whole range of oppressions. We do not have racial, sexual, heterosexual, or class privilege to rely upon, nor do we have even the minimal access to resources and power that groups who possess any one of these types of privileges have" (p. 18).

The CRC's cognizance of their unprivileged sociopolitical position as black lesbian socialist feminists ultimately led them to articulate a theory of revolution and liberation that emerged out of black women's lived-experiences and lived-endurances as, quite literally, the opposite of the white bourgeois heterosexual males who have for centuries dominated and deformed American culture, politics, and society. The CRC vowed to use their "position at the bottom . . . to make a clear leap into revolutionary action. If black women were free, it would mean that everyone else would have to be free since our freedom would necessitate the destruction of all the systems of oppression" (p. 18). The CRC's conception of black feminist politics complicated both white and conventional black feminist politics because they not only challenged what it meant to be a *feminist*, but also what it meant to be a *black feminist*. The CRC's awareness of the innovative nature of their insurgent intersectional politics is evident in the famous passage in which they acknowledge their extension and expansion of the feminist slogan "the personal is political":

> A political contribution that we feel we have already made is the expansion of the feminist principle that the personal is political. In our consciousness-raising sessions, for example, we have in many ways gone beyond white women's revelations because we are dealing with the implications of race and class as well as sex. . . . We have spent a great deal of energy delving into the cultural and experiential nature of our oppression out of necessity because none of these matters have ever been looked at before. No one before has ever examined the multilayered texture of black women's lives. (p. 17)

In a way, the CRC called into question both the "personal" and the "political," extending and expanding these categories beyond white bourgeois and black feminist heteronormative conceptions. As they correctly contended, "[n]o one before has ever examined the multilayered texture of black women's lives," especially not black lesbians' lives. Based on the above discussion of the origin and evolution of the black Women's Liberation movement of the late-1960s and 1970s it would appear that we have before us several central themes. First, and most obvious, is the critique of misogyny and patriarchy, which clearly connects their ideas and actions with the wider 1960s and 1970s Women's Liberation movement. Black women's liberationists did not merely critique the male supremacy of "the white man," but they also critiqued the pretensions to male supremacy on the part of the black nationalist masculinists leading the Black Power movement, as well as black men more generally. A second major theme is centered around the recurring critique of anti-black racism specifically, and white supremacy more generally. Black women's liberationists' critique of the "feminist racism" of the white Women's Liberation movement represents an important advance in nonwhite women's feminist theory insofar as it demonstrates their willingness to work with white feminists and their principled unwillingness to accept anti-black racism, however "unconscious" or subtle.

Another major theme that can be gathered from the above discussion of the black Women's Liberation movement involves black women's liberationists' critique of capitalism, class struggle, the political economy of anti-black racism, and the economic exploitation of nonwhite women at the hands of white women. This is an extremely important issue that seems to have only intensified over time, as currently many hip hop feminists' work speaks to nonwhite women's ongoing frustrations with most contemporary white feminists' "race and class unconsciousness" and unwillingness to acknowledge their race and class privilege when compared with the impoverished life-worlds and life-struggles of most nonwhite women. A direct discursive link can be shown to run between Frances Beal and the BWA/TWWA's intensely increasing black/multi-racial feminist socialism and the black lesbian socialist feminist radical politics of the Combahee River Collective. This brings us to the last major theme that should be noted, it encompasses the ways in which some black women—especially the members of the Combahee River Collective—raised the issue of the heteronormativity, as well as the homophobia and heterosexism, of most feminist thought and practice during the 1960s and 1970s Women's Liberation movement. Heterosexual women, to reiterate the CRC's position, do not have a monopoly on feminism, just as heterosexual men and women do not have a monopoly on hip hop culture, as was discussed in chapter 2. Taken together, then, the overarching contributions of the 1960s and 1970s black Women's Liberation movement to contemporary forms of feminism, not simply hip hop feminism, revolves around its innovative dialectical deconstruction and reconstruction of the "personal is political" paradigm into a more insurgent, inclusive, and intersectional feminist theory and praxis.

As this section has demonstrated, the black Women's Liberation movement of the late 1960s and 1970s was multidimensional and multiperspectival, not monolithic, and, or so it seems, a similar radical political and discursive diversity marks the hip hop feminist movement. Before turning to the hip hop feminist movement, however, it will be beneficial for us to very briefly engage the work of the black women artists who drew from and indelibly influenced the Feminist Art movement. Although often overlooked, these women's artistry provides several paradigms for what it means to be a black feminist artist-activist, a model very much in vogue within the hip hop feminist movement.

AESTHETIC APARTHEID: RACIAL AND GENDER SEGREGATION, THE FEMINIST ARTIST-ACTIVIST ARCHETYPE, AND THE FEMINIST ART MOVEMENT

The overlap between the Black Power, Black Arts, black Women's Liberation, and Feminist Art movements seems relatively apparent in hindsight (Bobo, 1995, 2001; Hassan, 1997; Pinder, 2002). However, from the late 1960s through to the late 1970s few concrete connections were made between the ways in which the radical politics of the black and white Women's Liberation movements impacted the work of black women artists. It is virtually undeniable that the black and white women who participated in the Women's Liberation movement shared similar conceptions of a world free from patriarchy and misogyny, where women could develop to their fullest potential, on their own terms, and in their own time.

As discussed above, for the most part black and white feminists struggled against patriarchy in linked but parallel Women's Liberation movements. They sought solidarity with, and to mobilize those they understood to be their kith and kin in order to disrupt and ultimately destroy unjust (especially patriarchal) power relations. They also struggled for the radical redistribution of social wealth and political power, as well as to validate and legitimate women's life-worlds and lived-experiences on women-centered—as opposed to male supremacist—terms. However, it is important to come back to the notion that the black and white feminists of the 1960s and 1970s essentially worked in "linked but parallel women's liberation movements" as a result of, as discussed above, what was perceived as the "race and class unconsciousness" and "feminist racism" of the white Women's Liberation movement and black women's acute emphasis on the critique of racism and classism. Where many white feminists understood their central struggle to be against patriarchy, many black feminists, at the very least, understood their central struggle to be against white supremacy *and* patriarchy. Even though they critiqued different aspects of imperialism from comparably different angles, and considering the divergent strategies and tactics they employed in identifying problems and offering up solutions, it is important to bear in mind that much like many of the other movements of the 1960s and 1970s, black and white feminists envisioned a similar end result for their respective movements: social, political, and psychological liberation and a world free from exploitation, oppression, and violence.

As the cultural corollaries of the Black Power and Women's Liberation movements, it could be said that the Black Arts and Feminist Art movements had similar, if not shared, aesthetic attributes, propensities, strategies, tactics, and objectives. Similar to the sociopolitical movements from within which they emerged, the Black Arts and Feminist Art movements were "linked but parallel" cultural aesthetic movements in which only a few black feminists, womanists, and black women who identified as neither feminist nor womanist drew from and importantly contributed to, were influenced by, and significantly impacted. Perhaps the most noteworthy black feminist artists and aesthetes whose work, whether consciously or unconsciously, build bridges from and demonstrably display the influence of both the Black Arts and Feminist Art movements include Audre Lorde, Angela Davis, Toni Cade Bambara, Sonia Sanchez, June Jordan, Frances Beal, Toni Morrison, Betye Saar, Faith Ringgold, Michele Wallace, Ntozake Shange, and Alice Walker, among others (Bambara, 1996; Byrd, 2010; L. G. Collins, 2002; Henkes, 1993; hooks, 1995a; Lorde, 1996, 2004; Morrison, 1994; Wallace, 2004). Although not as widely discussed as the masculinism of the Black Arts movement or the lack of anti-racism in the Feminist Art movement, it is important to acknowledge the work of the black women artists of the late 1960s, 1970s, and 1980s that not only built bridges between the Black Arts and Feminist Art movements, but whose work also continues to influence hip hop feminists and womanists' conceptions of feminism, womanism, feminist aesthetics, and/or womanist aesthetics.

Considering that the previous chapter provided a detailed discussion of the aesthetic criteria and major motifs of the Black Arts movement, here I will focus more attention on the Feminist Art movement and the ways in which black women artists synthesized aspects of black and feminist aesthetics to articulate their own distinct *black feminist aesthetic* (L. G. Collins, 2002; Farrington, 2005; Mitchell and Taylor, 2009; Raphael-Hernandez, 2008). The Feminist Art movement generally pertains to the work (theoretical and practical) to create art that reflects women's life-worlds and life-struggles. The movement sought to transform the principles upon which contemporary art was produced, received, and evaluated, as well as to emphasize women within art history, art pedagogy, and art practice. As the aesthetic outlet of the Women's Liberation movement of the 1960s and 1970s, the Feminist Art movement utilized "second wave" feminist strategies and tactics, such as consciousness-raising collectives, performance workshops, insurgent artistic experimentation, and comprehensive research into women's history, literature, and art (Broude and Garrard, 1994; Deepwell, 1995; Hess and Baker, 1973; Liss, 2009).

Drawing inspiration from the French feminist philosopher Simone de Beauvoir and her extremely influential 1949 book *Le deuxième sexe*, translated into English and titled *The Second Sex* in 1953, white feminist artists were enamored with Beauvoir's critique of the patriarchal construction of womanhood and the historical oppression and suppression of women.[8] *The Second Sex*, truth be told, was both brilliant and heartbreaking: brilliant in its innovative interdisciplinary exploration of the suffocating suppression of women in history, philosophy, politics, economics, biology, psychology, anthropology, folklore, religion, literature, and the arts; and, heartbreaking because her work seemed to reveal not only a bleak past, but an equally depressing present and future for "the second sex" (Evans, 1998; Simons, 1999). However, prescient and powerful, Beauvoir concluded *The Second Sex* with a proto-"second wave" feminist section entitled "Toward Liberation." Here, in the final few pages of *The Second Sex*, the seemingly more existentialist than feminist philosopher observed that up to the middle of the twentieth century women had not been able to develop to their fullest potential in the arts and humanities because of the patriarchal colonization of their life-worlds and lived-experiences, but, she assured her readers, there was hope on the horizon. The colonization of women's creativity, Beauvoir (1953) prophesied, would come to an end in the near future because, she famously intoned, "the free woman is just being born" (p. 715). The future liberated woman that she envisioned would at last be able to offer up women's insights and answers to life's big questions, as well as create noteworthy work that would not only give new meaning to the world but, perhaps, fundamentally alter it. Deeply believing that women's decolonization would indelibly extend and expand women's life-worlds and worldviews and, in turn, enhance their lifework, Beauvoir bellowed:

> Art, literature, philosophy, are attempts to found the world anew on a human liberty: that of the individual creator; to entertain such a pretension, one must first unequivocally assume the status of a being who has liberty. The restrictions that education and custom impose on woman now limit her grasp on the universe; when the struggle to find one's place in this world is too arduous, there can be no question of getting away from it. Now, one must first emerge from it into a sovereign solitude if one wants to try to regain a grasp upon it: what woman needs first of all is to undertake, in anguish and pride, her apprenticeship in abandonment and transcendence; that is, in liberty. (p. 711)

Observing the longstanding invisibility and outright historical erasure of women's critical thought and creative practices—all the while somehow holding back from arguing whether or not women's future thoughts and practices would be comparably different from men's—Beauvoir ended *The Second Sex* with a grim assessment of women's past accompanied by a sanguine proclamation on the prospects of women's future: "What is certain is that hitherto woman's possibilities have been suppressed and lost to humanity, and that it is high time she be permitted to take her chances in her own interest and in the interest of all" (p. 715). It is relatively easy to see how Beauvoir's constant references to women's past "restrictions" and women's future "possibilities" would resonate with second wave feminists. In addition, the fact that she lived her life with such verve, which seemed, not only informed by her unprecedented existentialist-feminist research and writings, but also to marvelously mirror her emphasis on the future possibilities of liberated women, was not lost on her second wave feminist progeny.

Perhaps the most noted second wave feminist artist to grapple with Beauvoir's work was Chicago-born but Los Angeles-based artist-activist Judy Chicago (1975), who had been born Judy Cohen, became Judy Gerowitz upon her first marriage, and then Judy Chicago in order to reflect the city of her birth and to represent her unrepentant "emerging position as a feminist" (pp. 62–63).[9] The sign announcing her name change famously read: "Judy Gerowitz hereby divests herself of all names imposed upon her through male dominance and freely chooses her own name Judy Chicago" (p. 63). In 1970 Chicago and fifteen female students established the first Feminist Art Education Program at Fresno State College, later California State University at Fresno. The Fresno feminist artists laid the foundation for several of the core principles and practices of the Feminist Art movement, including employing "female technologies" such as performance, video, and costume, as well as developing their own distinct critique of the media (i.e., feminist media studies) and the culture industries (i.e., feminist cultural studies)—this last point should not be lost to my readers and should be borne in mind when we discuss hip hop feminists' critique of the media and culture industries below. In direct response to Beauvoir's claims in *The Second Sex* concerning the "restrictions that education and custom impose on woman now limit her grasp on the universe" and that historically women had not been able to excel at and offer up their special truth in the arts and humanities, Chicago established women's *herstorical research* as the cornerstone of the first feminist art program's curriculum.

After her work at Frenso State, Judy Chicago, along with painter Miriam Schapiro, went on to establish the feminist art program at California Institute of the Arts (a.k.a. "Cal Arts") in Los Angeles in 1971. Undoubtedly the highlight of her tenure at Cal Arts was the work she and her students did creating a month-long installation in an empty house, which they dubbed

"WomanHouse" (Broude and Garrard, 1994). Running parallel with California feminist artwork were emerging feminist artist collectives in New York (e.g., the A.I.R. Gallery) and Chicago (e.g., the Artemisia Gallery). This explosion of feminist art activity inspired new work by women artists (Broude and Garrard, 2005; Ecker, 1985; Raven, Langer, and Fruech, 1988; Fruech, Langer, and Raven, 1994; Paglia, 1991, 1992, 1994). However, white feminist artists, for the most part, had greater access to patrons, publicity, studios, galleries, theaters, and other important venues in which to conceive, create, and exhibit their work. Consequently, black and other nonwhite women artists' work, whether visual, performing or literary art, was often omitted from the mainstream Feminist Art movement, and this is precisely where and why the black women artists working during the Black Arts and Feminist Art movements inaugurated their own black Feminist Art movement.

Where the white Feminist Art movement turned to Simone de Beauvoir, the black Feminist Art movement heavily drew from Zora Neale Hurston and Lorraine Hansberry for spiritual and aesthetic sustenance and guidance. Hurston's legacy in particular served as a source of inspiration for the black women artists of the late 1960s and 1970s. Playwright, novelist, and folklorist, Hurston is best known as the author of the 1937 classic *Their Eyes Were Watching God*, but many black women artists also looked to her work as a raconteur, ethnographer, and cultural anthropologist. Just as Judy Chicago emphasized *herstorical research* in her conception of feminist art in the early 1970s, Hurston endeavored ethnographic, *herstorical*, and cultural research in order to render her characters authentic or, rather, true to black life, language, and culture.[10]

All of this is also to say that even before Judy Chicago was born (in 1939), and more than a decade before Simone de Beauvoir published *The Second Sex* (in 1949), it is noteworthy to observe that Hurston had been developing her own unique *black feminist herstorical and cultural anthropological research method* at Howard University (1918–1924), Barnard College (1924–1927), and Columbia University (1927–1929). At Howard, she studied with Lorenzo Dow Turner, Dwight O. W. Holmes, Montgomery Gregory, and Alain Locke, and off campus she regularly attended Georgia Douglas Johnson's literary salon, where she came into contact with W. E. B. Du Bois, Alice Dunbar-Nelson, Jean Toomer, Marita Bonner, and Jessie Fauset, among other Harlem Renaissance luminaries; at Barnard she studied with and conducted fieldwork for Franz Boas; and, at Columbia she continued to work with Boas, as well as his colleagues Ruth Benedict and Otto Klineberg. It is also interesting to note that one of her classmates at Columbia was noted cultural anthropologist Margaret Mead.

Hurston is a unique figure in African American arts and letters in that of the leading lights of the Harlem Renaissance it was only she and W. E. B. Du

Bois who brought their training in the social sciences to bear on their literary output—of course, Hurston had a greater sense of the melody or, rather, the musicality of black vernacular culture than Du Bois, whose novels and short stories, truth be told, were often rather rigid and stylistically stiff. The 1930s were Hurston's most productive period, and she published her first three novels during this decade: *Jonah's Gourd Vine* (1934); *Their Eyes Were Watching God* (1937), which has long been hailed as her masterpiece; and, *Moses, Man of the Mountain* (1939). She also published a critically acclaimed volume of short stories entitled *Mules and Men* in 1935, which put her hard-won "literary anthropology" research and writing style on full display. Her articulation of "literary anthropology" was so well received that in 1937 Hurston was awarded a prestigious Guggenheim Fellowship to conduct ethnographic research on the retentions of African ritual culture in Jamaica and Haiti. She chronicled her Jamaican and Haitian fieldwork and extracurricular experiences in *Tell My Horse*, which was published in 1938.

Educated at the University of Wisconsin at Madison and The New School in New York City, playwright, novelist, and essayist Lorraine Hansberry was one of those rare and remarkable artists who defies quick categorization and lazy labeling.[11] Primarily known for her award-winning 1959 Broadway play *A Raisin in the Sun*, Hansberry's work frequently explicitly engaged racism, sexism, heterosexism, feminism, poverty, education, segregation, abortion, the Civil Rights movement, and African Americans' perception of Africa, among other issues (Hansberry, 1964, 1972, 1994, 1995; Laughlin and Schuler, 1995). Similar to Hurston, her work grew out of her lived-experiences and lived-endurances of being both black *and* a woman — something that continues to distinguish black feminist theory and praxis, as the added variable of anti-black racism is such that most black women cannot conceive of a form of feminism that is not simultaneously anti-sexist *and* anti-racist.

Although Hansberry succumbed to cancer at the tender age of thirty-four in 1965, her legacy and influence only increased during the Black Power period, partly as a result of Hansberry's ex-husband Robert Nemiroff, who adapted many of her writings into the 1968 off-Broadway hit play, *To Be Young, Gifted, and Black*. Nemiroff also edited and published a volume of Hansberry's writings in 1969 under the title *To Be Young, Gifted, and Black* (see Hansberry, 1995). Jazz singer and pianist Nina Simone, who was a close friend and confidante of Hansberry's, paid tribute to her fallen friend by writing a Civil Rights/Black Power-themed song entitled "To Be Young, Gifted, and Black" with the iconic African American composer, lyricist, and pianist Weldon Irvine. The song became one of Simone's greatest hits, reaching the top 10 on the R&B charts in 1969, and spawning cover versions by soul music superstars Donny Hathaway (on his 1970 album *Everything Is Everything*) and Aretha Franklin (on her 1972 album *Young, Gifted, and Black*).

Just as Hansberry's work seemed to have a life of its own well beyond her death, Hurston's work was also revived in the 1970s, particularly as a result of the efforts of a Georgia-born, Spelman College and Sarah Lawrence College-educated young writer by the name of Alice Walker. In 1975 Walker published an article in *Ms.* magazine entitled, "In Search of Zora Neale Hurston," which most African American literary critics agree helped to initiate the critical reevaluation of Hurston's work (Bates, 2005; Gates and Appiah, 1993a; L. P. Howard, 1993). In terms of the black Feminist Art movement, it is important to acknowledge that the reemergence of Hurston and Hansberry's work coincided with the blossoming of black women writers, such as Toni Morrison, Maya Angelou, Toni Cade Bambara, June Jordan, Nikki Giovanni, Sonia Sanchez, Audre Lorde, and, of course, Walker herself—all of whose works in one way or another focuses on African American experiences, but not necessarily on race or anti-black racism (Christian, 1985; M. Evans, 1983; Hernton, 1990; Tate, 1983; Wall, 2005; T. L. Walters, 2007).

One of the major overlapping areas of emphasis for both the black and white Feminist Art movements revolved around critically studying the past, audaciously addressing the present, and optimistically envisioning a liberated future. While black and white Feminist Art movement members took different intellectual herstories and aesthetic trajectories as their points of departure, their overarching shared goals for their "real" and "imagined" kith and kin—i.e., social, political, and psychological liberation and a world free from exploitation, oppression, and violence—caused members of both movements to place special emphasis on women's worldviews and new feminist knowledge(s), specifically new ways of viewing and knowing the individual self and women collectively in relation to U.S. society. Artist-activists in both the black and white Feminist Art movements were convinced that heightened self-consciousness coupled with political and ideological awakening would be extremely advantageous to oppressed and suppressed women by quelling the excruciating emotions of angst and alienation, healing deep-seated trauma, and moving them from an inward focus to an outward focus, which would ultimately enable them to embrace feminist solidarity and see other women as sisters and comrades in struggle. Contained within the calls for feminist/womanist consciousness-raising, self-reflection, self-criticism, and self-correction was the noble notion that critical and comprehensive knowledge of the self and the collective in society, past and present, would result in a new collective consciousness which, in turn, would yield an artist-activist community of struggle preoccupied with fundamentally altering the established order.

Both the black and white Feminist Art movements held fairly distinct conceptions of the role of the artist, and each put forward pivotal roles for the artists and their art or, rather, the creators and their creations, which was couched within a wider world of social and political struggle. Moreover, both movements ardently advocated the notion of *artist-activists* or, rather, *activist-artists* whose counter-ideology-informed and politically committed work would bring about not only women's liberation but also wider social transformation. Black and white women artists as a rule rejected the image of the usually white male artist whose idiosyncratic "genius" was supposedly far beyond the pale of common people's comprehension, especially women— and, even more, especially nonwhite women. On the contrary, both the black and white Feminist Art movements conceived of the ideal artist as someone who, intensely engrossed in the *herstory*, culture, and struggle of her community, produced important and exuberant work that exalted and empowered her new and non-elite audience through recognition, celebration, and consciousness-raising.

Renowned feminist art critic Lucy Lippard (1980b), perhaps, best articulated the white Feminist Art movement's critique of the dominant male-centered modernist myth of the ideal artist as aggressive and evasive, famously stating: "The history of the male avant-garde has been one of reverse (or perverse) response to society, with the artist seen as the opposition or as out-of-touch idealist" (p. 364). Instead of the ideal artist being seen as "the opposition or as out-of-touch idealist," the white Feminist Art movement advocated an egalitarian relationship between artist and audience, a relationship predicated on accountability, responsibility, and honesty, and not irreverence and belligerence. In her watershed work, *From the Center: Feminist Essays on Women's Art*, Lippard (1976) astutely argued that a more balanced and mutually respectful relationship between artist and audience would be beneficial to both, and also, she contended, it would reinvigorate the creation and reception of art: "I do not think it possible to make important or even communicable art without some strong sense of source and self on one hand and some strong sense of audience and communication on the other" (p. 148).

In complete agreement with the white Feminist Art movement's critique of the dominant male-centered modernist myth of the ideal artist, as well as its conception of a more balanced and mutually respectful relationship between artist and audience, the black Feminist Art movement's critique was distinguished in light of its emphasis on the life-worlds and life-struggles of those artists who were not only women, but also *black* women. Undeniably, one of the best articulations of the black Feminist Art movement's critique of the dominant white *and* male supremacist modernist myth of the ideal artist was put forward by Alice Walker in an essay, which was originally published in *Ms.* magazine in 1974, from her much-celebrated book *In Search of Our Mother's Gardens* (1983), where she critically queried:

How was the creativity of the black woman kept alive, year after year and century after century, when for most of the years black people have been in America, it was a punishable crime for a black person to read or write? And the freedom to paint, to sculpt, to expand the mind with action did not exist. Consider, if you can bear to imagine it, what might have been the result if singing, too, had been forbidden by law. Listen to the voices of Bessie Smith, Billie Holiday, Nina Simone, Roberta Flack, and Aretha Franklin, among others, and imagine those voices muzzled for life. Then you may begin to comprehend the lives of our "crazy" "Sainted" mothers and grandmothers. The agony of the lives of women who might have been Poets, Novelists, Essayists, and Short-Story Writers (over a period of centuries), who died with their real gifts stifled within them. (p. 234)

Here, Walker's words do not simply highlight the hardships of what it means to be a feminist artist, but also the ways in which black women's often ignored *racially gendered* use and abuse at the hands of both "white over-seers" and "lazy [white] backwater tramps" has "year after year and century after century" blocked black women artists from developing to their full creative potential (p. 233). It was the black Feminist Art movement's empha-sis on the added burden of battling anti-black racism that differentiated their womanist critique of the dominant ideal of the artist. As will be discussed below, Walker's query concerning how the creativity of black women has been kept alive in spite of the hardships and horrors of their lives unfortu-nately remains extremely relevant with respect to the hip hop feminist move-ment.

Additionally, here it is important to observe that the women artists of both the black and white Feminist Art movements sought to deconstruct and re-construct not only the role of the artist, but also to extend and expand the purpose and meaning of art. They challenged the ideal of "art for art's sake" by championing an ideal of "art for life and liberation's sake," especially *art for the sake of women's lives and women's liberation.* In essence, they aimed to contradict and replace the male-centered modernist myth of the artist, which they understood to be glaringly decadent and life-threatening, with a more non-indulgent and life-enhancing one. Lucy Lippard (1980b), possibly, put the premium on both the black and white Feminist Art movements' conception(s) of a more balanced and mutually respectful relationship be-tween artist and audience, as well as the creation of art grounded in and growing out of collective struggle and community life, when she astutely stated:

The feminist (and socialist) value system insists upon cultural workers supporting and responding to their constituencies. The three models of such interaction are: (1) group and/or public ritual; (2) public consciousness-raising and interaction through visual images, environments, and performances; and (3) cooperative/collaborative/ collective or anonymous art-making. . . . All three structures are in the most funda-mental sense collective, like feminism itself. And these three models are all characterized by an element of outreach, a need for connections beyond process or product, an element of *inclusiveness* which also takes the form of responsiveness and responsibility for one's own ideas and images—the outward and inward facets of the same impulse. (p. 364, emphasis in original)

Both the black and white Feminist Art movements repudiated what they perceived to be the decadent directives of male supremacist modernism, and instead put forward a radical feminist vision of an emancipated world where art was grounded in, and grew out of both the ordinary and the extraordinary in everyday life. Moreover, feminist modernism audaciously envisioned a liberated future world where ethics informed aesthetics, and aesthetics informed ethics. In the passage above, Lippard emphasized the importance of feminist artists' advancing their "own ideas and images," which points to both the black and white Feminist Art movements' critique of the exclusion of black and feminist aesthetics from "mainstream" (read: "malestream") modernism. This is to say, then, they not only critiqued the role of the artist and the purpose of art, but also the "mainstream" art world's incessant omission of black and white women artists, especially when women artists opted to unapologetically express their unique lived-experiences and lived-endurances, their distinct issues and identities in *their* art.

Although many women artists stridently struggled to integrate and transform the established male-centered art world, others diligently dedicated themselves to the inauguration of an alternative women-centered art world where feminist aesthetics informed how art was created, critiqued, and appreciated. In fact, so frustrated was Lucy Lippard (1976) with the male-centered and female-censuring art world of the 1970s that she advocated a separate women-centered art world in *From the Center*, candidly contending:

Why are we all still so afraid of being *other* than men? Women are still in hiding. We still find it difficult, even the young ones, to express ourselves freely in large groups of men. Since that art world is still dominated by men, this attitude pervades the art that is being made. In the process, feelings and forms are neutralized. For this reason, I am all in favor of a separate art world for the time being—separate women's schools, galleries, museums—until we reach the point when women are as at home in the world as men are. (p. 11, emphasis in original)

Lippard argued that ultimately women artists should be "as at home in the world as men are," but until the male-centered ideal of the modern artist is eradicated, "for the time being," it is extremely important for women artists to support and recognize each others' work. Something very similar could be said (and, perhaps, *should* be said) with respect to not only the artistry but also the feminist and/or womanist activism of the women of the hip hop generation. How many women, roughly born between 1965 and 1990, are "as at home in the world [of hip hop] as men are"? How many, whether con-

sciously or unconsciously, are currently building on the "personal is political" paradigm, feminist aesthetics, and feminist artist-activist archetype(s)
promoted during the heyday of second wave feminism and the Feminist Art
movement? This chapter will conclude by taking up these crucial questions.

"WE WANNA GIVE FEMINISM A FACELIFT!": HIP HOP FEMINISM AND THE HIP HOP FEMINIST MOVEMENT

It is only in the aftermath of the feminist aesthetics of the black and white
Feminist Art movements, as well as the black aesthetic of the Black Arts
movement, that the hip hop feminist movement emerged. Indeed, new forms
of politicization and mobilization have emerged among the African
American and other nonwhite women of the hip hop generation that speak to
the special ways they have remixed the "personal is political" paradigm.
Undoubtedly black and other nonwhite women are not *en masse* embracing
the "feminist" label, but this should not be taken as a rejection of feminism
on their part as much as it should serve as a sign of their repudiation of
feminism as espoused by the conservative feminist and anti-feminist forces
that co-opted feminism during the Reagan and Bush administration years
between 1980 and 1992 (Burack and Josephson, 2003; Heywood and Drake,
1997; Lynn, 1992; Põldsaar, 2006; Schreiber, 2008). Truth be told, feminism
is seen as something foreign to most nonwhite women's *herstories*, cultures,
and struggles because of the academization and embourgeoisement of feminism in the 1980s and 1990s. College-educated women are more likely to be
exposed to feminism than those women who do not attend college, or those
women whose lives are quarantined to their respective nonwhite world. Because nonwhite working-class and poor women have to overcome unfathom-
able obstacles in order to attend college it could be argued that contemporary
feminism has, to a certain extent, fallen prey to the political economy of U.S.
capitalism, which is also to sadly say that feminism, although it had such a
powerful public presence in the late 1960s and 1970s, by the 1980s and
1990s it became increasingly privatized and commodified (Dow, 1996; Maglin and Perry, 1996; Oakley and Mitchell, 1997).[12]

It would seem that the women of the hip hop generation do not reject the
fundamental tenets of feminism, but rather what has been done or not done in
the name of feminism. Here we have come back to the issue of nomenclature.
For instance, in my experience of teaching African American studies over the
last decade I have found most young black women extremely receptive to
black feminist thought in part, I believe, because (within the insurgent interdisciplinary and intersectional context of African American studies) they can
easily comprehend how a form of anti-racist feminism will help them *per-*

sonally, and the larger black community *politically*. In other words, these young women are still working within the "personal is political" paradigm, but doing so from the standpoint of *racially gendered women* from, quite often, poor and working-class communities. Above we observed that almost the exact same remix of cultural feminism and cultural nationalism was advanced by the members of the black Women's Liberation movement during the late 1960s and 1970s. One can only speculate how many more young black women would embrace feminism, womanism, and/or women's liberation if they were exposed early on to the specific forms of feminist/womanist struggle waged by their black feminist foremothers, and not simply the super-sanitized, whitewashed, one-token-woman-of-color version of feminism and the Women's Liberation movement that is offered in most women's studies classrooms.

In fact, my teaching experiences in African American studies have also exposed me to the fact that many (although certainly not all) young black men are equally as receptive to feminism when it is refracted through the lens of black women's lived-experiences and lived-endurances. For example, I can distinctly recall that once I gave an assignment where I asked my Introduction to Hip Hop Studies class to compare and contrast Rachel Raimist's documentaries *Nobody Knows My Name* (1999) and *A B-Girl Is . . . : A Celebration of Women in Hip Hop* (2005) with a classic black feminist text (e.g., autobiography, novel, collection of poetry, or volume of theory), with the only stipulation being that the "classic black feminist text" had to have been published prior to 1979, which, of course, is the year that most Hip Hop studies scholars agree hip hop began in earnest (S. Baker, 2006; Chang, 2005; Fricke and Ahearn, 2002; Light, 1999). I was truly amazed to see how my students enthusiastically took to the assignment. There were comparisons of the hip hop feminist themes in Raimist's documentaries with texts by Sojourner Truth, Maria Stewart, Anna Julia Cooper, Ida B. Wells, Ella Baker, Dorothy Height, Sonia Sanchez, Rita Dove, and Ntozake Shange, among others. What really struck me, however, was a collaboration between one of my female students and one of my male students where they put parts of a 1970s speech by Angela Davis to hip hop beats. The young lady rapped about the prison industrial complex, health care, rape, and women's rights in between and often along with Angela Davis's speech, while the young man scratched excerpts of the speech on two turntables behind her. It was an absolutely phenomenal performance.

Afterwards I asked them how their collaboration came about, and the young sister said that they had been discussing what they were learning in the class about hip hop feminism with each other and decided they wanted to "put a new face on feminism." She candidly continued: "It does not have to be what it was, right? We can take it, and just like we did with other things from our past, we can update it, we can remix it, right? Ain't that what you said hip hop was all about the other day in class Professor Rabaka?"

At this point, the young brother chimed in, saying: "Yeah, we wanted to give feminism a facelift! This right here is 'hood feminism! Ghetto feminism! You know what I mean, a feminism for the sisters on the block, like Joan Morgan say. It ain't about hatin' men. It's about women learning to love, respect, and appreciate themselves. Ain't that what you said? Really though, to be truthful with you, this hip hop feminism stuff made me realize I got some work to do in terms of my own gender politics—I mean, with my moms, my sister, my lady, and even my little daughter." Obviously, this was one of those rare and remarkable moments where a risky assignment paid off, pedagogically speaking. To see both of these students—both of whom just so happened to be first-generation college students—so "hyped" about hip hop feminism made me even more determined to expose the connections between the Women's Liberation movement of the 1960s and 1970s and the hip hop feminist movement of the 1990s and early 2000s.

I have found that exposing my students to hip hop feminism usually makes them more receptive to other forms of feminism, whether it be African American, Chicana, Native American, or Asian American feminism. Many of us working within women's studies find it extremely troubling that young women and young men can earn their college degrees and have absolutely no working knowledge of women's herstory, culture, and struggle. Again, whether or not young African American and other nonwhite women refer to themselves as "feminists" is superfluous at this point because, similar to the black women who began embracing the term "womanist" in the early 1980s, the women of the hip hop generation have a right to practice self-naming, self-definition, and self-determination on their own terms, and no group of high-handed "old school feminists" has a right to tell them otherwise (Houston and Davis, 2002; Hudson-Weems, 1995, 1997, 2004; Phillips, 2006; Prince, Silva-Wayne, and Vernon, 2004). What needs to be understood are the ways in which the 1980s and 1990s backlash against feminism defamed the label "feminist" to such a degree that now there is an entire generation of young women and young men who are reluctant to critically engage the herstory of Women's Liberation movements because they do not want to be typecast as "feminists." This practice is, perhaps, even more prickly in nonwhite communities because of the ways in which nonwhite cultural nationalism has been collapsed into the reductive either/or logic of nonwhite male chauvinism.[13] It would seem to me that those of us currently working in women's studies should open ourselves to the fact that although the women of the hip hop generation's feminism, womanism, or what have you, may not resemble our or our mother or grandmother's "feminism," their contributions are not only valid but extremely valuable for the future of the Women's

Liberation movement (Hernández and Rehman, 2002; Heywood and Drake, 1997; Labaton and Martin, 2004).

The nonwhite women of the hip hop generation whose gender consciousness has been heightened as a result of their exposure to feminist ideas within women's studies classrooms often use their newfound knowledge in ways comparably different than most of their contemporary white counterparts, because their daily lives and struggles, their lived-experiences and lived-endurances demand not only that they be fluent in womanist/feminist theory and praxis, but also in critical race theory and Marxist (and other anti-capitalist) theory (R. A. Bernard, 2009; M. Rojas, 2009; Sharpley-Whiting, 2007). Many of these women are able to detect early on the deficiencies of feminism as a stand-alone theory and usually they quickly tire of all of the "academic talk" of feminism. When they put feminist theory into praxis, they usually turn to the issues and terrain that they feel strongest about and are most familiar with. As a result of their coming of age during a period of intense technological revolution—for instance, from the Sony Walkman to Apple's iPod, from car phones to cellular phones, and from the Commodore 64 computer to Apple's iPad—the women of the hip hop generation, as with the hip hop generation in general, have been inundated with the explosion of social media and popular culture that took place during the 1980s, 1990s, and early 2000s. Consequently, social media and popular culture have become important sites and sources for hip hop feminism, and often these new-fangled feminists (albeit, many would argue, "feminists" nonetheless) make important connections between "old school" grassroots politics and hip hop generation cyber-politics, between 1960s and 1970s-styled politicization and late twentieth/early twenty-first century new social movement mobilization.

Even if we were to focus our discussion primarily on the hip hop feminists featured in Gwendolyn Pough, Elaine Richardson, Aisha Durham, and Rachel Raimist's groundbreaking edited volume, *Home Girls Make Some Noise!: A Hip Hop Feminism Anthology* (2007), we can deduce that hip hop feminism critically engages music, film, fashion, fiction, poetry, spoken-word, dance, theater, and visual art, as well as other aspects of popular culture, as essential arenas for feminist politicization and mobilization. Which is also to say, when compared with the feminist mobilization of the 1960s and 1970s, the majority of hip hop feminist mobilization at the present moment seems to emerge from cyber-social networks, mass media, and popular culture, rather than nationally networked women's organizations based in government, academic, or male-dominated leftist bureaucracies. Undeniably, hip hop culture touches the lives of many more young nonwhite women, and even the lives of many young white women, than the feminism coming out of women's studies classes and the American academy in general. This means, then, that those of us who would truly like to reach and radicalize the women of the hip hop generation will have to come to the realization that whether we like it or not hip hop feminists have (or, at the very least, they are in the process of), in the words of my student, *giving feminism a "facelift."* We might even go so far as to say that for many of the women of the hip hop generation their feminist politics reflect the fact that the majority of nonwhite women regularly receive substandard education in the public school system and, therefore, school has ceased to serve as the place where they learn literacy, sociality, and politics. Instead, for many, if not for most, cyber-social networks, mass media, and popular culture has, literally, become their classroom and, not seeking to sound supercilious, little or no distinction is made between uncritical information and authentic critical education (Dimitriadis, 2001; Hill, 2009; Parmar, 2009; Runell and Diaz, 2007).

In observing the fact that hip hop culture currently reaches more young nonwhite women, especially black and brown women, than the feminism found in the academy of the twenty-first century, I am not in any way arguing that hip hop, and specifically rap music and videos, are not full of controversy and contradictions when and where we come to the ways in which women (again, especially black and brown women) are represented or, rather, misrepresented within the world of hip hop. Instead, I am emphasizing the fact that hip hop culture and rap music are malleable and mobile enough to be adapted to a wide range of ideas and actions, a wealth of theories and praxes—some progressive, while others regressive; some truly remarkable, while others merely mediocre; and, some liberating, while others incarcerating. Taking into consideration the contradictory ability of hip hop culture to simultaneously imprison and emancipate women, most hip hop feminists' theory and praxis revolve around their relationships with and critiques of the racial-patriarchal-capitalist political economy of cyber-social networks, mass media, and popular culture. All of this makes perfect sense when one contemplates the hypermasculinism, misogyny, and embourgeoisement seemingly inherent in the most popular expressions of hip hop culture: commercial rap music and videos. Were we to focus specifically on African American women's ragged relationship with rap music and videos, then we would be able to easily see the often conflicted connections many women of the hip hop generation make between hip hop, feminism, and anti-racism.

It is important here to observe that whether hip hop feminists are aware of it or not, black women at the turn of the twentieth century faced a similar situation with respect to misrepresentations and gross mischaracterizations of African American women in what was then an emerging mass media and culture industry. As briefly touched on in chapter 2, Harriet Tubman, Margaret Murray Washington, Frances E. W. Harper, Ida B. Wells, Josephine Ruffin, and Mary Church Terrell established the National Association of Colored Women (NACW) in 1896, which was not only committed to the uplift of African American women, but also preoccupied with repudiating anti-black racist caricatures of black women in the then materializing mass media. Similar to their African American feminist foremothers in the Black Women's Club movement, then, the women of the hip hop feminist movement find themselves fighting the simultaneously racist and sexist stereotypes being hurled at them. Most of the women of the hip hop generation who have been able to engage and ultimately embrace feminism or womanism strongly stress the necessity of sensibly utilizing hip hop culture, especially rap music and videos, as a critical consciousness-raising caucus, an anti-racist feminist forum that exposes the young women (and men) of the hip hop generation to what nonwhite and non-elite feminism has to offer—that is, as we have seen above, the very kind of feminism put forward and practiced by most members of the black Women's Liberation movement in the 1960s and 1970s.

Most contemporary cultural critics and cultural studies scholars agree that hip hop is the late twentieth/early twenty-first century generation's signature sociocultural contribution (or "damned" deprivation, depending on who you ask), so it should not shock anyone, least of all those of us working in the field of new social movement theory, that a new form of feminism—i.e., hip hop feminism—has arisen from the underbelly or entrails of hip hop culture. In addition, none of this should shock and awe any of us when we bear in mind something that Frantz Fanon demonstrated in his discussion of the ways in which violence, exploitation, and oppression often unwittingly give rise to radical, if not revolutionary forms of resistance. Men, least of all the men of the hip hop generation, do not have a monopoly on radicalism or revolutionary thought and praxis, which is also to say that the hypermasculinism, misogyny, and male supremacy seemingly at the center of commercial hip hop culture has only intensified many young women's decolonial desire(s) to critique and combat patriarchy or, rather, *patriarchal colonialism*. Were we to "flip the script," to use hip hop lingo, and view commercial hip hop as a kind of racially gendered "colonial world" where women are the central radical/revolutionary anticolonial agents and actresses, then Fanon's caveat in *The Wretched of the Earth* (1968) concerning the "colonized's" right to violent resistance—or, rather, resistance "by any means necessary"—is plausibly even more relevant to the discussion at hand:

The violence which has ruled over the ordering of the colonial world, which has ceaselessly drummed the rhythm for the destruction of native social forms and broken up without reserve the systems of reference of the economy, the customs of dress and external life, that same violence will be claimed and taken over by the native at the moment when, deciding to embody history in his [or her] own person, he [or she] surges into forbidden quarters. To wreck the colonial world is henceforward a mental picture of action which is very clear, very easy to understand, and which may be assumed by each one of the individuals which constitute the colonized people. (pp. 40–41)

That is to say, then, that any woman—regardless of her age, race, class, sexual orientation, or religious affiliation—might at any moment come to a kind of critical feminist/womanist consciousness that compels her to "wreck the [racially gendered] colonial world" of hip hop. Fanon's conception of the "wreck" contained within the process of "true decolonization" can be shown to be connected to the "wreck" of contemporary hip hop feminist discourse (p. 59).[14] For instance, in her groundbreaking book, *Check It While I Wreck It!: Black Womanhood, Hip Hop Culture, and the Public Sphere*, Gwendolyn Pough (2004) explained that within hip hop feminist discourse "wreck" is "a hip hop term that connotes fighting, recreation, skill, boasting, or violence. The hip hop concept of wreck sheds new light on the things blacks have had to do in order to obtain and maintain a presence in the larger public sphere, namely fight hard and bring attention to their skill and right to be in the public sphere" (p. 17). By focusing exclusively on the trials and tribulations of black women within the world of hip hop we are able to more easily see not only how Pough's hip hop feminist conception of wreck connects with Fanon's insurrectionist anti-colonial conception of wreck, but also how, much like the larger bourgeois patriarchal "public sphere," commercial hip hop culture schizophrenically renders black women's sexuality hypervisible and their social and political struggles utterly invisible.

It is a known fact that women within the world of hip hop have had to "fight hard and bring attention to their skill and right to be" included in the world of hip hop—again, a world they undeniably helped to create and continue to cultivate. Their simultaneous struggles both within *and* without the world of hip hop is what distinguishes their form of feminism. Pough importantly continued: "Bringing wreck, for black participants in the public sphere historically, has meant reshaping the public gaze in such a way as to be recognized as human beings—as functioning and worthwhile members of society—and not to be shut out of or pushed away from the public sphere" (p. 17). It would seem that here we have come to the heart of hip hop feminism, and this primarily has to do with black and other nonwhite women's earnest efforts to refashion the "public gaze" of hip hop culture "in such a way as to be recognized as human beings" and "not to be shut out of or pushed away from" the world of hip hop as a consequence of male hip hoppers' hypermasculinism, misogyny, and male supremacy.

Many of the folk Joan Morgan referred to as "old school feminists" have taken issue with hip hop feminists' utilization of cyber-social networks, mass media, and popular culture, and because they do not use the more tried and true grassroots political methods popularized during the Women's Liberation movement(s) of the 1960s and 1970s, as well as the "old school" emphasis on integrating academe, many "old school feminists" have argued that the hip hop feminist movement is misconceived and often mealy-mouthed. Others argue, however, that the women of the hip hop generation with feminist sensibilities are actually dialectically deconstructing and reconstructing the bourgeois patriarchal public sphere, as well as cyber-social networks, mass media, and popular culture, in new womanist ways that are both novel and necessary. Here, then, it will be important for us to briefly examine how the hip hop feminists themselves define or, rather, radically redefine feminism (and womanism) to speak to the special needs of their life-worlds and life-struggles.

Perhaps one of the first major works on rap music and hip hop culture to provocatively broach the subject of hip hop and feminism was Tricia Rose's pioneering book *Black Noise: Rap Music and Black Culture in Contemporary America* (1994). Although the volume does not seem to directly draw from either the Black Arts or Feminist Art movements, it is interesting to observe that Rose conceives of and conceptualizes the work of women rappers loosely utilizing a combination of black and feminist aesthetic criteria. As with hip hop culture in general, hip hop feminism often only hints at its influences, past and present. However, here we should unambiguously acknowledge its influences, not only to determine what it has inherited from previous sociopolitical and cultural aesthetic movements, but also to ascertain how it has built on and, in many instances, gone beyond its influences and ancestral movements.

Undoubtedly the work of women rappers forces us to reevaluate our criteria for what constitutes feminist art, but the same could be said (and actually has been said) about the work of many of the major players in the Feminist Art movement of the 1960s and 1970s, such as Judy Chicago, Faith Ringgold, Sheila Levrant de Bretteville, Susan Lacy, Dara Birnbaum, June Wayne, Nancy Spero, Mary Kelly, Kate Millett, Martha Rosler, Faith Wilding and, later, the Guerrilla Girls. Just as the artist-activists of the Feminist Art movement sought to expand the range and meaning of the Women's Liberation movement by offering up alternative articulations of women's life-worlds and life-struggles, so too are the artist-activists of the hip hop feminist movement expanding the range and meaning of contemporary feminism and offering up alternative expressions of women's life-worlds and life-struggles. In a sense, hip hop feminists represent important elements of a new avant-garde in both hip hop and contemporary feminist theory and praxis.

Rose's *Black Noise* offers us an early glimpse of how hip hop feminists have blurred the supposed boundaries between hip hop and feminism, and why the hip hop feminist movement is one of the most salient forms of feminism in contemporary U.S. culture and society. However, having said all of this, it is important to remind my readers that even as Hip Hop studies scholars acknowledge and critically theorize the hip hop feminist movement, most of the folk we are referring to as "hip hop feminists" do not self-identify as feminists and do not subscribe to each and every "feminist" tenet that has been handed down by their womanist/feminist foremothers. As with so many other arenas of hip hop culture, labeling has been left to those who need such sobriquets in order to make sense of what has so long been regarded as nonsense.

After identifying three primary themes prevalent in the work of African American women rappers—"heterosexual courtship, the importance of the female voice, and mastery in women's rap and black female public displays of physical and sexual freedom"—Rose (1994) reveals that by the mid-1990s discussions of women rappers had been separated into two interrelated arguments: "(1) women rappers are feminist voices who combat sexism in rap; and/or (2) the sexist exclusion or mischaracterization of women's participation in rap devalues women's significance and must be countered by evidence of women's contributions" (pp. 147, 149). Returning to the idea articulated above concerning the contradictory ability of hip hop culture to simultaneously imprison and emancipate women, the facts and fictions of the one-dimensional argument that all or even most male rappers are sexist and all or even most female rappers are anti-sexist should be debunked without delay.

First, and most obviously, this kind of lazy logic is nothing but another contribution to the longstanding discourse surrounding the "battle of the sexes," and it situates *female-feminist rappers* in unbending binary opposition to *male-misogynist rappers*—which is also to say, this line of logic also sounds like nothing more than a re-articulation of the age-old male/female dichotomy. It could almost go without saying that many female rappers unflinchingly criticize the misogyny in rap music and hip hop culture, but it is completely incorrect to argue that their relationship with male rappers can be best depicted as one that is in absolute opposition to all or even most male rappers. Needless to say, like hip hop itself, many female rappers' critiques of misogynistic rap music frequently have been contradictory and extremely complicated: contradictory, insofar as many female hip hoppers have a love/hate relationship with hip hop, as discussed by Joan Morgan in *When Chickenheads Come Home to Roost* (1999) and, more recently, by Aya de Leon in "Lyrical Self-Defense and the Reluctant Female Rapper" (2007) and Shawan Worsley in "Loving Hip Hop When It Denies Your Humanity" (2007); and, extremely complicated, when and where we come to the fact that many of the most popular female rappers (e.g., Lil' Kim, Foxy Brown, Trina, Jacki-O, Khia, and Nicki Minaj) often unrepentantly embrace the hypersexualized and licentious images of black women endlessly promoted in commercial rap music and hip hop culture (Babb, 2002; Sharpley-Whiting, 2007; Thomas, 2009).

Second, the monolith of male-misogynist rappers versus female-feminist rappers also unwittingly overlooks the fact that almost all (hetero)sexual discourse at the turn of the twenty-first century could be said to be complex and contradictory; one, perhaps, need not raise the issue of the ever-increasing (heterosexual) divorce rate in the United States. Were we to turn to the ongoing dialogue between male and female rappers surrounding sex, love, and heterosexual relationships, then, we would probably be able to see that not all male rappers' sexual discourse is sexist and, by the same token, not all female rappers' sexual discourse is feminist and/or anti-sexist. Many of the more commercially popular female rappers, such as the aforementioned Lil' Kim, Foxy Brown, Trina, Jacki-O, Khia, and Nicki Minaj, frequently come across as going out of their way to defend male rappers' misogyny, and at times a lot of their own lyrics reflect and, therefore, ratify misogynistic hip hop masculinity, male supremacist conceptions of mothers, wives, and family life, and the socially accepted (i.e., within a patriarchal society) gender roles of men as protectors, providers, lovers, brothers, fathers, and husbands.

Quiet as it has been kept, just as there have been female rappers—such as MC Lyte, Queen Latifah, Monie Love, Bahamadia, Medusa, Mystic, Jean Grae, Ursula Rucker, and Sarah Jones—who have critiqued misogynistic rap music, there have been male rappers who have taken men to task for delinquent daddyism, domestic violence, rape, pressuring women to have abortions, and not recognizing and respecting the contributions of African American women to African American history, culture, and struggle. Many pro-women rap songs produced by males have sought to celebrate black womanhood, especially black motherhood. [15] To begin with the most obvious examples, male rappers have produced song after song singing the praises of their mothers: from Tupac Shakur's immortal "Dear Mama," to Mos Def's "Umi Says," to Kanye West's "Hey Mama." Examples of male rappers who have critically engaged rape and domestic violence include: A Tribe Called Quest's "Date Rape," De La Soul's "Millie Pulled a Pistol on Santa," Tupac Shakur's "Brenda's Got A Baby," Nas's "Black Girl Lost," Common's "Between Me, You & Liberation," Immortal Technique's "Dance With The Devil," and Damian Marley's "Pimpa's Paradise." Several male rappers have also, however tongue-in-cheek and crudely, critiqued stripping, pimping, and prostitution, and here Common's "A Film Called Pimp" (with MC Lyte), Wyclef Jean's "Perfect Gentleman," The Roots's "Pussy Galore," and Talib Kweli's "Black Girl Pain" quickly come to mind.

Again, hip hop's sexual politics is complex and contradictory and, therefore, it cannot be reduced to the simple male-misogynist rappers versus female-feminist rappers, or vice versa. Indeed, there is a need to critique the hypermasculine histories of hip hop that either exclude, co-opt, or devalue women's contributions, but even as we undertake these critiques it is important for us not to negate the contributions of male hip hoppers who have questioned and condemned misogynistic rap music and hip hop's sexism in general. Additionally, it is equally important for us not to overlook the fact that, although in *Black Studies, Rap, and the Academy* Houston Baker (1993) would have us believe that hip hop culture emerged in the late 1970s and early 1980s as a "resentment of disco culture and a reassertion of black

manhood," black women were undeniably at the heart of hip hop's inauguration and early evolution and it can just as easily be viewed as a new expression of black womanhood in the aftermath of the black Women's Liberation
movement and its cultural aesthetic corollary the black Feminist Art movement (p. 86).

In arguing that rap music is a "reassertion of black manhood," Baker's
analysis collapses rap music into an expression of black masculinity and, in
some ways, closes the door to the possibility that it could also be viewed as
an expression of African American women's newfangled femininity. What is
more, Baker seems to sidestep the notion that rap music specifically, and hip
hop culture more generally, could actually represent a transgender forum
where African American males and females voice their criticisms and put
forward their visions of healthy and unhealthy relationships (e.g., intimate,
interpersonal, intracommunal, and intercommunal relationships). By turning
black women's actual presence in the emergence of rap music into an absence, in this specific instance the otherwise gender progressive Baker contributes to the age-old male/female dichotomy and negates not only African
American women's contributions to hip hop culture, but he also erases the
ways in which female hip hoppers themselves might profit and derive pleasure from their participation in hip hop culture on their own feminist/woman-
ist terms—à la the black women artists who participated in both the Black
Arts and Feminist Art movements (Balton, 1991; DeBerry, 1995; Latifah,
2000; D. Perkins, 2000; Souljah, 1996).

Although rap is unmistakably the major musical expression of hip hop
culture, it is important for us not to overlook what has been termed "neo-
soul" music. Distinguished from the doldrums of digitized 1980s and 1990s
R&B by its incorporation of live instrumentation, as well as elements of rap,
jazz, fusion, funk, gospel, rock, reggae, and African music, neo-soul represents a soul music revival movement. As implied by its name (i.e., new soul),
neo-soul music is basically new century soul music, or, rather, twenty-first-
century music for the soul, with undeniable hip hop sensibilities. In other
words, it is a hybrid musical form that re-centers the autobiographical and
sociopolitical singer-songwriter style of classic soul and, consequently, many
of its critics have stressed that it has a greater emphasis on lyrical content or
"conscious lyrics" when compared with the pedestrian character of most
contemporary R&B. Also, neo-soul is known to be a concept album-oriented
genre that, by establishing and expiating lyrical and musical recurring themes
throughout the course of an album, directly draws from the more "organic"
and acoustic musical innovations and production techniques of classic soul
music. This, of course, is in stark contrast to contemporary R&B, which is a
more hit single–oriented genre based on catchy "hooks" (i.e., choruses),
cameos from commercial rappers, computerized music, live music samples,
and the pop-oriented super-polished sound of a recognized production team.

In an age of computerized and commercialized music, neo-soul artists' emphasis on an acoustic "band sound" and message-oriented music offers a much-needed alternative, not only to contemporary R&B, but also to the blandness of commercial rap. Frequently characterized as "musical bohemians" because their work draws from such a wide range of musical genres (not all of them distinctly African American musical genres), *Time* magazine writer Christopher John Farley (1998) went so far to as say that neo-soul artists, such as Lauryn Hill, D'Angelo, Erykah Badu, and Maxwell, "share a willingness to challenge musical orthodoxy" during an era (i.e., 1990–2000) dominated by the rise of gangsta rap. Putting forward a provocative working definition of neo-soul, Farley wrote further:

> Simply defined, neo-soul describes artists—like song-stylist Erykah Badu—who combine a palpable respect for and understanding of the classic soul of the '60s and '70s with a healthy appetite for '90s sonic experimentation and boundary-crossing. Neo-soul artists tend to create music that's a good deal more real, a good deal more edgy than the packaged pop of, say, teen-oriented groups like the Spice Girls and Cleopatra. And they tend to write lyrics that are more oblique and yet more socially and emotionally relevant than those of gangsta rappers. (p. 1)

Farley's work is extremely important in terms of the discussion at hand because his now "classic" *Time* article candidly captured the musical conceptions of several pioneering neo-soul artists in their own words and at the height of their popularity in the late 1990s. For instance, directly commenting on how she sought to both develop as an artist and break down barriers within the world of hip hop culture, Lauryn Hill said: "Sometimes it's hard to really make any statements when you know that the industry caters to hit singles rather than to developing artists," but "I definitely felt like I wanted to push the envelope of hip-hop. It was very important to me that the music be very raw . . . and there be a lot of live instrumentation." Echoing Hill, Maxwell criticized the music industry's condescending attitude toward consumers and explicitly stated that he intends his music to be an alternative to both contemporary R&B and commercial rap, saying: "I think people are a lot smarter than they are credited for being. I like to challenge what some people think most people will accept and listen to, particularly African Americans and particularly in the R&B genre. To me, it's important to reflect the alternative." And, finally, similar to Hill and Maxwell, D'Angelo likewise emphasized artistic integrity and musical innovation over all that "synthetic stuff," forcefully contending: "The mid-to-late '60s was the golden age of soul and funk. It wasn't like now, where you have one producer working for a slew of artists, who all sound the same. Artists are no longer self-contained and are more prone to conform. In the '60s, people were defying what people expected. That's what's missing now" (p. 2).

In a sense, then, neo-soul seeks to offer alternatives to, and highlight "what's missing now" in contemporary R&B and commercial rap music: edifying message-oriented music, acoustic instrumentation, sonic experimentation, etc. Consciously going against the musical grain, neo-soul artists' work is situated at the crossroads where the black musical past meets the black (and multicultural) musical present. Which is also to say, although rap music is regularly in the musical limelight and receives more media attention, much of the future of African American music may very well rest on the musical innovations and sonic experimentations of neo-soul artists, who have calmly and quietly become the conscience, even if not the "official" voices, of the hip hop generation. Where commercial rap music seems to have reached the point where it has begun to incessantly recycle itself, neo-soul's sonic experimentations have seemed to grow bolder and bolder with each new album. Of course, not all of the sonic experiments of neo-soul result in authentic musical innovations, but its fan base remains loyal and seems to greatly appreciate the restless spirit of the genre. In comparing neo-soul with contemporary R&B, it could be easily argued that by the 1980s and 1990s most R&B seems to have degenerated into the super-polished computerized and sonic seduction productions of name brand producers and powerful, pop-oriented production companies. Consequently, the uplifting and enlightening messages in classic R&B, soul, and funk music, not to mention musicianship in general, began to seriously decline, if not disappear altogether. As the noted *Vibe* magazine music critic Dimitri Ehrlich (2002) succinctly said:

> By definition, neo-soul is a paradox. Neo means new. Soul is timeless. All the neo-soul artists, in various ways, perform balancing acts, exploring classic soul idioms while injecting a living, breathing presence into time-tested formulas. They humanize R&B, which has often been reduced to a factory-perfected product. Like sushi, neo-soul is fresh enough to be served raw. (p. 72)

In response to the flash and splash of 1990s and early 2000s digitized R&B, neo-soul put forward "raw" messages more relevant to the soul of the hip hop generation, especially African American and other poor nonwhite youth. Indeed, commercial rap music might capture the quasi-political and sexual impulses of the hip hop generation, but it was left to neo-soul music to articulate hip hoppers' conceptions of love—and here my research has revealed that as a genre neo-soul music embodies all five major forms of love (at least as the ancient Greeks conceived of them): *epithumia* (deep desire/ passionate longing/lust); *eros* (romantic/sexual love); *storge* (familial love); *phile* (friendship/friendly love); and *agape* (selfless/unconditional love). Therefore, in neo-soul, in contradistinction to the blah of most contemporary R&B, love is conceptualized as something that extends well beyond intimate or sexual relationships (i.e., *epithumia*). Neo-soul artists frequently sing about and celebrate black life, black love, black culture, and the black community. Following in the musical footsteps of classic soul artists, such as Ray Charles, Aretha Franklin, James Brown, Smokey Robinson, Betty Davis, Bill Withers, Roberta Flack, Donnie Hathaway, Marvin Gaye, Stevie Wonder, Minnie Riperton, Curtis Mayfield, Gladys Knight, and Al Green, neo-soul artists do not privilege black sexuality over black spirituality (George, 2007; Guralnick, 1986; Hirshey, 1984; J. A. Jackson, 2004; Pruter, 1991; Ripani, 2006; Shaw, 1970; B. Ward, 1998).

Many neo-soul artists are also known to be musical innovators who, from my point of view, represent synthesized elements of the bohemian undergrounds of both R&B and hip hop. Their work, literally, offers deeper messages than contemporary R&B, and expands the range and meaning of hip hop beyond commercial rap music. In *Songs in the Key of Black Life: A Rhythm and Blues Nation*, my esteemed colleague Mark Anthony Neal (2003) echoes Ehrlich's above assertion concerning neo-soul being a "paradox" and "perform[ing] balancing acts, exploring classic soul idioms while injecting a living, breathing presence into time-tested formulas," when he asserted:

> Though neo-soul and its various incarnations have helped to redefine the boundaries and contours of black pop, often the most popular of these recordings, like Maxwell's *Urban Hang Suite*, India.Arie's *Acoustic Soul*, and Musiq Soulchild's *Aijuswanaseing*, exist comfortably alongside the trite blah, blah, blah of the 112s and Destiny's Childs of the world. Just a small reminder that "difference" is often valued only when it smells, tastes, and sounds like the same old same old. And even when artists break the mold, as Maxwell did with *Urban Hang Suite* and D'Angelo did with *Brown Sugar*, they are expected to remain true to that formula lest they risk the critical backlash that Maxwell and D'Angelo faced in the aftermath of artistically compelling projects like *Embrya* (1998) and *Voodoo* (2000), respectively. The bottom line is that contemporary R&B and the radio and video programmers responsible for making that music available to listeners and viewers remain trapped in a small black box largely informed by hip hop bottoms and Blige-like histrionics with small traces of Luther and Whitney and enough tone deafness to have Clara Ward, Mahailia Jackson, and Sam Cooke turn twice in their graves about every four and a half minutes. . . . With such a small margin to work with, the seminal hybrid-soul of Lenny Kravitz, the Family Stand, Seal, Corey Glover, Me'Shell Ndegéocello, Dionne Farris, Michael Franti (both the Disposable Heroes and Spearhead versions), and even Wyclef Jean has been consistently marginalized save an occasional MTV buzz clip and the hordes of "pomo-bohos" like myself who continue to crave great "black" music even if it don't sound like Marvin Gaye or Aretha Franklin. (pp. 117–18)

Neal's comment that neo-soul's "'difference' is often valued only when it smells, tastes, and sounds like the same old same old" should be accented, as it helps to highlight how even as neo-soul seeks to offer alternatives to contemporary R&B and commercial rap it, too, has been musically colonized and quarantined to a sphere of sonically and socially acceptable "difference" (and, dare I go even further to say, "blackness"). This, of course, makes one wonder how much more "different" could or would neo-soul be were it not for the incessant pressures placed on neo-soul artists to appeal to the political economy of a music industry dominated by the vulgarities of commercial rap? The free expression found in so much classic soul music is often buried beneath a barrage of musical fodder awkwardly aimed at placing neo-soul artists' work within the realms of either contemporary R&B or commercial rap. This is problematic for several reasons, but here I would like to emphasize how it ironically also offers a marginalized musical abode where the women of the hip hop generation have created a body of work that offers up feminist or womanist answers to many of the hip hop generation's most urgent interpersonal, cultural, social, and political issues.

NEW SOUL SISTAS & OLD BAD BRUTHAS: MOVING BEYOND THE FEMALE-FEMINIST RAPPER VS. MALE-MISOGYNIST RAPPER DICHOTOMY

Where women have come to be misogynistically marginalized within the rap genre, they have been ever-present and undeniably at the center of the neo-soul movement (Brooks, 2007; Furman and Furman, 1999; J. King, 1999; McIver, 2002; Nickson, 1999; Planer, 2002; G. Thomas, 2007; Whaley, 2002). Indeed, by centering their discussions almost exclusively around rap music over the past thirty years or so, most hip hop cultural critics have put into play a very subtle form of sexism that, once again, privileges the more male-centered musical genre (i.e., rap) over that of the more female-centered musical genre (i.e., neo-soul). Moreover, even if one disagrees that neo-soul seems to be more female-centered (especially considering the popularity of neo-soul Romeos, such as D'Angelo, Maxwell, Musiq Soulchild, Anthony Hamilton, Donnie, Raheem DeVaughn, Raphael Saadiq, Dwele, Cee Lo Green, and Nuwamba), at the very least, a convincing case could be made that it is far more *female-friendly* when compared with commercial rap. The unprecedented accomplishments of several neo-soul divas—such as Mary J. Blige, Angie Stone, Lauryn Hill, Erykah Badu, India.Arie, Jill Scott, Macy Gray, Alicia Keyes, Floetry, N'Dambi, Jaguar Wright, Chrisette Michele, Ledisi, Janelle Monáe, and Rhonda Nicole—lends even more credence to this line of logic. While it may very well be the case that none of the aforementioned neo-soul divas considers their work "feminist" or "womanist," and certainly not in the academic sense in which these terms are currently used, it is still important for us to acknowledge that collectively their work has: first, significantly contributed to hip hop culture; and, second, it indeed does unapologetically critique rap music and hip hop culture's hypermasculinism, misogyny, and male supremacy. Again, they may not use fly feminist theory terms, such as "patriarchy," "hypermasculinism," "misogyny," and "male supremacy" in their songs (or interviews), but if one listens to, and really hears the messages in their music it is almost impossible to argue that the women of the hip hop generation have not critiqued and combated hip hop culture's hypermasculinism, misogyny, and male supremacy.

Hypermasculinist interpretations of hip hop have long been regarded as the rule, but here I would like to touch on one of the more egregious examples to briefly give my readers a sense of what most of the lopsided and lame male-centered analyses of hip hop culture look and sound like. Making Baker's above lapse into the age-old male/female dichotomy almost seem minuscule, in *Hip Hop America* noted music critic Nelson George (1999) infamously wrote:

> Hip hop has produced no Bessie Smith, no Billie Holiday, no Aretha Franklin. You could make an argument that Queen Latifah has, as a symbol of female empowerment, filled Aretha's shoes for rap, though for artistic impact Latifah doesn't compare to the Queen of Soul. Similarly, you can make a case that Salt-N-Pepa's four platinum albums and clean-cut sexuality mirror the Supremes' pop appeal, though neither of the two MCs or their beautiful DJ Spinderella is ever gonna be Diana Ross. In twenty-plus years of hip hop history on record, a period that has produced black vocalists Chaka Khan, Whitney Houston, Anita Baker, Tracy Chapman, Mary J. Blige, and Erykah Badu, there are no women who have contributed profoundly to rap's artistic growth. Aside from Latifah and Salt-N-Pepa, MC Lyte has recorded for over a decade and Yo-Yo has garnered some respect. So has longtime spinner and mix tape star DJ Jazzy Joyce. In the late '90s Foxy Brown and Lil' Kim have proven that raw language and sex sells, but no one is mistaking them for innovators. (p. 184; see also George, 1989)

When George wrote, "there are no women who have contributed profoundly to rap's artistic growth" and, concerning those he deems the most noteworthy female rappers, "no one is mistaking them for innovators," one wonders what criteria he used to measure whether these female rappers have "contributed profoundly to rap's artistic growth." Let's "keep it real" here, as we say within the hip hop community. It ain't like measuring aesthetic contributions is some sort of exact, empirical science. This, of course, gives us grounds to critically call into question George's hip hop aesthetic. He dropped the names of several female rappers but, as we witnessed in the quote above, he claimed that none of them have significantly impacted "rap's artistic growth." This is primarily so, according to George, because "[t]here is an adolescent quality to hip hop culture that makes it clear that most of its expressions are aimed to please teenage boys, and this usually excludes women from the dialogue. The dynamics of *adult* relationships are the backbone of blues and soul music, in which both women and men tell stories of love, hate, infidelity, and lust." Whereas, hip hop's "typical narrator is a young, angry, horny male who is often disdainful of or, at least, uninterested in commitments of any kind." In fact, he continued, for most of hip hop's history, "it has been a truism that the male rap consumer, white and black, simply won't accept female rappers" (p. 185, emphasis in original). What is truly amazing here, however, is the fact that George does not in any way critically interrogate the reasons why female rappers are "exclude[d] . . . from the dialogue" and why "the male rap consumer, white and black, simply won't accept female rappers."

By not critically interrogating the reasons why female rappers are "exclude[d] . . . from the dialogue," isn't George himself continuing to quarantine them to a space outside of the world of rap music, thus silencing or, at the least, significantly disparaging female rappers and their contributions to hip hop culture? Building on the black feminist aesthetic bequeathed by the black Feminist Art movement to the hip hop feminist movement, here instead of simply observing hip hop culture's gender problems (e.g., the misogyny of both male rappers and male hip hop consumers) couldn't we offer a solution by suggesting a *hip hop feminist aesthetic*? As someone who has been listening to rap music and a student of hip hop culture since I first heard "Rapper's Delight" blast out of my older brother's boom-box speakers on a basketball court in 1979, it would seem to me that although it has often gone unacknowledged and, therefore, unnamed, a hip hop feminist aesthetic indeed has historically and currently continues to exist and, as a matter of fact, it stretches all the way back to the origins of rap music and hip hop culture.

Even if the current "male rap consumer, white and black, simply won't accept female rappers," it does not mean that male rappers and male rap consumers have not previously, especially before rap music's mid- to late-1980s cross-over success, accepted and respected the skills and contributions of female rappers. How else can we explain female MCs' (or the inclusion of female MCs on so many) early hit rap records (in fact, "rap classics!"), for instance: Paulette Tee and Sweet Tee, "Vicious Rap" (1978) and "Rhymin' and Rappin'" (1979); Lady B, "To the Beat Y'All!" (1979); Funky 4+1 More (featuring Sha Rock), "Rappin' and Rockin'" (1979), "That's the Joint!" (1981), "Do You Want to Rock (Before I Let You Go)?" (1982), and "Feel It!" (1984); Afrika Bambaataa and the Cosmic Force (featuring Lisa Lee), "Zulu Nation Throwdown!" (1980); Blondie, "Rapture" (1981); Sylvia, "It's Good to Be the Queen" (1982); Us Girls (featuring Sha Rock, Lisa Lee, and Debbie Dee), "Us Girls" (1984); and, of course, Sequence, "Funk You Up!" (1979), "Monster Jam" (1980), "And You Know That" (1980), "Funky Sound" (1981), "Simon Says" (1982), "I Don't Need Your Love" (1982),

"Here Comes the Bride" (1982), "I Just Want to Know" (1983), "Funk You Up '85" (1984), and "Control" (1985)?

However, even as we discuss the existence of a hip hop feminist aesthetic and the conventional hypermasculine histories of hip hop, female rappers' vexed rejection of the term "feminist" must be raised, as it sheds more light on hip hop's contradictory and complex character. For example, in *Black Noise*, Tricia Rose (1994) wrote, "during my conversation with Salt, MC Lyte, and Queen Latifah it became clear that these women were uncomfortable with being labeled feminist and perceived feminism as a signifier for a movement that related specifically to white women," which, as we saw above, eerily echoes the views of most members of the black Women's Liberation movement (p. 176). Rose further explained, "[t]hey also thought feminism involved adopting an anti-male position, and although they clearly express frustrations with men, they did not want to be considered or want their work to be interpreted as anti-black male" (p. 176). As it was with the women of the Black Women's Club movement at the turn of the twentieth century and the members of the black Women's Liberation movement during the 1960s and 1970s, most African American female rappers have a filial connection with African American men that stems from their shared experience of anti-black racism. We should be clear here, as Rose pointed out, black women "clearly express frustrations with [black] men," but—to paraphrase Fanon in *Black Skin, White Masks* (1967)—it is the "lived-experience of the black" or, rather, the "fact of [their] blackness" in a simultaneously white and male supremacist society that has brought generation after generation of black women to the confounding conclusion that black men's sufferings as a result of anti-black racism (from the African Holocaust and the Middle Passage to racial colonialism and enslavement, through to twenty-first-century segregation and ongoing American apartheid) binds them to black men ideally as allies and comrades in struggle. This, of course, is also a sentiment that is echoed in the songs of neo-soul divas.

For many black women siding with black men in anti-racist struggle, even though many anti-racist black men are yet and still sexist, is like reluctantly choosing between the lesser of two evils. Black feminist foremothers have handed down invaluable lessons concerning multicultural and transethnic feminist alliances: from the memoirs of Black Women's Club movement pioneers, such as Ida B. Wells (1969, 1970, 1991, 1993, 1995) and Mary Church Terrell (1932, 1940), to the theoretical works discussed above from the black Women's Liberation movement. Moreover, the recurring theme of denial and betrayal, which has long been at the heart of black feminist writings, whether that denial and betrayal is at the hands of black men or white women, continues to haunt the hip hop feminist movement. Which is to say, a similar suspicion characterizes female rappers, neo-soul sisters, and other female hip hoppers' perception of, and fractured relationships with feminism. Rose (1994) intrepidly asserts:

> For these women rappers, and many other black women, feminism is the label for members of a white women's social movement that has no concrete link to black women or the black community. Feminism signifies allegiance to historically specific movements whose histories have long been the source of frustration for women of color. Similar criticisms of women's social movements have been made vociferously by many black feminists. As they have argued, race and gender are inextricably linked for black women. This is the case for both black and white women. However, in the case of black women, the realities of racism link black women to black men in a way that challenges cross-racial sisterhood. Sisterhood among and between black and white women will not be achieved at the expense of black women's racial identity. (p. 177)

As was witnessed above, most nonwhite women have long been just as committed to women's liberation as white feminists, but it has been their lived-experience of white women's "feminist racism" that has caused them to consistently recoil from bourgeois white women-centered conceptions of feminism and women's liberation. Nonwhite women should not be expected to embrace a form of feminism or a movement that is rhetorically aimed at their liberation while in reality it contributes to, and continues their economic exploitation and racial oppression. Herein lies the frequently commented on frustration and terse tension between black and white feminists, as well as the reason why the vapid male-misogynist rappers versus female-feminist rappers, or vice versa, is quite simply not applicable to the hip hop feminist movement. To speak here specifically about black women rappers, it is important to observe the recurring themes of black identity and black unity that runs throughout most of their music. This means, then, if many of them perceive feminism to be anti-black male, it stands to reason that feminism is not seen as a viable option for black women or black liberation.

Black women rappers are not simply in dialogue with the women of the hip hop generation. They are also in dialogue with the men of the hip hop generation, and it is their shared lived-experience and shared lived-endurance of anti-black racism and anti-black economic exploitation, which they suffer along with black men, that makes them simultaneously critical of black men's misogyny, but also sympathetic to and appreciative of black men's ongoing efforts to combat anti-black racism and economic exploitation. Joan Morgan (1999), in characteristic fashion, articulated the seemingly inexplicable relationship between black women, feminism, and black men:

> White girls don't call their men "brothers" and that made their struggle enviably simpler than mine. Racism and the will to survive it creates a sense of intra-racial loyalty that makes it impossible for black women to turn our backs on black men—even in their ugliest and most sexist of moments. I needed a feminism that would

allow us to continue loving ourselves *and* the brothers who hurt us without letting race loyalty buy us early tombstones. (p. 36, emphasis in original)

Like generation after generation of black women before them, hip hop feminists find themselves in a situation where they understand it to be "impossible for black women to turn our backs on black men." Consequently, it will never be enough for black and other nonwhite women to desegregate white feminist discourse, or for white feminists to finally (and paternalistically) allow *the racially gendered other* to speak. Much more, a systematic deconstruction and reconstruction of feminism and women's liberation should be carried out and, even more specifically, one that takes into serious consideration the ways in which race, culture, class, religion, sexuality, and nationality discursively destabilize gender as an autonomous analytical category.

Noted hip hop feminist Heather Humann (2007) went so far as to say, "[a]lthough women's rights are undoubtedly important, a point of view that *only* considers gender can become problematic, because it mistakenly pits women against men instead of realizing that the system itself is flawed and encourages exploitation and oppression of large numbers of people" (pp. 101–02, emphasis in original). The emergence of intersectional studies (especially the critique of the ways in which race, gender, class, and sexuality overlap and intermesh) during the late 1970s, 1980s, and 1990s must be taken into consideration here, or else it will be very difficult to comprehend hip hop feminism. In other words, hip hop feminists critically comprehend that mass media interpretations of hip hop, as well as the mass media's widely disseminated distorted stories about hip hop, are actually part and parcel of the ongoing social construction and maintenance of race, gender, class, sexuality, nationality, and other identities. All of this is to say, *hip hop feminism is much more than feminism, and it focuses on more than feminist issues, misogyny, and patriarchy.* Hip hop feminists use hip hop culture as one of their primary points of departure to highlight serious social issues and the need for political activism aimed at racism, sexism, capitalism, and heterosexism as overlapping and interlocking systems of oppression. In this sense, then, hip hop feminism displays the influence not only of feminism, but of several new theories that have emerged within the last three decades and, even more, it arguably represents the most visible recent reminder that for feminism to really find footing in the twenty-first century and truly speak to the special needs of the women of the hip hop generation it will have to epistemically open itself to the theoretical and practical advances of several of the new theories and praxes that have emerged in the aftermath of various 1960s and 1970s social movements, for example: womanist theory, mestiza consciousness theory, critical race theory, critical race feminist theory, Africana critical theory, postcolonial theory, subaltern theory, queer theory, transnationalism, black Marxism, and hip hop aesthetics.

Hip hop feminism is not only critical of white women-centered feminism, but also super-strong black women-centered feminism. Discursively building on Michele Wallace's classic *Black Macho and the Myth of the Superwoman* (1979), Joan Morgan's (1999) work helps to highlight hip hop feminists' repudiation of the myth of the super-strong, self-sacrificing, and long-suffering black woman (pp. 83–112; see also James and Busia, 1993). As was the case with the members of the black Women's Liberation movement of the 1960s and 1970s, hip hop feminists are much less likely to embrace the myth of the super-strong black woman. In fact, hip hop feminists are highly critical of those black and other nonwhite women who resist the notion that, in so many words, the "personal is political," insofar as those women who demur and refuse to give full and uninhibited voice to their needs and deep desires not only perpetuate the myth of the super-strong, self-sacrificing, and long-suffering black woman, but they also impede black women's liberation and authentic African American emancipation. In their own way, hip hop feminists seem to be asking the very same question that so many of their foremothers in the Black Women's Club movement and the black Women's Liberation movement asked: Can authentic black liberation be achieved if black women, who roughly constitute half of the black folk in the United States, remain enslaved and imprisoned as a result of patriarchal gender roles and racially gendered social rules? To state it outright: black women's liberation is (or, rather, *should be*) an integral part of authentic African American emancipation. African Americans cannot and will not achieve true decolonization and lasting human liberation if black women are not freed from gender domination and discrimination in the midst of the overarching struggle for racial, social, and economic justice in the United States.

In the United States patriarchy is predicated on masculinist popular culture as much as it is on male-centered politics, economics, and social conventions, and this is one of the reasons hip hop feminists find it necessary to carry out their critiques within the wider world of mass media and popular culture.[16] However, and this is where the "old school feminists'" concerns critically come into play, it is quite often difficult to discern whether hip hop feminists in particular, and the women of the hip hop generation in general, are creating a new form of feminism and a new wing of the Women's Liberation movement to meet the novel needs of their generation, or simply being insidiously entertained by sexism's new, even more seductive, twenty-first century soundtrack. Within the world of hip hop many hip hoppers, female and male, with feminist sensibilities and anti-sexist politics live anguished existences, torn between the latest hip hop fad and radical anti-racist feminism. Many of us (myself included, to speak candidly) are guilty of being enamored with hip hop artists and their commercial and/or conscious cultural products, avowing the power, beauty, and—with a yelping yes—the ugliness of their poetry and artistry each and every time we mouth the wise/wack words of their rhymes, mimic their seductive dance moves, and bounce with abandon to their bodacious beats. It is as if we know but wanna hide the fact from ourselves that we have embraced a form of *hip hop bad faith*, because all of the murder-mouthing, mean-mugging, and rotund rump-shaking in contemporary hip hop culture regularly reminds us that no matter how hype hip hop used to be, no matter how it may have raised our consciousness and made us aware of important social and political issues in the past, now it frequently leaves us numb and desensitized to the pain and suffering of the present—and, especially, the pain and suffering of the women and girls of the hip hop generation.

I will openly admit that I have long been offended by the insults and indifference of most of what is taken to be hip hop in the world of popular music and culture. However, even as I write all of this I manage to steer clear of a deep depression in light of the fact that at this very moment I am in the process of deconstructing and reconstructing hip hop culture. I refuse to be imprisoned by the distorted and disturbing images of what it means to be a man who loves and is inspired by hip hop culture. There quite simply is no eleventh commandment that has been handed down that says that all males who are hip hoppers must be hypermasculinist, misogynist, and/or male supremacist. Instead of leading the youth to mindlessly adopt the most misogynistic thought and behavior available, real hip hop, what is commonly called "conscious" and/or "alternative" hip hop, can cause hip hoppers to call into question unjust social conventions, conservative politics, and the carpetbagger nature of corporate capitalism. What is more, when and where we agree that conscious hip hop has and continues to raise our consciousness about critical issues is precisely when and where we acknowledge that hip hop has the ability to highlight, critique, and disrupt power relations. Within the world of intersectional theory and praxis, power relations are not simply predicated on race and class, but gender and sexuality also play a pivotal role here, and this is where feminism and sexology importantly come into play.

A simultaneously intersectional and interdisciplinary critical theory of hip hop culture highlights the multidimensionality and polyvocality of hip hop identities and, it should be emphasized, hip hop identities are as racially gendered as any other social and/or cultural identity. Consequently, hip hop feminism focuses on, and forces hip hoppers to acknowledge the racially gendered discursive formations and discursive practices of hip hop culture, as well as the wider sociocultural world. Which is to say, hip hoppers' conceptions of manhood and womanhood or, rather, masculinity and femininity did not miraculously fall from the sky, and an intersectional and interdisciplinary critical theory of hip hop culture enables hip hoppers to cogently connect the dots between pre-existing race, gender, class, and sexual orientation oppression and their current forms within the world of hip hop. Instead of viewing hip hop as nothing more than another site where a simultaneously patriarchal and "pathological" culture distracts young women (and men) from feminist theory and praxis, hip hop feminism "wrecks" patriarchal power relations in hip hop by juxtaposing commercial and conscious hip hop and the ways in which women are represented and/or misrepresented in both.

Of course, there are few if any authentic feminist spaces within the world of popular culture in patriarchal societies, but for hip hop feminists this is all beside the point. The point is to offer the women of the hip hop generation feminist and womanist alternatives to the patriarchal (mis)representations of womanhood spewing out of the U.S. culture industries. As Gwendolyn Pough (2004) pointed out, because hip hop's sexism is so prevalent, and because there is only so long that the women of the hip hop generation can embrace either the super-strong black woman or video vixen identities, hip hop feminists have "found ways to deal with these issues within the larger public sphere and the counter-public sphere of hip hop by bringing wreck to stereotyped images through their continued use of expressive culture" (p. 74; see also jamila, 2002; Pough, 2002, 2003).

Patriarchs do not now, and have never had a monopoly on popular or expressive culture, and the hip hop feminists "flip the script" by using hip hop culture as a medium to raise awareness about women's life-worlds and life-struggles. By critically studying and participating in hip hop culture, hip hop feminists bring their intimate knowledge of hip hop to bear on the ways in which patriarchy plays itself out within the world of hip hop and the wider sociocultural world. Contradictory and controversial, in the final analysis hip hop feminism challenges both hip hop *and* feminism, and the work of the hip hop feminists discussed above, among others, offers proof-positive that U.S. feminism is not now and never has been the prime property or exclusive domain of middle-class white or college-educated women. In both the past and the present, the Women's Liberation movement in the United States has been built and maintained by women from a wide range of backgrounds who comprehend feminist theory to be an indispensible tool (albeit inadequate when it comes to the critique of racism, capitalism, and heterosexism) in their efforts to critically understand and explain their lived-experiences with, and lived-endurances of misogyny and patriarchy.

As was the case with the members of the black Women's Liberation movement of the 1960s and 1970s, most black women continue to reject bourgeois and white women-centered conceptions of feminism that, from black women's point of view, have absorbed several of the signatures of American society, such as Jeffersonian individualism, Jacksonian democracy, bourgeois materialism, allusive anti-black racism, and hedonism. As a strain of feminist theory and praxis primarily inspired by past nonwhite women's anti-racist and anti-capitalist feminism, hip hop feminism can be said to offer both a critique of, and a corrective for contemporary conceptions and articulations of U.S. feminism. It must be openly admitted, however, that because the women of the hip hop generation are also members of U.S. society, similar to many of the feminists who have gone before them, they too have been influenced by and often embrace Eurocentric, patriarchal, bourgeois, and heteronormative views and values—hence, my above characterization of hip hop feminism as "contradictory and controversial." With one foot in hip hop culture and one foot in feminism, even as hip hop feminism endeavors to critique hip hop *and* feminism it often shows itself to be culturally and conceptually incarcerated: critical of hip hop, yet basking in its boldness, and critical of "old school feminism," yet extremely appreciative (and often in awe) of its audacious commitment to women's liberation.

Truth be told, most nonwhite youth have been socialized to want the "American dream" (i.e., a "good" job, fancy clothes, shiny jewelry, a flashy car, and a big house with a two-car garage) just like their mainstream white counterparts. This means, then, that the young women of the hip hop generation are not immune to Americanisms, and hip hop feminism not only harbors many of the contradictions of hip hop and feminism, but also many of the contradictions of American history, culture, and society. This fact should shock no one, least of all the "old school feminists" of the previous generation, because, as quiet as it has been kept, their theories and praxes are also deeply rooted in Americanisms even though they are critical of patriarchy in U.S. society. By not denying the contradictions of hip hop culture, and by emphasizing the ways in which sexism overlaps and intersects with race, class, sexuality, and nationality in U.S. popular culture, hip hop feminists are simultaneously expanding the range and uses of intersectional theory and complicating what it means to be both a hip hopper and a feminist.

At this point it would seem that the hip hop feminist movement has laid to rest the question of whether it is possible for one to be both a hip hopper and a feminist. Unapologetically courting controversy, the hip hop feminist movement represents a revitalization of feminism from poor nonwhite women's perspectives, and a much needed deconstruction and reconstruction of hip hop culture from an anti-racist feminist perspective. Consequently, hip hop and feminism, both of which have historically marginalized, colonized, and co-opted the contributions of nonwhite women, have been and are being transformed by the poetry, artistry, intellectualism, and activism of non-elite and nonwhite women. For most of the women of the hip hop generation, then, their lived-experiences and lived-endurances resoundingly reaffirm that, however different from their feminist foremothers, *the personal is still political*, and the political continues to be bound up with patriarchal and racially gendered notions of "a woman's place" in U.S. culture and society. Even with all of its contradictions and seeming callousness toward other forms of feminism, hip hop feminism is innovatively continuing the Women's Liberation and Feminist Art movements. Whether we agree or disagree with hip hop feminists' articulations of hip hop or feminism—or, even more, *hip hop feminism*—is all beside the point: the point, to put it plainly, is that they are critically interpreting and explicating hip hop and feminism on their own terms and from their own distinct standpoints as hip hoppers *and* feminists and, I honestly believe, both hip hop culture and feminism have been and will continue to be enriched as a result of the seminal syntheses and critical contributions of hip hop feminism.

Bearing in mind our above discussion concerning the female-feminist rapper versus the male-misogynist rapper dichotomy, the next chapter critically explores the origins and evolution of arguably hip hop culture's most popular and controversial expression: rap music. Emphasis will be placed on the ways in which corporate America-created categories, such as "commercial" rap versus "conscious" rap, are part and parcel of what I have termed the "hyper-corporate colonization of hip hop culture." Let us purposely ponder this for a moment: What are the distinct differences between "commercial" and "conscious" rap, and who created these categories? How has the hardcore capitalist political economy of corporate America altered—i.e., discursively deformed—rap music and, even more, hip hop culture's evolution? How has rap music's emergence in the aftermath of the Civil Rights, Black Power, and Women's Liberation movements impacted its message, or lack of message? Furthermore, what has rap music *inherited*, or not inherited, from past sociopolitical movements? How did the popularity and politics of post-modernism in the late 1970s, 1980s, and 1990s impact and influence the creation and general reception of rap music? And, lastly, the question that seems to be on the tip of almost everyone's tongues these days: Is hip hop dead or, at the very least, dying? One sincerely wonders whether this book will be taken as a eulogy for hip hop rather than (as the author intended it) a work aimed at contributing to *critical Hip Hop studies*—that is, *insurgent interdisciplinary and intersectional Hip Hop studies*? It is these questions, among others, that will serve as the primary preoccupation of the final chapter.

NOTES

1. The contention that hip hop feminism seems to "simultaneously embrace and reject the fundamentals of feminism and the contradictions of hip hop culture" will serve as a recurring theme throughout this chapter. However, unlike most of the other work on hip hop feminism—save the aforementioned works by Pough (2004) and P. H. Collins (2005)—here a more dialectical approach will be undertaken, one that embraces Collins's (2005, p. 194) caveat that it is time for us to analyze and explore continuity and consensus rather than merely discontinuity and discord by developing critical analyses that consider "expressions of black women's activism as intersecting versus parallel spheres of activity."

2. For those unfamiliar with what Morgan is referring to as the "vital tradition of black feminist thought," and for samplings of the work of several of the black feminist authors she mentions in this excerpt, please see: P. H. Collins (2000), A. Y. Davis (1981, 1989, 1998a),

Guy-Sheftall (1995), hooks (1981, 1984, 1989, 1990, 1991, 1995b), Houston and Davis (2002), Hudson-Weems (1998a, 1998b, 1998c, 2000, 2001a, 2001b), Hull, Scott, and Smith (1982), James and Busia (1993), James, Foster, and Guy-Sheftall (2009), James and Sharpley-Whiting (2000), Lorde (1984, 1988, 1996), Phillips (2006), Prince, Silva-Wayne, and Vernon (2004), and Barbara Smith (1983, 1998).

3. For further discussion of the "unhappy marriage of Marxism and feminism," please see: Di Stephano (1991, 2011), Eisenstein (1979), Hartmann (1979), Hennessy (1993), Hennessy and Ingraham (1997), Kuhn and Wolpe (1978), Moi and Radway (1994), Nye (1989), Sargent (1981), and Weinbaum (1978).

4. The focus on the African American family here should be emphasized, as *The Negro Family: The Case for National Action* (also known as "The Moynihan Report on the Negro Family") was published in the year that marked the beginning of the Black Power movement and, ironically, the year commonly used to demarcate the first year hip hoppers began to be born, 1965. Arguably, African American male/female relationships have been in crisis since enslavement, but it is also important for us to acknowledge how the Moynihan report, among other policy reports, may have exacerbated preexisting issues within the black community. As a matter of fact, there is a substantial body of research that reveals the disproportionate and detrimental impact that seemingly "neutral" and "positive" public policy has historically had on African Americans. For further discussion, I refer my readers to a few of the more noteworthy studies in this area: Duchess Harris (2001), Herring (1997), Jewell (2003), R. W. Walters (2003), and W. J. Wilson (1987).

5. The body of literature on African American medical experimentation and medical mistrust is extensive and, much of it, well beyond the parameters of the present study. However, besides Washington's groundbreaking book, it is important to observe that my interpretation here has been indelibly informed by Gamble (1993), Reverby (2000), and Savitt (1982, 2007).

6. It is important here to emphasize the pioneering nature of Toni Cade Bambara's *The Black Woman*, which helped to discursively distinguish the literature of the black Women's Liberation movement from the literatures of both the Black Power and white Women's Liberation movements. For further discussion of *The Black Woman*, see Crow (2000), M. Crawford (2009), Griffin (2002), and Hernton (1984, 1990).

7. Considering the common mischaracterizations of black men as seemingly inherently predisposed to patriarchy and misogyny, it is important here to emphasize what has come to be called "black male feminism," which has roots in the lifework and legacies of black feminist forefathers such as Charles Lenox Remond, Frederick Douglass, W. E. B. Du Bois, and Frantz Fanon, among others (see Lemons, 2008, 2009; Rabaka 2007, 2010a, 2010b; Sharpley-Whiting, 1997). In fact, as quiet as it has been kept, many of the men of the Black Power and hip hop generations have made several important contributions to the continuation of black male feminism, women's liberation, and gender justice. For example, see Byrd and Guy-Sheftall (2001), Carbado (1999), Ikard (2007), Mutua (2006), M. A. Neal (2005), and A. M. White (2008).

8. Considering the wide range of works available on Beauvoir, I have been extremely selective in choosing the texts that inform my interpretation of her life and the evolution of her thought. With respect to my analysis here, the most noteworthy works are Marks (1987), Moi (1994), Simons (1995), and Whitmarsh (1981).

9. For further discussion of Judy Chicago's biography and artistry, as well as the works that I have relied on the most to develop my interpretation here, see Chicago (1996), Levin (2007), and Lucie-Smith (2000).

10. Hurston's life and legacy has a special place among black feminist artists, especially writers. Therefore, Hurston studies is a fairly developed field. My interpretation of Hurston's biography and artistry has been influenced by Bloom (2008), Croft (2002), Cronin (1998), Gates and Appiah (1993b), Hemenway (1977), Miles (2003), Plant (2007), and M. G. West (2005).

11. Still something of a mystery to many scholars and researchers, the following abbreviated interpretation of Hansberry's life and legacy has greatly benefited from critical readings of S. R. Carter (1991), A. Cheney (1984), and Scheader (1978).

12. As noted in the introduction to this chapter, my conception of the evolution of the Women's Liberation movement of the 1960s and 1970s, as well as its aftermath in the 1980s

and 1990s, is primarily based on the work of Verta Taylor and her colleagues (see also Rupp and Taylor, 1986, 1991; Schmidt and Taylor, 1997; Staggenborg and Taylor, 2005; Taylor and Rupp, 1991). In this section, along with Taylor and her collaborators' work, my analysis has been influenced by Berkeley (1999), Dicker (2008), S. Evans (1979), Ferree and Martin (1995), Freeman (1975), and Giardina (2010).

13. It is almost impossible to critically discuss hip hop feminism without also connecting it to and critically engaging hip hop (hyper)masculinism, which is, whether consciously or unconsciously, based on the brashness and braggadocio of Black Power movement (hyper)masculinism. As a matter of fact, Charise Cheney's groundbreaking *Phallic/ies and Hi(s)stories: Masculinity and the Black Nationalist Tradition, from Slave Spirituals to Rap Music* (1999) and *Brothers Gonna Work It Out!: Sexual Politics in the Golden Age of Rap Nationalism* (2005) both astutely illustrate several of the ways in which past forms of nationalist masculinism inform present forms of nationalist masculinism, especially "rap nationalism." Other noteworthy works on hip hop masculinity that have directly influenced my analysis here include Greene (2008), Hopkinson and Moore (2006), Hurt (2006), Osayande (2008), and J. K. Smith (2002).

14. For those skeptical of my use of Fanon's critical theory in the interest of women's decolonization and women's liberation, it is important to acknowledge feminists and womanists' longstanding critical relationship with his radical politics and revolutionary humanist praxis. Admittedly, Fanon has a contradictory, controversial, and regularly contested relationship with feminism, womanism, and women's studies (Dubey, 1998; Fuss, 1995; Gopal, 2002; McClintock, 1995; Sharpley-Whiting, 1997). As the growing body of criticism on Fanon's "feminism" demonstrates, it would be extremely difficult to deny his contributions—again, however contradictory, controversial, and contested—to women's quest to decolonize their distinct life-worlds and lived-experiences in the male supremacist world in which they find themselves. As I argued in *Forms of Fanonism: Frantz Fanon's Critical Theory and the Dialectics of Decolonization*, Fanon's commitment to women's liberation was deeply connected to, and, even more, inextricable from his commitments to revolutionary decolonization, democratic socialism, and human liberation, and, as with each of the aforementioned, his theory of women's liberation has progressive and retrogressive aspects (Rabaka, 2010b). There has long been a knee-jerk tendency among theorists, both male and female, who engage Fanon's contributions to feminism, womanism, and women's liberation to argue *either* that Fanon was gender progressive *or* that Fanon was gender regressive. I openly acknowledge, in all intellectual honesty, that Fanon was *both*: in his texts he seems to be schizophrenically, at times, a staunch advocate for women's rights and women's liberation, and, at other times, completely oblivious of his "Freudian slips" and blind-spots with regard to gender justice and the ways in which his work—that is, his own words—speak to, not the *decolonization* of women's life-worlds and lived-experiences, but the *recolonization* of women's life-worlds and lived-experiences. In a sense, then, Fanon's contributions to feminism prefigure and mirror much of the contradictory and controversial character of hip hop feminism by containing some progressive and some retrogressive elements.

15. While it can be considered progressive for men to recognize women's life-struggles, it is extremely problematic when "genuine" womanhood is quickly collapsed into motherhood. When one carefully and critically listens to male rappers' odes to their mothers from a womanist and/or feminist perspective what one mostly hears are *mythic idealizations of the maternal*. In other words, it often seems as though male rappers' mothers (and other older women) are somehow exceptions to hip hop's hypermasculinist and misogynist rules that regularly reduce young women to "baby mamas," "gold diggers," "skeezers," "bitches," and "hoes." African American men's mythic idealization of the maternal did not begin with the men of the hip hop generation but, interestingly, this species of thought can be shown to extend all the way back to the men of the New Negro movement and the Harlem Renaissance. Engaging this issue by focusing on a specific New Negro/Harlem Renaissance luminary, I have treated W. E. B. Du Bois's simultaneous contributions to, and critique of the mythic idealization of black motherhood in my book *W. E. B. Du Bois and the Problems of the Twenty-First Century*, see especially chapter 5, "Du Bois and 'The Damnation of Women': Critical Social Theory and the Souls of Black Female Folk" (Rabaka, 2007, 137–87).

16. As is well known, hip hop feminists are not the only group of contemporary feminists whose feminist critique centers on the ways that patriarchy plays itself out in mass media and popular culture (see Buszek, 2006; Genz, 2009; Gillis and Hollows, 2009; Hollows, 2000; Hollows and Moseley, 2006; Worsley, 2010; Zeisler, 2008). However, hip hop feminism is distinguished by its use of hip hop culture as its primary point of departure in its efforts to develop a newfangled anti-racist feminist critique of, not simply contemporary popular culture, but also contemporary politics, economics, and society.

Chapter Five

Is Hip Hop Dead? or, At the Very Least, Dying?: On the Pitfalls of Postmodernism, the Riddles of Contemporary Rap Music, and the Continuing Conundrums of Hip Hop Culture

Everything is permitted in the dance circle. . . . Everything is permitted, for in fact the sole purpose of the gathering is to let the supercharged libido and the stifled aggressiveness spew out volcanically. Symbolic killings, figurative cavalcades, and imagined multiple murders, everything has to come out. The ill humors seep out, tumultuous as lava flows. —Frantz Fanon, *The Wretched of the Earth*, p. 20

"EVERY SHUT EYE AIN'T SLEEP, AND EVERY GOODBYE AIN'T GONE!": ON HIP HOP'S LIFE, DEATH, AND POTENTIAL RADICAL POLITICAL RESURRECTION

Obviously there is more to hip hop culture than meets the untrained or overly critical eye, and I have carefully come to the conclusion that the major soundtrack of hip hop, rap music, however controversially and contradictorily, speaks volumes about both what is good and what is bad, what is beautiful and what is undeniably ugly within the world of hip hop. Hip hop culture, especially rap music, is like a large panoramic mirror reflecting contemporary culture, politics, and society. Whatever issues and ills rap music raises are not simply the products of tortured and twisted young black folks' minds,

189

but more musical responses to current *intra-communal* and *extra-communal* pressing problems. Therefore, the search for solutions to hip hop's problems cannot and will not be found exclusively within the world of hip hop, but also within the wider world of contemporary U.S. culture, politics, and society. In other words, hip hop does not now, and never has existed in a social, political, and cultural vacuum. This means, then, that in the aftermath of our critical discussions of what hip hop has *inherited* from previous cultural aesthetic and sociopolitical movements we have reached the crucial point where we must critically examine how it has been, truth be told, both informed and deformed by the moorings and overall "postmodern" mood of late twentieth-century and early twenty-first-century America.

This chapter, which will also serve as the book's conclusion, brings the disparate discourses from the previous chapters together in the interest of highlighting how the aesthetic advances and political breakthroughs of the past have impacted and influenced hip hop's aesthetics and politics in the present, especially the origins and evolution of rap music. We begin by exploring the interrelation between hip hop culture and postmodernism. This is an important point of departure because previous Hip Hop studies scholars have had a tendency to either make too much, or too little of the connections between 1980s and 1990s postmodern aesthetics and hip hop aesthetics, especially the influence of postmodernism on rap music's poetics and politics.

The next section critically engages what I have termed the "hyper-corporate colonization of hip hop culture," intensely exploring how late 1970s and early 1980s African American underclass and other working-poor youth culture, which was initially thought to be nothing more than a mere passing ghetto fad and poor young folks' foolishness, evolved into an artistic and sociopolitical force of great significance, not only nationally but internationally. However with its increasing cultural clout, by the mid-1980s corporate America began to take notice and perceive the money-making potential in hip hop culture, elevating rapping and break-dancing over the other five fundamental elements of hip hop culture: DJing, graffiti-writing, and beat-boxing (S. Baker, 2006; Chang, 2006; Forman and Neal, 2011; Fricke and Ahearn, 2002; Lommel, 2000). After a brief period of competing with rap music as the most identifiable public emblem or social symbol of hip hop culture, break-dancing fell to the wayside and the "hyper-corporate colonization of hip hop culture," mostly centering around all manner of schemes to market and commercialize rap music, began in earnest.[1] A tug-of-war of sorts soon took place or, rather, is taking place between those who see rap music as a pop cultural and commercial gold mine and those who believe that rap music should radically reflect the politics, culture, and impecunious communities that created and contributed it. In short, this section will tackle the contentious dichotomy between "commercial" and "conscious" rap, revealing that these forms represent much more than "ghetto music" and that they discursively converge and diverge more often than previously perceived or critically commented on.

The last section of this chapter brings *Hip Hop's Inheritance* to a close by building on and going beyond the critique of the "conscious" versus "commercial" rap dichotomy, solemnly emphasizing that what should really matter with regard to rap music, and hip hop culture more generally, is not whether a hip hopper's artistry falls within the corporate America–created categories of "commercial" or "conscious" rap but, even more, whether the messages in the hip hopper's work reflect the "real" issues and ills, as well as the hopes, dreams, and deep-seated desires, of the hip hop generation. That is to say, the historic *idyllic impulse* that has informed the best of African American history, culture, and struggle is emphasized in this section and the ongoing ritual of the *European Americanization of African American popular music and culture* is critically called into question. Highlighting what I have termed "African Americans' culture of resistance and restitution" and "African Americans' tradition of transcendence and opposition," this book concludes as it began, advancing a critical theory of hip hop culture and placing hip hop's controversies and contradictions into historical perspective. We now turn, then, to one of the often overlooked contributors to hip hop's aesthetic palette, 1980s and 1990s U.S. postmodernism, and the place where 1980s and 1990s so-called high culture met 1980s and 1990s so-called low culture, and vice versa.

HIP HOP'S HOMESPUN POSTMODERNISM: BETWIXT AND BETWEEN BLACK AMERICA'S POST-CIVIL RIGHTS POLITICS AND WHITE AMERICA'S POSTMODERN POLITICS

It would seem that the hip hop generation has either come too late, or too early. Too late, from the point of view of the postmodernists, to witness "modernity" in all of its Eurocentric and imperial glory and splendor. Too early, from the point of view of the already emerging post-hip hop generation, to participate in the deeply hoped for future renaissance of the twenty-first century. In fact, for many hip hop is quickly becoming a relic and reminder of the failure of the post–Civil Rights, post–Black Power, and post–Women's Liberation generation. What is more, many hip hoppers themselves (the present author notwithstanding) have begun to question the overarching direction, mission, and message of hip hop culture. Considering both the breakthroughs and setbacks of the Harlem Renaissance, the Black Arts movement, and the Feminist Art movement we are now in a position to critically call into question what the hip hop generation has and has not done with its unique inheritance. Indeed, it has boldly backslid when and where we come to sexism, heterosexism, and bourgeois materialism. However, especially when one considers "conscious" and "alternative" hip hop communities and cultures, it has also persevered and contributed to contemporary anti-sexism, anti-heterosexism, and anti-capitalism. In other words, and rather ironically, hip hop is as political as it is perceived to be apolitical.[2]

Emerging during a period when many of the major social, political, cultural, and aesthetic theorists of (or, at the very least, associated with) the Eurocentric established order were propounding "postmodern" thesis after thesis on the "death of man" (Michel Foucault), the "death of the author" (Roland Barthes), the "panoply of symbols and signs" (Jacques Derrida), the "libidinal economy" of contemporary culture and society (Jean-François Lyotard), the "linguistic, semiotic, and social construction of the feminine" (Julia Kristeva, Luce Irigaray, and Judith Butler), and the "end of history" (Jean Baudrillard and Francis Fukuyama), the world of hip hop—its culture, politics, literature, language, fashion, and aesthetics—is situated somewhere between and, at times, beyond the mainstream and the margin. For example, notice here how hip hop culture could be said to be thoroughly "postmodern" based on Jean-François Lyotard's articulation of postmodernism in his groundbreaking classic *The Postmodern Condition* (1984), where he argued that the "postmodern condition" is

> the condition of knowledge in the most highly developed societies. I have decided to use the word *postmodern* to describe that condition. The word is in current use on the American continent among sociologists and critics; it designates the state of our culture following the transformations which, since the end of the nineteenth century, have altered the game rules for science, literature, and the arts. (p. xxiii, emphasis in original)[3]

Making a critical distinction between *postmodernity* (i.e., the historical, cultural, social, and political epoch emerging after European modernity), *postmodernism* (i.e., a set of aesthetic theories and praxes and a combination of art emerging both after and often against European modernism), and *postmodern knowledge* (i.e., thought critical of modern European epistemology), hip hop culture only loosely fits within the web of the conventional definitions of postmodernity, postmoderism, and postmodern knowledge because its points of departure primarily stem from the history, culture, and thought of those whose ancestors were decimated and dominated, *not* exalted and liberated, during European modernity.[4] As a matter of fact, much of hip hop culture—especially conscious rap and alternative hip hop culture—continues historic critiques and is currently aimed at critiquing the hegemony of European American thought, culture, and politics. Because the bulk of its primary points of departure are rooted in historical and cultural realities long marginalized in both European and U.S. modern *and* postmodern circles, hip hop culture often decidedly stands outside of the orbit of postmodernism. That is to say, while hip hop may appear to have some of the outer trappings and harbor other accoutrements associated with postmodernism, it might be more properly interpreted as nonwhite youths', especially African American underclass and working-poor youths', anguished expressions of their efforts to make sense of the mayhem that followed in the wake of the Civil Rights, Black Power, and Women's Liberation movements—and, most especially, the offshoot Black Arts and Feminist Art movements.

To speak calmly, although candidly, here, the origins of hip hop culture do not lie in Europe or European America, but in the *ghettos* (from the Italian word *borghetto*, a diminutive of *borgo*, meaning "village"), *barrios*, and other impoverished areas of non-European America, especially *African* America. Moreover, for all of the postmodernists' conversations and contentions concerning moving away from the "master narratives" of European modernity I have long been amazed by the fact that they seem to be completely oblivious to the arguable issue that their new or, rather, "postmodern" narratives have debatably done nothing more than continue the colonization and marginalization of nonwhites, women and, for the most part, homosexuals in the postmodern period. The previous chapters clearly reveal that I do not believe hip hop culture to be the most welcoming or egalitarian space when we come to the life-worlds and life-struggles of women and homosexuals. However, and refusing to throw the baby out with the bathwater, I believe that the more recent Hip Hop Feminist and Homo-Hop movements discursively demonstrate that hip hop culture is a lot more aesthetically, intellectually, and politically elastic than previously thought. Needless to say, postmodernism—even with its stress on multiplicity and plurality, emphasis on micropolitics over macropolitics, and critique of postindustrial society and modernity's "bourgeois humanist subject"—has neither included nor gone out of its way to make nonwhites feel welcome within its discursive circles and aesthetic communities. In fact, one of the great ironies of postmodernists' critique of modern European history, culture, and thought revolves around their, whether intentional or not, rote refusal to create authentic radical humanist relationships with the history, culture, and thought of the descendants of those whom their ancestors culturally decimated and racially colonized during European modernity.

Postmodernists' identification of, and pontification about a "politics of difference" theoretically should include the *vox populi* of the wretched of the earth, those marginalized, racially colonized, exploited and oppressed by European modernity's "slave masters" and their "master narratives." It is rather ironic, then, that the same contemporary discourse which endlessly emphasizes hybridity, heterogeneity, the decentered subject, and constantly calls our attention to the importance of recognizing and embracing the "Other," for all intents and purposes, continues to couch its "postmodern" voice in an obscure Eurocentric academic language (i.e., "academese") and in discursive directions that grow out of, and often surreptitiously congratulates and continues the very same modern "master narratives" it proudly professes to be challenging. If, indeed, postmodernist thought is to really and truly have a transformative impact on contemporary culture, politics, and society, then it will have to move beyond radical rhetorical posturing and actually get down to the business of developing serious dialogues with the critical theories and radical praxes emanating from the non-European world, many of which revolve around the discourses of decolonization, postcolonialism, subaltern studies, critical race theory, critical race feminism, and queer theory, etc. Moreover, if postmodernism is to have any lasting meaning beyond a handful of highbrow Eurocentric critics and academics, it must bring its novel aesthetics of existence, artistic expressions, and cultural criticisms into discursive dialogue with the most pressing social and political problems emerging from contemporary non-European life-worlds and life-struggles. In short, non-Europeans and their so-called postcolonial histories, cultures, and ongoing struggles must be rendered the same *radical subjectivity* that a wide range of modern and postmodern European peoples, histories, cultures, and ongoing struggles have been granted since the genesis of postmodernism after World War II (i.e., circa 1945) (Farrell, 1994; Pieterse, 1992; Schnitman and Schnitman, 2002; Seidman, 1994).

The non-European proletariat and bourgeoisie, as with the European and European American proletariat and bourgeoisie, who indifferently imbibe cultural imperialist and otherwise white supremacist thought and practices, and who racially (re)colonize and ghettoize "postmodern"/"postcolonial" non-European and non-European American history, culture, and contemporary struggles, should not be counted on to produce or somehow provide the wretched of the earth of the twenty-first century with decolonialist discursive thought and practices or, even more, to promote the radical disruption of conventional Eurocentric ways of being, seeing, and thinking because, truth be told, they have been brutally brainwashed into believing that the current configuration of the world is the only possible configuration of the world at this point. Hence, here I wish to highlight the undertone of pessimism that pervades so much of the thought and practices of the "postmodern"/"postcolonial" non-European proletariat and bourgeoisie—a prevalent and predatory form of pessimism that is frequently found in rap music, and hip hop culture more generally, and which stands today as one of the staunchest deterrents to the *idyllic impulse* (to be discussed in detail below) that has historically housed generation after generation of African Americans' most hallowed hopes, dreams, and deep-seated desires.

An alternate interpretation of the relationship between hip hop culture and postmodernism understands the "postmodern" to be that which is no longer modern or, rather, that which succeeds European modernity and, therefore, builds on and goes beyond it. However, drawing on Jürgen Habermas's

(1975, 1984, 1987a, 1987b, 1989) pioneering critique of postmodernism and critical theory of legitimation, it does not necessarily mean that the "postmodern," that which follows the modern, is always and in every sense "postmodern," insofar as many aspects of European modernity continue to shape and shade contemporary history, culture, thought, and behavior. We might even go so far as to say that the more "postmodern" one is, ironically the more "modern" one is, to the exact degree to which one consciously seeks to build on and/or break with past conceptions of what it meant to be modern. By placing "post" in front of "modern" one is still to a certain extent carrying past conceptions of what it meant to be "modern" forward. In acknowledging this, then, it is also important to highlight lines of continuity from the colonizations and marginalizations of European modernity to the continued colonizations and marginalizations of European and European American postmodernity. In other words, as the work of the Nigerian philosopher Emmanuel Eze (1997, 2001, 2008) and the Eritrean philosopher Tsenay Serequeberhan (1994, 2000, 2007) suggest, what might register as a rupture within European and European American history, culture, and thought does not necessarily nicely and neatly translate into a rupture within—and certainly not a resumption of precolonialist and precapitalist or, rather, "indigenous" and "traditional"—non-European and non-European American history, culture, and thought. This is so, to state the obvious, because of the different timelines and topographies European modernity discontinued, interrupted, and spuriously spawned within the non-European world.

Where the appellation "modernity" might very well mean the conglomeration of Europe's fabled advances in marine travel, agricultural manufacturing, industrialization, urbanization, state consolidation, and bureaucratization, for most non-Europeans Europe's age of "modernity" meant rote racialization, colonization, cultural decimation, physical degradation, and sexual violation (Abu-Lughod, 1989; Blaut, 1993; Dussel, 1995, 1996; Marable, 1983; Mignolo, 2000, 2003, 2005; Prashad, 2007; Rodney, 1972; Said, 1979, 1993; Zinn, 2003). Lofty ideals like the democratic responsibility and accountability of social institutions and the dignity of individual persons and all classes of citizens were put forward and popularized during this period. These ideals led to penetrating critiques of what was then perceived to be illegitimate officialdom—in the realm of religion, the Protestant Reformation against the Roman Catholic Church, and the Enlightenment against state churches; in politics and government, liberal movements against megalomaniacal monarchal states and feudalism; in labor and economics, the proletariat against the petit-bourgeoisie and bourgeoisie; in gender relations, women against sexist social conventions and patriarchal practices; in race and ethnic relations, non-whites and Jews against white and Gentile supremacist sentiments and sanctions; and, in sexual relations, homosexuals against homophobic practices and heterosexist social conventions. It was the sheer range and reach of these critiques that led to both the rise and decline of European modernity and also the glaring discrepancies between hallowed words (e.g., the U.S. Declaration of Independence, Constitution, and Bill of Rights, etc.) and dastardly deeds (e.g., Native American holocaust, African holocaust, African American enslavement, Japanese internment, and the Tuskegee syphilis experiment, etc.) in the name of these consecrated words that contributed to the beleaguered birth of postmodernism and, in turn, hip hop culture's contradictory and controversial nature or, rather, *hip hop's homespun postmodernism.* In short, as Russell Potter emphasized in *Spectacular Vernaculars: Hip Hop and the Politics of Postmodernism* (1995), it could be said that the inconsistency between hip hop's arguably progressive principles and its actual retrogressive practices continues to loom large because, as quiet as it has been kept, a very similar conundrum continues to haunt contemporary U.S. aesthetics, politics, culture, and society.

If postmodern theory is to have a discursive life beyond the twentieth century, then it must not merely—in the most panderingly "politically correct" manner imaginable—appropriate the experiences of Europe's non-European "Others" to enrich its discourse or to be the epitome of the latest (neo)liberal or Eurocentric version of radical chic. It is important for postmodernists, who are primarily European and European American academics and critics, to come to terms with the fact that for most postcolonial, subaltern, and critical race theorists Eurocentric postmodernists' discourse on the "politics of difference" is inextricable from the continued politics of racial colonialism or, rather, the politics of racism. Critically engaging racism, as the critical race theorists have revealed, means that the life-worlds and life-struggles of non-Europeans is, on principle, dragged from the discursive margins to the discursive center.

Speaking specifically of the origins and evolution of hip hop culture in the postmodern era, it is important for us to emphasize the African American roots of rap music and hip hop culture more generally. Without in any way deny the seminal contributions of Caribbean and Latin American working-poor youth with regard to the origins and evolution of hip hop culture, the overall musical, cultural, and discursive direction of hip hop has been dictated by African American underclass and working-poor youth, primarily young African American males.[5] This is also one of the reasons that contemporary hip hop culture has retained some of the feel and funk of early hip hop culture, because once we move beyond pseudo-sociological discussions concerning the 1980s and 1990s growing black bourgeoisie we may quickly conclude that based on the serious sociological data and literature presently available very little with regard to the sociopolitical situation of African Americans has changed since the late 1970s and early 1980s inception of hip hop. As a matter of fact, there is a growing body of economic, political science, sociological, and criminal justice data and literature that sadly suggests that the sociopolitical situation of most African Americans has actually worsened since the end of the Black Power period (E. Anderson, 1999, 2008; Conley, 1999; Massey and Denton, 1993; Oliver and Shapiro, 2006; T. M. Shaprio, 2004; W. J. Wilson, 1978, 1987, 1997, 2009).

If one hears mind-numbing nihilism, anguished-filled alienation, dreaded despair and the like in rap music (and even in many neo-soul songs), perhaps, it is because African American life and culture continues to be filled with hopelessness, futility, and chronic misery. However, it is also possible to hear desperate calls for *the re-politicization of African American music and popular culture* in even the most seemingly mindless rap music. In point of fact, the music that might sound like nothing more than "black noise" or a "bunch of gibberish" to hip hop's critics could very well contain coded cultural messages for hip hoppers (Banfield, 2010; Peretti, 2009; Shaw, 1986). Indeed, there is a certain inescapable irony to be found in the fact that so much of Eurocentric postmodernist thought revolves around pastiche, play, the critique of modern "master narratives," and the deconstruction of modern dichotomies, but yet where these same traits are to be found within the world of hip hop, especially in rap music, they are somehow seen as nihilistic nonsense and nothing other than the misguided musings of, for the most part, "angry" young misogynistic and hypermasculinist black men. Little or no thought is given to the historical fact that at the very moment that the *vox populi* of the wretched of the earth (i.e., rap music) takes the cultural aesthetic and sociopolitical national and, now, international center stage Eurocentric postmodern critics, who have virtually no relationship with authentic African American culture, not simply corporatized African American music and popular culture, quickly clamor for hip hop culture's, especially rap music's, censure and silencing. It almost seems as though "anything goes" in postmodern white America, but nothing—at least "nothing" postmodern white America does not high-handedly approve of or understand—is allowed in post–Civil Rights and post–Black Power black America that might even potentially radicalize or re-politicize the *recolonized* and even more profoundly racialized progeny of the 1950s, 1960s, and 1970s Black Freedom movements.

One of the often overlooked ironies of the national and international impact of postmodernism is that now Europeans and European Americans, especially European and European American youth, seem to have some far-flung sense of the uncertainty, despair, deep alienation, and heartfelt hopelessness that non-Europeans and non-European Americans have been fiendishly forced to live in since the onslaught of European global imperialism some five hundred years ago (circa 1450) (Epstein, 1998; Giroux, 1996; Strickland, 2002). That is to say, although hip hop culture, especially rap music, is an undeniable expression of African American's particular and peculiar history, culture, and struggle, because it touches on an abundance of issues, views, and values shared by postmodern and/or postcolonial national and international youth it has increasingly become the most salient musical, cultural, social, and political idiom for those of us born in the aftermath of the Civil Rights, Black Power, and Women's Liberation movements. Unlike the highbrow and Eurocentric postmodern pontifications on the "politics of difference," and as we have witnessed in the preceding chapters, hip hop culture is hybrid, heterogeneous, and elastic enough to accommodate a wide range of "Others" excluded from both modernity *and* postmodernity's "master narratives." Even with all of its infamous issues and ills, its scandalous controversies and contradictions, hip hop culture has provided and, I honestly believe, will continue to provide, a *terreno comune* (i.e., common ground) and *lingua franca* (i.e., common language) that cuts across the modern and postmodern borders and boundaries surrounding race, gender, class, sexual orientation, religious affiliation, and nation. In other words, hip hop culture has been and can continue to be utilized as a tool and decisive terrain for radical re-politicization and critical consciousness-raising, helping to highlight shared progressive sensibilities and common commitments, as well as serving as a foundation for anti-imperialist community, camaraderie, and coalition.[6]

Above when Lyotard wrote that the moniker "postmodern" should be taken to mean "the state of our culture following the transformations which, since the end of the nineteenth century, have altered the game rules for science, literature, and the arts," his words could be seemingly easily applied to hip hop culture. However, faithfully following W. E. B. Du Bois, Frantz Fanon, Enrique Dussel, Edward Said, Walter Mignolo and Vijay Prashad, here we are given grounds to question whether Lyotard was including the histories, cultures, and thoughts of those racially colonized by the very same imperial expansion that European modernity symbolizes to the majority of non-Europeans when he wrote of "our culture" being transformed by the aftermath of modernity. I doubt very seriously that Lyotard, or any other Eurocentric postmodern theorist for that matter, seriously (i.e., in discursive depth and detail) considered how the cultural decimation and racial colonization of Africa, the Americas, the Caribbean Islands, Australia, and India, among other cultures, countries, and continents, transformed "our" (i.e., non-Europeans') precapitalist and precolonialist cultures at both the beginning and the end of European modernity—quick corollary question: has European modernity really and truly come to an end since the progeny of the very same Europeans and European Americans who rose to power during modernity, for the most part, remain in unprecedented global power in postmodernity or, rather, post-postmodernity? It is only when we move away from Eurocentric, bourgeois, patriarchal, and heterosexist conceptions of history, culture, and thought that we are able to more clearly detect some of the problems involved in projecting postmodernism, especially its "politics of difference," onto hip hop culture, and Europe's non-European "Others" more generally.

Hip hop culture is, indeed, more malleable, free-floating, and fluid than many critics have been previously willing to concede. Ironically, it is its very malleability and motive nature that makes it, literally, simultaneously postmodern and anti-postmodern, postcolonial and anti-postcolonial, postfeminist and anti-postfeminist, and on and on *ad infinitum*. Furthermore, to say that hip hop is post–Civil Rights obscures the ways in which some aspects of it, especially its more radical political elements, may also be indicative of or, at the very least, contributive to a kind of neo–Civil Rights movement—of course, not our grandparents or parents' idea of a civil right movement, but arguably a twenty-first-century movement that focuses on civil rights and social justice nonetheless. To say that hip hop is post–Black Power also masks and mystifies many of the ways in which African Americans continue to explore their *Africanity* (i.e., their African identities) and seek the ongoing *empowerment* of black folk in an even more illusively anti-black racist and neocolonialist contemporary U.S. society. Something similar, as was witnessed in the previous chapter, could be said about the assertion that hip hop is postfeminist: because authentic feminism—as opposed to a benevolently bigoted bourgeois feminism—has *herstorically*, and continues currently, to take many forms and is, therefore, both multifarious and malleable.

When we take stock of what hip hop has inherited from previous cultural aesthetic movements, as we have in the preceding chapters, questions concerning hip hop's current mission and message seem all the more relevant. Obviously I believe hip hop actually has what might be very loosely defined as a "mission and message," but because of the barrage of Eurocentric postmodern media and telecommunications, as well as the rise of technological and corporate capitalism in the last quarter of the twentieth century (i.e., the time period that gave birth to hip hop culture), much of that "mission and message" has been, at best, muffled and, at worst, manipulated by the carpetbaggers of corporate capitalism. As W. E. B. Du Bois persuasively and eloquently argued in his 1924 classic *The Gift of Black Folk*, U.S. society has arguably always been a consumer society centered on the buying, selling, and policing of black folk—their bodies, behavior, labor, language, culture, art, and image—so it should not come as a surprise to anyone that the postmodern reconfiguration of U.S. culture, politics, economics, and society at the end of the twentieth century nefariously found new uses for black folk, especially the most visible and visceral expression of blackness during the 1980s and 1990s: rap music and hip hop culture.

Although long overlooked, in many senses hip hop culture represents African Americans' confrontation with both the politics of the so-called post- –Civil Rights period and the politics of postmodernism. One of the most evident examples of the hip hop generation's dialogue with both the intracommunal politics of the post–Civil Rights period of African America and the extra-communal postmodern politics of European America is to be found in their Deleuzean and Guattarian schizophrenic rejection and open embrace of the *hyper-corporate colonization of hip hop culture* and, even more, the dichotomous distinctions that are currently and quite commonly being made between "conscious" and "commercial" rap music. What does the evolving dichotomy and distinctions being made between "conscious" and "commercial" rap tell us about the current state of, not just hip hop culture, but also black America? What does it tell us about the current state of white America and, even more, multicultural and transethnic America? Is this dichotomy indicative of the maturation of the hip hop generation, or yet another sign that hip hop's hyper-corporate colonization has crippled it and transformed it into nothing more than another meaningless "American" pop cultural commodity clamoring for more and more space in the national and international market-places? It is these questions and concerns that will serve as the primary preoccupation for the subsequent section of this chapter.

THE HYPER-CORPORATE COLONIZATION OF HIP HOP CULTURE: ON THE "CONSCIOUS" VERSUS "COMMERCIAL" RAP DICHOTOMY

Inextricably linked to the Harlem Renaissance, Black Arts movement, and Feminist Art movement, the real significance of hip hop culture lies in the fact that, similar to each of the aforementioned movements, it is emblemati-cally symptomatic of a shift in sensibilities and moods among the youth in the United States, primarily working-poor nonwhite youth, and especially black youth. This shift in sensibilities and moods is most certainly connected to the fact that the hip hop generation is the first generation of U.S. citizens born in the wake of the socio-legal breakthroughs of the Civil Rights move-ment. However, as the previous chapters have emphasized, the hip hop gen-eration has also benefited from the advances made by the 1960s and 1970s Black Power, Women's Liberation, and Homophile movements, among oth-er, sociopolitical movements. Were we to cautiously turn to, and critically focus on the most popular form of hip hop culture, rap music and videos, then we might be presented with a more tangible metaphor for hip hop's historical hybridity and its possible contributions to post–hip hop genera-tions. In a sense, rap music *re-Africanizes* and reanimates African American music, all the while continuing *the African Americanization of mainstream American music and popular culture*. That is to say, rap music unrepentantly returns African American music to its roots in the African aesthetic, with its emphasis on frantic spirituality, unrestrained sexuality, dancing orality, piercing polyvocality, discursive dissonance and, of course, accenting syncopated polyrhythms.[7]

Rap music, and hip hop culture more generally, is virtually incomprehensible without critically engaging its inheritance from *both* cultural aesthetic and sociopolitical movements—that is, *both* continental and diasporan African cultural aesthetic and sociopolitical movements. For instance, as hip hop cultural linguist H. Samy Alim (2004, 2006) has illustrated, the fact that rap music's virtuosity lies in its linguistic versatility and vocal dexterity, as opposed to its technical facility and sonic fluency, speaks volumes about what hip hop has inherited from the roaring oratory and rhetorical radicalism popularized in the 1960s and 1970s by Civil Rights and Black Power movement members (see also Adjaye and Andrews, 1997; Alim, Awad, and Pennycook, 2009; Campbell, 2005). In short, rap music resuscitates and revises the African American oratorical tradition by synthesizing it with advances in the African American musical tradition in light of its interface with the technological, political, and economic changes that defined and deformed the twilight years of the twentieth century and the dawn of the twenty-first century. Indeed, much of rap music's popularity stems from its intense emphasis on rhyme and rhythm, which represent and register as an updated articulation of the two major aesthetic tropes of the African American experience: African American rhetoric and African American music.

Rap music's *re-Africanization* of African American music, if you will, is connected to its unique relationship with the entirety of African American musical history and its initial desire to speak directly to and about the life-struggles of ghetto youth, as opposed to creating bland cross-over musical blah-blah for suburban white youth consumption. Because of its willingness to build on a wide range of older African American musical styles—not simply soul and rhythm & blues, but also gospel, blues, jazz, and rock—rap music is sonically synoptic, frequently deconstructing and reconstructing past black musical forms to speak to present sociopolitical problems and intercultural issues. It would seem that where the hip hop generation exhibits a historical amnesia when and where we come to all but the most popular figures and events of African American social and political history, they are quite well versed when and where we come to the panorama of African American musical history. Nonetheless, it is the depth and multidimensionality of rap music's relationship with older African American musical styles and the distinctly "black" messages conveyed through classic African American music that, for the most part, has enabled it to resist being completely co-opted by the contemporary carpetbaggers of corporate capitalism. Although there has been increased imitation and trite emulation of rap music over the last three decades of its existence, hip hop's discourse on authenticity (although not without its own set of serious problems), as well as the fact that it has increasingly become fashionable to make critical distinctions between "commercial" and "conscious" hip hop (or, rather, *hip pop* versus "real" hip hop), indicates that rap music in specific, and hip hop culture in general, continues to combat, however contradictorily and politically incorrectly, complete cooptation by corporate America (Amoaku, 2005; Hess, 2007; Miranda, 2003; E. O. Patton, 2009; Watkins, 2005).

My use of the term "commercial" rap or "commercial" hip hop culture here follows the lead of other like-minded black popular culture (especially Hip Hop studies) scholars who are similarly concerned about racial colonial caricatures and other wrongheaded representations of African Americans within the contemporary hyper-corporatized world of hip hop. The critique of "commercial" rap and "commercial" hip hop culture throughout this chapter is meant to emphasize and elucidate the insidious influence and political economy of corporate and, therefore, "mainstream" America's anti-black racist cultural imperatives *and* cultural imperialism in relationship to the current course and content of what is considered rap music and hip hop culture. Instead of merely blaming black youth for the crassness of some of their sociocultural expressions, which seems to be an often overlooked African American intracommunal tradition dating back to at least the Niggerati of the Harlem Renaissance, I believe that it is important to critically engage the complicity and culpability of both the hip hoppers *and* corporate America. All too often, both within and without the African American community, the bulk of the blame for the postmillennial minstrelism within the world of hip hop is aimed exclusively at black youth without in any way connecting it to the racial colonial whims and wishes of white corporations and white consumers, currently the primary peddlers and purchasers of hyper-corporatized or commercial hip hop culture.

In contrast to commercial rap music and hip hop culture those deeply concerned about the direction and discourse of hip hop have come to contentiously distinguish between "commercial" and "conscious" rap music and hip hop culture, with the latter designation supposedly signifying an "alternative" or "underground" world of hip hop where cultural criticism, social commentary, and political analysis are the *sine qua non* of "real" hip hop (Eure and Spady, 1991; McQuillar, 2007; Spady, Lee, and Alim, 1999; Spady, Alim, and Meghelli, 2006). The distinctions made between commercial and conscious hip hop usually have to do with whether or not a specific hip hop artist incorporates cultural criticism, social commentary, and political analysis into their aesthetic expressions. It is not uncommon for conscious rappers to have record deals or, at the least, distribution deals with high-profile and powerful record companies. However, what tends to set their music apart from commercial rappers (frequently on the same record label) is that their work generally sidesteps postmillennial minstrelism, gravitates toward sociopolitically conscious content, and is most often poorly promoted when compared with commercial rappers working within *the ghetto/gangsta/*

pimp/whore paradigm. In other words, the world of hip hop, particularly rap
music, has been disputably divided into commercial rappers, who seem quite
content to resuscitate and mimic blackface minstrelism, and conscious rappers, who allegedly really "keep it real" by rapping about sociopolitical
issues that are currently relevant to black and other racially colonized and
economically impoverished communities.

That being said, however, what has come to be the conventional split
between commercial and conscious rap is not without its pronounced problematics. Such a distinction, whether unwittingly or not, in many instances
ironically limits the alternatives to, and actual insurgency against the hyper-
corporatized commercial hip hop that nowadays dominates, defines, and de-
forms what counts as hip hop. It should be emphasized that conscious rap is
not the only alternative to commercial rap, and those who dogmatically push
this dichotomous line of logic would do well to bear in mind early rap
music's emphasis on *politics* (e.g., "The Message" by Grandmaster Flash and
the Furious Five and "The Breaks" by Kurtis Blow) and *partying* (e.g.,
"Rapper's Delight" by the Sugar Hill Gang and "Basketball" by Kurtis
Blow). Hip hop culture is more discursively diverse than the simple-minded
dichotomy "conscious versus commercial rap" could ever dream of captur-
ing. Such a dichotomy makes it seem as though the only viable solution to
the problem of corporate-conceived postmillennial minstrelism and commercial rappers' parades of pathos is to lamentably and long-sufferingly "fight
the power," as Public Enemy said some twenty years ago on their classic
Fear of a Black Planet (1990).

Adhering to this wrongheaded and heavy-handed dichotomy within the
contemporary world of hip hop glosses over the fact that many of the major
and most legendary hip hop artists, especially rappers, might have work that
contentiously falls within the realm of both commercial *and* conscious hip
hop culture. For instance, and continuing the focus on rap, Tupac Shakur,
Nas, Common, Mos Def, Talib Kweli, Wyclef Jean, Michael Franti, and The
Roots have all produced songs with commercial sensibilities, but each of the
aforementioned have been consistently characterized as "conscious" or "political" rappers. The "conscious versus commercial rap" dichotomy has developed to the point where the so-called conscious rappers themselves have
come to critique these labels, in essence questioning who created the labels
and the real reasons for their creation. To take this line of logic further, on the
title track from his innovative album *The Beautiful Struggle* (2004), to cite a
well-known example, Talib Kweli explained: "They call me the political
rapper / Even after I tell 'em I don't fuck with politics / I don't even follow it
/ I'm on some KRS, Ice Cube, Chris Wallace shit / Main Source, De La Soul,
bumpin' *2Pacalypse Now.*" On "I Try," a track produced by Kanye West
with a heavenly Mary J. Blige hook from the same album, Kweli continued
his critique of the corporatization of rap music, revealingly rhyming: "The

label want a song about a bubbly life / I have trouble tryin' to write some shit / To bang in the club through the night / When people suffer tonight." Obviously Kweli understands some of the limitations involved in embracing corporate-conceived labels and song or album concepts that seem to only lyrically quarantine and sonically segregate "conscious rappers" from the wide range of hip hop styles, issues, and approaches currently available to genre-jumping rappers and hip hoppers (e.g., Queen Latifah, Michael Franti, Mos Def, Jill Scott, Lauryn Hill, Wyclef Jean, Cee Lo Green, Janelle Monáe, and Phonté, among others).

Because of *the overexposure of commercial rap* and *the underexposure of conscious rap*, there is a political economy at play on the contemporary hip hop scene that makes being labeled a "conscious" or "political" rapper a virtual commercial/career death sentence in light of the fact that conscious rap does not have the kind of artist visibility or casual fan appreciation that commercial rap does. Of course, this means less enthusiasm and lower record sales for conscious rappers and, therefore, logically it is less lucrative to be labeled a conscious rapper. Looking at rap music from this angle, then, it would seem that more "mainstream" rappers are not only able to achieve fame and fortune, but also have the option to offer crude, often tongue-in-cheek cultural criticism, social commentary, and political analysis from time to time. In short, many of the commercial rappers working within the ghetto/gangsta/pimp/whore paradigm seem to not only be having all the fun (from the point of view of their extremely impressionable tween, teen, and twenty-something fans), but also, because of their solid record sales, they are able to occasionally comment on social and political issues (e.g., Jay-Z, Lil' Wayne, Kanye West, Drake, Nelly, Master P., Ice Cube, N.W.A., Snoop Dogg, etc.).

Sad to say, no matter how breathtakingly brilliant their rhymes and sonically seductive their beats, broadly speaking, for all intents and purposes conscious rappers have been lyrically quarantined and sonically segregated to the musical margins, to the musical ghetto of commercial radio and the music industry's promotional programs. The musical marginalization of socially and politically conscious rap dictates fan appreciation and consumption, which ultimately determines its value and longevity within the political economy of the musical marketplace. Considering the advertising explosion that has both defined and deformed contemporary society, there is a tendency to gravitate toward that which is given pride of place within the larger world of the market-driven media and economy. The musical marginalization of conscious rap, therefore, is inextricable from the fiction that authentic African American culture really is nothing more than the gruesomeness of ghetto existence, dogged familial dysfunction, perpetual promiscuity, wallowing in welfarism, and sonic celebrations of "thug life" that so many of the "I'm-just-keepin'-it-real" commercial rappers routinely rhyme about.

As W. E. B. Du Bois famously observed in *The Philadelphia Negro* (1899) and *The Souls of Black Folk* (1903), among other works, African American life and culture cannot and should not be roguishly reduced to figments of white folks' racial colonial imaginations. African American culture, as with contemporary hip hop culture, is more complex—as a matter of fact, a lot more complicated—than the racial colonial caricatures and postmillennial minstrelism incessantly presented as black life and culture within the world of the contemporary national and international culture and media industries. Just as the "I'm-holier-than-thou" attitude of many conscious rappers is off-putting and outright false, the "I'm-just-keepin'-it-real" attitude of most commercial rappers registers as a fundamental lie and fiction that only resuscitates and reinforces a form of "postmodern" or, rather, postmillennial blackface minstrelism. It is the faulty features and ideological insinuations of both conscious and commercial rappers' articulations and (mis)representations of African American life and culture that must be dialectically deconstructed in order to not only move "real" conscious rap from the musical margins to the center of hip hop culture, but to provide hip hoppers with truly transformative and politically progressive (i.e., both appreciative and critical) visions of themselves and society.

I am arguing here, then, that contemporary African American popular music must be simultaneously innovative and exciting, serious and playful, challenging and accessible. Indeed, at times this will assuredly mean radical political rap with searing social commentary but, truth be told, no one can be expected to listen to tale after tale of the social trauma and political drama of black life and culture all the time. Ultimately, this means that neither the "commercial" nor "conscious" rap camps should be allowed to lyrically and musically colonize what rap or hip hop is or isn't definitively—that is to say, once and for all. Hip hop's continuation, which is to say its ongoing life and not its death, may very well depend on hip hoppers' ability to open their minds and ears to the new hip hop (or, rather, *the new politics of hip hop*) on the horizon. Codifying hip hop culture, whether within the realm of "conscious" or "commercial" rap, will only colonize and, in the end, kill it. This is so because hip hop has always been about organic open-ended dualities, as opposed to rigid corporate-conceived dichotomies.

Truth be told, progressive pronouncements in rap music should not be quarantined to the realm of conscious rap. That is to say, a really "fly-funky-fresh" rap artist, whether a "conscious" or "commercial" rapper, ought to be able to rap about a wide range of topics—from police brutality to sexuality, from women's liberation to the current social and political direction of the nation, from the ups and downs of college dorm life to the rush one gets when they rhyme on the mic. As the work of Lauryn Hill, Wyclef Jean, The Roots, Ursula Rucker, Michael Franti, Common, Mos Def, Talib Kweli, Bahamadia, Dead Prez, Jean Grae, and Little Brother illustrate, so-called conscious rappers' rhymes can be just as explicit, egocentric, misogynistic, ghettocentric, and viciously violent as gangsta and thug life-loving rappers' lyrics. Conscious rappers cannot be expected to simply focus on the social and political in every rhyme, disregarding the violence, (legal and illegal) drug addictions, alcoholism, sadomasochism, bling-blingism, and other self-destructive "ghetto fabulous" behaviors that have increasingly engulfed their (or, at the very least, their family and friends') life-worlds and lived-experiences. Speaking directly to this issue in a recent interview with Jerry Barrow (2010) in *The Urban Daily*, Phonté of Little Brother said that he has resisted being labeled a "conscious" rapper because it seems as though it has become convenient and conventional to focus more attention on what "conscious" rappers are *against* rather than what they are *for*. He candidly continued: "Just because I don't rap about guns or pimpin' doesn't necessarily make me a better choice for your children to listen to. . . . That's why the whole conscious rap thing we just kind of wanted to keep ourselves out of it." Then, unequivocally calling the "conscious" rap label into question, he sternly stated: "It didn't represent the full scope of who we were" (p. 1). One of the more recent leading lights of contemporary "conscious" rap, Phonté of the iconic rap group Little Brother (who offered game-changing albums such as *The Listening, The Chitlin Circuit, The Minstrel Show, Separate But Equal,* and *And Justus For All*), makes it clear that the label "conscious rap" simply does not "represent the full scope" of who he is and what his work is really about.

How many other hip hoppers, not just rappers, find the corporate-conceived labels and promotional programs created to quickly generate as much money as possible from hip hop culture extremely limiting or, rather, aesthetically asphyxiating? Hence, is it any wonder that there is so much discussion surrounding "the death of hip hop" and whether, as Nas said, "hip hop is dead" (Hess, 2007). When one listens to either commercial or conscious rap, are there transformative and progressive visions of African American culture and community being articulated, perhaps not in every instance, but at least some (maybe even the bulk) of the time? Based on this music, what principles for treating ourselves and others is being elucidated and advocated? Topically speaking, then, the current distinction between conscious and commercial rap does not always, or in any hard and fast fashion, revolve around the subject matter of the music, but rather more often than not it has to do with corporate-conceived accessibility and frequency: *accessibility,* insofar as the musical masses are concerned—will the imagined musical "everyman" be able to quickly and easily digest the topic of the music, bearing in mind the corporate American advertising mantra "sex sells" and "if it bleeds it leads"?—and *frequency,* insofar as it must fit into the already existing musical scheme of things and both lyrically and sonically resemble most of the music currently on the scene so as to be well received on the radio and fit the longstanding advertising formulas created by corporate America's multitude of marketing teams.

As Talib Kweli and Phonté both emphasize above, progressive rappers and hip hoppers have resisted *the hyper-corporate colonization of hip hop culture*, refusing to give in to a kind of hip hop cultural elitism that insinuates that commercial rappers and hip hop consumers are unintelligent and unsophisticated and, even more, that hit rap songs and club-bangers are automatically illegitimate when compared with the conscious rap not routinely played on the radio or in heavy video rotation on cable television. As a matter of fact, most conscious rappers at one point or another acknowledge and express solemn solidarity with the ghetto realities and sensual fantasies that most commercial rappers rhyme about. Consequently, and we should be clear here, African American music has historically and consistently taken up the topics of *ghetto reality* and *black sexuality*. In terms of ghetto reality as a musical topic we need to look no further than the compositions of the Last Poets, the Watts Prophets, Nina Simone, James Brown, Abbey Lincoln, Donny Hathaway, Stevie Wonder, Isaac Hayes, and Tracy Chapman. Moreover, with regard to black sexuality as a musical topic obvious examples include Aretha Franklin, Marvin Gaye, Otis Redding, Al Green, Donna Summer, Teddy Pendergrass, Gladys Knight, George Clinton and, of course, Prince. This means, then, that the conscious versus commercial rap dichotomy and distinctions might be nothing more than the result of one genre of rappers privileging the political stream of early rap over the party stream of early rap, and vice versa. However, no matter which genre of rap one might favor it is important to earnestly ask what the musical landscape would sound like without the duality of social consciousness *and* sensuousness that has so long characterized the best of, not simply rap music, but hip hop culture? It is important for us to bear in mind that our critiques of rap music and hip hop culture must always be *constructive*, as opposed to *destructive*, or else every word that we speak or write to critique hip hop will ultimately be nothing more than discursive deathblows and disingenuous eulogies, surreptitious censuring, and clandestine conservatism hiding behind the hallowed name of "hip hop cultural criticism" or "critical Hip Hop studies."

HIP HOP & THE IDYLLIC IMPULSE: ON AFRICAN AMERICANS' ONGOING CULTURE OF RESISTANCE & RESTITUTION AND TRADITIONS OF TRANSCENDENCE & OPPOSITION

Unlike previous African American musical forms (e.g., blues, jazz, and rock) that have fallen to the whims and wishes of white consumption and black get-rich-quick schemes and cross-over dreams, conscious rap music, and "real" hip hop culture more generally, is essentially the musical and cultural expression of the paradoxical scream of desperation and perplexed cry of celebration emanating from the African American underclass and working poor. This simultaneous scream and cry unequivocally acknowledges and acutely confronts the stream of racialized stress, blatant betrayals, gnawing self-negation, manufactured self-mutilation, planned pathos, and criminal cruelty that have all but become the hallmarks of black life in U.S. ghettos. In clear contrast to what could be termed *the European Americanization of African American music* (especially blues, jazz, and rock), rap music is fundamentally a class-specific musical form and cultural aesthetic re-articulation of longstanding African diasporan dichotomies, such as spirituality/sexuality, rhyme/rhythm, and academic/organic intellectualism, that masks and mystifies, and sometimes eliminates altogether, the homespun hope and unfaltering faith that has historically characterized African American life-worlds and life-struggles.

Rap music's resistance to unmitigated corporate cooptation may have something to do with the fact that its most immediate and major cultural aesthetic ancestral movement is the Black Arts movement. As discussed in chapter 3, whether we are speaking of spoken-word or rap, the soundtracks of the hip hop generation have been indelibly influenced by the rhetorical radicalism of the Black Power movement and, even more, by the black aesthetic, especially the scathingly political poetry, of the Black Arts movement. Mention has already been made of the poetic presence and aesthetic influence otherwise of Amiri Baraka, Sonia Sanchez, Haki Madhubuti, Nikki Giovanni, Ishmael Reed, and Maya Angelou, among others, within the world of hip hop. Truth be told, however, rap music most resembles and, therefore, its real roots could be said to lie in, the radical political poetry-cum-musical musings of Sun Ra, Gil Scott-Heron, Jayne Cortez, Isaac Hayes, Millie Jackson, Archie Shepp, June Tyson, the Last Poets, and the Watts Prophets, among other 1960s and 1970s poetic singer-songwriters, whose work could be collectively characterized as simultaneously lyrically and musically innovative, fiercely funky, melancholically moving, and hauntingly hopeful.

Although rap music, and hip hop culture more generally, was founded on and continues to be deeply grounded in African diasporan dichotomies—again, such as spirituality/sexuality, rhyme/rhythm, and academic/organic intellectualism—certain rogue strands of rap music have emerged that patently privilege sexuality over spirituality, banging rhythms over reason-filled rhymes, and anti-intellectualism over both academic and organic intellectualism. The aforementioned forms of rap usually fall within the realm of what could be called "commercial" or "cross-over" rap and, as was witnessed in chapter 2, this music and its messages are very often, however unwittingly, predicated on and preoccupied with variants of the very anti-black racist minstrelesque myths and sexual stereotypes that most of the members of the

New Negro movement, the Black Women's Club movement, and the Harlem Renaissance found utterly appalling and righteously railed against at the turn of the twentieth century. Both the monotony and vulgarity of much of what passes now days as commercial rap is outright offensive (both morally and musically), and on a deeper level it actually calls into question core values that have helped countless generations of African Americans have hope for a better future and hold on to some semblance of their humanity—not to mention their *Africanity* (i.e., their African identity).

It is no secret that one of the main messages of African American music has historically revolved around what could plausibly be called "utopian" hopes and dreams. Indeed, there is an *idyllic impulse* that colors and courses through every major form of African American music: from the spirituals and gospel to blues and jazz, from rhythm & blues and soul to funk and rap (S. A. Floyd, 1995; T. L. Reed, 2003; Southern, 1997; Spencer, 1993, 1995). This "idyllic impulse," if you will, is not simply unsophisticated superstition or starry-eyed stupidity on the part of African Americans but, more profoundly, it hits at the very heart of African American life and culture—which is to say, *African Americans' culture of resistance and restitution* and *African Americans' tradition of transcendence and opposition* (M. Ellison, 1989; Ramsey, 2003; Sanger, 1995; Spencer, 1990; B. Ward, 1998). Bearing in mind Amiri Baraka's assertion in chapter 1, where he stated "if the music of the Negro in America, in all its permutations, is subjected to a socio-anthropological as well as musical scrutiny, something about the essential nature of the Negro's existence in this country ought to be revealed, as well as something about the essential nature of this country, *i.e.*, society as a whole," here we have come back to the question of what rap music, and hip hop culture more generally, says about contemporary society. Indeed, there are messages in black music—some positive, and others negative—and serious Hip Hop studies scholars would do well not to ignore those messages in rap music that contradict their personal and/or petit-bourgeois academic conceptions of what hip hop is, and what hip hop is not or, even more, who black youth are, and who they are not. In fact, genuinely *critical* Hip Hop studies would interpret the vices and vulgarities of hip hop culture in general, and rap music in specific, as W. E. B. Du Bois did African American criminality in *The Philadelphia Negro* (1899), where he sternly stated:

Above all, we must remember that crime is not normal; that the appearance of crime among Southern Negroes is a symptom of wrong social conditions—of a stress of life greater than a large part of the community can bear. The Negro is not naturally criminal; he is usually patient and law-abiding. If slavery, the convict-lease system, the traffic in criminal labor, the lack of juvenile reformatories, together with the unfortunate discrimination and prejudice in other walks of life, have led to that sort of social protest and revolt which we call crime, then we must look for remedy in the sane reform of these wrong social conditions, and not in intimidation, savagery, or the legalized slavery of men. (pp. 8–9; see also Rabaka, 2010a, pp. 293–336)

Based on Du Bois's sociology of crime, here we are given grounds to not simply ask what contemporary black crime says about contemporary black America, but also what contemporary black criminality says about the failure(s) of contemporary American society as a whole. Black youth are not born "bad," or inherently criminal anymore than all Asian youth excel at math and science, all Mexican youth are immigrants or "illegal aliens," and all white youth spend the bulk on their time in tanning booths, listening to heavy metal, drinking beer, and doing drugs. Critical Hip Hop studies challenges myths and stereotypes not only about black youth, but also about youth in general. However, since ghetto-dwelling black youth have always been and continue to be the "poster children" for hip hop culture, the life-worlds and life-struggles of African American underclass and working-poor youth should have pride of place in critical Hip Hop studies, as other youth, white and nonwhite, continue to gauge their own and others' *hip hop authenticity* based on cultural aesthetic criteria primarily bequeathed by African American artists and activists. If, indeed, the longstanding idyllic impulse in African American music is seemingly nonexistent in postmillennial popular rap music, and if we concede that African American music is really and truly indicative of the current conditions of African American life and culture, then, as Du Bois declared above, "we must look for remedy in the sane reform of these wrong social conditions, and not in intimidation, savagery, or the legalized slavery of men." How much of hip hop culture's—especially young black males'—ostensible existential hopelessness and ontological anguish is connected to the twenty-first-century "legalized slavery of men," which is otherwise known as the prison industrial complex.[8]

Although African Americans only account for 12 percent of the U.S. population, 47 percent of all prisoners in the United States are black. The U.S. census data for 2000, which offered statistical data based on the race of all incarcerated individuals in the United States, divulged the alarming racial disproportion of the prison population in each state: the proportion of black incarcerated individuals dramatically exceeded their proportion among state residents in all fifty states. Moreover, in twenty states, the black prison population was at least five times greater than the black state resident population. With respect to unemployment, between 2000 and 2010 the black unemployment rate went from being twice that of the white unemployment rate to nearly thrice that of the white unemployment rate, which means that many black youth continue to live below the poverty line and, from their desperate point of view, are forced to participate in the illegal and underground economy of the ghetto. Is it any wonder, then, why so much rap music reflects the illicit ills and underbelly of, not only black America, but also—although it has long been, and I fear will continue to be, doggedly denied—the morbid moorings and clandestinely crass culture of mainstream America?

In *The Philadelphia Negro* when Du Bois contended that black crime was "a symptom of wrong social conditions," he appears to have been, yet again, prophetic, considering that at present of the 2.3 million prisoners in the United States almost a million of them are black, and primarily black men. This means, then, that close to 10.5 percent of the entire African American male population in the United States between the ages of 21 and 30 are incarcerated—undeniably the largest racial or ethnic group of incarcerated individuals when compared with 2.5 percent of Latino men and 1.2 percent of white men in the same age demographic. In short, over the last thirty years of hip hop's existence the number of black men in prison has quintupled.

Of course, there remain those among us who believe that black men are quite simply innately evil or inherently immoral, as was witnessed with the first wave of the blackface minstrel phenomenon that spanned from the 1830s to the 1930s, but I would calmly beg to differ, especially considering cutting-edge black criminal justice research, which extends from Du Bois's late nineteenth-century sociology of crime through to the contemporary groundbreaking criminological contributions of Dee Cook and Barbara Hudson (1993), Anne Sulton (1996), Shaun Gabbidon, Helen Greene, and Vernetta Young (2002), Everette Penn (2003), Darnell Hawkins and Kimberly Kempt-Leonard (2005), and Shaun Gabbidon (2010). Statistically speaking, then, there are more black men in prison than in college, and it does not take a degree in criminology, sociology, or ethnomusicology to come to the conclusion that the bulk of contemporary rap music (both conscious and commercial rap) provides a soundtrack for black youths' blighted lives. Those who think that rap music is vulgar and violent simply for the sake of being vulgar and violent should think long and hard about the ways in which this music—music the rappers and their audiences believe authentically and realistically—captures most black youths' lamentable life-worlds and life-struggles. What if the bulk of these rappers really are "keepin' it real" and actually describing the vulgarity and violence of their life-worlds and life-struggles? Who will not simply hear, but seriously heed the existential hopelessness emerging from these, however crude, narratives? Also, how do these narratives help to highlight the anguished absurdities of African American life and culture at the turn of the twenty-first century and the eerie ironies of transitioning from arguably one of the most pious people in the past to one of the most exploited, oppressed, and sometimes self-sabotaging people in the present?

We see here, then, that African American music, and black popular culture more generally, devoid of the idyllic impulse of the African American experience—which is to say, bereft of the black tradition of transcendence from and open opposition to the irony and misery of American imperialism—essentially means that the august African American struggle, and the hope and meaning that has historically been wrenched from that anti-imperial struggle, ceases. It could go without saying that conscious or radical political rap, especially in light of its celebratory lyrics and unapologetically continental and diasporan African-derived polyrhythms, breathes new life into the idyllic impulse and inspires many at the present moment—this writer notwithstanding. Nonetheless, as of late it would seem that for every conscious rap album there are a hundred commercial rap albums that, in the most contrived manner imaginable, lyrically and sonically see-saw between violent vulgarity (usually aimed at young black and brown women) and sadomasochistic celebrations of newly acquired power and privilege (i.e., "power" and "privilege" only when compared with those suffering souls the commercial rappers left behind in the ghetto or, rather, the "domestic colonies" of the United States).[9]

To speak generally here, where conscious rap often offers life-affirming and liberation-preoccupied lyrics, it could be said that most commercial rap offers dignity-denying and postmillennial minstrelism-embracing lyrics. When juxtaposed with the fundamental elements of the former, the latter appears to essentially serve a ritualistic function: music (or, rather, a soundtrack) for a collective cathartic release in the realm of the age-old African American rituals of parties and dances. That being said, there is a sense in which even the most seemingly mindless rap music and hip hop dances may very well serve a function for the African American underclass and working-poor youth who, I have a hunch, only want what every other young person in the United States wants on the weekend or on their day off from their dream-destroying jobs—that is, to, however temporarily, be free from their problems and party with their friends by "living it up" and dancing with abandon. In short, even the rhymes, rhythms and, let it be said, the ribaldry and roguishness of commercial rap music may contain coded messages that conceal an unprecedented and ongoing phenomena in African American life and culture—that is, the subtle but definite genocidal and otherwise insidious impact of contemporary U.S. racism, sexism, capitalism, and heterosexism on the African American underclass and working-poor youth, and the existential hopelessness of their inability to summon enough spiritual, not to mention political and economic, resources to not simply survive, but to live the "good life" that so many preachers, teachers, politicians and, yes, even rappers, tirelessly talk about. Ironically, it was Frantz Fanon's discourse on the dance culture and recreational practices of the racially colonized in *The Wretched of the Earth* that forced me to rethink the cultural aesthetic functionality and ritualism of commercial rap music. Fanon (2005) famously wrote:

Any study of the colonial world therefore must include an understanding of the phenomena of dance and possession. The colonized's way of relaxing is precisely this muscular orgy during which the most brutal aggressiveness and impulsive violence are channeled, transformed, and spirited away. The dance circle is a permissive circle. It protects and empowers. At a fixed time and a fixed date men and women assemble in a given place, and under the solemn gaze of the tribe launch themselves into a seemingly disarticulated, but in fact extremely ritualized, pantomime where the exorcism, liberation, and expression of a community are grandiosely and spontaneously played out through shaking of the head, and back and forth thrusts of the body. Everything is permitted in the dance circle. . . . Everything is permitted, for in fact the sole purpose of the gathering is to let the supercharged libido and the stifled aggressiveness spew out volcanically. Symbolic killings, figurative cavalcades, and imagined multiple murders, everything has to come out. The ill humors seep out, tumultuous as lava flows. (pp. 19–20)[10]

Who could possibly deny the obvious connections between Fanon's discourse on decolonization and Hip Hop studies, specifically critiques of the mindlessness and monotony of commercial rap music, after reading his discussion of the "[s]ymbolic killings, figurative cavalcades, and imagined multiple murders" that cathartically "come out" during the racially colonized's dance and party rituals? Only my most stubborn and stiff-necked critics will refuse to concede the connections between commercial rap and hip hop culture and Fanon's contention that the racially colonized's "way of relaxing is precisely this muscular orgy during which the most brutal aggressiveness and impulsive violence are channeled, transformed, and spirited away." Because the racially colonized, and here I specifically have in mind African American underclass and working-poor youth, were quite literally born into a society that claims to be both democratic and racially neutral, but yet this same society incessantly violates black and other nonwhites' human and civil rights, violence (i.e., various forms of violence: physical, psychological and verbal, among other insidious incarnations of, violence) has become a normalized and naturalized part of almost each and every one of their lived-experiences.

As was witnessed with Du Bois's discussion of black crime above, much of the verbal violence of rap music is indicative of larger, long looming superstructural (particularly political and economic) problems and contradictions within U.S. culture and society. Without in any way condoning rap music's verbal violence (especially with respect to its insufferable expressions of sexism and heterosexism), it is important for Hip Hop studies scholars not to overlook the ways in which rap music and videos, in their own discursively distorted way, speak volumes about both contemporary African American *and* contemporary mainstream American social issues and cultural ills. Ironically, as *Hip Hop's Inheritance* has illustrated, many of these social issues and cultural ills were handed down to the hip hop generation from previous generations, which is to say that certain injustices and forms of violence visited on previous generations not only continue to plague the hip hop generation, but have diabolically combined to become even more egregious forms of violence within hip hoppers' life-worlds.

One wonders whether hip hop's uncritical critics have ever taken the time to objectively study the social and political problems confronting the hip hop generation; a set of social and political problems unlike (and, perhaps, even more harmful than) those that challenged any previous generation of U.S. citizens. Were the uncritical critics of hip hop to calmly conduct serious (i.e., empirical social scientific) studies of the hip hop generation's social and political problems they would no doubt come to see that many of the hip hop generation's problems actually overlap with wider social and political problems in contemporary U.S. culture and society. Indeed, and I should state this outright, rappers are wrong, dead wrong (or, rather, "as wrong as two left shoes," as my Grandmama might say), for unrepentantly embracing sexism, heterosexism, and bourgeois materialism, but—and, again, in no way attempting to excuse rappers' inexcusable immorality—the question begs: how has mainstream America's modern (and even "postmodern") expressions of sexism, heterosexism, and bourgeois materialism inspired and influenced hip hop's sexism, heterosexism, and bourgeois materialism? We should be clear here: this is not a case of "the chicken or the egg" or Aristotelean *petitio principii* (i.e., "begging the question"), because everyone knows that U.S. culture and society was historically obsessed with the most barbarous forms of bourgeois materialism, the most sadistic forms of sexism, and horribly heterosexist long before the genesis of the hip hop generation—and, just for the funk of it, anyone with the unmitigated gall to deny this, as we say within the hip hop lexicon, has got it all seriously twisted and is truly trippin'.

Believe it or not, rap music, and hip hop culture more generally, may very well represent the last bastion of transcendence and opposition available to the African American underclass and working-poor youth at the turn of the twenty-first century, yet it, revealingly and rather ironically, is also quite frequently utilized to subvert, sabotage, and satirize black transcendence and opposition, both past and present. In other words, the most pressing social and political problems confronting black America are often routinely ridiculed and made to seem insignificant or antiquated in most commercial rap music and videos—that is, if "real" black issues are engaged at all. These innovative artistic, although often tacit, tactics—those such as pastiche, play, collage, silence, and apolitical avant-garde performance—ironically seem to fit nicely and neatly within the framework of postmodernism, especially that strain of postmodern thought that was taken up by Eurocentric petit-bourgeois artists, intellectuals, and critics in the United States. However, hip hoppers' homespun "postmodernism," if you will, with its ahistorical and apolitical pastiche (especially its parody of black historical and political events, movements, and figures), increasing in popularity every second urban radio and cable television stations play commercial rap songs, is arguably one of the most alarming and enormously amnesiac issues currently confronting black America.

It is rather ironic that at the exact same moment that we witness the African Americanization of popular music and culture around the globe *African Americans' culture of resistance and restitution*, as well as *African Americans' tradition of transcendence and opposition* is being challenged by the very heirs or, rather, the discursive descendants of this culture and tradition. Here, then, we have come full circle, back to what I characterized as the hip hop generation's historical amnesia in chapter 1, and their embrace of the *ritual of repudiation* in chapters 2, 3, and 4. As discussed in detail in chapters 2, 3, and 4, the hip hop generation is not the first generation of young black folk to take up the *ritual of repudiation*. However, what distinguishes their embrace of the *ritual of repudiation* is that, unlike previous generations of black youth, and ironically even with the academization of African American studies having been discursively developed to the extent to where one can actually earn a Ph.D. in the field, the hip hop generation as a whole arguably has the most acute form of historical amnesia of any generation of young black folk since the issuing of the Emancipation Proclamation. Why, my readers may earnestly ask? Because, to put it plainly, one of the great ironies of American apartheid—I honestly cannot believe that I am about to write this, as it is exactly what my grandparents used to tell me when I was a schoolboy, and what I have been able to gather from my more recent research—is that prior to desegregation in the United States both the urban and rural exclusively black enclaves grounded black youth in their particular and peculiar history, culture, and struggle. For instance, African American churches, schools, secret societies, and other social uplift organizations prior to desegregation instilled in black youth a sense of self, exposed them to the hallowed history of their people, and provided them with the tools to contribute to both African American and mainstream American culture and society.

For many (i.e., the misguided) in the United States, desegregation meant nothing more than black assimilation into white America. Few considered the costs of *assimilationist desegregation* on black folk (i.e., their *Africanity*—which is to say, their humanity, identity, and psyche). Not only did *assimilationist racial desegregation and integration* rupture African Americans' relationship with their unique history, culture, and struggle, but it also led to an intensification of most African Americans' inferiority complex (i.e., what Du Bois famously dubbed "double-consciousness" in *The Souls of Black Folk*) in light of their past enslavement and their present faux freedom. Let us meditate on this most important matter for a moment: How can one be truly free in a racially segregated society? With the symbols of American apartheid blazoned on every government building, school, college, restaurant, theater, park, swimming pool, beach, restroom, and water fountain, who would dare to be so cruel as to call African American life between 1863 and 1963—that is, between the issuing of the Emancipation Proclamation and the March on Washington—"freedom"? It is this century of American apartheid—the very century in which the bulk of the hip hop generation's grandparents and parents were born—that hip hoppers know so little about or, what is worse, ridicule what little they think they know about it.

Indeed, and this should be emphasized, hip hoppers, especially most conscious or alternative rappers, have an authentic relationship with African American history, culture, and struggle. However, it is the historical amnesia of the forms of commercial rap music that have risen to prominence since the "Golden Age of Rap" (1987–1999) that I am calling into question and that I am most critical of here. As a matter of fact, my own insurgent intellectual expressions and avant-garde artistry speak volumes about the ways in which conscious or alternative rap provided a working-poor youth in the ghetto with a sense of black pride, historical memory, social justice, and political direction. Not to sound too nostalgic, coming of age during the Golden Age of Rap, that period before the floodgates of corporate America opened and almost completely co-opted and commercialized it, it was a time when rap music was instrumental in exposing black and other youth to African American history, culture, and struggle. Back then hip hop culture had a greater sense of history, and rap music was most often utilized to rescue and reclaim the historic thought, leaders, movements, and events from the black past that hip hoppers believed best spoke to the bleakness of the black present.

Even the most cursory content analysis of rap music produced during its so-called Golden Age will reveal that it essentially served an archaeological function for African American underclass and working-poor youth. Critically taking into consideration the rise of the Reagan Right after the presidential election of 1980 and arguably the extension and expansion of Reaganism under President George H. W. Bush between 1988 and 1992, rap music was utilized as a retaliatory tool to combat the rising tide of anti-black racism then sweeping the nation and the increasing historical and cultural amnesia in black America since the end of the Black Power movement. In short, Golden Age rap music, employing what I am wont to call an *archaeological aesthetic*, sonically sifted through black history, culture, and struggle in its efforts to offer up anything and everything that might be useful in combating the political economy of anti-black racism extra-communally, and historical and cultural amnesia intra-communally. We witness here, then, that there was a dialectic at play in Golden Age rap music that cannot be easily or quickly reduced to the lame and lopsided critique that it was merely hateful or rage-filled music or, worse, "black noise" with no social or political substance, because its cultural criticism, social commentary, and political analysis was aimed at both external *and* internal issues and ills.

Hip hop studies is desperately in need of critical studies that examine the impact of conscious rap music on African American identity development and intellectual achievement. I personally can say that it impacted my growth and development, but I am curious to know what others who also came of age during the Golden Age think of its influence on their adolescence and later life-choices. Beyond providing a sense of pride, rap music during the Golden Age also exposed hip hoppers to the black intellectual tradition, especially black nationalist and black radical thought. Perhaps there is no Golden Age rap group that represents the nationalist impulse better than Public Enemy, although I continue to believe that rap groups like Boogie Down Productions, X Clan, Tribe Called Quest, De La Soul, Jungle Brothers, Arrested Development, Spearhead, Poor Righteous Teachers, Dream Warriors, and Freestyle Fellowship, among many others, have not been given the respect and critical acclaim they are due.

Touting African American insurgent activists and organizations, from Malcolm X and the Black Panther Party to Louis Farrakhan and the resuscitated 1980s and 1990s Nation of Islam, Golden Age rap—as with contemporary "conscious" rap—is not without its controversies and contradictions. However, what is commendable about conscious rap's historical and cultural revival is that it combats historical and cultural amnesia by raising historical and cultural consciousness, perceptively providing hip hoppers with historical and cultural paradigms and prompting them to put forward their own distinct visions of and views on both black and white America. Conscious rap's reinvigorated black historicism and black cultural consciousness enables black youth—who, without one word of hyperbole, as late as the close of the first decade of the twenty-first century, have little or no access to *authentic African American studies* (as opposed to *Eurocentric African American studies*)—to comprehend and connect the conditions of the past with the parlous circumstances of their present, archaeologically and aesthetically utilizing the past as a seminal source for cultural creation, social reflection, political resistance, and movement rallying in the present. Again, it must be openly acknowledged, there is much that is commendable when and where we come to conscious rap.

Yet and still, conscious rap, much like the wider world of hip hop from whence it emerged, has also inspired paltry perspectives on the past that are as ahistorical and apolitical as anything to be found in commercial rap. For example, many so-called conscious rappers mindlessly mimic past thought and practices without in any meaningful way bringing the dialectic to bear on it in ways that would simultaneously appreciate *and* critique it, as well as extend and expand it to meet the novel needs of the present moment. Hence, and this is where irony finds its way into the fray once again, many conscious rappers' black history lessons are ultimately ahistorical and apolitical, as they are discursively devoid of *the dialectic of deconstruction and reconstruction* and *tradition of appropriation and translation* (i.e., *Africanization* or *re-Africanization*) emphasized within Africana critical theory that would not only enable them to illuminate the issues of the past but also apply their illuminations to the ills of the present. Consequently, even those black (among other) youth who embrace and gain sustenance from conscious rap frequently have extremely fragmented views of African American history, culture, and contemporary struggle, because their uncritical acceptance of past thought and practices never calls into question whether such thought and practices, as viable as they may have been within the specific time and space in which they were put forward, are applicable to the special circumstances and novel needs confronting African Americans at the turn of the twenty-first century. This is, I honestly believe, a consequence of the absence of comprehension and communication between differing constituents of the contemporary African American community, specifically revolving around age and economics or, rather, generational and class issues, pressing problems most readily observed in the older African American community's contentious and condescending response to rap music and hip hop culture. In other words, conscious rappers' black history lessons are a good initial effort to combat historical and cultural amnesia, but songs—no matter how laudable the lyrics and seductive the beats—are no substitute for the serious study, *authentic African American studies*, which must be undertaken in order for African Americans (as well as multicultural and transethnic others) to develop a truly dialectical relationship and critical rapport with African American history, culture, and struggle. Ultimately this means, then, that African American elders and youth will have to build bridges from the past to the present, and vice versa, which will require *transgenerational transcendence* and *compassionate communication*—which is also to say, deep dialogue that allows the elders to historicize their lived-experiences and lived-endurances (i.e., primarily the past) and the youth to contextualize their life-worlds and life-struggles (i.e., primarily the present). Needless to say, none of this will occur if significant segments of the African American community continue their *black generational segregation*—that is, Civil Rights, Black Power, and Women's Liberation movement elders segregating themselves from hip hop youth and, by the same token, hip hop youth segregating themselves from Civil Rights, Black Power, and Women's Liberation movement elders.

With the erosion of the idyllic impulse of African American life and culture on the one hand, and hip hoppers' invention of their own homespun postmodernism on the other hand, African American's historic tradition of transcendence and opposition is currently, and rather ironically I believe, being radically challenged, not by white sheet–wearing and snuff-dipping rural racists, but by baggy pants and baseball cap–wearing urban rappers.

This challenge registers not simply as a lack of will or loss of nerve on the part of the African American underclass and working-poor youth, but it also represents the roguishness of ruling-class politicians and their policies, the condescending and callous attitude of the black bourgeoisie, and the historical amnesia and consequent erasure of African Americans' longstanding culture of resistance and restitution. To put it plainly, the real roots of the idyllic impulse of African American life and culture—from Harriet Tubman and Frederick Douglass to Malcolm X and Angela Davis—are predicated on the belief that someone—God, Grandmama, Mama, church folk, or neighbors—really and truly cares. At present, many of the most popular expressions of rap music and hip hop culture radically challenge this solemn supposition. Consequently, it seems as though the future of, not only African Americans' idyllic impulse, but African Americans themselves may very well rest on the caution and caliber of the response to this challenge. In this sense, then, the real vitality and value of rap music and hip hop culture is not simply based on the talents, techniques, or expressions of testosterone on the part of rappers and other hip hop artists, but even more on the moral visions, ethical alternatives, social analyses, and political strategies their lifework and legacies offer up which accent individual enlightenment, stress collective struggle, emphasize shared responsibility, highlight social justice, provide political promise, and impart existential hope to the underclass and working-poor youth of black America, the United States, and the world.

NOTES

1. It is important to emphasize the prominence of break-dancing and b-boys and b-girls (i.e., "break-dancing boys" and "break-dancing girls") in early hip hop culture. Some of my readers may be too young to recall how break-dancing films—such as *Wild Style* (1983), *Breakin'* (1984), *Breakin' 2: Electric Boogaloo* (1984), *Beat Street* (1984), *Body Shock* (1984), *Krush Groove* (1985), and *Rappin'* (1985)—took the nation, and later the world, by storm. Along with several of the major scholarly studies of break-dancing (e.g., Bramwell and Green, 2003; Franklin and Watkins, 1984; Hazzard-Gordon, 1990; Huntington, 2007; Schloss, 2009), I have relied on the following critically acclaimed documentaries for my interpretation of "breakin'" here: Celia Ipiotis's *Popular Culture in Dance: The World of Hip Hop* (1984), Israel's *The Freshest Kids: A History of the B-Boy* (2002), and Benson Lee's *Planet B-Boy: Break-dancing Has Evolved* (2008).

2. Within the world of Hip Hop studies there has long been a tendency to downplay hip hop's politics. As with the cultural aesthetic movements it draws from and builds on, hip hop culture is contentiously political even when and where it aspires to be apolitical. On the one hand, this is partly due to the ways in which race, gender, class, and sexuality have historically overlapped and intersected in U.S. culture, politics, and society: from antebellum and post-Reconstruction blackface minstrelism through to 1990s and early 2000s "postfeminist" art. On the other hand, hip hop's seemingly ever-increasing popularity means that frequently local or regional issues are lost in translation as they travel at digital download speed to the national and international marketplace. Indeed, much is lost but, as Edward Said (1999, 2000) contends with his conception of "traveling theory," something is also gained as ideas and theories move from one intellectual context to the next. In the succeeding section I utilize the "commercial" rap

versus "conscious" rap dichotomy as a point of departure to explore how hip hop's politics have evolved over the last thirty years and how the *hyper-corporate colonization of hip hop culture* has influenced more and more rappers to mute and mask the sociopolitical messages in their music. For further discussion of hip hop's politics in general, and for a few of the most noteworthy works that influenced my interpretation of hip hop's politics here, please see: A. Anderson (2003), Banjoko (2004), Butler (2009), Bynoe (2004), Goff (2008), McWhorter (2008), Ogbar (2007), Perry (2004), Potter (1995), and Watkins (2005).

3. At this point, the terms "postmodernity" and "postmodernism" mean many different things to many different people. Following groundbreaking Hip Hop studies by Potter (1995), Lhamon (1998), and Grandt (2009), which bring hip hop culture into dialogue with postmodernism, I would be remiss if I did not make mention of the other postmodern studies that have informed my analysis here, please see Best and Kellner (1991, 1997, 2001), Dirlik (2000), Harvey (1990), Jameson (1991), Jordan and Weedon (1995), Nicholson (1990), Sadar (1998), and Smart (1992, 1993).

4. The discursive distinctions that I am making here between "postmodernity," "postmodernism," and "postmodern knowledge" have been informed by Appleby et al. (1996), Bertens (1995), Connor (2004), Hutcheon (1988, 2002), Hutcheon and Natoli (1993), and Sim (2005). Also, with regard to the contention that non-Europeans—who were, for the most part, racially colonized within the context of European modernity—have comparably different points of departure in terms of postmodernity and postmodernism, my assertion is predicated on pioneering postcolonial studies, such as Ashcroft, Griffiths, and Tiffin (2006), Lazarus (2004), McLeod (2007), and Schwarz and Ray (2000).

5. With regard to the African American roots of rap music and hip hop culture more generally, in *Prophets of the Hood: Politics and Poetics in Hip Hop* (2004), Princeton African American studies professor Imani Perry sternly stated: "Hip hop music is black music. Even with its hybridity: the consistent contributions from nonblack artists, and the borrowings from cultural forms of other communities, it is nevertheless black American music. It is constituted as such because of four central characteristics: (1) its primary language is African American Vernacular English (AAVE); (2) it has a political location in society distinctly ascribed to black people, music, and cultural forms; (3) it is derived from black oral culture; and (4) it is derived from black American musical traditions" (p. 10). It will be important to bear Perry's assertions in mind, as the following sections of this chapter emphasize rap music's roots deep within both the African American rhetorical and musical traditions, both of which are considered extremely "political" within the wider world of U.S. culture, politics, and society.

6. International Hip Hop studies has exponentially increased over the last decade and, consequently, my analysis here is based on several of the better works within this new area of inquiry, please see Kato (2007), T. Mitchell (2001), Neate (2004), Nilan and Feixa (2006), Osumare (2007), Price (2006), and Spady, Alim, and Meghelli (2006).

7. My interpretation of the African aesthetic has obviously been informed by Halifu Osumare's innovative *The Africanist Aesthetic in Global Hip Hop* (2007). However, more general scholarship on the African aesthetic has also indelibly influenced my analysis here. Please see, for example, Cole (1989), Fiagbedzi (2005), L. A. Johnson (1982), Magnin and Soulillou (1996), Visona (2001), and Welsh-Asante (1992).

8. My interpretation of the prison industrial complex, especially with regard to the African American males of the hip hop generation, has been informed by Boothe (2007), Dyer (2000), Herivel and Wright (2003), Marable, Steinberg, and Middlemass (2007), May and Pitts (2000), and Sudbury (2005).

9. Considering that the previous chapter offered an extended discussion of misogyny in rap music, and hip hop culture more generally, there is no need to rehash this issue here. However, for further discussion of nonwhite America essentially constituting a series of "domestic colonies" or "internal colonies," please see Hahn (2003), Pulido (2006), Singh (2004), and C. A. Young (2006).

10. For further discussion of Frantz Fanon's views on violence, the art of the oppressed, and the recreational activities of the wretched of the earth, see Rabaka (2010b, esp., pp. 49–216).

Bibliography

Abbott, Lynn, and Seroff, Doug. (2002). *Out of Sight: The Rise of African American Popular Music, 1889–1895.* Jackson: University Press of Mississippi.

Abelove, Henry, Barale, Michele Aina, and Halperin, David M. (Eds.). (1993). *The Lesbian and Gay Studies Reader.* New York: Routledge.

Abod, Jennifer. (Dir.). (1990). *Edge of Each Other's Battles: The Vision of Audre Lorde.* Long Beach, CA: Profile Productions.

Abu-Lughod, Janet L. (1989). *Before European Hegemony: The World System A.D. 1250–1350.* Oxford, UK: Oxford University Press.

Adjaye, Joseph K., and Andrews, Adrianne R. (Eds.). (1997). *Language, Rhythm, & Sound: Black Popular Cultures into the Twenty-First Century.* Pittsburgh, PA: University of Pittsburgh Press.

Ajalon, Jamika. (Dir.). (1993). *Intro to Cultural Skitzo-Frenia.* New York: Third World Newsreel.

Aldridge, Delores P., and James, E. Lincoln. (Eds.). (2007). *Africana Studies: Philosophical Perspectives and Theoretical Paradigms.* Pullman: Washington State University Press.

Aldridge, Delores, and Young, Carlene. (Eds.). (2000). *Out of the Revolution: An Africana Studies Anthology.* Lanham, MD: Lexington Books.

Alexander, Bryant K. (2006). *Performing Black Masculinity: Race, Culture, and Queer Identity.* Lanham, MD: AltaMira Press.

Algarín, Miguel, and Holman, Bob. (Eds.). (1994). *Aloud: Voice from the Nuyorican Poets Café.* New York: Henry Holt.

Alim, H. Samy. (2004). *You Know My Steez!: An Ethnographic and Sociolinguistic Study of Style-Shifting in a Black American Speech Community.* Durham, NC: Duke University Press.

———. (2006). *Roc the Mic Right!: The Language of Hip Hop Culture.* New York: Routledge.

Alim, H. Samy, Ibrahim, Awad, and Pennycook, Alastair. (Eds.). (2009). *Global Linguistic Flows: Hip Hop Cultures, Youth Identities, and the Politics of Language.* New York: Routledge.

Alkebulan, Paul. (2007). *Survival Pending Revolution: The History of the Black Panther Party.* Tuscaloosa: University of Alabama Press.

Amani, Khalil. (2007) *Hip Hop Homophobes: Origins and Attitudes Towards Gays and Lesbians in Hip Hop Culture.* Bloomington, IN: iUniverse, Inc.

Amoaku, Kwame. (Dir.). (2005). *The Industry: The Real Story Behind Hip Hop.* Chatsworth, CA: Imagine Entertainment.

Amoo-Adare, Epifania Akosua. (2006). "Critical Spatial Literacy: A Womanist Positionality and the Spatio-Temporal Construction of Black Family Life." In Layla Phillips (Ed.), *The Womanist Reader* (pp. 347–60). New York: Routledge.

Amos, Valerie, and Parmar, Pratibha. (2005). "Challenging Imperial Feminism." *Feminist Review* 80:44–63.

Anderson, Adrienne. (2003). *Word!: Rap, Politics and Feminism.* Lincoln, NE: Writers Club Press.

Anderson, Elijah. (1999). *Code of the Street: Decency, Violence, and the Moral Life of the Inner City.* New York: W.W Norton.

———. (Ed.). (2008). *Against the Wall: Poor, Young, Black, and Male.* Philadelphia: University of Pennsylvania Press.

Anderson, Linda R. (1997). *Women and Autobiography in the Twentieth Century: Remembered Futures.* New York: Prentice Hall.

Anderson, Perry. (1998). *The Origins of Postmodernity.* New York: Verso.

Anderson, Talmadge, and Stewart, James B. (2007). *Introduction to African American Studies: Transdisciplinary Approaches and Implications.* Baltimore, MD: Black Classic Press.

Anderson-Bricker, Kristin. (1999). "'Triple Jeopardy': Black Women and the Growth of Feminist Consciousness in SNCC, 1964–1975." In Kimberly Springer (Ed.), *Still Lifting, Still Climbing: Contemporary African American Women's Activism* (pp. 49–69). New York: New York University Press.

Andrews, William L., and Gates, Henry Louis. (Eds.). (1999). *The Civitas Anthology of African American Slave Narratives.* Washington, DC: Civitas/Counterpoint.

———. (2000). *Slave Narratives.* New York: Library of America.

Anner, John. (Ed.). (1996). *Beyond Identity Politics: Emerging Social Justice Movements in Communities of Color.* Boston, MA: South End Press.

Appleby, Joyce, Covington, Elizabeth, Hoyt, David, Latham, Michael, and Snieder, Allison. (Eds.). (1996). *Knowledge and Postmodernism in Historical Perspective.* New York: Routledge.

Aptheker, Herbert. (1983). *American Negro Slave Revolts.* New York: International Publishers.

Arthur, Paul. (2005). *Line of Sight: American Avant-Garde Film since 1965.* Minneapolis: University of Minnesota Press.

Asante, M. K., Jr. (2008). *It's Bigger Than Hip Hop: The Rise of the Post–Hip Hop Generation.* New York: St. Martin's Press.

Asante, Molefi K., and Karenga, Maulana. (Eds.). (2006). *The Handbook of Black Studies.* Thousand Oaks, CA: Sage.

Asante, Molefi Kete, and Mazama, Ama. (Eds.). (2005). *Encyclopedia of Black Studies.* Thousand Oaks, CA: Sage.

Ashcroft, Bill, Griffiths, Gareth, and Tiffin, Helen. (Eds.). (2006). *The Post-Colonial Studies Reader.* New York: Routledge.

Austin, Curtis J. (2006). *Up Against the Wall: Violence in the Making and Unmaking of the Black Panther Party.* Fayetteville: University of Arkansas Press.

Avery, Byllye. (1990). "Abortion and Black Women's Health." In Marlene Gerber Fried (Ed.), *From Abortion to Reproductive Freedom: Transforming a Movement* (pp. 75–82). Boston: South End Press.

Azevedo, Mario. (Ed.). (2005). *Africana Studies: A Survey of Africa and the African Diaspora.* Durham, NC: Carolina Academic Press.

Babb, Tracie. (2002). *The Treatment of Women in the Hip-Hop Community: Past, Present, and Future.* New York: Fordham University Press.

Baker, Houston A., Jr. (1980). *The Journey Back: Issues in Black Literature and Criticism.* Chicago: University of Chicago Press.

———. (1983). *Singers of Daybreak: Studies in Black American Literature.* Washington, DC: Howard University Press.

———. (1984). *Blues, Ideology, and Afro-American Literature: A Vernacular Theory.* Chicago: University of Chicago Press.

———. (1987). *Modernism and the Harlem Renaissance.* Chicago: University Chicago Press.

———. (1988). *Afro-American Poetics: Revisions of Harlem and the Black Aesthetic*. Madison: University of Wisconsin Press.

———. (1990). *Long Black Song: Essays in Black American Literature and Culture*. Charlottesville: University Press of Virginia.

———. (1991). *Workings of the Spirit: The Poetic Voices of Afro-American Women's Writing*. Chicago: University of Chicago Press.

———. (1993). *Black Studies, Rap, and the Academy*. Chicago: University of Chicago Press.

———. (2001). *Turning South Again: Re-Thinking Modernism*. Durham, NC: Duke University Press.

———. (2007). *I Don't Hate the South: Reflections on Faulkner, Family, and the South*. Oxford, UK: Oxford University Press.

———. (2008). *Betrayal: How Black Intellectuals Have Abandoned the Ideals of the Civil Rights Era*. New York: Columbia University Press.

Baker, Houston A., Jr., and Redmond, Patricia. (Eds.). (1989). *Afro-American Literary Study in the 1990s*. Chicago: University of Chicago Press.

Baker, Soren. (2006). *A History of Rap and Hip Hop*. Thousand Oaks, CA: Thomson-Gale.

Balbus, Isaac D. (1984). "Habermas and Feminism: (Male) Communication and the Evolution of (Patriarchal) Society." *New Political Science* 5 (1): 27–47.

Baldwin, Katherine A. (2002). *Beyond the Color-Line and the Iron Curtain: Reading Encounters Between Black and Red, 1922–1963*. Durham, NC: Duke University Press.

Ball, Howard. (2000). *Bakke Case: Race, Education, and Affirmative Action*. Lawrence: University Press of Kansas.

Balton, Chris. (Dir.). (1991). *Sisters in the Name of Rap*. Los Angeles: PolyGram Video.

Bambara, Toni Cade. (Ed.). (1970). *The Black Woman: An Anthology*. New York: New American Library.

———. (1996). *Deep Sightings and Rescue Missions: Fiction, Essays, and Conversations* (Toni Morrison, Ed.). New York: Pantheon Books.

Banfield, William C. (2010). *Cultural Codes: The Makings of a Black Music Philosophy—An Interpretive History*. Lanham, MD: Scarecrow Press.

BaNikongo, Nikongo. (Ed.). (1997). *Leading Issues in African American Studies*. Durham, NC: Carolina Academic Press.

Banjoko, Adisa. (2004). *Lyrical Swords: Hip Hop and Politics in the Mix*. San Jose, CA: YinSumi Press.

Baraka, Amiri. (1963). *Blues People: Black Music in White America*. New York: Morrow.

———. (1967). *Black Music*. New York: Quill.

———. (1970). "Black Women." *Black World* (July): 7–11.

———. (1987). *The Music: Reflections on Jazz and Blues*. New York: Morrow.

———. (2009). *Digging: The African American Soul of American Classical Music*. Berkeley: University of California Press.

Barrett, Michele. (1980). *Women's Oppression Today: Problems in Marxist Feminist Analysis*. London: Verso.

Barrow, Jerry. (2010). "Phonté Speaks on the Hypocrisy of 'Conscious' Rappers." *The Urban Daily*. http://theurbandaily.com/music/jbarrow/phonte-speaks-on-hypocrisy-of-conscious-rappers/.

Bascom, Lionel C. (Ed.). (1999). *Renaissance in Harlem: Lost Voices of an American Community*. New York: Bard.

Basu, Dipannita, and Lemelle, Sidney J. (Eds.). (2006).*The Vinyl Ain't Final: Hip Hop and the Globalization of Black Popular Culture*. London: Pluto Press.

Bates, Gerri. (Ed.). (2005). *Alice Walker: A Critical Companion*. Westport, CT: Greenwood Press.

Bauman, Zygmunt. (1992). *Intimations of Postmodernity*. New York: Routledge.

———. (1997). *Postmodernity and Its Discontents*. New York: New York University Press.

Beal, Frances M. (1975). "Slave of a Slave No More: Black Women in Struggle." *Black Scholar* 6 (6): 2–10.

———. (1995). "Double Jeopardy: To Be Black and Female." In Beverly Guy-Sheftall (Ed.), *Words of Fire: An Anthology of African American Feminist Thought* (pp. 146–56). New York: Free Press.

Bean, Annemarie, Hatch, James V., and McNamara, Brooks. (Eds.). (1996). *Inside the Minstrel Mask: Readings in Nineteenth-Century Blackface Minstrelsy*. Hanover, NH: Wesleyan University Press.

Beauvoir, Simone de. (1953). *The Second Sex* (H. M. Parshley, ed.). New York: Vintage.

Beemyn, Brett, and Eliason, Mickey. (Eds.). (1996). *Queer Studies: A Lesbian, Gay, Bisexual & Transgender Anthology*. New York: New York University Press.

Bell-Scott, Patricia. (1999). "Barbara Smith: A Home Girl with a Mission." In Kimberly Springer (Ed.), *Still Lifting, Still Climbing: Contemporary African American Women's Activism* (pp. 17–24). New York: New York University Press.

Benhabib, Seyla. (1986). *Critique, Norm, and Utopia*. New York: Columbia University Press.

———. (1992). *Situating the Self: Gender, Community, and Postmodernism in Contemporary Ethics*. New York: Routledge.

Benhabib, Seyla, and Cornell, Drucilla. (1987). *Feminism as Critique: Essays on the Politics of Gender in Late-Capitalist Societies*. London: Polity Press.

Benston, Margaret. (1969)."The Political Economy of Women's Liberation." *Monthly Review* 21 (4): 13–27.

Berkeley, Kathleen C. (1999). *Women's Liberation in America*. Westport, CT: Greenwood Press.

Bernard, Emily. (2006). "A Familiar Strangeness: The Spectre of Whiteness in the Harlem Renaissance and the Black Arts Movement." In Lisa Gail Collins and Margo Natalie Crawford (Eds.), *New Thoughts on the Black Arts Movement* (pp. 255–72). New Brunswick, NJ: Rutgers University Press.

Bernard, Regina A. (2009). *Black & Brown Waves: The Cultural Politics of Young Women of Color and Feminism*. Boston, MA: Sense Publishers.

Bertens, Johannes W. (1995). *Idea of the Postmodern: A History*. New York: Routledge.

Best, Steven. (1995). *The Politics of Historical Vision: Marx, Foucault, Habermas*. New York: Guilford.

Best, Steven, and Kellner, Douglas. (1991). *Postmodern Theory: Critical Interrogations*. New York: Guilford.

———. (1997). *The Postmodern Turn*. New York: Guilford.

———. (2001). *The Postmodern Adventure*. New York: Guilford.

Blackett, Richard J. M. (1983). *Building an Anti-Slavery Wall: Black Americans in the Atlantic Abolitionist Movement, 1830–1860*. Baton Rouge: Louisiana State University Press.

Blassingame, John. (Ed). (1973). *New Perspectives on Black Studies*. Chicago: University of Illinois Press.

Blaut, James M. (1993). *The Colonizer's Model of the World: Geographical Diffusionism and Eurocentric History*. New York: Guilford.

Bloom, Harold. (Ed.). (1994). *Black American Women Fiction Writers*. New York: Chelsea House Publishers.

———. (Ed.). (2008). *Zora Neale Hurston*. New York: Chelsea House Publishers.

Bloom, Leslie R. (1998). *Under the Sign of Hope: Feminist Methodology and Narrative Interpretation*. Albany: State University of New York Press.

Blount, Marcellus, and Cunningham, George P. (Eds.). (1996). *Representing Black Men*. New York: Routledge.

Bobo, Jacqueline. (1995). *Black Women as Cultural Readers*. New York: Columbia University Press.

———. (Ed.). (2001). *Black Feminist Cultural Criticism*. Malden, MA: Blackwell.

Bobo, Jacqueline, and Michel, Claudine. (Eds.). (2000). *Black Studies: Current Issues, Enduring Questions*. Dubuque, IA: Kendall/Hunt.

Bobo, Jacqueline, Hudley, Cynthia, and Michel, Claudine. (Eds.). (2004). *The Black Studies Reader*. New York: Routledge.

Bodunde, Charles. (2001). *Oral Traditions and Aesthetic Transfer: Creativity and Social Vision in Contemporary Black Poetry*. Bayreuth, Germany: Bayreuth University.

Bogues, Anthony. (2003). *Black Heretics, Black Prophets: Radical Political Intellectuals*. New York: Routledge.

Bolden, Tony (Ed.). (2008). *Funk Era and Beyond: New Perspectives on Black Popular Culture*. New York: Palgrave Macmillan.

Bonilla-Silva, Eduardo, and Zuberi, Tukufu. (Eds.). (2008). *White Logic, White Methods: Racism and Methodology*. Lanham, MD: Rowman & Littlefield.

Boothe, Demico. (2007). *Why Are So Many Black Men in Prison?: A Comprehensive Account of How and Why the Prison Industry Has Become a Predatory Entity in the Lives of African-American Men*. Memphis, TN: Full Surface Publishing.

Bounds, Elizabeth M., Brubaker, Pamela K., Hobgood, Mary E. (Eds.). (1999). *Welfare Policy: Feminist Critiques*. Cleveland, OH: Pilgrim Press.

Boyd, Todd. (1997). *Am I Black Enough for You?: Popular Culture from the 'Hood and Beyond*. Indianapolis: Indiana University Press.

———. (2002). *The New H.N.I.C.: The Death of Civil Rights and the Reign of Hip Hop*. New York: New York University Press.

———. (2003). *Young, Black, Rich, and Famous: The Rise of the NBA, the Hip Hop Invasion and the Transformation of American Culture*. New York: Doubleday.

Bracey, Earnest N. (2003). *On Racism: Essays on Black Popular Culture, African American Politics, and the New Black Aesthetics*. Lanham, MD: University Press of America.

Bracey, John H., Meier, August, and Rudwick, Elliott. (Ed.). (1970). *Black Nationalism in America*. Indianapolis, IN: Bobbs-Merrill.

Brack, Charles B. (Dir.). (2008). *Dreams Deferred: The Sakia Gunn Film Project*. New York: Third World Newsreel.

Bradley, Adam. (2009). *Book of Rhymes: The Poetics of Hip Hop*. New York: Basic/Civitas.

Bradley, Adam, and DuBois, Andrew. (Eds.). (2010). *The Anthology of Rap*. New Haven, CT: Yale University Press.

Bramwell, David, and Green, Jairus. (2003). *Breakdance: Hip Hop Handbook*. New York: Street Style Publications.

Branch, Taylor. (1988). *Parting the Waters: America in the King Years, 1954–1963*. New York: Simon & Schuster.

———. (1998). *Pillar of Fire: America in the King Years, 1963–1965*. New York: Simon & Schuster.

———. (2006). *At Canaan's Edge: America in the King Years, 1965–1968*. New York: Simon & Schuster.

Brandt, Eric. (Ed.). (1999). *Dangerous Liaisons: Blacks, Gays, and the Struggle for Equality*. New York: New Press.

Breines, Winifred. (2002). "What's Love Got to Do with It?: White Women, Black Women, and Feminism in the Movement Years." *Signs: Journal of Women in Culture and Society* 27 (4): 1095–133.

———. (2006). *Trouble Between Us: An Uneasy History of White and Black Women in the Feminist Movement*. Oxford, UK: Oxford University Press.

Brooks, TaKeshia. (2007). *Dream Factory Deferred: Black Womanhood, History, and Music Video*. Bloomington, IN: iUniverse.

Broude, Norma, and Garrard, Mary D. (Eds.). (1994). *The Power of Feminist Art: The American Movement of the 1970s, History and Impact*. New York: H. N. Abrams.

———. (2005). *Reclaiming Female Agency: Feminist Art History After Postmodernism*. Berkeley: University of California Press.

Browder, Laura. (2000). *Slippery Characters: Ethnic Impersonators and American Identities*. Chapel Hill: University of North Carolina Press.

Brown, Fahamisha P. (1999). *Performing the Word: African American Poetry as Vernacular*. New Brunswick, NJ: Rutgers University Press.

Brown, Ruth Nicole. (2008). *Black Girlhood Celebration: Toward a Hip-Hop Feminist Pedagogy*. New York: Peter Lang Publishing.

Brown, Timothy J. (2006). "Welcome to the Terrordome!: Exploring the Contradictions of Hip Hop Black Masculinity." In Athena D. Mutua (Ed.), *Progressive Black Masculinities* (pp. 191–214). New York: Routledge.

Brown, Wendy. (Ed.). (2006). "Feminist Theory and the Frankfurt School." *Differences: A Journal of Feminist Cultural Studies* [Special Edition] 17 (1): 1–160.

Brundage, W. Fitzhugh. (1993). *Lynching in the New South: Georgia and Virginia, 1880–1930.* Urbana: University of Illinois Press.

———. (Ed.). (1997). *Under Sentence of Death: Lynching in the South.* Chapel Hill: University of North Carolina Press.

Buchanan, Ian. (2006). *Fredric Jameson: Live Theory.* New York: Continuum.

Buechler, Steven M. (1990). *Women's Movements in the United States: Woman Suffrage, Equal Rights, and Beyond.* New Brunswick, NJ: Rutgers University Press.

Bulmer, Martin, and Solomos, John. (Eds.). (2004). *Researching Race and Racism.* New York: Routledge.

Burack, Cynthia, and Josephson, Jyl J. (Eds.). (2003). *Fundamental Differences: Feminists Talk Back to Social Conservatives.* Lanham, MD: Rowman & Littlefield.

Burns, Kate. (Ed.). (2008). *Rap Music and Culture.* Detroit, MI: Greenhaven Press.

Buszek, Maria Elena. (2006). *Pin-Up Girrrls: Feminism, Sexuality, Popular Culture.* Durham, NC: Duke University Press.

Butler, Paul. (2009). *Let's Get Free!: A Hip-Hop Theory of Justice.* New York: New Press.

Bynoe, Yvonne. (2004). *Stand and Deliver: Political Activism, Leadership, and Hip Hop Culture.* Brooklyn, NY: Soft Skull Press.

Byrd, Rudolph P. (Ed.). (2010). *The World Has Changed: Conversations with Alice Walker.* New York: New Press.

Byrd, Rudolph P., and Guy-Sheftall, Beverly. (Eds.). (2001). *Traps: African American Men on Gender and Sexuality.* Indianapolis: Indiana University Press.

Cabral, Amilcar. (1972). *Revolution in Guinea: Selected Texts.* New York: Monthly Review Press.

———. (1973). *Return to the Source: Selected Speeches of Amilcar Cabral.* New York: Monthly Review Press.

———. (1979). *Unity and Struggle: Speeches and Writings of Amilcar Cabral.* New York: Monthly Review Press.

Cahn, Steven M. (Ed.). (2002). *The Affirmative Action Debate.* New York: Routledge.

Campbell, Kermit E. (2005). *Gettin' Our Groove On: Rhetoric, Language, and Literacy for the Hip Hop Generation.* Detroit, MI: Wayne State University Press.

Carbado, Devon W. (Ed.). (1999). *Black Men on Race, Gender, and Sexuality: A Critical Reader.* New York: New York University Press.

Carby, Hazel V. (1996). "White Woman Listen!: Black Feminism and the Boundaries of Sisterhood." In Houston A. Baker, Jr., Manthia Diawara, and Ruth H. Lindeborg (Eds.), *Black British Cultural Studies: A Reader* (pp. 67–86). Chicago: University of Chicago Press.

Carmichael, Stokely. (2003). *Ready for Revolution!: The Life and Struggles of Stokely Carmichael (Kwame Ture)* (with Ekwueme Michael Thelwell). New York: Scribner.

———. (2007). *Stokely Speaks: From Black Power to Pan-Africanism.* Chicago: Lawrence Hill Books.

Carmichael, Stokely, and Hamilton, Charles V. (1967). *Black Power: The Politics of Liberation in America.* New York: Vintage.

Carroll, Ann Elizabeth. (2005). *Word, Image, and the New Negro: Representation and Identity in the Harlem Renaissance.* Bloomington: Indiana University Press.

Carter, David C. (2009). *Music Has Gone Out of the Movement: Civil Rights and the Johnson Administration, 1965–1968.* Chapel Hill: University of North Carolina Press.

Carter, Steven R. (1991). *Hansberry's Drama: Commitment Amid Complexity.* Urbana: University of Illinois Press.

Carver, Terrell. (1982). *Marx's Social Theory.* Oxford, UK: Oxford University Press.

———. (Ed.). (1991). *The Cambridge Companion to Marx.* Cambridge, UK: Cambridge University Press.

Cash, Floris Loretta. (2001). *African American Women and Social Action: The Clubwomen and Volunteerism from Jim Crow to the New Deal, 1896–1936.* Westport, CT: Greenwood Press.

Cepeda, Raquel. (Ed.). (2004). *And It Don't Stop!: The Best American Hip Hop Journalism of the Last 25 Years.* New York: Faber & Faber.

Chambers, Veronica. (1996). *Mama's Girl*. New York: Riverhead Books.

Chang, Jeff. (2005). *Can't Stop Won't Stop!: A History of the Hip Hop Generation*. New York: St. Martin's Press.

———. (Ed.). (2006). *Total Chaos: The Art and Aesthetics of Hip-Hop*. Cambridge, MA: Basic/Civitas Books.

Cheney, Anne. (1984). *Lorraine Hansberry*. Boston, MA: Twayne.

Cheney, Charise L. (1999). *Phallic/ies and Hi(s)stories: Masculinity and the Black Nationalist Tradition, from Slave Spirituals to Rap Music*. Champaign: University of Illinois Press.

———. (2005). *Brothers Gonna Work It Out!: Sexual Politics in the Golden Age of Rap Nationalism*. New York: New York University Press.

Chicago, Judy. (1975). *Through the Flower: My Struggle as a Woman Artist*. Garden City, NY: Doubleday.

———. (1996). *Beyond the Flower: The Autobiography of a Feminist Artist*. New York: Viking.

Choi, Jung Min, Callaghan, Karen A., and Murphy, John W. (1995). *The Politics of Culture: Race, Violence, and Democracy*. Westport, CT: Praeger.

Christian, Barbara. (1985). *Black Feminist Criticism: Perspectives on Black Women Writers*. New York: Pergamon Press.

———. (1988). "The Race for Theory." *Feminist Studies* 14 (1): 67–79.

Churchill, Ward, and Wall, Jim V. (1988). *Agents of Repression: The FBI's Secret Wars Against the Black Panther Party and the American Indian Movement*. Boston, MA: South End Press.

Clarke, Cheryl. (2005). *"After Mecca": Women Poets and the Black Arts Movement*. New Brunswick, NJ: Rutgers University Press.

Clay, Adreana. (2007). "'I Used to Be Scared of the Dick': Queer Women of Color and Hip Hop Masculinity." In Gwendolyn D. Pough, Elaine Richardson, Aisha Durham, and Rachel Raimist (Eds.), *Home Girls Make Some Noise!: The Hip Hop Feminism Anthology* (pp. 148–65). Mira Loma, CA: Parker Publishing.

Cleaver, Kathleen, and Katsiaficas, George. (Eds.). (2001). *Liberation, Imagination, and the Black Panther Party*. New York: Routledge.

Clinton, Catherine. (2004). *Harriet Tubman: The Road to Freedom*. New York: Little, Brown.

Cobb, William Jelani. (2007). *To the Break of Dawn: A Freestyle on the Hip Hop Aesthetic*. New York: New York University.

Cohn, Nik. (2005). *Triksta: Life and Death and New Orleans Rap*. New York: Knopf.

Cockrell, Dale. (1997). *Demons of Disorder: Early Blackface Minstrels and Their World*. Cambridge, UK: Cambridge University Press.

Cole, Herbert M. (1989). *Icons: Ideals and Power in the Art of Africa*. Washington, DC: Smithsonian Institution Press.

Cole, Johnnetta B., and Guy-Sheftall, Beverly. (2003). *Gender Talk: The Struggle for Women's Equality in African American Communities*. New York: Ballantine.

Collier-Thomas, Betty, and Franklin, V. P. (Eds.). (2001). *Sisters in the Struggle: African American Women in the Civil Rights–Black Power Movement*. New York: New York University Press.

Collins, Lisa Gail. (2002). *Art of History: African American Women Artists Engage the Past*. New Brunswick, NJ: Rutgers University Press.

Collins, Lisa Gail, and Crawford, Margo Natalie. (Eds.). (2006). *New Thoughts on the Black Arts Movement*. New Brunswick, NJ: Rutgers University Press.

Collins, Patricia Hill. (1998). *Fighting Words: Black Women and the Search for Social Justice*. Minneapolis: University of Minnesota Press.

———. (2000). *Black Feminist Thought: Knowledge, Consciousness, and the Politics of Empowerment* (Second Edition). New York: Routledge.

———. (2003). "Some Group Matters: Intersectionality, Situated Standpoints, and Black Feminist Thought." In Tommy L. Lott and John P. Pittman (Eds.), *A Companion to African American Philosophy* (pp. 205–30). Malden, MA: Blackwell.

———. (2005). *Black Sexual Politics: African Americans, Gender, and the New Racism*. New York: Routledge.

————. (2006). *From Black Power to Hip Hop: Racism, Nationalism, and Feminism.* Philadelphia, PA: Temple University Press.

————. (2007). "Pushing Boundaries or Business as Usual?: Race, Class, and Gender Studies and Sociological Inquiry." In Craig J. Calhoun (Ed.), *Sociology in America: A History* (pp. 572–604). Chicago: University of Chicago Press.

Combahee River Collective. (1982). "A Black Feminist Statement." In Gloria T. Hull, Patricia Bell Scott, and Barbara Smith (Eds.), *All the Women Are White, All the Blacks Are Men, But Some of Us Are Brave: Black Women's Studies* (pp. 13–23). New York: The Feminist Press at CUNY.

Conley, Dalton. (1999). *Being Black, Living in the Red: Race, Wealth, and Social Policy in America.* Berkeley: University of California Press.

Connor, Steve. (Ed.). (2004). *Cambridge Companion to Postmodernism.* Cambridge, UK: Cambridge University Press.

Conyers, James L. (Ed.). (2005). *Africana Studies: A Disciplinary Quest for Both Theory and Method.* Jefferson, NC: McFarland & Co.

Conyers, James L. (Ed.). (2005). *Africana Studies: A Disciplinary Quest for Both Theory and Method.* Jefferson, NC: McFarland & Co.

Cook, Dee, and Hudson, Barbara. (Eds.). (1993). *Racism and Criminology.* Thousand Oaks, CA: Sage.

Cooks, Carla, and Garner, Antonio. (Eds.). (2004). *Lyrical Madness: An Anthology of Contemporary Poetry by African American Poets.* Bloomington, IN: AuthorHouse.

Costello, Mark, and Wallace, David Foster. (1990). *Signifying Rappers: Rap and Race in the Urban Present.* New York: Ecco Press.

Cowan, Rosemary. (2003). *Cornel West: The Politics of Redemption.* Cambridge, UK: Polity.

Crawford, Margo N. (2009). "Must Revolution Be a Family Affair?: Revisiting the Black Woman." In Dayo F. Gore, Jeanne Theoharis, and Komozi Woodard (Eds.), *Want to Start a Revolution?: Radical Women in the Black Freedom Struggle* (pp. 185–204). New York: New York University Press.

Crawford, Richard. (2005). *America's Musical Life: A History.* New York: Norton.

Crenshaw, Kimberle, Gotanda, Neil, Peller, Gary, and Thomas, Kendall. (Eds.). (1995). *Critical Race Theory: The Key Writings That Formed the Movement.* New York: New Press.

Croft, Robert W. (Ed.). (2002). *Zora Neale Hurston Companion.* Westport, CT: Greenwood Press.

Cronin, Gloria L. (Ed.). (1998). *Critical Essays on Zora Neale Hurston.* New York: G. K. Hall.

Cross, Brian. (1993). *It's Not About a Salary: Rap, Race, and Resistance in Los Angeles.* New York: Verso.

Crow, Barbara A. (Ed.). (2000). *Radical Feminism: A Documentary Reader.* New York: New York University Press.

Cruse, Harold. (1965). *Marxism and the Negro Struggle.* New York: Pioneer Publishers.

————. (1967). *The Crisis of the Negro Intellectual: A Historical Analysis of the Failure of Black Leadership.* New York: Quill.

————. (1969). *Rebellion or Revolution?* New York: Morrow.

————. (2002). *The Essential Harold Cruse: A Reader* (William J. Cobb, Ed.). New York: Palgrave.

Darby, Derrick, and Shelby, Tommie. (Eds.). (2005). *Hip Hop and Philosophy: Rhyme to Reason.* New York: Open Court.

Davis, Angela Y. (1981). *Women, Race and Class.* New York: Vintage.

————. (1989). *Women, Culture, and Politics.* New York: Vintage.

————. (1990). "Racism, Birth Control, and Reproductive Rights." In Marlene Gerber Fried (Ed.), *From Abortion to Reproductive Freedom: Transforming a Movement* (pp. 15–26). Boston: South End Press.

————. (1995). "Reflections on the Black Woman's Role in the Community of Slaves." In Beverly Guy-Sheftall (Ed.), *Words of Fire: An Anthology of African American Feminist Thought* (pp. 200–18). New York: Free Press.

————. (1998a). *The Angela Y. Davis Reader* (Joy James, Ed.). Malden, MA: Blackwell.

———. (1998b). "Attacking the Prison Industrial Complex." *Time*. www.time.com/time/community/transcripts/chattr092298.html (accessed May 25, 2005).

———. (1998c). *Blues Legacies and Black Feminism: Gertrude "Ma" Rainey, Bessie Smith, and Billie Holiday*. New York: Pantheon.

Davis, David Brion. (2006). *Inhuman Bondage: The Rise and Fall of Slavery in the New World*. Oxford, UK: Oxford University Press.

Davis, Elizabeth L. (1996). *Lifting As They Climb: The National Association of Colored Women*. New York: G. K. Hall.

Dawahare, Anthony. (2003). *Nationalism, Marxism, and African American Literature Between the Wars: A New Pandora's Box*. Jackson: University Press of Mississippi.

Dean, Terrance. (2009). *Hiding in Hip Hop: On the Down Low in the Entertainment Industry, from Music to Hollywood*. New York: Atria.

DeBerry, Stephen. (1995). *Gender Noise: Community Formation, Identity and Gender Analysis in Rap Music*. Master's Thesis, Graduate School of Education & Information Studies, University of California, Los Angeles.

Deepwell, Katy. (Ed.). (1995). *New Feminist Art Criticism: Critical Strategies*. Manchester, UK: Manchester University Press.

Dei, George J. Sefa, and Singh Johal, Gurpreet. (Eds.). (2005). *Critical Issues in Anti-Racist Research Methodologies*. New York: Peter Lang.

Delgado, Richard. (Ed.). (1995). *Critical Race Theory: The Cutting Edge*. Philadelphia, PA: Temple University Press.

Delgado, Richard, and Stefancic, Jean. (Eds.). (1997). *Critical White Studies: Looking Behind the Mirror*. Philadelphia, PA: Temple University Press.

———. (2001). *Critical Race Theory: An Introduction*. New York: New York University Press.

Dent, Gina. (Ed.). (1992). *Black Popular Culture*. Seattle: Bay Press.

DeVeaux, Alexis. (2004). *Warrior Poet: A Biography of Audre Lorde*. New York: Norton.

Dicker, Rory. (2008). *History of U.S. Feminism*. Berkeley, CA: Seal Press.

Dicker, Rory, and Piepmeier, Alison. (Eds.). (2003). *Catching a Wave: Reclaiming Feminism for the 21st Century*. Boston: Northeastern University Press.

Dill, Bonnie Thornton. (1994). *Across the Boundaries of Race and Class: An Exploration of Work and Family Among Black Female Domestic Servants*. New York: Garland.

Dimitriadis, Greg. (Ed.). (2001). *Performing Identity/Performing Culture: Hip Hop as Text, Pedagogy, and Lived Practice, Vol. 1*. New York: Peter Lang Publishing.

Dirlik, Arif. (2000). *Postmodernity's Histories: The Past as Legacy and Project*. Lanham, MD: Rowman & Littlefield.

Di Stephano, Christine. (1991). "Masculine Marx." In Mary Lyndon Shanley and Carole Pateman (Eds.), *Feminist Interpretations and Political Theory* (pp. 146–64). University Park, PA: Pennsylvania State University Press.

———. (Ed.). (2011). *Feminist Interpretations of Karl Marx*. University Park: Pennsylvania State University Press.

Donovan, Josephine. (2000). "Feminism and Marxism." In Josephine Donovan, *Feminist Theory: The Intellectual Traditions of American Feminism* (pp. 65–90). London: Continuum.

Dorsey, Brian. (1997). *Who Stole the Soul?: Blaxploitation Echoed in the Harlem Renaissance*. Salzburg, Austria: Institut für Anglistik und Amerikanistik.

Dow, Bonnie J. (1996). *Prime-Time Feminism: Television, Media Culture, and the Women's Movement since 1970*. Philadelphia: University of Pennsylvania Press.

Drake, Alfred J. (Ed.). (2009). *New Essays on the Frankfurt School of Critical Theory*. Newcastle upon Tyne, UK: Cambridge Scholars.

Dreyfuss, Joel, and Lawrence, Charles. (1979). *Bakke Case: The Politics of Inequality*. New York: Harcourt Brace Jovanovich.

Dubey, Madhu. (1994). *Black Women Novelists and the Nationalist Aesthetic*. Bloomington: Indiana University Press.

———. (1998). "The 'True Lie' of the Nation: Fanon and Feminism." *Differences: A Journal of Feminist Cultural Studies* 10 (2): 1–29.

Dublin, Thomas, Arias, Franchesca, and Carreras, Debora. (2003). *What Gender Perspectives Shaped the Emergence of the National Association of Colored Women, 1895–1920?* Alexandria, VA: Alexander Street Press.

Du Bois, W. E. B. (1897). "The Conservation of Races." *The American Negro Academy Occasional Papers* 2:1–15.

———. (1899). *The Philadelphia Negro: A Social Study.* Philadelphia: University of Pennsylvania Press.

———. (1903). *The Souls of Black Folk: Essays and Sketches.* Chicago: McClurg.

———. (1911). *The Quest of the Silver Fleece: A Novel.* Chicago: McClurg.

———. (1920). *Darkwater: Voices from within the Veil.* New York: Harcourt, Brace and Howe.

———. (1924). *The Gift of Black Folk: The Negroes in the Making of America.* Boston: Stratford.

———. (1985a). *Against Racism: Unpublished Essays, Papers, Addresses, 1887–1961* (Herbert Aptheker, Ed.). Amherst: University of Massachusetts Press.

———. (1985b). *Creative Writings by W. E. B. Du Bois: A Pageant, Poems, Short Stories and Playlets* (Herbert Aptheker, Ed.). Millwood, NY: Kraus-Thomson.

———. (1985c). *Selections from Horizon* (Herbert Aptheker, Ed.). White Plains, NY: Kraus-Thomson.

———. (1986). *Du Bois: Writings* (Nathan Irvin Huggins, Ed.). New York: Library of America Press.

———. (1995a). *Black Reconstruction in America, 1860–1880.* New York: Touchstone.

———. (1995b). *W. E. B. Du Bois Reader* (David Levering Lewis, Ed.). New York: Henry Holt.

Dunn, Stephane. (2008). *Baad Bitches and Sassy Supermamas: Black Power Action Films.* Urbana: University of Illinois Press.

Durand, Alain-Phillippe. (Ed.). (2002). *Black, Blanc, Beur: Rap Music and Hip Hop Culture in the Francophone World.* Lanham, MD: Scarecrow Press.

Durr, Marlese, and Hill, Shirley A. (Eds.). (2006). *Race, Work, and Family in the Lives of African Americans.* Lanham, MD: Rowman & Littlefield.

Dussel, Enrique. (1995). *The Invention of the Americas: Eclipse of the "Other" and the Myth of Modernity.* New York: Continuum.

———. (1996). *The Underside of Modernity: Apel, Ricoeur, Rorty, Taylor, and the Philosophy of Liberation* (Eduardo Mendieta, Ed.). New York: Prometheus.

Dyer, Joel. (2000). *Perpetual Prisoner Machine: How America Profits from Crime.* Boulder, CO: Westview Press.

Dyson, Michael Eric. (1997). *Between God and Gangsta Rap: Bearing Witness to Black Culture.* Oxford, UK: Oxford University Press.

———. (2002). *Holler If You Hear Me: Searching for Tupac Shakur.* New York: Basic/Civitas.

———. (2007). *Know What I Mean?: Reflections on Hip Hop.* New York: Basic/Civitas.

Ecker, Gisela. (Ed.). (1985). *Feminist Aesthetics.* London: Women's Press.

Egar, Emmanuel E. (2003). *Black Women Poets of the Harlem Renaissance.* Lanham, MD: University of America Press.

Ehrlich, Dimitri. (2002). "Young Soul Rebels." *Vibe* 72 (February).

Eisenstein, Zillah. (Ed.). (1979). *Capitalist Patriarchy and the Case for Socialist Feminism.* New York: Monthly Review Press.

Ellison, Mary. (1989). *Lyrical Protest: Black Music's Struggle Against Discrimination.* New York: Praeger.

Ellison, Ralph. (1964). *Shadow and Act.* New York: Random House.

———. (1995a). *Collected Essays of Ralph Ellison* (John F. Callahan, Ed.). New York: Modern Library.

———. (1995b). *Conversations with Ralph Ellison* (Maryemma Graham and Amritjit Singh, Eds.). Jackson: University Press of Mississippi.

———. (2001). *Living With Music: Ralph Ellison's Jazz Writings* (Robert G. O'Meally, Ed.). New York: Modern Library.

Entman, Robert M., and Rojecki, Andrew. (2000). *Black Image in the White Mind: Media and Race in America.* Chicago: University of Chicago Press.

Epstein, Jonathan S. (Ed.). (1998). *Youth Culture: Identity in a Postmodern World.* Malden, MA: Blackwell.

Essed, Philomena, and Goldberg, David Theo. (Eds.). (2001). *Race Critical Theories: Texts and Contexts.* Malden, MA: Blackwell.

Essed, Philomena, Goldberg, David Theo, and Kobayashi, Audrey. (Eds.). (2005). *Companion to Gender Studies.* Malden, MA: Blackwell.

Eure, Joseph D., and Spady, James G. (Eds.). (1991). *Nation Conscious Rap: The Hip Hop Vision.* New York: PC International Press.

Evans, Mari. (Ed.). (1983). *Black Women Writers, 1950–1980: A Critical Evaluation.* Garden City, NY: Anchor/Doubleday.

Evans, Ruth. (Ed.). (1998). *Simone de Beauvoir's* The Second Sex: *New Interdisciplinary Essays.* Manchester, UK: Manchester University Press.

Evans, Sara. (1979). *Personal Politics: The Roots of Women's Liberation in the Civil Rights Movement.* New York: Vintage.

Eze, Emmanuel Chukwudi. (Ed.). (1997). *(Post)Colonial African Philosophy: A Critical Reader.* Malden, MA: Blackwell.

———. (2001). *Achieving Our Humanity: The Idea of the Post-Racial Future.* New York: Routledge.

———. (2008). *On Reason: Rationality for a World of Cultural Conflict and Racism.* Durham, NC: Duke University Press.

Fabre, Geneviève, and Feith, Michel. (Ed.). (2001). *Temples for Tomorrow: Looking Back at the Harlem Renaissance.* Bloomington: Indiana University Press.

Fairclough, Adam. (1987). *To Redeem the Soul of America: The Southern Christian Leadership Conference and Martin Luther King, Jr.* Athens: University of Georgia Press.

———. (1995). *Martin Luther King, Jr.* Athens: University of Georgia Press.

Fanon, Frantz. (1965). *A Dying Colonialism.* New York: Grove.

———. (1967). *Black Skin, White Masks.* New York: Grove.

———. (1968). *The Wretched of the Earth.* New York: Grove.

———. (1969). *Toward the African Revolution.* New York: Grove.

———. (2005). *The Wretched of the Earth* (Richard Philcox, Trans.). New York: Grove.

———. (2008). *Black Skin, White Masks* (Richard Philcox, Trans.). New York: Grove.

Farley, Christopher John. (1998). "Music: Neo-Soul on a Roll. *Time.* www.time.com/time/magazine/article/0,9171,988672,00.html (accessed May 9, 2010).

Farr, Jory. (1994). *Moguls and Madmen: The Pursuit of Power in Popular Music.* New York: Simon & Schuster.

Farrell, Frank B. (1994). *Subjectivity, Realism, and Postmodernism: The Recovery of the World.* Cambridge, UK: Cambridge University Press.

Farrington, Lisa E. (2005). *Creating Their Own Image: The History of African American Women Artists.* New York: Oxford University Press.

Favor, Martin J. (1999). *Authentic Blackness: The Folk in the New Negro Movement.* Durham, NC: Duke University Press.

Ferguson, Ann. (1998). "Socialism." In Alison M. Jaggar and Iris Marion Young (Eds.), *A Companion to Feminist Philosophy* (pp. 520–40). Malden, MA: Blackwell.

Ferguson, Roderick A. (2004). *Aberrations in Black: Toward a Queer of Color Critique.* Minneapolis: University of Minnesota Press.

Fernando, Stephen H. (1994). *The New Beats: Exploring the Music, Culture, and Attitudes of Hip Hop.* New York: Anchor/Doubleday.

Ferree, Myra Marx, and Martin, Patricia Y. (Eds.). (1995). *Feminist Organizations: Harvest of the New Women's Movement.* Philadelphia, PA: Temple University Press.

Fiagbedzi, Nissio. (2005). *Essay on the Nature of the Aesthetic in the African Musical Arts.* Accra, Ghana: Sankofa Press.

Findlen, Barbara. (Ed.). (2001). *Listen Up!: Voices from the Next Feminist Generation.* Seattle: Seal Press.

Firth, Simon. (Ed.). (2004). *Popular Music: Critical Concepts in Media and Cultural Studies*. New York: Routledge.

Fisch, Audrey. (Ed.). (2007). *Cambridge Companion to the African American Slaves Narrative*. Cambridge, UK: Cambridge University Press.

Fleming, Cynthia G. (2001). "Black Women and Black Power: The Case of Ruby Doris Smith Robinson and the Student Nonviolent Coordinating Committee." In Bettye Collier-Thomas and V. P. Franklin (Eds.), *Sisters in the Struggle: African American Women in the Civil Rights-Black Power Movement* (pp. 280–305). New York: New York University Press.

Flores, Juan. (2000). *From Bomba to Hip-Hop: Puerto Rican Culture and Latino Identity*. New York: Columbia University Press.

Flowers, Sandra H. (1996). *African American Nationalist Literature of the 1960s: Pens of Fire*. New York: Garland.

Floyd, Kevin. (2009). *Reification of Desire: Toward a Queer Marxism*. Minneapolis: University of Minnesota Press.

Floyd, Samuel A. (1995). *Power of Black Music: Interpreting Its History from Africa to the United States*. New York: Oxford University Press.

Foley, Barbara. (2003). *Spectres of 1919: Class and Nation in the Making of the New Negro*. Urbana: University of Illinois Press.

Foner, Philip S. (Ed.). (2002). *The Black Panthers Speak*. New York: Da Capo Press.

Fong, Timothy. (Ed.). (2008). *Ethnic Studies Research: Approaches and Perspectives*. Lanham, MD: AltaMira Press.

Foreman, Ann. (1977). *Femininity and Alienation: Women and the Family in Marxism and Psychoanalysis*. London: Pluto.

Forman, Murray. (2002). *The Hood Comes First: Race, Space, and Place in Rap and Hip Hop*. Middletown, CT: Wesleyan University Press.

Forman, Murray, and Neal, Mark Anthony. (Eds.). (2011). *That's the Joint!: The Hip Hop Studies Reader*. New York: Routledge.

Foster, Stephen C. (1980). *Minstrel Show Songs*. New York: Da Capo Press.

Foucault, Michel. (1971). *The Order of Things: An Archaeology of the Human Sciences*. New York: Pantheon.

———. (1973). *Madness and Civilization: A History of Insanity in the Age of Reason*. New York: Vintage.

———. (1974). *The Archaeology of Knowledge and the Discourse on Language*. New York: Pantheon.

———. (1979). *Discipline and Punish: The Birth of the Prison*. New York: Vintage.

———. (1984). *The Foucault Reader* (Paul Rabinow, Ed.). New York: Pantheon.

———. (1990a). *The History of Sexuality, Volume 1: The Will to Knowledge*. New York: Vintage.

———. (1990b). *The History of Sexuality, Volume 2: The Use of Pleasure*. New York: Vintage.

———. (1990c). *The History of Sexuality, Volume 3: The Care of the Self*. New York: Vintage.

———. (1994). *The Birth of the Clinic: An Archaeology of Medical Perception*. New York: Vintage.

———. (1996). *Foucault Live: Interviews, 1961–1984* (Sylvère Lotringer, Ed.). New York: Semiotext(e).

———. (2009). *The History of Madness in the Classical Age*. New York: Routledge.

Franklin, Eric N., and Watkins, William H. (1984). *Breakdance*. Chicago: NTC/Contemporary Publishing.

Fraser, Nancy. (1989). *Unruly Practices: Power, Discourse, and Gender in Contemporary Social Theory*. Minneapolis: University of Minnesota Press.

———. (1991). "What's Critical About Critical Theory?: The Case of Habermas and Gender." In David Ingram and Julia Simon-Ingram (Eds.), *Critical Theory: The Essential Readings* (pp. 357–87). New York: Paragon House.

———. (1997). *Justice Interruptions: Critical Reflections on the "Postsocialist" Condition*. New York: Routledge.

———. (1998). "Another Pragmatism: Alain Locke, Critical 'Race' Theory, and the Politics of Culture." In Morris Dickstein (Ed.), *The Revival of Pragmatism: New Essays on Social Thought, Law, and Culture* (pp. 157–75). Durham, NC: Duke University Press.

Fredrickson, George. (1981). *White Supremacy: A Comparative Study in American and South African History.* New York: Oxford University Press.

———. (1987). *The Black Image in the White Mind: The Debate on Afro-American Character and Destiny, 1817–1914.* Hanover, NH: Wesleyan University Press.

———. (1995). *Black Liberation: A Comparative History of Black Ideologies in the United States and South Africa.* New York: Oxford University Press.

———. (2002). *Racism: A Short History.* Princeton, NJ: Princeton University Press.

Freeman, Joreen. (1975). *Politics of Women's Liberation: A Case Study of an Emerging Social Movement and Its Relation to the Policy Process.* New York: Longman.

Freire, Paulo. (1993). *Pedagogy of the Oppressed.* New York: Continuum.

———. (1994). *Pedagogy of Hope: Reliving* Pedagogy of the Oppressed. New York: Continuum.

———. (1996). *Education for Critical Consciousness.* New York: Continuum.

Fricke, Jim, and Ahearn, Charlie. (Eds.). (2002). *Yes Yes Y'all!: The Experience Music Project Oral History of Hip-Hop's First Decade.* New York: Da Capo Press.

Frilot, Shari. (Dir.). (1995). *Black Nations/Queer Nations?: Lesbian and Gay Sexualities in the African Diaspora.* New York: Third World Newsreel.

Fromm, Erich. (1947). *Man for Himself: An Inquiry into the Psychology of Ethics.* New York: Rhinehart.

———. (1955). *The Sane Society.* New York: Rhinehart.

———. (1970). *The Crisis of Psychoanalysis.* New York: Holt, Rhinehart and Winston.

Fruech, Joanna, Langer, Cassandra L., and Raven, Arlene. (Eds.). (1994). *New Feminist Criticism: Art, Identity, Action.* New York: IconEditions.

Funk, Rainer. (1982). *Erich Fromm: The Courage to Be Human.* New York: Continuum.

Furman, Leah, and Furman, Elina. (1999). *Heart of Soul: The Lauryn Hill Story.* New York: Ballantine Books.

Fuss, Diana. (1995). *Identification Papers: Readings on Psychoanalysis, Sexuality, and Culture.* New York: Routledge.

Gabbidon, Shaun L. (2010). *Race, Ethnicity, Crime, and Justice: An International Dilemma.* Los Angeles, CA: Sage.

Gabbidon, Shaun L., Greene, Helen T., and Young, Vernetta D. (Eds). (2002). *African American Classics in Criminology & Criminal Justice.* Thousand Oaks, CA: Sage.

Gamble, Vanessa N. (1993). "A Legacy of Distrust: African Americans and Medical Research." *American Journal of Preventive Medicine* 9 (6): 35–38.

Garrow, Davis J. (1981). *The FBI and Martin Luther King, Jr.: From "Solo" to Memphis.* New York: Morrow.

———. (1986). *Bearing the Cross: Martin Luther King, Jr., and the Southern Christian Leadership Conference.* New York: Morrow.

Gaspar, David B., and Hine, Darlene Clark. (Eds.). (1996). *More Than Chattel: Black Women and Slavery in the Americas.* Bloomington: Indiana University Press.

Gates, Henry Louis, Jr. (1987). *Figures in Black: Words, Signs, and the "Racial" Self.* New York: Oxford University Press.

———. (1988). *The Signifying Monkey: A Theory of African American Literary Criticism.* New York: Oxford University Press.

———. (1993). "The Black Man's Burden." In Michael Warner (Ed.), *Fear of a Queer Planet: Queer Politics and Social Theory* (pp. 230–39). Minneapolis: University of Minnesota Press.

Gates, Henry Louis, Jr., and Appiah, Kwame A. (Eds.). (1993a). *Alice Walker: Critical Perspectives Past and Present.* New York: Amistad.

———. (1993b). *Zora Neale Hurston: Critical Perspectives Past and Present.* New York: Amistad.

Gates, Henry Louis, Jr., and Jarrett, Gene Andrew. (Eds.). (2007). *The New Negro: Readings on Race, Representation, and African American Culture, 1892–1938.* Princeton, NJ: Princeton University Press.

Gayle, Addison, Jr. (Ed.). (1969). *Black Expression: Essays by and about Black Americans in the Creative Arts.* New York: Weybright & Talley.

———. (Ed.). (1970). *Black Situation.* New York: Horizon Press.

———. (Ed.). (1971). *The Black Aesthetic.* Garden City, NY: Doubleday.

———. (2009). *Addison Gayle Jr. Reader* (Nathaniel Norment, Jr., Ed.). Urbana: University of Illinois Press.

Genovese, Eugene D. (1992). *From Rebellion to Revolution: Afro-American Slave Revolts in the Making of the Modern World.* Baton Rouge: Louisiana State University Press.

Genz, Stéphanie. (2009). *Postfemininities in Popular Culture.* New York: Palgrave Macmillan.

George, Nelson. (1989). "Rap's Tenth Birthday." *Village Voice* 24 (October): 40.

———. (Ed.). (1990). *Stop the Violence: Overcoming Self-Destruction.* New York: Pantheon.

———. (1992). *Buppies, B-Boys, Baps & Bohos: Notes on Post-Soul Black Culture.* New York: HarperCollins.

———. (1994). *Blackface: Reflections on African Americans and the Movies.* New York: HarperCollins.

———. (1999). *Hip Hop America.* New York: Viking.

———. (2007). *Where Did Our Love Go?: The Rise and Fall of the Motown Sound.* Urbana: University of Illinois Press.

Giardina, Carol. (2010). *Freedom for Women: Forging the Women's Liberation Movement, 1953–1970.* Gainesville: University Press of Florida.

Gilbert, Derrick I. M. (Ed.). (1998). *Catch the Fire!!!: A Cross-Generational Anthology of Contemporary African American Poetry.* New York: Riverhead Books.

Gillis, Stacy, and Hollows, Joanne. (Eds.). (2009). *Feminism, Domesticity, and Popular Culture.* New York: Routledge.

Gilyard, Keith. (1997). *Spirit and Flame: An Anthology of Contemporary African American Poetry.* Syracuse, NY: Syracuse University Press.

———. (2008). *Composition and Cornel West: Notes Toward a Deep Democracy.* Carbondale: Southern Illinois University Press.

Giroux, Henry A. (1992). *Border Crossings: Cultural Workers and the Politics of Education.* New York: Routledge.

———. (1996). *Fugitive Cultures: Race, Violence, and Youth.* New York: Routledge.

Girshick, Lori B. (2002). *Woman-to-Woman Sexual Violence: Does She Call It Rape?* Boston: Northeastern University Press.

Glaude, Eddie S., Jr. (Ed.). (2002). *Is It Nation Time?: Contemporary Essays on Black Power and Black Nationalism.* Chicago: University of Chicago Press.

Goff, Keli. (2008). *Party Crashing: How the Hip Hop Generation Declared Political Independence.* New York: Basic Books.

Goldberg, David Theo. (Ed.). (1990). *Anatomy of Racism.* Minneapolis: University of Minnesota Press.

———. (1993). *Racist Culture: Philosophy and the Politics of Meaning.* Cambridge, UK: Blackwell.

———. (Ed.). (1994). *Multiculturalism: A Critical Reader.* Cambridge, UK: Blackwell.

———. (1997). *Racial Subjects: Writing on Race in America.* New York: Routledge.

———. (2001). *The Racial State.* Malden, MA: Blackwell.

———. (2008). *The Threat of Race: Reflections on Racial Neoliberalism.* Malden, MA: Blackwell-Wiley.

Goldberg, David Theo, Musheno, Michael, and Bower, Lisa. (Eds.). (2001). *Between Law and Culture: Relocating Legal Studies.* Minneapolis: University of Minnesota Press.

Goldberg, David Theo, and Solomos, John. (Eds.). (2002). *A Companion to Racial and Ethnic Studies.* Malden, MA: Blackwell.

Gonzales-Day, Ken. (2006). *Lynching in the West, 1850–1935.* Durham, NC: Duke University Press.

Gopal, Priyamvada. (2002). "Frantz Fanon, Feminism, and the Question of Relativism." *New Formations* 47:38–42.

Gordon, Lewis R., and Gordon, Jane Anna. (Eds). (2006a). *A Companion to African American Studies*. Malden, MA: Blackwell.

———. (2006b). *Not Only the Master's Tools: African American Studies in Theory and Practice*. Boulder, CO: Paradigm.

Gordon, Vivian V. (1985). *Black Women, Feminism, and Black Liberation*. Chicago: Third World Press.

Gore, Dayo F., Theoharis, Jeanne, and Woodard, Komozi. (Eds.). (2009). *Want to Start a Revolution?: Radical Women in the Black Freedom Struggle*. New York: New York University Press.

Gottlieb, Roger S. (1992). *Marxism, 1844–1990: Origins, Betrayal, Rebirth*. New York: Routledge.

Grandt, Jürgen E. (2009). *Shaping Words to Fit the Soul: The Southern Ritual Grounds of Afro-Modernism*. Columbus: Ohio State University Press.

Grassian, Daniel. (2009). *Writing the Future of Black America: Literature of the Hip Hop Generation*. Columbia: University of South Carolina Press.

Grayson, Sandra M. (Ed.). (2008). *Literary Revolution: In the Sprit of the Harlem Renaissance*. Lanham, MD: University Press of America.

Greene, Jasmin S. (2008). *Beyond Money, Cars, and Women: Examining Black Masculinity in Hip Hop Culture*. Newcastle, UK: Cambridge Scholars.

Griffin, Ada G., and Parkerson, Michelle. (Dirs.). (1996). *Litany for Survival: The Life and Work of Audre Lorde*. New York: Third World Newsreel.

Griffin, Farah Jasmine. (2002). "Conflict and Chorus: Reconsidering Toni Cade's *The Black Woman: An Anthology*." In Eddie Glaude, Jr. (Ed.), *Is It Nation Time?: Contemporary Essays on Black Power and Black Nationalism* (pp. 113–29). Chicago: University of Chicago Press.

Gubar, Susan. (1997). *Race-Changes: White Skin, Black Face in American Culture*. Oxford, UK: Oxford University Press.

Gueraseva, Stacy. (2005). *Def Jam, Inc.: Russell Simmons, Rick Rubin, and the Extraordinary Story of the World's Most Influential Hip Hop Label*. New York: Random House.

Guerrero, Edward. (1993). *Framing Blackness: The African American Image in Film*. Philadelphia, PA: Temple University Press.

Guettel, Charnie. (1974). *Marxism and Feminism*. Toronto: Women's Educational Press.

Guevara, Nancy. (1996). "Women Writin', Rappin', Breakin.'" In William E. Perkins (Ed.), *Droppin' Science: Critical Essays on Rap Music and Hip Hop Culture* (pp. 48–62). Philadelphia, PA: Temple University Press.

Guillory, Monique, and Green, Richard C. (Eds.). (1998). *Soul: Black Power, Politics, and Pleasure*. New York: New York University Press.

Gunaratnam, Yasmin. (2003). *Researching Race and Ethnicity: Methods, Knowledge, and Power*. Thousand Oaks, CA: Sage.

Gundaker, Grey. (1998). *Signs of Diaspora/Diaspora of Signs: Literacies, Creolization, and Vernacular Practice in African America*. Oxford, UK: Oxford University Press.

Guralnick, Peter. (1986). *Sweet Soul Music: Rhythm & Blues and the Southern Dream of Freedom*. New York: Harper & Row.

Guy-Sheftall, Beverly. (1990). *Daughters of Sorrow: Attitudes Toward Black Women, 1880–1920*. Brooklyn, NY: Carlson.

———. (Ed.). (1995). *Words of Fire: An Anthology of African American Feminist Thought*. New York: The Free Press.

Habermas, Jürgen. (1975). *Legitimation Crisis*. Boston: Beacon.

———. (1984). *Theory of Communicative Action, Volume 1*. Boston: Beacon.

———. (1987a). *The Philosophical Discourse on Modernity*. Cambridge, MA: MIT Press.

———. (1987b). *Theory of Communicative Action, Volume 2*. Boston: Beacon.

———. (1989). *The Structural Transformation of the Public Sphere: An Inquiry into a Category of Bourgeois Society*. Cambridge, MA: MIT Press.

Hagedorn, John. (2008). *World of Gangs: Armed Young Men and Gangsta Culture.* Minneapolis: University of Minnesota Press.

Haggerty, George E., and McGarry, Molly. (Eds.). (2007). *Companion to Lesbian, Gay, Bisexual, Transgender, and Queer Studies.* Malden, MA: Blackwell.

Hahn, Steven. (2003). *Nation Under Our Feet: Black Political Struggles in the Rural South, from Slavery to the Great Migration.* Cambridge, MA: Harvard University Press.

Halberstam, Judith. (1997). "Mackdaddy, Superfly, Rapper: Gender, Race, and Masculinity in the Drag King Scene." *Social Text* 52/53:104–31.

———. (1998). *Female Masculinity.* Durham, NC: Duke University Press.

———. (2003). "What's That Smell?: Queer Temporalities and Subcultural Lives." *International Journal of Cultural Studies* 6 (3): 313–33.

———. (2005). *In a Queer Time and Place: Transgender Bodies, Subcultural Lives.* New York: New York University Press.

Hames-Garcia, Michael. (2001). "Can Queer Theory Be Critical Theory?" In William S. Wilkerson and Jeffrey Paris (Eds.), *New Critical Theory: Essays on Liberation* (pp. 201–22). Lanham, MD: Rowman & Littlefield.

Hane, Audrey Curtis. (1999). "Metaphor for Negotiating Work and Family." In Trevy McDonald and T. Ford-Ahmed (Eds.), *Nature of a Sistuh: Black Women's Lived Experiences in Contemporary Culture* (pp. 113–32). Durham, NC: Carolina Academic Press.

Haney-López, Ian. (2003). *Racism on Trial: The Chicano Fight for Justice.* Cambridge, MA: Belknap Press of Harvard University Press.

Hansberry, Lorraine. (1964). *Movement: Documentary of a Struggle for Equality.* New York: Simon & Schuster.

———. (1972). *Les Blancs: The Collected Last Plays of Lorraine Hansberry* (Robert Nemiroff, Ed.). New York: Random House.

———. (1994). *Collected Last Plays by Lorraine Hansberry* (Robert Nemiroff, Ed.). New York: Vintage.

———. (1995). *To Be Young, Gifted, and Black: A Portrait of Lorraine Hansberry in Her Own Words* (Robert Nemiroff, Ed.). New York: Vintage.

Haralambos, Michael. (1974). *Right On!: From Blues to Soul in Black America.* London: Eddison Press.

Harlan, Louis R. (1972). *Booker T. Washington: The Making of a Black Leader, 1856–1901.* New York: Oxford University Press.

———. (1982). "Booker T. Washington and the Politics of Accommodation." In John Hope Franklin and August Meier (Eds.), *Black Leaders of the Twentieth Century* (pp. 1–18). Chicago: University of Illinois Press.

———. (1983). *Booker T. Washington: The Wizard of Tuskegee, 1901–1915.* New York: Oxford University Press.

Harley, Sharon. (Ed.). (2002). *Sister Circle: Black Women and Work.* New Brunswick, NJ: Rutgers University Press.

Harper, Phillip Brian. (1994). *Framing the Margins: The Social Logic of Postmodern Culture.* New York: Oxford University Press.

———. (1996). *Are We Not Men?: Masculine Anxiety and the Problem of African American Identity.* New York: Oxford University Press.

Harris, Cheryl I. (1993). "Whiteness as Property." *Harvard Law Review* 106 (8): 1707–91.

Harris, Dean A. (Ed.). (1995). *Multiculturalism from the Margins: Non-Dominant Voices on Difference and Diversity.* Westport, CT: Bergin & Garvey.

Harris, Duchess. (2001). "From the Kennedy Commission to the Combahee River Collective: Black Feminist Organizing, 1960–1980." In Bettye Collier-Thomas and V. P. Franklin (Eds.), *Sisters in the Struggle: African American Women in the Civil Rights–Black Power Movement* (pp. 197–213). New York: New York University Press.

Harris, Keith M. (2006). *Boys, Boyz, Bois: An Ethics of Black Masculinity in Film and Popular Media.* New York: Routledge.

Hartmann, Heidi I. (1979). "The Unhappy Marriage of Marxism and Feminism." *Capital and Class* 8:1–33.

Harvey, David. (1990). *Condition of Postmodernity: An Enquiry into the Origins of Cultural Change*. Cambridge, MA: Blackwell.

Haskins, James. (2002).*The Story of Hip Hop: From Africa to America, Sugarhill to Eminem*. New York: Penguin.

Hassan, Salah M. (Ed.). (1997). *Gendered Visions: The Art of Contemporary Africana Women Artists*. Trenton, NJ: Africa World Press.

Hawkins, Darnell F., and Kempt-Leonard, Kimberly. (Eds.). (2005). *Our Children, Their Children: Confronting Racial and Ethnic Differences in American Juvenile Justice*. Chicago: University of Chicago Press.

Hazzard-Gordon, Katrina. (1990). *Jookin': The Rise of Social Dance Formations in African American Culture*. Philadelphia, PA: Temple University Press.

Heaggans, Raphael. (2009). *The Twenty-First-Century Minstrel Show: Are We Continuing the Blackface Tradition?* San Diego, CA: University Readers.

Hearn, Jeff. (1987). *The Gender of Oppression: Men, Masculinity, and the Critique of Marxism*. New York: St. Martin's Press.

———. (1991). "Gender: Biology, Nature, and Capitalism." In Terrell Carver (Ed.), *The Cambridge Companion to Marx* (pp. 222–45). Cambridge, UK: Cambridge University Press.

Heath, Julia A., and Ciscel, David H. (1988). "Patriarchy, Family Structure and the Exploitation of Women's Labor." *Journal of Economic Issues* 22 (3): 781–94.

Heberle, Renee J. (Ed.). (2006). *Feminist Interpretations of Theodor Adorno*. University Park, PA: Pennsylvania State University Press.

Held, David. (1980). *Introduction to Critical Theory: Horkheimer to Habermas*. Berkeley: University of California Press.

Hemenway, Robert E. (1977). *Zora Neale Hurston: A Literary Biography*. Urbana: University of Illinois Press.

Henkes, Robert. (1993). *Art of Black American Women: Works of Twenty-Four Artists of the Twentieth Century*. Jefferson, NC: McFarland.

Hennessy, Rosemary. (1993). *Materialist Feminism and the Politics of Discourse*. London: Routledge.

Hennessy, Rosemary, and Ingraham, Chrys. (Eds.). (1997). *Materialist Feminism: A Reader in Class, Difference, and Women's Lives*. London: Routledge.

Henry, Astrid. (2004). *Not My Mother's Sister: Generational Conflict and Third Wave Feminism*. Bloomington: Indiana University Press.

Herek, Gregory M. (Ed.). (1998). *Stigma and Sexual Orientation: Understanding Prejudice Against Lesbians, Gay Men, and Bisexuals*. Thousand Oaks, CA: Sage.

Herivel, Tara, and Wright, Paul. (Eds.). (2003). *Prison Nation: The Warehousing of America's Poor*. New York: Routledge.

Hernández, Daisy, and Rehman, Bushra (Eds.). (2002). *Colonize This!: Young Women of Color on Today's Feminism*. New York: Seal Press.

Hernton, Calvin C. (1984). "The Sexual Mountain and Black Women Writers." *Black American Literature Forum* 18 (4): 139–45.

———. (1990). *Sexual Mountain and Black Women Writers: Adventures in Sex, Literature, and Real Life*. New York: Anchor Books.

Herring, Cedric. (Ed.). (1997). *African Americans and the Public Agenda*. Thousand Oaks, CA: Sage.

Hess, Mickey. (2007). *Is Hip Hop Dead?: The Past, Present, and Future of America's Most Wanted Music*. Westport, CT: Praeger.

Hess, Thomas B., and Baker, Elizabeth C. (Eds.). (1973). *Art and Sexual Politics: Women's Liberation, Women Artists, and Art History*. New York: Macmillan.

Heywood, Leslie, and Drake, Jennifer. (Eds.). (1997). *Third Wave Agenda: Being Feminist, Doing Feminism*. Minneapolis: University of Minnesota Press.

Higginbotham, Evelyn Brooks. (1993). *Righteous Discontent: The Women's Movement in the Black Baptist Church, 1880–1920*. Cambridge, MA: Harvard University Press.

Hill, Marc Lamont. (2009). *Beats, Rhymes, and Classroom Life: Hip-Hop Pedagogy and the Politics of Identity*. New York: Teachers College Press.

Himmelweit, Susan. (1991). "Reproduction and the Materialist Conception of History: A Feminist Critique." In Terrell Carver (Ed.), *The Cambridge Companion to Marx* (pp. 196–221). Cambridge, UK: Cambridge University Press.

Hine, Darlene Clark, and Jenkins, Earnestine. (Eds.). (1999). *A Question of Manhood: A Reader in U.S. Black Men's History and Masculinity (Volume 1)*. Bloomington: Indiana University Press.

———. (Eds.). (2001). *A Question of Manhood: A Reader in U.S. Black Men's History and Masculinity (Volume 2)*. Bloomington: Indiana University Press.

Hinton, Alex. (Dir.) (2006). *Pick Up the Mic!: The (R)Evolution of the Homo-Hop Movement*. Los Angeles, CA: Planet Janice/Rhino Films.

Hirshey, Gerri. (1984). *Nowhere to Run: The Story of Soul Music*. New York: Times Books.

Hobbs, Stuart D. (1997). *End of the American Avant-Garde*. New York: New York University Press.

Holcomb, Gary E. (2007). *Claude McKay, Code Name Sasha: Queer Black Marxism and the Harlem Renaissance*. Gainesville: University Press of Florida.

Hollows, Joanne. (2000). *Feminism, Femininity, and Popular Culture*. Manchester: Manchester University Press.

Hollows, Joanne, and Moseley, Rachel. (Eds.). (2006). *Feminism in Popular Culture*. New York: Berg.

Holmstrom, Nancy. (1982). "'Women's Work,' the Family and Capitalism." *Science and Society* 45 (2): 186–211.

Homer, Sean. (1998). *Fredric Jameson: Marxism, Hermeneutics, Postmodernism*. Cambridge, UK: Polity.

Honey, Maureen. (Ed.). (2006). *Shadowed Dreams: Women's Poetry of the Harlem Renaissance*. New Brunswick, NJ: Rutgers University Press.

hooks, bell. (1981). *Ain't I a Woman: Black Women and Feminism*. Boston: South End.

———. (1984). *Feminist Theory: From Margin to Center*. Boston: South End.

———. (1989). *Talking Back: Thinking Feminist, Thinking Black*. Boston: South End.

———. (1990). *Yearning: Race, Gender, and Cultural Politics*. Boston: South End.

———. (1991). *Black Looks: Race and Representation*. Boston: South End.

———. (1992). *Sisters of the Yam: Black Women and Self-Recovery*. Boston: South End.

———. (1994a). *Outlaw Culture: Resisting Representation*. New York: Routledge.

———. (1994b). *Teaching to Transgress: Education as the Practice of Freedom*. New York: Routledge.

———. (1995a). *Art on My Mind: Visual Politics*. New York: New Press.

———. (1995b). *Killing Rage: Ending Racism*. New York: Henry Holt.

———. (1996). *Reel to Real: Race, Sex, and Class at the Movies*. New York: Routledge.

———. (2000a). *Where We Stand: Class Matters*. New York: Routledge.

———. (2000b). *Feminism Is for Everybody: Passionate Politics*. New York: Routledge.

———. (2004a). *We Real Cool: Black Men and Masculinity*. New York: Routledge.

———. (2004b). *The Will to Change: Men, Masculinity, and Love*. New York: Atria.

Hooyman, Nancy R., and Gonyea, Judith. (1995). *Feminist Perspectives on Family Care: Policies for Gender Justice*. Thousand Oaks, CA: Sage.

Hopkinson, Natalie, and Moore, Natalie Y. (2006). *Deconstructing Tyrone: A New Look at Black Masculinity in the Hip Hop Generation*. San Francisco: Cleis Press.

Horkheimer, Max, and Adorno, Theodor W. (1995). *Dialectic of Enlightenment*. New York: Continuum.

Houston, Marsha, and Davis, Olga I. (Eds.). (2002). *Centering Ourselves: African American Feminist and Womanist Studies of Discourse*. Cresskill, NJ: Hampton Press.

Howard, Josiah. (2007). *Blaxploitation Cinema: The Essential Reference Guide*. Guildford, UK: FAB.

Howard, Lillie P. (1993). *Alice Walker and Zora Neale Hurston: The Common Bond*. Westport, CT: Greenwood Press.

Hudson-Weems, Clenora. (1995). *Africana Womanism: Reclaiming Ourselves*. Boston: Bedford.

————. (1997). "Africana Womanism and the Critical Need for Africana Theory and Thought." *Western Journal of Black Studies* 21 (2): 79–84.

————. (1998a). "Africana Womanism: An Historical, Global Perspective for Women of African Descent." In Patricia Liggins Hill (Ed.), *Call and Response: The Riverside Anthology of the African American Literary Tradition* (pp. 1811–1815). Boston: Houghton Mifflin.

————. (1998b). "Africana Womanism, Black Feminism, African Feminism, Womanism." In Obioma Nnaemeka (Ed.), *Sisterhood, Feminisms, and Power: From Africa to the Diaspora* (pp. 149–62). Trenton, NJ: Africa World Press.

————. (1998c). "Self-Naming and Self-Defining: An Agenda for Survival." In Obioma Nnaemeka (Ed.), *Sisterhood, Feminisms, and Power: From Africa to the Diaspora* (pp. 449–52). Trenton, NJ: Africa World Press.

————. (2000). "Africana Womanism: An Overview." In Delores Aldridge and Carlene Young (Eds.), *Out of the Revolution: The Development of Africana Studies* (pp. 205–17). Lanham, MD: Lexington Books.

————. (2001a). "Africana Womanism, Black Feminism, African Feminism, Womanism." In William Nelson, Jr., (Ed.), *Black Studies: From the Pyramids to Pan-Africanism and Beyond.* New York: McGraw-Hill.

————. (2001b). "Africana Womanism: Entering the New Millennium." In Jemadari Kamara and T. Menelik Van Der Meer (Eds.), *State of the Race, Creating Our 21st Century: Where Do We Go from Here?* Amherst: University of Massachusetts Press.

————. (2004). *Africana Womanist Literary Theory.* Trenton, NJ: Africa World Press.

————. (Ed). (2007). *Contemporary Africana Theory, Thought, and Action: A Guide to Africana Studies.* Trenton, NJ: Africa World Press.

Huggins, Nathan I. (1971). *The Harlem Renaissance.* New York: Oxford University Press.

————. (Ed.). (1976). *Voices from the Harlem Renaissance.* New York: Oxford University Press.

Hughes, Langston. (Ed.). (1958). *The Langston Hughes Reader.* New York: G. Braziller.

————. (1995). *Langston Hughes and the Chicago Defender: Essays on Race, Politics, and Culture, 1942–1962* (Christopher C. De Santis, Ed.). Urbana: University of Illinois Press.

————. (1997). "The Negro Artist and the Racial Mountain." In William L. Van Deburg (Ed.), *Modern Black Nationalism: From Marcus Garvey to Louis Farrakhan* (pp. 52–58). New York: New York University Press.

Hull, Gloria T. (1987). *Color, Sex & Poetry: Three Women Writers of the Harlem Renaissance.* Bloomington: Indiana University Press.

Hull, Gloria T., Scott, Patricia Bell, and Smith, Barbara. (Eds.). (1982). *All the Women Are White, All the Blacks Are Men, but Some of Us Are Brave: Black Women's Studies.* New York: The Feminist Press at CUNY.

Humann, Heather D. (2007). "Feminist and Material Concerns: Lil' Kim, Destiny's Child, and Questions of Consciousness." In Gwendolyn D. Pough, Elaine Richardson, Aisha Durham, and Rachel Raimist (Eds.), *Home Girls Make Some Noise!: The Hip Hop Feminism Anthology* (pp. 94–105). Mira Loma, CA: Parker Publishing.

Huntington, Carla S. (2007). *Hip Hop Dance: Meanings and Messages.* Jefferson, NC: McFarland & Co.

Hurdis, Rebecca. (2002). "Heartbroken: Women of Color Feminism and the Third Wave." In Daisy Hernández and Bushra Rehman (Eds.), *Colonize This!: Young Women of Color on Today's Feminism* (pp. 279–94). New York: Seal Press.

Hurston, Zora Neale. (1934). *Jonah's Gourd.* London: Virago.

————. (1935). *Mules and Men.* Philadelphia, PA: J. B. Lippincott Company.

————. (1937). *Their Eyes Were Watching God: A Novel.* New York: Negro University Press.

————. (1938). *Tell My Horse.* Philadelphia, PA: J. B. Lippincott Company.

————. (1939). *Moses, Man of the Mountain.* Urbana: University of Illinois Press.

————. (1979). *I Love Myself When I Am Laughing . . . And Then When I Am Looking Mean and Impressive: A Zora Neale Hurston Reader* (Alice Walker, Ed.). Old Westbury, NY: Feminist Press.

Hurt, Byron. (Dir.). (2006). *Hip-Hop: Beyond Beats & Rhymes.* Northampton, MA: Media Education Foundation and God Bless the Child Productions.

Hutcheon, Linda. (1988). *Poetics of Postmodernism: History, Theory, Fiction*. New York: Routledge.

———. (2002). *Politics of Postmodernism*. New York: Routledge.

Hutcheon, Linda, and Natoli, Joseph. (Eds.). (1993). *Postmodern Reader*. Albany: State University of New York Press.

Hutchinson, George. (1995). *The Harlem Renaissance in Black and White*. Cambridge, MA: Harvard University Press.

———. (2007). (Ed.). *The Cambridge Companion to the Harlem Renaissance*. Cambridge, UK: Cambridge University Press.

Ifill, Sherrilyn A. (2007). *On the Courthouse Lawn: Confronting the Legacy of Lynching in the Twenty-First Century*. Boston: Beacon Press.

Ikard, David. (2007). *Breaking the Silence: Toward a Black Male Feminist Criticism*. Baton Rouge: Louisiana State University Press.

Ipiotis, Celia. (Dir.). (1984). *Popular Culture in Dance: The World of Hip Hop*. New York: ARC Videodance.

Israel. (Dir.). (2002). *The Freshest Kids: A History of the B-Boy*. Los Angeles: QD3 Entertainment.

Iton, Richard. (2008). *In Search of the Black Fantastic: Politics and Popular Culture in the Post–Civil Rights Era*. New York: Oxford University Press.

Jackson, John A. (2004). *House of Fire: The Rise and Fall of Philadelphia Soul*. New York: Oxford University Press.

Jackson, Lawrence. (2007). "'The Aftermath': The Reputation of the Harlem Renaissance Twenty Years Later." In George Hutchinson (Ed.), *The Cambridge Companion to the Harlem Renaissance* (pp. 239–53). Cambridge, UK: Cambridge University Press.

Jackson, Ronald L. (2006). *Scripting the Black Masculine Body: Identity, Discourse, and Racial Politics in Popular Media*. Albany: State University of New York Press.

James, C. R. L. (1963). *The Black Jacobins: Toussaint L'Ouverture and the San Domingo Revolution*. New York: Vintage.

James, Joy A. (1996). *Resisting State Violence: Radicalism, Gender, and Race in U.S. Culture*. Minneapolis: University of Minnesota Press.

———. (1997). *Transcending the Talented Tenth: Black Leaders and American Intellectuals*. New York: Routledge.

———. (1999). *Shadow Boxing: Representations of Black Feminist Politics*. New York: St. Martin's Press.

James, Joy A., and Sharpley-Whiting, T. Denean. (Eds.). (2000). *The Black Feminist Reader*. Malden, MA: Blackwell.

James, Stanlie, and Busia, Abena. (Eds.). (1993). *Theorizing Black Feminism: The Visionary Pragmatism of Black Women*. New York: Routledge.

James, Stanlie M., Foster, Frances Smith, and Guy-Sheftall, Beverly. (Eds.). (2009). *Still Brave: The Evolution of Black Women's Studies*. New York: Feminist Press.

James, Winston. (1998). *Holding Aloft the Banner of Ethiopia: Caribbean Radicalism in Early Twentieth-Century America*. New York: Verso.

Jameson, Fredric. (1971). *Marxism and Form: Twentieth-Century Dialectical Theories of Literature*. Princeton, NJ: Princeton University Press.

———. (1981). *Political Unconscious: Narrative as a Socially Symbolic Act*. Ithaca, NY: Cornell University Press.

———. (1988). "Cognitive Mapping." In Cary Nelson and Lawrence Grossberg (Eds.), *Marxism and the Interpretation of Culture* (pp. 347–60). Chicago: University of Illinois Press.

———. (1990). *Late Marxism: Adorno, or, The Persistence of the Dialectic*. London: Verso.

———. (1991). *Postmodernism, or, The Cultural Logic of Late Capitalism*. Durham, NC: Duke University Press.

———. (1998). *Cultural Turn: Selected Writings on the Postmodern, 1983–1998*. New York: Verso.

———. (2000). *The Jameson Reader* (Michael Hardt and Kathi Weeks, Eds.). Malden, MA: Blackwell.

————. (2007). *Jameson on Jameson: Conversations on Cultural Marxism* (Ian Buchanan, Ed.). Durham, NC: Duke University Press.

jamila, shani. (2002). "Can I Get a Witness?: Testimony from a Hip Hop Feminist." In Daisy Hernández and Bushra Rehman (Eds.), *Colonize This!: Young Women of Color on Today's Feminism* (pp. 279–94). New York: Seal Press.

Jarrett, Gene Andrew. (2005). "The Black Arts Movement and Its Scholars." *American Quarterly* 57 (4): 1243–51.

Jarrett, Robin L. (1994). "Living Poor: Family Life Among Single Parent, African-American Women." *Social Problems* 41 (1): 30–49.

Jarrett-Macauley, Delia. (Ed.). (1996). *Reconstructing Womanhood, Reconstructing Feminism.* New York: Routledge.

Jay, Martin. (1984). *Marxism and Totality: The Adventures of a Concept from Lukács to Habermas.* Berkeley: University of California Press.

————. (1996). *The Dialectical Imagination: A History of the Frankfurt School and the Institute of Social Research, 1923–1950.* Berkeley: University of California Press.

Jeffries, Judson L. (2002). *Huey P. Newton, The Radical Theorist.* Jackson: University Press of Mississippi.

————. (Ed.). (2006). *Black Power in the Belly of the Beast.* Urbana: University of Illinois.

Jewell, K. Sue. (2003). *Survival of the African American Family: The Institutional Impact of U.S. Social Policy.* Westport, CT: Praeger.

Johnson, Cedric. (2007). *Revolutionaries to Race Leaders: Black Power and the Making of African American Politics.* Minneapolis: University of Minnesota Press.

Johnson, Clarence S. (2003). *Cornel West and Philosophy: The Quest for Social Justice.* New York: Routledge.

Johnson, Eloise E. (1997). *Rediscovering the Harlem Renaissance: The Politics of Exclusion.* New York: Garland Publishing.

Johnson, E. Patrick. (2003). *Appropriating Blackness: Performance and the Politics of Authenticity.* Durham, NC: Duke University Press.

Johnson, E. Patrick, and Henderson, Mae G. (Eds.). (2005). *Black Queer Studies: A Critical Anthology.* Durham, NC: Duke University Press.

Johnson, Lemuel A. (Ed.). (1982). *Toward Defining the African Aesthetic.* Washington, DC: Three Continents Press.

Johnson, Louise C. (1990). "Socialist Feminisms." In Sneja Gunew (Ed.), *Feminist Knowledge: Critique and Construct* (pp. 304–31). London: Routledge.

Johnson, Pauline. (2001). "Distorted Communications: Feminism's Dispute with Habermas." *Philosophy & Social Criticism* 27 (1): 39–62.

Johnson, Vernon, and Lyne, Bill. (Eds.). (2002). *Walkin' the Talk: An Anthology of African American Studies.* Upper Saddle River, NJ: Prentice Hall.

Jones, Charles E. (Ed.). (1998). *Black Panther Party (Reconsidered).* Baltimore, MD: Black Classic Press.

Jones, Howard. (1987). *American Abolition, Law, and Diplomacy.* Oxford, UK: Oxford University Press.

Jones, Jacqueline. (1985). *Labor of Love, Labor of Sorrow: Black Women, Work and the Family from Slavery to the Present.* New York: Basic Books.

Jones, Kathleen B. (1988). "Socialist-Feminist Theories of the Family." *Praxis International* 8:284–300.

Jones, Lisa. (1994). *Bulletproof Diva: Tales of Race, Sex, and Hair.* New York: Doubleday.

Jordan, Winthrop D. (1974). *The White Man's Burden: Historical Origins of Racism in the United States.* New York: Oxford University Press.

————. (1977). *White Over Black: Images of Africa and Blacks in Western Popular Culture.* New York: Norton.

Jordan, Glenn, and Weedon, Chris. (Eds.). (1995). *Cultural Politics: Class, Gender, Race, and the Postmodern World.* Cambridge, MA: Blackwell.

Joseph, Gloria I. (1981). "The Incompatible Menage a Trois: Marxism, Feminism, and Racism." In Lydia Sargent (Ed.), *Women and Revolution: A Discussion of the Unhappy Marriage of Marxism and Feminism* (pp. 91–108). Boston: South End Press.

Joseph, Gloria I., and Lewis, Jill. (1981). *Common Differences: Conflicts in Black and White Feminist Perspectives*. New York: Anchor/Doubleday.

Joseph, Peniel E. (Ed.). (2001). "Black Power Studies I." *The Black Scholar* 31 (Fall/Winter): 3–4.

———. (Ed.). (2002). "Black Power Studies II." *The Black Scholar* 32 (Spring): 1.

———. (Ed.). (2006a). *Black Power Movement: Rethinking the Civil Rights–Black Power Era*. New York: Routledge.

———. (2006b). *Waiting 'Til the Midnight Hour: A Narrative History of Black Power in America*. New York: Henry Holt.

———. (2008). "Revolution in Babylon: Stokely Carmichael and America in the 1960s." *Souls: A Critical Journal of Black Politics, Culture, and Society* 9 (4): 281–301.

———. (Ed.). (2010). *Neighborhood Rebels: Black Power at the Local Level*. New York: Palgrave Macmillan.

Judy, R. A. T. (2004). "On the Question of Nigga Authenticity." In Murray Forman and Mark Anthony Neal (Eds.), *That's the Joint!: The Hip Hop Studies Reader* (pp. 105–18). New York: Routledge.

Jung, Patricia B., and Smith, Ralph F. (1993). *Heterosexism: An Ethical Challenge*. Albany: State University of New York Press.

Kalamka, Juba, and West, Tim'm. (2006). "It's All One: A Conversation." In Jeff Chang (Ed.), *Total Chaos: The Art and Aesthetics of Hip Hop* (pp. 198–208). New York: Basic/Civitas.

Kann, Mark E. (1999). *The Gendering of American Politics: Founding Mothers, Founding Fathers, and Political Patriarchy*. Westport, CT: Praeger.

Kantor, Martin. (1998). *Homophobia: Description, Development, and Dynamics of Gay Bashing*. Westport, CT: Praeger.

———. (2009). *Homophobia: The State of Sexual Bigotry Today*. Westport, CT: Praeger.

Karcher, Carolyn L. (1980). *Shadow Over the Promised Land: Slavery, Race, and Violence in Melville's America*. Baton Rouge: Louisiana State University Press.

Karenga, Maulana. (1968). "Black Art: A Rhythmic Reality of Revolution." *Negro Digest* 3:5–9.

———. (1972). "Black Cultural Nationalism." In Addison Gayle, Jr., (Ed.), *The Black Aesthetic* (pp. 32–38). Garden City, NY: Doubleday.

———. (1997). "Black Art: Mute Matter Given Force and Function." In Henry Louis Gates, Jr., and Nellie Y. McKay (Eds.), *The Norton Anthology of African American Literature* (pp. 1972–1977). New York: W.W. Norton and Company.

———. (2002). *Introduction to Black Studies* (3rd Edition). Los Angeles, CA: University of Sankore Press.

———. (2010). *Introduction to Black Studies* (4th Edition). Los Angeles, CA: University of Sankore Press.

Kato, M. T. (2007). *From Kung Fu to Hip Hop: Globalization, Revolution, and Popular Culture*. Albany: State University of New York Press.

Kebede, Ashenafi. (1995). *The Roots of Black Music: The Vocal, Instrumental, and Dance Heritage of Africa and Black America*. Trenton, NJ: Africa World Press.

Kelley, Robin D. G. (1997). *Yo' Mama's Disfunktional!: Fighting the Culture Wars in Urban America*. Boston: Beacon.

———. (2002). *Freedom Dreams: The Black Radical Imagination*. Boston: Beacon.

Kellner, Douglas. (1984). *Herbert Marcuse and the Crisis of Marxism*. Berkeley: University of California Press.

———. (1989). *Critical Theory, Marxism, and Modernity*. Baltimore, MD: Johns Hopkins University Press.

———. (1992). "Erich Fromm, Feminism, and the Frankfurt School." In Michael Kessler and Rainer Funk (Eds.), *Erich Fromm und die Frankfurter Schule* (pp. 111–30). Tubingen: Francke Verlag.

———. (1993). "Critical Theory and Social Theory: Current Debates and Challenges." *Theory, Culture, and Society* 10 (2): 43–61.

————. (1995). "The Obsolescence of Marxism?" In Bernard Magnus and Stephen Cullenberg (Eds.), *Whither Marxism?: Global Crises in International Perspective* (pp. 3–30). New York: Routledge.

————. (1996). *Media Culture: Cultural Studies, Identity, and Politics Between the Modern and the Postmodern*. New York: Routledge.

————. (2003). *Media Spectacle*. New York: Routledge.

Kellner, Douglas, and Homer, Sean. (Eds.). (2004). *Fredric Jameson: A Critical Reader*. New York: Palgrave Macmillan.

Keyes, Cheryl L. (2002). *Rap Music and Street Consciousness*. Urbana: University of Illinois Press.

King, Deborah K. (1988). "Multiple Jeopardy, Multiple Consciousness: The Context of a Black Feminist Ideology." *Signs* 14 (1): 42–72.

King, Jason. (1999). "When Autobiography Becomes Soul: Erykah Badu and the Cultural Politics of Black Feminism." *Women & Performance: A Journal of Feminist Theory* 10 (1& 2): 211–43.

Kirschke, Amy Helene. (2007). *Art in Crisis: W. E. B. Du Bois and the Struggle for African Identity and Memory*. Bloomington: Indiana University Press.

Kitwana, Bakari. (2002). *The Hip Hop Generation: Young Blacks and the Crisis in African American Culture*. New York: Basic/Civitas.

————. (2005). *Why White Kids Love Hip Hop: Wangstas, Wiggers, Wannabes, and the New Reality of Race in America*. New York: Basic/Civitas.

Kopano, Baruti N., and Williams, Yohuru R. (Eds.). (2004). *Treading Our Ways: Selected Topics in Africana Studies*. Dubuque, IA: Kendall/Hunt Publishing.

Kramer, Victor A. (Ed.). (1987). *Harlem Renaissance Re-Examined*. New York: AMS Press.

Krims, Adam. (2000). *Rap Music and the Poetics of Identity*. Cambridge, UK: Cambridge University Press.

Kuhn, Annette, and Wolpe, Ann Marie. (Eds.). (1978). *Feminism and Marxism: Women and Modes of Production*. Boston: Routledge & Kegan.

Labaton, Vivien, and Martin, Dawn L. (Eds.). (2004). *Fire This Time!: Young Activists and the New Feminism*. New York: Anchor Books.

Lamothe, Daphne M. (2008). *Inventing the New Negro: Narrative, Culture, and Ethnography*. Philadelphia: University of Pennsylvania Press.

Landes, Joan B. (1977). "Women, Labor, and Family Life: A Theoretical Perspective." *Science and Society* 41 (1): 386–409.

Landry, Bart. (2000). *Black Working Wives: Pioneers of the American Family*. Berkeley: University of California Press.

Latifah, Queen. (2000). *Ladies First: Revelations of a Strong Woman*. New York: Perennial Currents.

Laughlin, Karen, and Schuler, Catherine. (Eds.). (1995). *Theatre and Feminist Aesthetics*. Rutherford, NJ: Fairleigh Dickinson University Press.

Lawrence, Novotny. (2008). *Blaxploitation Films of the 1970s: Blackness and Genre*. New York: Routledge.

Lazarus, Neil. (Ed.). (2004). *Cambridge Companion to Postcolonial Literary Studies*. Cambridge, UK: Cambridge University Press.

Lazerow, Jama, and Williams, Yohuru. (Eds.). (2006). *In Search of the Black Panther Party: New Perspectives on a Revolutionary Movement*. Durham, NC: Duke University Press.

————. (2008). *Liberated Territory: Untold Local Perspectives on the Black Panther Party*. Durham, NC: Duke University Press.

Leadbeater, Bonnie J. R., and Way, Niobe. (Eds.). (1996). *Urban Girls: Resisting Stereotypes, Creating Identities*. New York: New York University Press.

Lee, Benson. (Dir.). (2008). *Planet B-Boy: Breakdancing Has Evolved*. New York: Arts Alliance America.

Lemelle, Anthony J. (2010). *Black Masculinity and Sexual Politics*. New York: Routledge.

Lemons, Gary L. (2001). "'When and Where [We] Enter': In Search of a Feminist Forefather— Reclaiming the Womanist Legacy of W. E. B. Du Bois." In Rudolph P. Byrd and Beverly

Guy-Sheftall (Eds.), *Traps: African American Men on Gender and Sexuality* (pp. 71–89). Indianapolis: Indiana University Press.

———. (2008). *Black Male Outsider: Teaching as a Pro-Feminist Man: A Memoir.* Albany: State University of New York Press.

———. (2009). *Womanist Forefathers: Frederick Douglass and W. E. B. Du Bois.* Albany: State University of New York Press.

Leon, Aya de. (2007). "If Women Ran Hip Hop." In Gwendolyn D. Pough, Elaine Richardson, Aisha Durham, and Rachel Raimist (Eds.), *Home Girls Make Some Noise!: The Hip Hop Feminism Anthology* (pp. 185–86). Mira Loma, CA: Parker Publishing.

Leonard, Keith. (2009). "African American Women Poets and the Power of the Word." In Angelyn Mitchell and Danille K. Taylor (Eds.), *The Cambridge Companion to African American Women's Literature* (pp. 168–86). Cambridge, UK: Cambridge University Press.

Levin, Gail. (2007). *Becoming Judy Chicago: A Biography of the Artist.* New York: Harmony Books.

Lewis, David Levering. (1989). *When Harlem Was in Vogue.* New York: Oxford University Press.

———. (1993). *W. E. B. Du Bois: Biography of a Race, 1868–1919.* New York: Henry Holt.

———. (Ed.). (1994). *Portable Harlem Renaissance Reader.* New York: Viking.

———. (2000). *W. E. B. Du Bois: The Fight for Equality and the American Century, 1919–1963.* New York: Henry Holt.

Lewis, Diane K. (1977). "A Response to Inequality: Black Women, Racism, and Sexism." *Signs* 3 (2): 339–61.

Lewis, Robert M. (Ed.). (2003). *From Traveling Show to Vaudeville: Theatrical Spectacle in America, 1830–1910.* Baltimore, MD: Johns Hopkins University Press.

Lhamon, W. T. (1998). *Raising Cain: Blackface Performance from Jim Crow to Hip Hop.* Cambridge, MA: Harvard University Press.

———. (Ed.). (2003). *Jump Jim Crow: Lost Plays, Lyrics, and Street Prose of the First Atlantic Popular Culture.* Cambridge, MA: Harvard University Press.

Light, Alan. (Ed.). (1999). *The Vibe History of Hip Hop.* New York: Random House.

Lippard, Lucy R. (1976). *From the Center: Feminist Essays on Women's Art.* New York: Dutton.

———. (Ed.). (1980a). *Issue: Social Strategies by Women Artists.* London: Institute of Contemporary Arts.

———. (1980b). "Sweet Exchanges: The Contributions of Feminism to the Art of the 1970s." *Art Journal* 40 (1–2): 360–69.

Liss, Andrea. (2009). *Feminist Art and the Maternal.* Minneapolis: University of Minnesota Press.

Lloyd, Sally A., Few, April L., and Allen, Katherine R. (Eds.). (2009). *Handbook of Feminist Family Studies.* Los Angeles: Sage.

Locke, Alain L. (Ed.). (1925). *The New Negro.* New York: Boni.

———. (1933). *The Negro in America.* Chicago: American Library Association.

———. (1936a). *Negro Art: Past and Present.* Washington, DC: Howard University Press.

———. (1936b). *The Negro and His Music.* New York: Arno Press.

———. (1940). *The Negro in Art: A Pictorial Record on the Negro Artists and of the Negro Theme in Art.* New York: Hacker Art Books.

———. (1949). *When Peoples Meet: A Study in Race and Culture.* New York: Hinds, Hayden, and Eldredge.

———. (Ed.). (1968). *The New Negro.* New York: Antheneum.

———. (1983). *The Critical Temper of Alain Locke: A Selection of His Essays on Art and Culture* (Jeffrey C. Stewart, Ed.). New York: Garland Publishing.

———. (1989). *The Philosophy of Alain Locke: Harlem Renaissance and Beyond* (Leonard Harris, Ed.). Philadelphia, PA: Temple University Press.

———. (1992). *Race Contacts and Interracial Relations: Lectures on the Theory and Practice of Race* (Jeffrey C. Stewart, Ed.). Washington, DC: Howard University Press.

Logan, Rayford W. (1954). *The Negro in American Life and Thought: The Nadir, 1877–1901.* New York: Dial Press.

Lommel, Cookie. (2000). *The History of Rap Music*. New York: Chelsea House.

Lorde, Audre. (1984). *Sister Outsider: Essays and Speeches by Audre Lorde*. Freedom, CA: The Crossing Press Feminist Series.

———. (1988). *A Burst of Light: Essays by Audre Lorde*. Ithaca, NY: Firebrand.

———. (1996). *The Audre Lorde Compendium: Essays, Speeches, and Journals*. London: Pandora.

———. (2004). *Conversations with Audre Lorde* (Joan Wylie Hall, Ed.). Jackson: University Press of Mississippi.

———. (2009). *I Am Your Sister: The Collected and Unpublished Writings of Audre Lorde* (Rudolph P. Byrd, Johnnetta B. Cole, and Beverly Guy-Sheftall, Eds.). New York: Oxford University Press.

Lott, Eric. (1995). *Love and Left: Blackface Minstrelsy and the American Working Class*. New York: Oxford University Press.

Lowry, Beverly. (2007). *Harriet Tubman: Imagining a Life*. New York: Doubleday.

Lucie-Smith, Edward. (2000). *Judy Chicago: An American Vision*. New York: Watson-Guptill Publications.

Lundy, Sandra E., and Leventhal, Beth. (1999). *Same-Sex Domestic Violence: Strategies for Change*. Thousand Oaks, CA: Sage.

Lynn, Susan. (1992). *Progressive Women in Conservative Times: Racial Justice, Peace, and Feminism, 1945 to the 1960s*. New Brunswick, NJ: Rutgers University Press.

Lyotard, Jean-François. (1984). *The Postmodern Condition: A Report on Knowledge*. Minneapolis: University of Minnesota Press.

Mabee, Carleton. (1970). *Black Freedom: The Nonviolent Abolitionists from 1830 through the Civil War*. New York: Macmillan.

Madhubuti, Haki R. (1971a). *Directionscore: Selected and New Poems*. Detroit, MI: Broadside Press.

———. (Ed.). (1971b). *Dynamite Voices: Black Poets of the 1960s*. Detroit, MI: Broadside Press.

Maeda, Daryl J. (2009). *Chains of Babylon: The Rise of Asian America*. Minneapolis: University of Minnesota Press.

Maglin, Nan Bauer, and Perry, Donna. (Eds.). (1996). *"Bad Girls"/"Good Girls": Women, Sex, and Power in the Nineties*. New Brunswick, NJ: Rutgers University Press.

Magnin, Andre, and Soulillou, Jacques. (Eds.). (1996). *Contemporary Art of Africa*. New York: H. N. Abrams.

Mahar, William J. (1999). *Behind the Burnt Cork Mask: Early Blackface Minstrelsy and Antebellum American Popular Culture*. Urbana: University of Illinois Press.

Malcolm X. (1967). *Malcolm X on Afro-American History*. New York: Pathfinder.

———. (1971). *The End of White World Supremacy: Four Speeches*. Merlin House/Seaver Books.

———. (1989). *Malcolm X: The Last Speeches*. New York: Pathfinder.

———. (1990). *Malcolm X Speaks: Selected Speeches and Statements*. New York: Grove-Weidendfeld.

———. (1991a). *Malcolm X Talks to Young People: Speeches in the U.S., Britain, and Africa*. New York: Pathfinder.

———. (1991b). *Malcolm X Speeches at Harvard* (Archie Epps, Ed.). New York: Paragon House.

———. (1992a). *The Autobiography of Malcolm X*. New York: Ballantine Books.

———. (1992b). *By Any Means Necessary*. New York: Pathfinder.

———. (1992c). *The Final Speeches, February 1965*. New York: Pathfinder.

Mance, Ajuan Maria. (2007). *Inventing Black Women: African American Women Poets and Self-Representation, 1877–2000*. Knoxville: University of Tennessee Press.

Marable, Manning. (1983). *How Capitalism Underdeveloped Black America*. Boston: South End Press.

———. (1995). *Beyond Black and White: Transforming African American Politics*. New York: Verso.

————. (1996). *Speaking Truth to Power: Essays on Race, Resistance, and Radicalism*. Boulder, CO: Westview.

————. (1997). *Black Liberation in Conservative America*. Boston: South End Press.

————. (Ed.). (2000). *Dispatches from the Ebony Towers: Intellectuals Confront the African American Experience*. New York: Columbia University Press.

————. (Ed). (2005). *The New Black Renaissance: The Souls Anthology of Critical African American Studies*. Boulder, CO: Paradigm Publishers.

————. (2011). *Malcolm X: A Life of Reinvention*. New York: Viking Press.

Marable, Manning, Steinberg, Ian, and Middlemass, Keesha. (Eds.). (2007). *Racializing Justice, Disenfranchising Lives: The Racism, Criminal Justice, and Law Reader*. New York: Palgrave/Macmillan.

Marcuse, Herbert. (1967). "The Obsolescence of Marxism." In Nikolaus Lobkowicz (Ed.), *Marxism in the Western World* (pp. 409–17). Notre Dame: University of Notre Dame Press.

————. (1971). "Dear Angela." *Ramparts* 9:22.

————. (1972). *Counter-Revolution and Revolt*. Boston: Beacon.

————. (1974). "Marxism and Feminism." *Women's Studies* 2 (3): 279–88.

————. (1978). "BBC Interview: Marcuse and the Frankfurt School." In Bryan Magee (Ed.), *Man of Ideas* (pp. 62–73). London: BBC Publishing.

Mariscal, George. (2005). *Brown-Eyed Children of the Sun: Lessons from the Chicano Movement, 1965–1975*. Albuquerque: University of New Mexico Press.

Marsh, James L. (2001). "Toward a New Critical Theory." In William S. Wilkerson and Jeffrey Paris (Eds.), *New Critical Theory: Essays on Liberation* (pp. 49–64). Lanham, MD: Rowman & Littlefield.

Markovitz, Jonathan. (2004). *Legacies of Lynching: Racial Violence and Memory*. Minneapolis: University of Minnesota Press.

Marks, Carole, and Edkins, Diana. (Eds.). (1999). *Power of Pride: Style-makers and Rule-breakers of the Harlem Renaissance*. New York: Crown Publishers.

Marks, Elaine. (Ed.). (1987). *Critical Essays on Simone de Beauvoir*. Boston, MA: G. K. Hall.

Massey, Douglas S., and Denton, Nancy A. (1993). *American Apartheid: Segregation and the Making of the Underclass*. Cambridge, MA: Harvard University Press.

Massood, Paula J. (2003). *Black City Cinema: African American Urban Experiences in Film*. Philadelphia, PA: Temple University Press.

Maxwell, Ian. (2003). *Phat Beats, Dope Rhymes: Hip Hop Down Under Comin' Upper*. Middletown, CT: Wesleyan University Press.

Maxwell, William J. (1999). *New Negro, Old Left: African American Writing and Communism Between the Wars*. New York: Columbia University Press.

May, John P., and Pitts, Khalid R. (Eds.). (2000). *Building Violence: How America's Rush to Incarcerate Creates More Violence*. Thousand Oaks, CA: Sage.

McClintock, Anne. (1995). *Imperial Leather: Race, Gender, and Sexuality in the Colonial Conquest*. New York: Routledge.

McDermott, Monica. (2006). *Working-Class White: The Making and Unmaking of Race Relations*. Berkeley: University of California Press.

McDonough, Roisin, and Rachel Harrison. (1978). "Patriarchy and Relations of Production." In Annette Kuhn and Ann Marie Wolpe (Eds.), *Feminism and Materialism: Women and Modes of Production* (pp. 11–41). New York: Routledge and Kegan Paul.

McIver, Joel. (2002). *Erykah Badu: The First Lady of Soul*. London: Sanctuary Publishing.

McLeod, John. (Ed.). (2007). *The Routledge Companion to Postcolonial Studies*. New York: Routledge.

McKivigan, John R., and Harrold, Stanley. (Eds.). (1999). *Anti-Slavery Violence: Sectional, Racial, and Cultural Conflict in Antebellum America*. Knoxville: University of Tennessee Press.

McLennan, Gregor. (1981). *Marxism and the Methodologies of History*. New York: Verso.

McQuillar, Tayannah L. (2007). *When Rap Music Had a Conscience: The Artists, Organizations, and Historic Events That Inspired and Influenced the "Golden Age" of Hip Hop, from 1987 to 1996*. New York: Thunder's Mouth.

McWhorter, John H. (2008). *All About the Beat: Why Hip Hop Can't Save Black America*. New York: Gotham Books.

Medina, Tony, and Rivera, Reyes. (Eds.). (2001). *Bum Rush the Page!: A Def Poetry Jam*. New York: Three Rivers Press.

Medina, Tony, Bashir, Samiya A., and Lansana, Quarishi Ali. (Eds.). (2002). *Role Call: A Generational Anthology of Social and Political Black Art and Literature*. Chicago: Third World Press.

Meehan, Johanna. (Ed.). (1995). *Feminists Read Habermas: Gendering the Subject of Discourse*. New York: Routledge.

————. (2000). "Feminism and Habermas's Discourse Ethics." *Philosophy & Social Criticism* 26 (3): 39–52.

Meer, Sarah. (2005). *Uncle Tom Mania: Slavery, Minstrelsy, and Trans-Atlantic Culture in the 1850s*. Athens: University of Georgia Press.

Meier, August. (1963). *Negro Thought in America, 1880–1915: Racial Ideologies in the Age of Booker T. Washington*. Ann Arbor: University of Michigan Press.

Meulenbelt, Anja. (Ed.). (1984). *A Creative Tension: Explorations in Socialist Feminism*. London: Pluto Press.

Mignolo, Walter. (2000). *Local Histories/Global Designs: Coloniality, Subaltern Knowledges, and Border Thinking*. Princeton, NJ: Princeton University Press.

————. (2003). *The Darker Side of the Renaissance: Literacy, Territoriality and Colonization*. Ann Arbor: University of Michigan Press.

————. (2005). *The Idea of Latin America*. Malden, MA: Blackwell.

Miles, Diana. (2003). *Women, Violence & Testimony in the Works of Zora Neale Hurston*. New York: Peter Lang.

Mills, Charles W. (1987). "Race and Class: Conflicting or Reconcilable Paradigms?" *Social and Economic Studies* 36 (2), 69–108.

————. (1997). *The Racial Contract*. Ithaca: Cornell University Press.

————. (1998). *Blackness Visible: Essays on Philosophy and Race*. Ithaca: Cornell University Press.

————. (1999). "The Racial Polity." In Susan E. Babbitt and Susan Campbell (Eds.), *Racism and Philosophy* (pp. 13–31, [endnotes] 255–57). Ithaca, NY: Cornell University Press.

————. (2003a). *From Class to Race: Essays in White Marxism and Black Radicalism*. Lanham, MD: Rowman & Littlefield.

————. (2003b). "White Supremacy." In Tommy L. Lott and John P. Pittman (Eds.), *A Companion to African American Philosophy* (pp. 269–84). Malden, MA: Blackwell.

Mills, Patricia J. (Eds). (1996). *Feminist Interpretations of G.W.F. Hegel*. University Park: Pennsylvania State University Press.

Miranda, Marcos A. (Dir.). (2003). *Inside Hip Hop*. Chatsworth, CA: Imagine Entertainment.

Mitchell, Angelyn. (Ed.). (1994). *Within the Circle: An Anthology of African American Literary Criticism from the Harlem Renaissance to the Present*. Durham, NC: Duke University Press.

Mitchell, Angelyn, and Taylor, Danille K. (Eds.). (2009). *Cambridge Companion to African American Women's Literature*. Cambridge, UK: Cambridge University Press.

Mitchell, Tony. (Ed.). (2001). *Global Noise: Rap and Hip Hop Outside the USA*. Hanover, NH: University Press of New England.

Mixon, Gregory. (2005). *The Atlanta Riot: Race, Class, and Violence in a New South City*. Gainesville: University Press of Florida.

Moi, Toril. (1994). *Simone de Beauvoir: The Making of an Intellectual Woman*. Cambridge, MA: Blackwell.

Moi, Toril, and Radway, Janice. (Eds.). (1994). *Materialist Feminism*. Durham, NC: Duke University Press.

Mongia, Padmini. (Ed.). (1997). *Contemporary Postcolonial Theory: A Reader*. Oxford, UK: Oxford University Press.

Mook, Richard. (2007). *Rap Music and Hip Hop Culture: A Critical Reader*. Dubuque, IA: Kendall/Hunt.

Moraga, Cherríe, and Anzaldúa, Gloria. (Eds.). (1984). *This Bridge Called My Back: Writings by Radical Women of Color*. New York: Kitchen Table Women of Color Press.

Morgan, Joan. (1995). "Fly-Girls, Bitches, and Hoes: Notes of a Hip Hop Feminist." *Social Text* 45:151–57.

———. (1999). *When Chickenheads Come Home to Roost: A Hip Hop Feminist Breaks It Down*. New York: Simon & Schuster.

———. (2007). "Afterword." In Gwendolyn D. Pough, Elaine Richardson, Aisha Durham, and Rachel Raimist (Eds.), *Home Girls Make Some Noise!: The Hip Hop Feminism Anthology* (pp. 475–80). Mira Loma, CA: Parker Publishing.

Morrison, Toni. (1994). *Conversations with Toni Morrison* (Danille Taylor-Guthrie, Ed.). Jackson: University Press of Mississippi.

Morton, Donald. (Ed.). (1996). *Material Queer: A LesBiGay Cultural Studies Reader*. Boulder, CO: Westview Press.

Moses, Wilson Jeremiah. (1978). *The Golden Age of Black Nationalism, 1850–1925*. New York: Oxford University Press.

———. (1990). *The Wings of Ethiopia: Studies in African American Life and Letters*. Ames: Iowa State University Press.

———. (1993). *Black Messiahs and Uncle Toms: Social and Literary Manipulations of a Religious Myth*. University Park: Pennsylvania State University Press.

———. (1998). *Afrotopia: The Roots of African American Popular History*. New York: Cambridge University Press.

———. (2004). *Creative Conflict in African American Thought: Frederick Douglass, Alexander Crummell, Booker T. Washington, W. E. B. Du Bois, and Marcus Garvey*. Cambridge, UK: Cambridge University Press.

Moten, Fred. (2003). *In the Break: The Aesthetics of the Black Radical Tradition*. Minneapolis: University of Minnesota Press.

Moynihan, Daniel Patrick. (1965). *The Negro Family: The Case for National Action*. United States Department of Labor, Office of Policy Planning and Research, Washington, DC: U.S. Government Printing Office.

Mullen, Bill V., and Smethurst, James. (Eds.). (2003). *Left of the Color-Line: Race, Radicalism, and Twentieth-Century Literature of the United States*. Chapel Hill: University of North Carolina Press.

Murray, Stephen O., and Roscoe, Will. (Eds.). (1998). *Boy-Wives and Female-Husbands: Studies in African Homosexualities*. New York: St. Martin's Press.

Mutua, Athena D. (Ed.). (2006). *Progressive Black Masculinities*. New York: Routledge.

Naison, Mark. (2005). *Communists in Harlem During the Depression*. Urbana: University of Illinois Press.

Napier, Winston. (Ed.). (2000). *African American Literary Theory: A Reader*. New York: New York University Press.

National Black Women's Health Project. (1990). "Reproductive Rights Position Paper: The National Black Women's Health Project." In Marlene Gerber Fried (Ed.), *From Abortion to Reproductive Freedom: Transforming a Movement* (pp. 291–93). Boston: South End Press.

Neal, Larry P. (1968). "The Black Arts Movement." *Drama Review* 12 (4): 29–39.

———. (1989). *Visions of a Liberated Future: Black Arts Movements Writings* (Michael Schwartz, Ed.). New York: Thunder's Mouth Press.

Neal, Mark Anthony. (1998). *What the Music Said: Black Popular Music and Black Public Culture*. New York: Routledge.

———. (2002). *Soul Babies: Black Popular Culture and the Post-Soul Aesthetic*. New York: Routledge.

———. (2003). *Songs in the Key of Black Life: A Rhythm and Blues Nation*. New York: Routledge.

———. (2005). *New Black Man: Rethinking Black Masculinity*. New York: Routledge.

Nealon, Jeffrey T., and Irr, Caren. (Eds.). (2002). *Rethinking the Frankfurt School: Alternative Legacies of Cultural Critique*. Albany: State University of New York Press.

Neate, Patrick. (2004). *Where Ya At?!: Notes from the Frontline of a Hip Hop Planet*. New York: Riverhead.

Nel, Philip. (2002). *Avant-Garde and American Postmodernity: Small Incisive Shocks*. Jackson: University Press of Mississippi.

Nelson, Angela M. S. (Ed.). (1999). *This Is How We Flow!: Rhythm in Black Cultures*. Columbia: University of South Carolina Press.

Nelson, Emmanuel S. (Ed.). (1993). *Critical Essays: Gay and Lesbian Writers of Color*. London: Haworth Press.

Nevels, Cynthia S. (2007). *Lynching to Belong: Claiming Whiteness Through Racial Violence*. College Station: Texas A&M University Press.

Newton, Huey P. (2002). *Huey P. Newton Reader* (David Hilliard and Donald Weise, Eds.). New York: Seven Stories Press.

Newton, Judith L., and Rosenfelt, Deborah. (1978)."Toward a Materialist-Feminist Criticism." In Judith Newton and Deborah Rosenfelt (Eds.), *Feminist Criticism and Social Change: Sex, Class, and Race in Literature and Culture* (pp. xv–xxxix). London: Methuen.

Nicholson, Linda J. (Ed.). (1990). *Feminism/Postmodernism*. New York: Routledge.

Nickson, Chris. (1999). *Lauryn Hill: She's Got That Thing*. New York: St. Martin's Press.

Nielsen, Aldon Lynn. (1997). *Black Chant: Languages of African American Postmodernism*. Cambridge, UK: Cambridge University Press.

Nilan, Pam, and Feixa, Carles. (Ed.). (2006). *Global Youth?: Hybrid Identities, Plural Worlds*. New York: Routledge.

Norment, Nathaniel, Jr. (2007a). *An Introduction to African American Studies: The Discipline and Its Dimensions*. Durham, NC: Carolina Academic Press.

———. (Ed.). (2007b). *The African American Studies Reader*. Durham, NC: Carolina Academic Press.

Nugent, Richard Bruce. (2002). *Gay Rebel of the Harlem Renaissance: Selections from the Work of Richard Bruce Nugent* (Thomas H. Wirth, Ed.). Durham, NC: Duke University Press.

Nye, Andrea. (1989). "A Community of Men: Marxism and Women." In Andrea Nye, *Feminist Theory and the Philosophies of Man* (pp. 31–72). New York: Routledge.

Oakley, Ann, and Mitchell, Juliet. (Eds.). (1997). *Who's Afraid of Feminism?: Seeing Through the Backlash*. New York: New Press.

O'Brien, Gail W. (1999). *The Color of the Law: Race, Violence, and Justice in the Post–World War II South*. Chapel Hill: University of North Carolina Press.

Ogbar, Jeffrey O.G. (2004). *Black Power: Radical Politics and African American Identity*. Baltimore, MD: Johns Hopkins University Press.

———. (2007). *The Hip Hop Revolution: The Culture and Politics of Rap*. Lawrence: University of Kansas Press.

Ogg, Alex. (2001). *The Hip Hop Years: A History of Rap* (with David Upshal). New York: Fromm International.

Okere, Theophilus. (1971). "Can There Be an African Philosophy?: A Heremeneutical Investigation with Special Reference to Igbo Culture." Ph.D. dissertation, Louvain University.

———. (1991). *African Philosophy: A Historico-Hermeneutical Investigation of the Conditions of Its Possibility*. Lanham, MD: University of America Press.

Okolo, Okondo. (1991). "Tradition and Destiny: Horizons of an African Philosophical Hermeneutics." In Tsenay Serequeberhan (Ed.), *African Philosophy: The Essential Readings* (pp. 201–11). New York: Paragon House.

Oliver, Melvin L., and Shapiro, Thomas M. (2006). *Black Wealth, White Wealth: A New Perspective on Racial Inequality*. New York: Routledge.

Olson, Joel. (2004). *The Abolition of White Democracy*. Minneapolis: University of Minnesota Press.

Ongiri, Amy Abugo. (2010). *Spectacular Blackness: The Cultural Politics of the Black Power Movement and the Search for a Black Aesthetic*. Charlottesville: University of Virginia Press.

Osayande, Ewuare X. (2008). *Misogyny & the Emcee: Sex, Race, & Hip Hop*. Philadelphia, PA: Talking Drum Communications.

Osumare, Halifu. (2007). *The Africanist Aesthetic in Global Hip-Hop*. New York: Palgrave/Macmillan.

Outlaw, Lucius T., Jr. (1990). "Toward a Critical Theory of 'Race.'" In David Theo Goldberg (Ed.), *Anatomy of Racism* (pp. 58–82). Minneapolis: University of Minnesota Press.

———. (1996). *On Race and Philosophy*. New York: Routledge.

———. (1997a). "African, African American, Africana Philosophy." In John P. Pittman (Ed.), *African American Perspectives and Philosophical Traditions* (pp. 63–93). New York: Routledge.

———. (1997b). "Is There a Distinctive African American Philosophy?" *Academic Questions* 10 (2): 29–46.

———. (2005). *Critical Social Theory in the Interests of Black Folk*. Lanham, MD: Rowman & Littlefield.

Paglia, Camille. (1991). *Sexual Personae: Art and Decadence from Nefertiti to Emily Dickinson*. New York: Vintage.

———. (1992). *Sex, Art, and American Culture: Essays*. New York: Vintage.

———. (1994). *Vamps & Tramps: New Essays*. New York: Vintage.

Parascandola, Louis J. (Ed.). (2005). *Look for Me All Around You: Anglophone Caribbean Immigrants in the Harlem Renaissance*. Detroit, MI: Wayne State University Press.

Parmar, Priya. (2009). *Knowledge Reigns Supreme: The Critical Pedagogy of Hip Hop Activist KRS-ONE*. Rotterdam, The Netherlands: Sense Publishers.

Patterson, James T. (2010). *Freedom Is Not Enough: The Moynihan Report and America's Struggle Over Black Family Life, From LBJ to Obama*. New York: Basic Books.

Patterson, Robert J. (2009). "African American Feminist Theories and Literary Criticism." In Angelyn Mitchell and Danille K. Taylor (Eds.), *The Cambridge Companion to African American Women's Literature* (pp. 87–106). Cambridge, UK: Cambridge University Press.

Patton, Erin O. (2009). *Under the Influence: Tracing the Hip-Hop Generation's Impact on Brands, Sports, & Pop Culture*. Ithaca, NY: Paramount Publishing.

Patton, Venetria K., and Honey, Maureen. (Eds.). (2001). *Double-Take: A Revisionist Harlem Renaissance Anthology*. New Brunswick, NJ: Rutgers University Press.

Pearson, Hugh. (1994). *Shadow of the Panther: Huey Newton and the Price of Black Power in America*. Reading, MA: Addison-Wesley.

Penn, Everette B. (2003). "On Black Criminology: Past, Present, and Future." *Criminal Justice Studies: A Critical Journal of Crime, Law, and Society* 16 (4): 317–27.

Peplow, Michael W., and Davis, Arthur Paul. (Eds.). (1975). *The New Negro Renaissance: An Anthology*. New York: Holt, Rinehart, and Winston.

Peretti, Burton W. (2009). *Lift Every Voice: The History of African American Music*. Lanham, MD: Rowman & Littlefield Publishers.

Perkins, Danila. (Dir.). (2000). *Miss M.C.: Women in Rap*. Thousand Oaks, CA: Ventura Distribution.

Perkins, William E. (Ed.). (1996). *Droppin' Science: Critical Essays on Rap Music and Hip Hop Culture*. Philadelphia, PA: Temple University Press.

Perkinson, James W. (2005). *Shamanism, Racism, and Hip Hop Culture: Essays on White Supremacy and Black Subversion*. New York: Palgrave/Macmillan.

Perry, Imani. (2004). *Prophets of the Hood: Politics and Poetics in Hip Hop*. Durham, NC: Duke University Press.

Pfeifer, Michael J. (2004). *Rough Justice: Lynching and American Society, 1874–1947*. Urbana: University of Illinois Press.

Pieterse, Jan N. (Ed.). (1992). *Emancipations, Modern, and Postmodern*. Newbury Park, CA: Sage.

Pinder, Kymberly N. (Ed.). (2002). *Race-ing Art History: Critical Readings in Race and Art History*. New York: Routledge.

Pinn, Anthony B. (2003). *Noise and Spirit: The Religious and Spiritual Sensibilities of Rap Music*. New York: New York University Press.

Phillips, Layli. (Ed.). (2006). *The Womanist Reader*. New York: Routledge.

Phillips, Layli, Reddick-Morgan, Kerri, and Stephens, Dionne P. (2005). "Oppositional Consciousness within an Oppositional Realm: The Case of Feminism and Womanism in Rap and Hip Hop, 1976–2004." *Journal of African American History* 90 (3): 253–77.

Phipps, Cyrille. (Dir.). (1992). *Respect Is Due!: Black Women in Rap Lyrics and Music Videos*. New York: Third World Newsreel.

———. (Dir.). (1993). *Our House: Lesbians and Gays in the Hood*. New York: Third World Newsreel.

Piontek, Thomas. (2006). *Queering Gay and Lesbian Studies*. Urbana: University of Illinois Press.

Planer, Rhonda. (2002). "Jill Scott: Words and Wisdom from a Neo-Soul Princess." *Black Collegian* 32 (2). www.black-collegian.com/issues/2ndsem02/jillscott2002-2nd.shtml (accessedDecember 9, 2003).

Plant, Deborah G. (2007). *Zora Neale Hurston: A Biography of the Spirit*. Westport, CT: Praeger.

Plummer, Ken. (2005). "Living with the Tensions: Critical Humanism and Queer Theory." In Norman K. Denzin and Yvonna S. Lincoln (Eds.), *The Sage Handbook of Qualitative Research* (pp. 357–75). Thousand Oaks, CA: Sage.

Põldsaar, Raili. (2006). *Critical Discourse Analysis of Anti-Feminist Rhetoric as a Catalyst in the Emergence of the Conservative Universe of Discourse in the United States in the 1970s–1980s*. Tartu, Estonia: Tartu University Press.

Potter, Russell A. (1995). *Spectacular Vernaculars: Hip Hop and the Politics of Postmodernism*. Albany: State University of New York Press.

Pough, Gwendolyn. (2002). "Love Feminism but Where's My Hip Hop?: Shaping a Black Identity." In Daisy Hernández and Bushra Rehman (Eds.), *Colonize This!: Young Women of Color on Today's Feminism* (pp. 85–98). New York: Seal Press.

———. (2003). "Do the Ladies Run This . . . ?: Some Thoughts on Hip Hop Feminism." In Rory Dicker and Alison Piepmeier (Eds.), *Catching a Wave: Reclaiming Feminism for the 21st Century* (pp. 232–43). Boston: Northeastern University Press.

———. (2004). *Check It While I Wreck It!: Black Womanhood, Hip Hop Culture, and the Public Sphere*. Boston: Northeastern University Press.

Pough, Gwendolyn D., Richardson, Elaine, Durham, Aisha, and Raimist, Rachel. (Eds.). (2007). *Home Girls Make Some Noise!: The Hip Hop Feminism Anthology*. Mira Loma, CA: Parker Publishing.

Powell, Kevin. (2003). *Who Gonna Take the Weight?: Manhood, Race, and Power in America*. New York: Three Rivers Press.

Powell, Kevin, and Baraka, Ras. (Eds.). (1992). *In the Tradition: An Anthology of Young Black Writers*. New York: Harlem River Press.

Prashad, Vijay. (2007). *Darker Nations: A People's History of the Third World*. New York: New Press.

Price, Emmett G. (2006). *Hip Hop Culture*. Santa Barbara, CA: ABC-CLIO.

Price, Richard. (Ed.). (1996). *Maroon Societies: Rebel Slave Communities in the Americas*. Baltimore, MD: Johns Hopkins University Press.

Prince, Althea, Silva-Wayne, Susan, and Vernon, Christian. (Eds.). (2004). *Feminisms and Womanisms: A Women's Studies Reader*. Toronto: Women's Press.

Pritchard, Eric, and Bibbs, Maria. (2007). "Sista Outsider: Queer Women of Color and Hip Hop." In Gwendolyn D. Pough, Elaine Richardson, Aisha Durham, and Rachel Raimist (Eds.), *Home Girls Make Some Noise!: The Hip Hop Feminism Anthology* (pp. 19–40). Mira Loma, CA: Parker Publishing.

Pruter, Robert. (1991). *Chicago Soul*. Urbana: University of Illinois Press.

Pulido, Laura. (2006). *Black, Brown, Yellow, and Left: Radical Activism in Los Angeles*. Berkeley: University of California Press.

Quarles, Benjamin. (1969). *Black Abolitionists*. Oxford, UK: Oxford University Press.

Quinn, Eithne. (2001). "'Pimpin' Ain't Easy'": Work, Play, and 'Lifestylization' of the Black Pimp Figure in Early 1970s America." In Brian Ward (Ed.), *Media, Culture, and the Modern African American Freedom Struggle* (pp. 211–32). Gainesville: University Press of Florida.

———. (2005). *Nuthin' but a "G" Thang: The Culture and Commerce of Gangsta Rap*. New York: Columbia University Press.

Rabaka, Reiland. (2006). "Africana Critical Theory of Contemporary Society: Ruminations on Radical Politics, Social Theory, and Africana Philosophy." In Molefi K. Asante and Maulana Karenga (Eds.), *The Handbook of Black Studies* (pp. 130–52). Thousand Oaks, CA: Sage.

———. (2007). *W. E. B. Du Bois and the Problems of the Twenty-First Century: An Essay on Africana Critical Theory*. Lanham, MD: Lexington Books.

———. (2008a). *Du Bois's Dialectics: Black Radical Politics and the Reconstruction of Critical Social Theory*. Lanham, MD: Lexington Books.

———. (2008b). "Malcolm X and Africana Critical Theory: Rethinking Revolutionary Black Nationalism, Black Radicalism, and Black Marxism." In James L. Conyers and Andrew P. Smallwood (Eds.), *Malcolm X: A Historical Reader* (pp. 281–98). Durham, NC: Carolina Academic Press.

———. (2009). *Africana Critical Theory: Reconstructing the Black Radical Tradition, from W. E. B. Du Bois and C. L. R. James to Frantz Fanon and Amilcar Cabral*. Lanham, MD: Lexington Books.

———. (2010a). *Against Epistemic Apartheid: W. E. B. Du Bois and the Disciplinary Decadence of Sociology*. Lanham, MD: Lexington Books.

———. (2010b). *Forms of Fanonism: Frantz Fanon's Critical Theory and the Dialectics of Decolonization*. Lanham, MD: Lexington Books.

———. (Ed.). (2010c). *W. E. B. Du Bois: A Critical Reader*. Fanham, UK: Ashgate Publishing.

———. (forthcoming). *Hip Hop's Historical Amnesia: On the Origins and Evolution of Contemporary Black Popular Culture*. Lanham, MD: Lexington Books.

Radford-Hill, Sheila. (2000). *Further to Fly: Black Women and the Politics of Empowerment*. Minneapolis: University of Minnesota Press.

Raimist, Rachel. (Dir.). (1999). *Nobody Knows My Name*. New York: Women Make Movies.

———. (Dir.). (2005). *A B-Girl Is . . . : A Celebration of Women in Hip Hop*. Minneapolis, MN: Intermedia Arts.

Ramji, Hasmita. (2009). *Researching Race: Theory, Methods, and Analysis*. Maidenhead, UK: Open University Press.

Rampersad, Arnold. (2002a). *The Life of Langston Hughes: I, Too, Sing America, 1902–1941, Vol. 1* (2nd Edition). New York: Oxford University Press.

———. (2002b). *The Life of Langston Hughes: I Dream a World, 1941–1967, Vol. 2* (2nd Edition). New York: Oxford University Press.

Ramsey, Guthrie P. (2003). *Race Music: Black Cultures from Be-Bop to Hip Hop*. Berkeley: University of California Press.

Randolph, Sherie M. (2009). "'Women's Liberation or . . . Black Liberation, You're Fighting the Same Enemies': Florynce Kennedy, Black Power, and Feminism." In Dayo F. Gore, Jeanne Theoharis, and Komozi Woodard (Eds.), *Want to Start a Revolution?: Radical Women in the Black Freedom Struggle* (pp. 223–47). New York: New York University Press.

Raphael-Hernandez, Heike. (Ed.). (2004). *Blackening Europe: The African American Presence*. New York: Routledge.

———. (2008). *The Utopian Aesthetics of Three African American Women (Toni Morrison, Gloria Naylor & Julie Dash): The Principle of Hope*. Lewiston, NY: Mellen Press.

Raven, Arlene, Langer, Cassandra L., and Fruech, Joanna. (Eds.). (1988). *Feminist Art Criticism: An Anthology*. Ann Arbor, MI: UMI Research Press.

Reed, Evelyn. (1975). *Woman's Evolution from Matriarchal Clan to Patriarchal Family*. New York: Pathfinder Press.

Reed, Teresa L. (2003). *The Holy Profane: Religion in Black Popular Music*. Lexington: University Press of Kentucky.

Reeves, Marcus. (2008). *Somebody Scream!: Rap Music's Rise to Prominence in the Aftershock of Black Power*. New York: Farber & Farber.

Renzetti, Claire M., and Miley, Charles H. (Eds.). (1996). *Violence in Gay and Lesbian Domestic Partnerships*. New York: Harrington Park Press.

Reverby, Susan M. (Ed.). (2000). *Tuskegee's Truths: Rethinking the Tuskegee Syphilis Study*. Chapel Hill: University of North Carolina Press.

Rhodes, Jane. (2007). *Framing the Black Panthers: The Spectacular Rise of a Black Power Icon*. New York: New Press.

Richardson, Diane, and Seidman, Steven. (Eds.). (2002). *Handbook of Lesbian and Gay Studies*. Thousand Oaks, CA: Sage.

Richardson, Heather Cox. (2001). *Death of Reconstruction: Race, Labor, and Politics in the Post–Civil War North, 1865–1901*. Cambridge, MA: Harvard University Press.

Riggs, Marlon T. (Dir.). (1986). *Ethnic Notions: Exploring Stereotypes About Blacks*. San Francisco, CA: California Newsreel.

———. (Dir). (1991). *Color Adjustment: Blacks in Prime Time, 1948–1988*. San Francisco, CA: California Newsreel.

———. (Dir.). (1995). *Black Is . . . Black Ain't*. San Francisco, CA: California Newsreel.

Ripani, Richard J. (2006). *New Blue Music: Changes in Rhythm & Blues, 1950–1999*. Jackson: University Press of Mississippi.

Rivera, Raquel Z. (2003). *New York Ricans from the Hip Hop Zone*. New York: Palgrave/Macmillan.

Rizzo, Albertina, and McCall, Amanda. (2005). *Hold My Gold: A White Girl's Guide to the Hip Hop World*. New York: Simon & Schuster.

Roberts, Adam C. (2000). *Fredric Jameson*. New York: Routledge.

Robinson, Cedric J. (2000). *Black Marxism: The Making of the Black Radical Tradition*. Chapel Hill: University of North Carolina Press.

———. (2001). *An Anthropology of Marxism*. Aldershot, UK: Ashgate.

———. (2007). *Forgeries of Memory and Meaning: Blacks and the Regimes of Race in American Theater and Film Before World War II*. Chapel Hill: University of North Carolina Press.

Robnett, Belinda. (1997). *How Long? How Long?: African American Women in the Struggle for Civil Rights*. New York: Oxford University Press.

Rodney, Walter. (1972). *How Europe Underdeveloped Africa*. Washington, DC: Howard University Press.

Rodriguez, Richard T. (2003). "The Verse of the Godfather: Signifying Family and Nationalism in Chicano Rap and Hip Hop Culture." In Alicia Gaspar de Alba (Ed.), *Velvet Barrios: Popular Culture and Chicana/o Sexualities*. New York: Palgrave/Macmillan.

———. (2006). "Queering the Homeboy Aesthetic." *Aztlan: A Journal of Chicano Studies* 31 (2): 127–137.

———. (2009). *Next of Kin: The Family in Chicago/a Cultural Politics*. Durham, NC: Duke University Press.

Roediger, David R. (1994). *Towards the Abolition of Whiteness: Essays on Race, Politics, and Working-Class History*. New York: Verso.

———. (Ed.). (1998). *Black on White: Black Writers on What It Means to Be White*. New York: Schocken.

———. (2002). *Colored White: Transcending the Racial Past*. Berkeley: University of California Press.

———. (2005). *Working Toward Whiteness: How America's Immigrants Became White—The Strange Journey from Ellis Island to the Suburbs*. New York: Basic Books.

———. (2007). *The Wages of Whiteness: Race and the Making of the American Working Class*. New York: Verso.

Rojas, Fabio. (2007). *From Black Power to Black Studies: How a Radical Social Movement Became an Academic Discipline*. Baltimore, MD: Johns Hopkins University Press.

Rojas, Maythee. (2009). *Women of Color and Feminism*. Berkeley, CA: Seal Press.

Rome, Dennis. (2004). *Black Demons: The Media's Depiction of the African American Male Criminal Stereotype*. Westport, CT: Praeger.

Rooks, Noliwe M. (2006). *White Money/Black Power: The Surprising History of African American Studies and the Crisis of Race in Higher Education*. Boston: Beacon Press.

Rosales, Francisco A. (1996). *Chicano!: The History of the Mexican American Civil Rights Movement*. Houston, TX: Arte Público Press.

Rose, Tricia. (1989). "Orality and Technology: Rap Music and Afro-American Cultural Resistance." *Popular Music and Society* 13 (4): 35–44.

———. (1990). "Never Trust a Big Butt and a Smile." *Camera Obscura: Feminism, Culture, and Media* 8 (2/23): 108–31.

————. (1991). "Fear of a Black Planet: Rap Music and Black Cultural Politics in the 1990s." *The Journal of Negro Education* 60 (3): 276–90.

————. (1994). *Black Noise: Rap Music and Black Culture in Contemporary America*. Middletown, CT: Wesleyan University Press.

————. (Ed.). (2003). *Longing to Tell: Black Women Talk About Sexuality and Intimacy*. New York: Farrar, Straus & Giroux.

————. (2008). *The Hip Hop Wars: What We Talk About When We Talk About Hip Hop—And Why It Matters*. New York: Basic/Civitas.

Roses, Lorraine E., and Randolph, Ruth E. (Eds.). (1996). *Harlem's Glory: Black Women Writing, 1900–1950*. Cambridge, MA: Harvard University Press.

Ross, Andrew, and Rose, Tricia. (Eds.). (1994). *Microphone Fiends: Youth Music and Youth Culture*. New York: Routledge.

Roth, Benita. (1999a). "Race, Class, and the Emergence of Black Feminism in the 1960s and 1970s." *Womanist Theory and Research* 2:1 (Fall).

————. (1999b). "The Vanguard Center: Intra-movement Experience and the Emergence of African-American Feminism." In Kimberly Springer (Ed.), *Still Lifting, Still Climbing: Contemporary African American Women's Activism* (pp. 70–90). New York: New York University Press.

————. (2004). *Separate Roads to Feminism: Black, Chicana, and White Feminist Movements in America's Second Wave*. New York: Cambridge University Press.

Rowbotham, Sheila. (1973). *Woman's Consciousness, Man's World*. Harmondsworth, UK: Penguin.

————. (1979). *Beyond the Fragments: Feminism and the Making of Socialism*. London: Merlin.

Rucker, Walter C. (2006). *River Flows On: Black Resistance, Culture, and Identity Formation in Early America*. Baton Rouge: Louisiana State University Press.

Runell, Marcella and Diaz, Martha. (2007). *The Hip Hop Education Guidebook: Volume 1*. New York: Hip Hop Association Publications.

Rupp, Leila J., and Taylor, Verta. (1986). "The Women's Movement: Strategies and New Directions." In Robert H. Bremner, Richard Hopkins, and Gary W. Reichard (Eds.), *American Choices: Social Dilemmas and Public Policy Since 1960* (pp. 75–104). Columbus: Ohio State University Press.

————. (1991). "Women's Culture and the Continuity of the Women's Movement." In Tayo Andreasen (Ed.), *Moving On: New Perspectives on the Women's Movement* (pp. 68–89). Aarhus, Denmark: Aarhus University Press.

Rutherford, Charlotte. (1992). "Reproductive Freedoms and African American Women." *Yale Journal of Law & Feminism* 4 (2): 255–90.

Sadar, Ziauddin. (1998). *Postmodernism and the Other: The New Imperialism of Western Culture*. London: Pluto Press.

Said, Edward W. (1979). *Orientalism*. New York: Vintage.

————. (1993). *Culture and Imperialism*. New York: Knopf.

————. (1999). "Traveling Theory Reconsidered." In Nigel C. Gibson (Ed.), *Rethinking Fanon* (pp. 197–214). Amherst, NY: Humanity Books.

————. (2000). "Traveling Theory." In Moustafa Bayoumi and Andrew Rubin (Eds.), *The Edward Said Reader* (pp. 195–217). New York: Vintage.

Salaam, Kalamu ya. (2002). "The Last Movement." *Mosaic* 13:40–43.

Sale, Maggie M. (1997). *Slumbering Volcano: American Slave Ship Revolts and the Production of Rebellious Masculinity*. Durham, NC: Duke University Press.

Salem, Dorothy. (1990). *To Better Our World: Black Women in Organized Reform, 1890–1920*. Brooklyn, NY: Carlson.

Sampson, Henry T. (1980). *Blacks in Blackface: A Sourcebook on Early Black Musical Shows*. Metuchen, NJ: Scarecrow Press.

Sandoval, Chela. (2000). *Methodology of the Oppressed*. Minneapolis: University of Minnesota Press.

Sanger, Kerran L. (1995). *"When the Spirit Says Sing!": The Role of Freedom Songs in the Civil Rights Movement*. New York: Garland.

Sanneh, Lamin O. (1999). *Abolitionists Abroad: American Blacks and the Making of Modern West Africa*. Cambridge, MA: Harvard University Press.

Sargent, Lydia. (Ed.). (1981). *Women and Revolution: A Discussion of the Unhappy Marriage of Marxism and Feminism*. Boston: South End Press.

Savitt, Todd L. (1982). "The Use of Blacks for Medical Experimentation and Demonstration in the Old South." *Journal of Southern History* 48 (3): 331–48.

———. (2007). *Race and Medicine in Nineteenth and Early-Twentieth Century*. Kent, OH: Kent State University Press.

Saxton, Alexander. (1990). *Rise and Fall of the White Republic: Class, Politics, and Mass Culture in Nineteenth-Century America*. New York: Verso.

Scheader, Catherine. (1978). *Lorraine Hansberry*. Chicago: Campus Publications.

Schloesser, Pauline E. (2002). *Fair Sex: White Women and Racial Patriarchy in the Early American Republic*. New York: New York University Press.

Schloss, Joseph. (2009). *Foundation: B-Boys, B-Girls, and Hip Hop Culture in New York*. New York: Oxford University Press.

Schmidt, Martha, and Taylor, Verta. (1997). "Women's Movements." In Janet J. Montelaro and Patricia M. Ulbrich (Eds.), *Introduction to Women's Studies* (pp. 1–9). New York: McGraw-Hill.

Schnitman, Dora F., and Schnitman, Jorge. (Ed.). (2002). *New Paradigms, Culture, and Subjectivity*. Cresskill, NJ: Hampton Press.

Schreiber, Ronnee. (2008). *Righting Feminism: Conservative Women and American Politics*. Oxford, UK: Oxford University Press.

Schwarz, A. B. Christa. (2003). *Gay Voices of the Harlem Renaissance*. Bloomington: Indiana University Press.

———. (2007). "Transgressive Sexuality and the Literature of the Harlem Renaissance." In George Hutchinson (Ed.), *The Cambridge Companion to the Harlem Renaissance* (pp. 141–54). Cambridge, UK: Cambridge University Press.

Schwarz, Henry, and Ray, Sangeeta. (Eds.). (2000). *A Companion to Postcolonial Studies*. Malden, MA: Blackwell.

Sears, James T., and Williams, Walter L. (Eds.). (1997). *Overcoming Heterosexism and Homophobia: Strategies That Work*. New York: Columbia University Press.

Seidman, Steven. (Ed.). (1994). *Postmodern Turn: New Perspectives on Social Theory*. Cambridge UK: Cambridge University Press.

———. (1995). "Deconstructing Queer Theory, or the Under-Theorization of the Social and the Ethical." In Linda J. Nicholson and Steven Seidman (Eds.), *Social Postmodernism: Beyond Identity Politics*. Cambridge, UK: Cambridge University Press.

———. (Ed.). (1996). *Queer Theory/Sociology*. Cambridge, MA: Blackwell.

———. (1997). *Difference Troubles: Queering Social Theory and Sexual Politics*. Cambridge, UK: Cambridge University Press.

Seidman, Steven, Fischer, Nancy, and Meeks, Chet. (Eds.). (2006). *Handbook of New Sexuality Studies*. New York: Routledge.

Serequeberhan, Tsenay. (Ed.). (1991). *African Philosophy: The Essential Readings*. New York: Paragon House.

———. (1994). *The Hermeneutics of African Philosophy: Horizon and Discourse*. New York: Routledge.

———. (2000). *Our Heritage: The Past in the Present of African American and African Existence*. Lanham, MD: Rowman & Littlefield.

———. (2007). *Contested Memory: The Icon of the Occidental Tradition*. Trenton, NJ: Africa World Press.

Sévéon, Julien. (2008). *Blakpoitation: 70s Soul Fever*. Paris: Bazaar & Co.

Sexton, Adam. (Ed.). (1995). *Straight-Up Talk on Hip Hop Culture*. New York: Delta.

Shapiro, Herbert. (1988). *White Violence and Black Response: From Reconstruction to Montgomery*. Amherst: University of Massachusetts Press.

Shapiro, Thomas M. (2004). *The Hidden Cost of Being African American: How Wealth Perpetuates Inequality*. New York: Oxford University Press.

256 Bibliography

Sharpley-Whiting, Tracy D. (1997). *Frantz Fanon: Conflicts and Feminisms*. Lanham, MD: Rowman & Littlefield.

———. (2007). *Pimps Up, Ho's Down: Hip Hop's Hold on Young Black Women*. New York: New York University Press.

Sharpley-Whiting, Tracy D., and White, Renée T. (Eds.). (1997). *Spoils of War: Women of Color, Culture, and Revolutions*. Lanham, MD: Rowman & Littlefield.

Shaw, Arnold. (1970). *World of Soul: Black America's Contributions to the Pop Music Scene*. New York: Cowles Book Co.

———. (1986). *Black Popular Music in America: From the Spirituals, Minstrels, and Ragtime to Soul, Disco, and Hip Hop*. New York: Schirmer Books.

Shaw, Harry B. (Ed.). (1990). *Perspectives of Black Popular Culture*. Bowling Green, Ohio: Bowling Green State University Popular Press.

Shaw, Stephanie J. (1991). "Black Club Women and the Creation of the National Association of Colored Women." *Journal of Women's History* 3 (2): 1–25.

Shaw, William. (2000). *Westside: Young Men and Hip Hop in LA*. New York: Simon & Schuster.

Sherrard-Johnson, Cherene. (2007). *Portraits of the New Negro Woman: Visual and Literary Culture in the Harlem Renaissance*. New Brunswick, NJ: Rutgers University Press.

Sim, Stuart. (Ed.). (2005). *Routledge Companion to Postmodernism*. New York: Routledge.

Simon, Richard. (1998). "The Stigmatization of 'Blaxplotation.'" In Monique Guillory and Richard C. Green (Eds.), *Soul: Black Power, Politics, and Pleasure* (pp. 236–49). New York: New York University Press.

Simons, Margaret A. (Ed.). (1995). *Feminist Interpretations of Simone de Beauvoir*. University Park, PA: Pennsylvania State University Press.

———. (1999). *Beauvoir and The Second Sex: Feminism, Race, and the Origins of Existentialism*. Lanham, MD: Rowman & Littlefield.

Sims, Yvonne D. (2006). *Women of Blaxploitation: How the Black Action Film Heroine Changed American Popular Culture*. Jefferson, NC: McFarland.

Singh, Nikhil Pal. (2004). *Black Is a Country: Race and the Unfinished Struggle for Democracy*. Cambridge, MA: Harvard University Press.

Sizemore, Barbara. (1973). "Sexism and the Black Male." *Black Scholar* 4 (6/7): 2–11.

Slaughter, Jane, and Kern, Robert. (Eds.). (1981). *European Women on the Left: Socialism, Feminism, and the Problems Faced by Political Women, 1880 to the Present*. Westport, CT: Greenwood.

Smart, Barry. (1992). *Postmodernity*. New York: Routledge.

———. (1993). *Modern Conditions, Postmodern Controversies*. New York: Routledge.

Smethurst, James Edward. (1999). *The New Red Negro: The Literary Left and African American Poetry, 1930–1946*. New York: Oxford University Press.

———. (2005). *The Black Arts Movement: Literary Nationalism in the 1960s and 1970s*. Chapel Hill: University of North Carolina Press.

Smith, Barbara. (Ed.). (1983). *Home Girls: A Black Feminist Anthology*. New York: Kitchen Table: Women of Color Press.

———. (1993). "Combahee River Collective." In Darlene Clark Hine, Elsa Barkley Brown, and Rosalyn Teborg-Penn (Eds.), *Black Women in America: An Historical Encyclopedia* (Volume 1, pp. 269–70). Brooklyn, NY: Carlson.

———. (1998). *The Truth That Never Hurts: Writings on Race, Gender, and Freedom*. New Brunswick: Rutgers University Press.

Smith, Beverly. (1990). "Choosing Ourselves: Black Women and Abortion." In Marlene Gerber Fried (Ed.), *From Abortion to Reproductive Freedom: Transforming a Movement* (pp. 83–87). Boston: South End Press.

Smith, David Lionel. (1991). "The Black Arts Movement and Its Critics." *American Literary History* 3 (1): 93–110.

Smith, Jason K. (2002). *Counter-Hegemonic Masculinity in Hip Hop Music: An Analysis of The Roots' Construction of Masculinity in Their Music and in the Media Culture*. Hartford, CT: University of Hartford Press.

Smith, Linda Tuhiwai. (1999). *Decolonizing Methodologies: Research and Indigenous Peoples*. Dunedin, New Zealand: University of Otago Press.

Smith, Lorrie. (2006). "Black Arts to Def Jam: Performing Black 'Spirit Work' Across Generations." In Lisa Gail Collins and Margo Natalie Crawford (Eds.), *New Thoughts on the Black Arts Movement* (pp. 349–68). New Brunswick, NJ: Rutgers University Press.

Smith, Shawn M. (2004). *Photography on the Color-Line: W. E. B. Du Bois, Race, and Visual Culture*. Durham, NC: Duke University Press.

Smith-Cooper, Tia. (2002). *Contradictions in a Hip Hop World: An Ethnographic Study of Black Women Hip Hop Fans in Washington, DC*. Columbus: Ohio State University.

Solomon, Irvin D. (1989). *Feminism and Black Activism in Contemporary America: An Ideological Assessment*. New York: Greenwood Press.

Solomon, Mark I. (1998). *The Cry Was Unity: Communists and African American, 1917–1936*. Jackson: University Press of Mississippi.

Somerville, Siobhan B. (2000). *Queering the Color-Line: Race and the Invention of Homosexuality in American Culture*. Durham, NC: Duke University Press.

Sotiropoulos, Karen. (2006). *Staging Race: Black Performance in Turn of the Century America*. Cambridge, MA: Harvard University Press.

Souljah, Sister. (1996). *No Disrespect*. New York: Vintage.

Southern, Eileen. (1997). *Music of Black Americans: A History*. New York: W.W. Norton.

Spady, James G., Alim, H. Samy, and Meghelli, Samir. (Ed.). (2006). *The Global Cipha: Hip Hop Culture and Consciousness*. Philadelphia, PA: Black History Museum Press.

Spady, James G., Lee, Charles G., and Alim, H. Samy. (1999). *Street Conscious Rap*. Philadelphia, PA: Black History Museum Press/LOH Publishers.

Spencer, Jon Michael. (1990). *Protest & Praise: Sacred Music of Black Religion*. Minneapolis, MN: Fortress Press.

———. (1993). *Blues & Evil*. Knoxville: University of Tennessee Press.

———. (1995). *The Rhythms of Black Folk: Race, Religion, and Pan-Africanism*. Trenton, NJ: Africa World Press.

Springer, Kimberly. (Ed.). (1999). *Still Lifting, Still Climbing: Contemporary African American Women's Activism*. New York: New York University Press.

———. (2001). "The Interstitial Politics of Black Feminist Organizations." *Meridians: Feminism, Race, Transnationalism* 1 (2): 155–91.

———. (2002). "Third Wave Black Feminism?" *Signs: Journal of Women in Culture and Society* 27 (4): 1059–82.

———. (2005). *Living for the Revolution: Black Feminist Organizations, 1968–1980*. Durham, NC: Duke University Press.

———. (2006). "Black Feminists Respond to Black Power Masculinism." In Peniel E. Joseph (Ed.), *The Black Power Movement: Rethinking the Civil Rights–Black Power Era* (pp. 105–18). New York: Routledge.

Springhall, John. (2008). *Genesis of Mass Culture: Show Business Live in America, 1840 to 1940*. New York: Palgrave/Macmillan.

Staggenborg, Suzanne, and Taylor, Verta. (2005). "Whatever Happened to the Women's Movement?" *Mobilization: International Journal of Theory and Research About Social Movements and Collective Behavior* 10:37–52.

Stanley, Tarshia L. (Ed.). (2009). *Encyclopedia of Hip Hop Literature*. Westport, CT: Greenwood Press.

Starr, Larry, and Waterman, Christopher. (2003). *American Popular Music: From Minstrelsy to MTV*. New York: Oxford University Press.

Stauffer, John. (2001). *Black Hearts of Men: Radical Abolitionists and the Transformation of Race*. Cambridge, MA: Harvard University Press.

Stephens, Vincent. (2005). "Pop Goes the Rapper: A Close Reading of Eminem's Genderphobia." *Popular Music* 24 (1): 21–36.

Stewart, Jeffrey C. (2007). "The New Negro as Citizen." In George Hutchinson (Ed.), *The Cambridge Companion to the Harlem Renaissance* (pp. 13–27). Cambridge, UK: Cambridge University Press.

Stockton, Kathryn B. (2006). *Beautiful Bottom, Beautiful Shame: Where "Black" Meets "Queer."* Durham, NC: Duke University Press.

Stokes, Mason B. (2001). *Color of Sex: Whiteness, Heterosexuality, and the Fictions of White Supremacy.* Durham, NC: Duke University Press.

Strausbaugh, John. (2006). *Black Like You: Blackface, Whiteface, Insult & Imitation in America Popular Culture.* New York: Penguin.

Strickland, Ronald. (Ed.). (2002). *Growing Up Postmodern: Neoliberalism and the War on the Young.* Lanham, MD: Rowman & Littlefield.

Sudbury, Julia. (Ed.). (2005). *Global Lockdown: Race, Gender, and the Prison-Industrial Complex.* New York: Routledge.

Sulton, Anne T. (Ed.). (1996). *African American Perspectives on Crime Causation, Criminal Justice Administration, and Crime Prevention.* Boston, MA: Butterworth/Heinemann.

Swindells, Julia. (Ed.). (1995). *Uses of Autobiography.* London: Taylor & Francis.

Tan, Joël Barraquiel. (2006). "Homothugdragsterism." In Jeff Chang (Ed.), *Total Chaos: The Art and Aesthetics of Hip Hop* (pp. 209–18). New York: Basic/Civitas.

Tanz, Jason. (2007). *Other People's Property: A Shadow History of Hip-Hop in White America.* New York: Bloomsbury.

Tarver, Australia, and Barnes, Paula C. (Eds.). (2006). *New Voices on the Harlem Renaissance: Essays on Race, Gender, and Literary Discourse.* Madison, NJ: Fairleigh Dickinson University Press.

Tate, Claudia. (Ed.). (1983). *Black Women Writers at Work.* New York: Continuum.

Taylor, Eric R. (2006). *If We Must Die: Shipboard Insurrections in the Era of the Atlantic Slave Trade.* Baton Rouge: Louisiana State University Press.

Taylor, Verta. (1989a). "The Future of Feminism: A Social Movement Analysis." In Laurel Richardson and Verta Taylor (Eds.), *Feminist Frontiers II* (pp. 473–90). New York: Random House.

———. (1989b). "Social Movement Continuity: The Women's Movement in Abeyance." *American Sociological Review* 54:761–75.

Taylor, Verta, and Rupp, Leila. (2008). "Preface." In Marian Sawyer and Sandra Grey (Eds.), *Women's Movements: Flourishing or in Abeyance.* New York: Routledge.

———. (1991). "Researching the Women's Movement: We Make Our Own History, but Not Just as We Please." In Mary Margaret Fonow and Judith A. Cook (Eds.), *Beyond Methodology: Feminist Scholarship as Lived Research* (pp. 119–32). Bloomington: Indiana University Press.

Taylor, Verta, and Whittier, Nancy. (1993). "The New Feminist Movement." In Laurel Richardson and Verta Taylor (Eds.), *Feminist Frontiers III: Rethinking Sex, Gender, and Society* (pp. 533–48). New York: McGraw-Hill.

———. (1995). "Analytical Approaches to Social Movement Culture: The Culture of the Women's Movement." In Hank Johnston and Bert Klandermans (Eds.), *Social Movements and Culture* (pp. 163–87). Minneapolis: University of Minnesota Press.

Taylor, Verta, Whittier, Nancy, and Pelak, Cynthia. (2001). "The Women's Movement in the Twenty-First Century: Persistence Through Transformation." In Laurel Richardson, Verta Taylor, and Nancy Whittier (Eds.), *Feminist Frontiers V* (pp. 559–74). New York: McGraw-Hill.

Taylor, Yuval. (Ed.). (1999a). *I Was Born a Slave: An Anthology of Classic Slave Narratives—Volume 1, 1772–1849.* Chicago: Lawrence Hill Books.

———. (Ed.). (1999b). *I Was Born a Slave: An Anthology of Classic Slave Narratives—Volume 2, 1849–1866.* Chicago: Lawrence Hill Books.

Terrell, Mary Church. (1932). *Colored Women and World Peace.* Philadelphia, PA: Women's International League for Peace and Freedom Press.

———. (1940). *A Colored Woman in a White World.* Salem, NH: Ayer.

Terrill, Robert E. (Ed.). (2010). *The Cambridge Companion to Malcolm X.* Cambridge, UK: Cambridge University Press.

Third World Women's Alliance. (1970). *Black Woman's Manifesto.* New York: Third World Women's Alliance Press.

Thomas, Greg. (2007). "Queens of Consciousness & Sex-Radicalism in Hip-Hop: On Erykah Badu & The Notorious K.I.M." *Journal of Pan-African Studies* 1 (7): 23–37.

———. (2009). *Hip-Hop Revolution in the Flesh: Power, Knowledge, and Pleasure in Lil' Kim's Lyricism*. New York: Palgrave/Macmillan.

Thorne, Barrie, and Yalom, Marilyn. (Eds.). (1992). *Rethinking the Family: Some Feminist Questions*. Boston: Northeastern University Press.

Thurman, Wallace. (2003). *Collected Writing of Wallace Thurman: A Harlem Renaissance Reader* (Amritjit Singh and Daniel M. Scott III, Eds.). New Brunswick, NJ: Rutgers University Press.

Tobias, Sheila. (1997). *Faces of Feminism: An Activist's Reflections on the Women's Movement*. Boulder, CO: Westview Press.

Toll, Robert C. (1974). *Blacking Up: The Minstrel Show in Nineteenth-Century America*. Oxford, UK: Oxford University Press.

Traylor, Eleanor W. (2009). "Women Writers of the Black Arts Movement." In Angelyn Mitchell and Danille K. Taylor (Eds.), *The Cambridge Companion to African American Women's Literature* (pp. 50–70). Cambridge, UK: Cambridge University Press.

Tucker, Linda G. (2007). *Lockstep and Dance: Images of Black Men in Popular Culture*. Jackson: University Press of Mississippi.

Twine, Frances W., and Blee, Kathleen M. (Eds.). (2001). *Feminism and Anti-Racism: International Struggles for Justice*. New York: New York University Press.

Twine, France Winddance, and Warren, Jonathan W. (Eds.). (2000). *Racing Research, Researching Race: Methodological Dilemmas in Critical Race Studies*. New York: New York University Press.

Usher, Carlton A. (2005). *A Rhyme Is a Terrible Thing to Waste: Hip Hop Culture and the Creation of a Political Culture*. Trenton, NJ: Africa World Press.

Valdes, Francisco, Culp, Jerome M., and Harris, Angela P. (Eds.). (2002). *Crossroads, Directions, and a New Critical Theory of Race*. Philadelphia: Temple University Press.

Valk, Anne M. (2008). *Radical Sisters: Second-Wave Feminism and Black Liberation in Washington, DC*. Urbana: University of Illinois Press.

Van Deburg, William L. (1992). *New Day in Babylon: The Black Power Movement and American Culture, 1965–1975*. Chicago: University of Chicago Press.

———. (1997). *Black Camelot: African American Culture Heroes in Their Times, 1960–1980*. Chicago: University of Chicago Press.

———. (2001). "Villains, Demons, and Social Bandits: White Fear of the Black Cultural Revolution." In Brian Ward (Ed.), *Media, Culture, and the Modern African American Freedom Struggle* (pp. 197–210). Gainesville: University Press of Florida.

———. (2004). *Hoodlums: Black Villains and Social Bandits in American Life*. Chicago: University of Chicago Press.

Vaz, Kim Marie. (Ed.). (1995). *Black Women in America*. Thousand Oaks, CA: Sage.

Vibe magazine. (Ed.). (2001). *Hip Hop Divas*. New York: Three Rivers Press.

Visona, Monica B. (2001). *History of Art in Africa*. New York: Harry N. Abrams, Inc.

Vogel, Lise. (1983). *Marxism and the Oppression of Women: Towards a Unitary Theory*. New Brunswick, NJ: Rutgers University Press.

Waldrep, Christopher. (Ed.). (2006). *Lynching in America: A History in Documents*. New York: New York University Press.

Walker, Alice. (1983). *In Search of Our Mother's Gardens: Womanist Prose*. San Diego, CA: Harcourt Brace Jovanovich.

———. (1990). "The Right to Life: What Can the White Man Say to the Black Woman?" In Marlene Gerber Fried (Ed.), *From Abortion to Reproductive Freedom: Transforming a Movement* (pp. 65–70). Boston: South End Press.

Walker, David, Rausch, Andrew J., and Watson, Chris. (Eds.). (2009). *Reflections on Blaxploitation: Actors and Directors Speak*. Lanham, MD: Scarecrow Press.

Walker, Rebecca. (Ed.). (1995). *To Be Real: Telling the Truth and Changing the Face of Feminism*. New York: Anchor Books.

Wall, Cheryl A. (1995). *Women of the Harlem Renaissance*. Bloomington: Indiana University Press.

———. (2005). *Worrying the Line: Black Women Writers, Lineage, and Literary Tradition.* Chapel Hill: University of North Carolina Press.

Wallace, Michele. (1979). *Black Macho and the Myth of the Superwoman.* New York: Dial Press.

———. (1990). *Invisibility Blues: From Pop to Theory.* New York: Verso.

———. (2004). *Dark Designs and Visual Culture.* Durham, NC: Duke University Press.

Walters, Ronald W. (2003). *White Nationalism, Black Interests: Conservative Public Policy and the Black Community.* Detroit, MI: Wayne State University Press.

Walters, Tracey L. (2007). *African American Literature and the Classicist Tradition: Black Women Writers from Wheatley to Morrison.* New York: Palgrave/Macmillan.

Ward, Brian. (1998). *Just My Soul Responding: Rhythm & Blues, Black Consciousness, and Race Relations.* Berkeley: University of California Press.

———. (Ed.). (2001). *Media, Culture, and the Modern African American Freedom Struggle.* Gainesville: University Press of Florida.

Ward, Stephen. (2006). "The Third World Women's Alliance." In Peniel E. Joseph (Ed.), *The Black Power Movement: Rethinking the Civil Rights–Black Power Era* (pp. 119–44). New York: Routledge.

Washington, Harriet A. (2006). *Medical Apartheid: The Dark History of Medical Experimentation on Black Americans from Colonial Times to the Present.* New York: Doubleday.

Washington, Robert E. (2001). *Ideologies of African American Literature: From the Harlem Renaissance to the Black Nationalist Revolt—A Sociology of Literature Perspective.* Lanham, MD: Rowman & Littlefield.

Watkins, S. Craig. (1998). *Representing: Hip Hop Culture and the Production of Black Cinema.* Chicago: University of Chicago Press.

———. (2005). *Hip Hop Matters: Politics, Pop Culture, and the Struggle for the Soul of a Movement.* Boston: Beacon.

Watson, Elwood. (Ed.). (2009). *Pimps, Wimps, Studs, Thugs, and Gentlemen: Essays on Media Images of Masculinity.* Jefferson, NC: McFarland.

Watson, Steven. (1995). *Harlem Renaissance: Hub of African American Culture, 1920–1930.* New York: Pantheon Books.

Wehbi, Samantha. (Ed.). (2004). *Community Organizing Against Homophobia and Heterosexism: The World Through Rainbow-Colored Glasses.* New York: Harrington Park Press.

Weinbaum, Batya. (1978). *The Curious Courtship of Women's Liberation and Socialism.* Boston: South End Press.

Welbon, Yvonne. (Dir.). (1993). *Sisters in the Life: First Love.* New York: Third World Newsreel.

Wells, Ida B. (1969). *On Lynchings.* New York: Arno Press.

———. (1970). *Crusade for Justice: The Autobiography of Ida B. Wells* (Alfreda Duster, Ed.). Chicago: University of Chicago Press.

———. (1991). *The Selected Works of Ida B. Wells-Barnett* (Trudier Harris, Ed.). New York: Oxford University Press.

———. (1993). *A Red Record: Lynchings in the U.S.* Salem, NH: Ayer & Co.

———. (1995). *The Memphis Dairy of Ida B. Wells* (Miriam Decosta-Willis, Ed.). Boston: Beacon.

Welsh-Asante, Kariamu. (Ed.). (1992). *The African Aesthetic: Keeper of the Traditions.* New York: Greenwood Press.

Werner, Craig H. (2006). *Change Is Gonna Come: Music, Race & the Soul of America.* Ann Arbor: University of Michigan Press.

Wesley, Charles H. (1984). *The History of the National Association of Colored Women's Clubs: A Legacy of Service.* Washington, DC: National Association of Colored Women.

West, Cornel. (1982). *Prophesy Deliverance!: An Afro-American Revolutionary Christianity.* Philadelphia, PA: Westminster.

———. (1993). *Keeping Faith: Philosophy and Race in America.* New York: Routledge.

West, Margaret Genevieve. (2005). *Zora Neale Hurston & American Literary Culture.* Gainesville: University Press of Florida.

West, Michael R. (2005). *The Education of Booker T. Washington: American Democracy and the Idea of Race Relations.* New York: Columbia University Press.

West, Tim'm T. (2003). *Red Dirt Revival: A Poetic Memoir in Six Breaths.* Castro Valley, CA: Poz'trophy Publishing.

——. (2005). "Keepin' It Real: Disidentification and Its Discontents." In Harry J. Elam, Jr., and Kennell Jackson (Eds.), *Black Cultural Traffic: Crossroads in Global Performance and Popular Culture* (pp. 162–84). Ann Arbor: University of Michigan Press.

——. (2007). *BARE: Notes from a Porchdweller.* Houston, TX: Red Dirt Publishing.

——. (2008). *Flirting.* Houston, TX: Red Dirt Publishing.

Whaley, Deborah E. (2002). "The Neo-Soul Vibe and the Post-Modern Aesthetic: Black Popular Music and Culture for the Soul Babies of History." *American Studies* 43 (3): 75–81.

Whelehan, Imelda. (1995). *Modern Feminist Thought: From the Second Wave to "Post-Feminism."* New York: New York University Press.

White, Aaronette M. (1999). "Talking Black, Talking Feminist: Gendered Micromobilization Processes in a Collective Protest Against Rape." In Kimberly Springer (Ed.), *Still Lifting, Still Climbing: Contemporary African American Women's Activism* (pp. 189–218). New York: New York University Press.

——. (Ed.). (2008). *Ain't I a Feminist: African American Men Speak Out on Fatherhood, Friendship, Forgiveness, and Freedom.* Albany: State University of New York Press.

White, Deborah G. (1985). *Aren't I a Woman?: Female Slaves in the Plantation South.* New York: Norton.

——. (1999). *Too Heavy a Load: Black Women in Defense of Themselves, 1894–1994.* New York: Norton.

Whiteley, Sheila, and Andy, Bennett. (2004). *Music, Space, and Place: Popular Music and Cultural Identity.* Aldershot, UK: Ashgate Publishing.

Whitmarsh, Anne. (1981). *Simone de Beauvoir and the Limits of Commitment.* Cambridge, UK: Cambridge University Press.

Whitten, Norman E., Jr., and Torres, Arlene. (Eds.). (1998). *Blackness in Latin America and the Caribbean: Social Dynamics and Cultural Transformations* (2 Volumes). Indianapolis: Indiana University Press.

Whittier, Nancy. (1995). *Feminist Generations: The Persistence of the Radical Women's Movement.* Philadelphia, PA: Temple University Press.

Wiggerhaus, Rolf. (1995). *The Frankfurt School: Its History, Theories, and Political Significance.* Cambridge, MA: MIT Press.

Wilkerson, William S., and Paris, Jeffrey. (Eds.). (2001). *New Critical Theory: Essays on Liberation.* Lanham, MD: Rowman & Littlefield.

Williams, Eric E. (1966). *Capitalism and Slavery.* New York: Capricorn Books.

Williams-Myers, Albert J. (1995). *Destructive Impulses: An Examination of an American Secret in Race Relations: White Violence.* Lanham, MD: University Press of America.

Williams, Rhonda Y. (2004). *The Politics of Public Housing: Black Women's Struggles Against Urban Inequality.* Oxford, UK: Oxford University Press.

——. (2006). "Black Women, Urban Politics, and Engendering Black Power." In Peniel E. Joseph (Ed.), *The Black Power Movement: Rethinking the Civil Rights–Black Power Era* (pp. 79–104). New York: Routledge.

Wilson, Sondra K. (Ed.). (1999). *The Crisis Reader: Stories, Poetry, and Essays from the NAACP's Crisis Magazine.* New York: Modern Library.

Wilson, William J. (1978). *The Declining Significance of Race: Blacks and Changing America Institutions.* Chicago: University of Chicago Press.

——. (1987). *Truly Disadvantaged: The Inner City, the Underclass, and Public Policy.* Chicago: University of Chicago Press.

——. (1997). *When Work Disappears: The World of the New Urban Poor.* New York: Vintage.

——. (2009). *More Than Just Race: Being Black and Poor in the Inner City.* New York: W.W. Norton.

Wilton, Tamsin. (1995). *Lesbian Studies: Setting an Agenda.* New York: Routledge.

Wimsatt, William Upski. (2003). *Bomb the Suburbs: Graffiti, Race, Freight-Hopping, and the Search for Hip Hop's Moral Center*. New York: Soft Skull Press.

Wintz, Cary D. (1988). *Black Culture and the Harlem Renaissance*. Houston, TX: Rice University Press.

———. (Ed.). (1996a). *African American Political Thought, 1890–1930: Washington, Du Bois, Garvey, and Randolph*. Armonk, NY: M.E. Sharpe.

———. (Ed.). (1996b). *Black Writers Interpret the Harlem Renaissance*. New York: Garland.

———. (Ed.). (1996c). *Critics and the Harlem Renaissance*. New York: Garland.

———. (Ed.). (1996d). *Emergence of the Harlem Renaissance*. New York: Garland.

———. (Ed.). (1996e). *The Harlem Renaissance: Analysis and Assessment, 1940–1979*. New York: Garland.

———. (Ed.). (1996f). *The Harlem Renaissance: Analysis and Assessment, 1980–1994*. New York: Garland.

———. (Ed.). (1996g). *The Politics and Aesthetics of "New Negro" Literature*. New York: Garland.

———. (Ed.). (1996h). *Remembering the Harlem Renaissance*. New York: Garland.

———. (Ed.). (2003). *The Harlem Renaissance: A History and an Anthology*. New York: Wiley.

Witalec, Janet. (Ed.). (2003). *Harlem Renaissance: A Gale Critical Companion*. Detroit, MI: Gale.

Wood, David. (2000). *Cornel West and the Politics of Prophetic Pragmatism*. Urbana: University of Illinois Press.

Woods, Gregory. (1998). *The History of Gay Literature: The Male Tradition*. New Haven, CT: Yale University Press.

Worsley, Shawan M. (2007). "Loving Hip Hop When It Denies Your Humanity." In Gwendolyn D. Pough, Elaine Richardson, Aisha Durham, and Rachel Raimist (Eds.), *Home Girls Make Some Noise!: The Hip Hop Feminism Anthology* (pp. 274–300). Mira Loma, CA: Parker Publishing.

———. (2010). *Audience, Agency, and Identity in Black Popular Culture*. New York: Routledge.

Wright, William D. (1997). *Black Intellectuals, Black Cognition, and a Black Aesthetic*. Westport, CT: Praeger.

Wu, Jin-Ping. (2000). *Frederick Douglass and the Black Liberation Movement: The North Star of American Blacks*. New York: Garland.

Yancy, George. (Ed.). (2001). *Cornel West: A Critical Reader*. Malden, MA: Blackwell.

———. (Ed.). (2004). *What White Looks Like: African American Philosophers on the Whiteness Question*. New York: Routledge.

———. (Ed.). (2005). *White on White/Black on Black*. Lanham, MD: Rowman & Littlefield.

———. (2008). *Black Bodies, White Gazes*. Lanham, MD: Rowman & Littlefield.

Yearwood, Gladstone L. (2000). *Black Film as a Signifying Practice: Cinema, Narration, and the African American Aesthetic Tradition*. Trenton, NJ: Africa World Press.

Yee, Shirley J. (1992). *Black Women Abolitionists: A Study in Activism, 1828–1860*. Knoxville: University of Tennessee Press.

Young, Cynthia A. (2006). *Soul Power: Culture, Radicalism, and the Making of a U.S. Third World*. Durham, NC: Duke University Press.

Young, John K. (2006). *Black Writers, White Publishers: Marketplace Politics in Twentieth-Century African American Literature*. Jackson: University Press of Mississippi.

Young, Vershawn A. (2007). *Your Average Nigga: Performing Race, Literacy, and Masculinity*. Detroit, MI: Wayne State University Press.

Yu, Timothy. (2009). *Race and the Avant-Garde: Experimental and Asian American Poetry since 1965*. Stanford, CA: Stanford University Press.

Zangrando, Robert L. (1980). *The NAACP Crusade Against Lynching, 1909–1950*. Philadelphia, PA: Temple University Press.

Zeisler, Andi. (2008). *Feminism and Pop Culture*. Berkeley, CA: Seal Press.

Zinn, Howard. (2003). *People's History of the United States: 1492–Present*. New York: HarperCollins.

Index

About the Author

Reiland Rabaka is associate professor of Africana studies in the Department of Ethnic Studies at the University of Colorado at Boulder, where he is also affiliate professor in the Women and Gender Studies program and a research fellow at the Center for Studies of Ethnicity and Race in America (CSERA). His research has been published in *Journal of African American Studies, Journal of Black Studies, Western Journal of Black Studies, Africana Studies Annual Review, Ethnic Studies Review, Jouvert: A Journal of Postcolonial Studies, Socialism & Democracy,* and *Journal of Southern Religion,* among others. He is an editorial board member of *Journal of African American Studies, Journal of Black Studies,* and *Africana Studies Annual Review.* Rabaka is the author of several books, including *W. E. B. Du Bois and the Problems of the Twenty-First Century* (2007); *Du Bois's Dialectics: Black Radical Politics and the Reconstruction of Critical Social Theory* (2008); *Africana Critical Theory* (2009); *Forms of Fanonism: Frantz Fanon's Critical Theory and the Dialectics of Decolonization* (2010); and, *Against Epistemic Apartheid: W. E. B. Du Bois and the Disciplinary Decadence of Sociology* (2010). In addition, he is the editor of *W. E. B. Du Bois: A Critical Reader* (2010) and coeditor of *Telling Our Stories: Ethnic Histories and Cultures of Colorado* (2011). His research has been recognized with several awards, including the National Council for Black Studies' W. E. B. Du Bois-Anna Julia Cooper Award for Outstanding Publications in Africana Studies. He has conducted archival research and lectured extensively both nationally and internationally, and has been the recipient of numerous community service citations, distinguished teaching awards, and research fellowships. His cultural criticism, social commentary, and political analysis has been featured in print, radio, television, and online media venues such as NPR, PBS,

BBC, ABC, NBC, BET, *The Tom Joyner Morning Show*, *The Philadelphia Tribune*, and *The Denver Post*, among others.

Professor Rabaka, who received his BFA in aesthetics and performing arts under the tutelage of Camille Paglia at the University of the Arts, is also a cultural critic, poet, and musician. His poetry has been published in *Talking Drum*, *Uhuru!*, *Harambee Notes*, *Imhotep*, *Stilt-Walkers*, *Ujima*, and *The Voice*, among others. He is a jazz drummer and percussionist, and has recorded three compact discs of his spoken-word/poetry with the be-bop to hip hop experimental music ensemble, Collective Consciousness. His ongoing teaching and research interests in the arts, specifically the social and political implications of African, African American, and Caribbean music and popular culture, include: Harlem Renaissance studies; Jazz studies; Negritude studies; the Black Arts movement; the Feminist Art movement; reggae music and the Rastafari movement; Hip Hop studies; and the Hip Hop Feminist movement.

Made in the USA
Coppell, TX
12 August 2023

20272173R00184